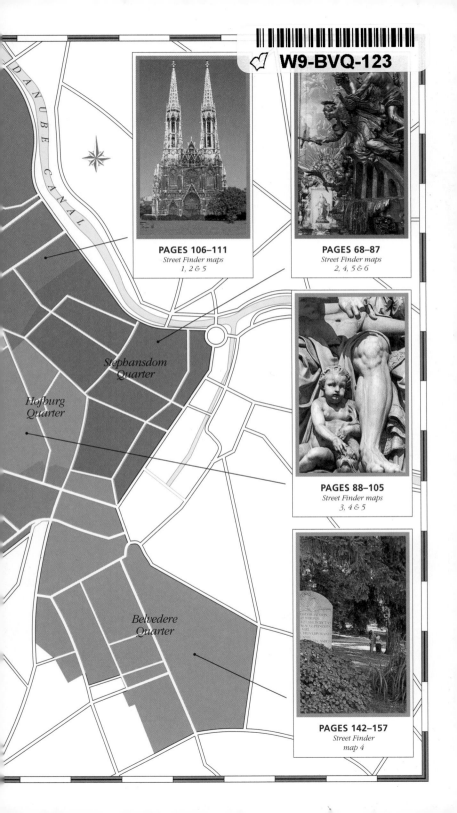

W9-BVQ-123

DANUBE CANAL

PAGES 106–111
Street Finder maps
1, 2 & 5

PAGES 68–87
Street Finder maps
2, 4, 5 & 6

Stephansdom
Quarter

Hofburg
Quarter

PAGES 88–105
Street Finder maps
3, 4 & 5

Belvedere
Quarter

PAGES 142–157
Street Finder
map 4

EYEWITNESS TRAVEL

VIENNA

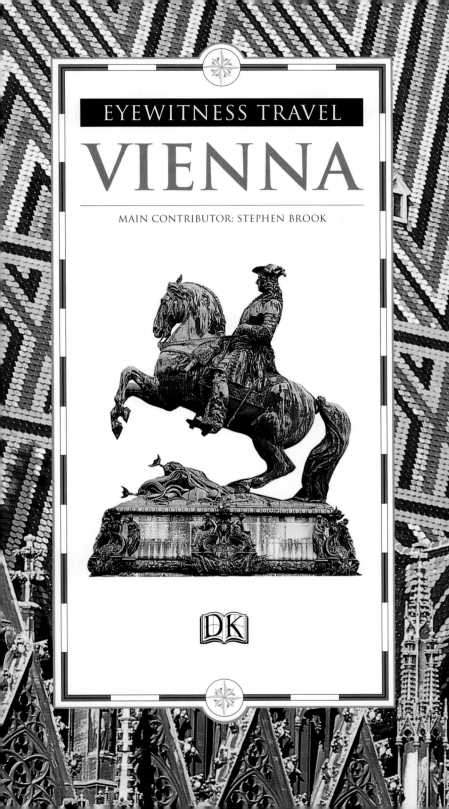

EYEWITNESS TRAVEL

VIENNA

MAIN CONTRIBUTOR: STEPHEN BROOK

DK

LONDON, NEW YORK,
MELBOURNE, MUNICH AND DELHI
www.dk.com

PROJECT EDITOR Carolyn Pyrah
ART EDITOR Sally Ann Hibbard
EDITORS Marcus Hardy, Kim Inglis
USEDITOR Mary Ann Lynch
DESIGNERS Vanessa Hamilton, Andy Wilkinson
DESIGN ASSISTANT Elly King

PRODUCTION Hilary Stephens
PICTURE RESEARCH Ellen Root
DTP DESIGNER Adam Moore

CONTRIBUTORS
Gretel Beer, Rosemary Bircz, Caroline Bugler,
Deirdre Coffey, Fred Mawer

PHOTOGRAPHER
Peter Wilson

ILLUSTRATORS
Richard Draper, Stephen Gyapay, Chris Orr,
Robbie Polley, Ann Winterbotham

Reproduced by Colourscan, Singapore
Printed and bound by L. Rex Printing Company Limited, China

First American Edition, 1994
10 11 12 13 10 9 8 7 6 5 4 3 2 1

Published in the United States by DK Publishing,
375 Hudson Street, New York, New York 10014
**Reprinted with revisions 1996, 1997 (twice), 2000, 2001,
2002, 2003, 2004, 2006, 2008, 2010**

Copyright © 1994, 2010 Dorling Kindersley Ltd

Published in Great Britain by Dorling Kindersley Limited

ISSN 1542-1554
ISBN 978-0-7566-6101-4

THROUGHOUT THIS BOOK, FLOORS ARE REFERRED TO IN ACCORDANCE WITH
EUROPEAN USAGE, I.E., THE "FIRST FLOOR" IS THE FLOOR ABOVE GROUND LEVEL.

*Front cover main image: Kunsthistorisches Museum at
Maria-Theresien-Platz*

We're trying to be cleaner and greener:
- • we recycle waste and switch things off
- • we use paper from responsibly managed
  forests whenever possible
- • we ask our printers to actively reduce
  water and energy consumption
- • we check out our suppliers' working
  conditions – they never use child labour

**Find out more about our values and
best practices at www.dk.com**

**The information in this
DK Travel Guide is checked regularly.**
Every effort has been made to ensure that this book is as up-to-date
as possible at the time of going to press. Some details, however,
such as telephone numbers, opening hours, prices, gallery hanging
arrangements and travel information are liable to change. The
publishers cannot accept responsibility for any consequences arising
from the use of this book, nor for any material on third party
websites, and cannot guarantee that any website address in this
book will be a suitable source of travel information. We value the
views and suggestions of our readers very highly. Please write to:
Publisher, DK Eyewitness Travel Guides,
Dorling Kindersley, 80 Strand, London WC2R 0RL, Great Britain.

◁ Close-up of Stephansdom roof

CONTENTS

**Karl V, Holy Roman Emperor
from 1519 to 1556 (see p24)**

INTRODUCING
VIENNA

**Bronze and copper Anker Clock in
Hoher Markt (see p84)**

Façade of Schönbrunn Palace *(see pp172–75)*

Grinzing restaurant *(see pp186–7)*

Dobostorte *(see p206)*

The Vienna Boys' Choir *(see p39)*

Karlskirche in the Belvedere Quarter *(see pp148–49)*

HOW TO USE THIS GUIDE

This Eyewitness Travel Guide helps you get the most from your stay in Vienna with the minimum of difficulty. The opening section, *Introducing Vienna*, locates the city geographically, sets modern Vienna in its historical context and describes events through the entire year. *Vienna at a Glance* is an overview of the city's main attractions. *Vienna Area by Area* starts on page 66. This is the main sightseeing section,

Plotting the route

which covers all the important sights, with photographs, maps and illustrations. It also includes day trips from Vienna, a river trip and four walks around the city. Carefully researched tips for hotels, restaurants, cafés and bars, markets and shops, entertainment and sports are found in *Travellers' Needs*. The *Survival Guide* has advice from how to make a telephone call to using the transport system and its ticket machines.

FINDING YOUR WAY AROUND THE SIGHTSEEING SECTION

Each of the six sightseeing areas in the city is colour-coded for easy reference. Every chapter opens with an introduction to the part of Vienna it covers, describing its history and character, followed by a Street-by-Street

map illustrating a typical part of the area. Finding your way around each chapter is made simple by the numbering system used throughout. The most important sights are covered in detail in two or more full pages.

Each area has colour-coded thumb tabs.

Locator map

A locator map shows where you are in relation to other areas in the city centre.

A suggested route takes in some of the most interesting and attractive streets in the area.

1 Introduction to the area
For easy reference, the sights in each area are numbered and plotted on an area map. To help the visitor, this map also shows underground stations, train stations and parking areas. The area's key sights are listed by category: Churches and Cathedrals; Museums and Galleries; Streets and Squares; Markets; Historic Buildings and Parks and Gardens.

The area shaded pink is shown in greater detail on the Street-by-Street map on the following pages.

2 Street-by-Street map
This gives a bird's eye view of interesting and important parts of each sightseeing area. The numbering of the sights ties in with the area map and the fuller descriptions on the pages that follow.

The list of star sights recommends the places that no visitor should miss.

VIENNA AREA MAP

The coloured areas shown on this map *(see inside front cover)* are the six main sightseeing areas used in this guide. Each is covered in a full chapter in *Vienna Area by Area (pp66–179)*. They are highlighted on other maps throughout the book. In *Vienna at a Glance (pp40–61)*, for example, they help you locate the top sights. They are also used to help you find the position of the three guided walks *(pp180–87)*.

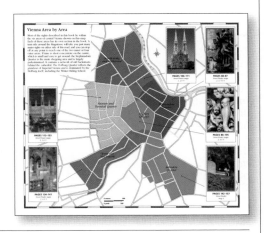

Numbers refer to each sight's position on the area map and its place in the chapter.

Practical information provides all the information you need to visit every sight. Map references pinpoint each sight's location on the *Street Finder* map *(pp262–7)*.

The visitors' checklist provides all the practical information needed to plan your visit.

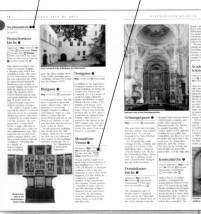

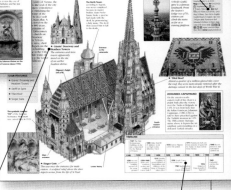

3 Detailed information on each sight

All the important sights in Vienna are described individually. They are listed in order, following the numbering on the area map at the start of the section. Practical information includes a map reference, opening hours, telephone numbers, admission charges and facilities available for each sight. The key to the symbols used is on the back flap.

Stars indicate the features no visitor should miss.

4 Vienna's major sights
Historic buildings are dissected to reveal their interiors; museums and galleries have colour-coded floorplans to help you find important exhibits.

A timeline charts the key events in the history of the building.

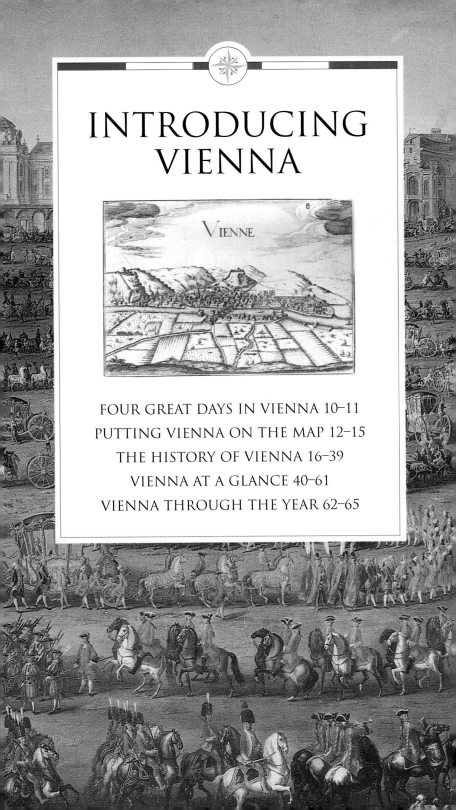

INTRODUCING
VIENNA

FOUR GREAT DAYS IN VIENNA

Whether you are a history buff, an art lover, an outdoors' enthusiast or a fan of thrill rides, in Vienna you will be sure to find something that appeals to you. From imperial palaces and art galleries to parks and a funfair, Vienna has

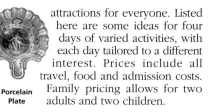

Porcelain Plate

attractions for everyone. Listed here are some ideas for four days of varied activities, with each day tailored to a different interest. Prices include all travel, food and admission costs. Family pricing allows for two adults and two children.

Schönbrunn Palace, whose formal gardens contain a palm house and zoo

VIENNA OF THE HABSBURGS

- **Hofburg: Habsburg Winter Residence**
- **Dine on Emperor's Pancakes**
- **Schönbrunn: Habsburg Summer Home**

TWO ADULTS allow at least 110 euros

Morning
Start the day early with a visit to the huge **Hofburg Complex** *(see pp96-7)*, which includes the former Habsburg winter residence, a church, chapel, the **Spanish Riding School** *(see pp98–9)*, museums and the Austrian National Library. Take a tour of the former **Habsburg State Apartments** *(see pp100–1)*, the **Sisi Museum** (dedicated to Empress Elisabeth of Austria) and the Silberkammer, which houses the Imperial Silver Collection. For lunch, dine in the complex at the **Café Hofburg** *(see p213)*, where traditional specialities such as *Kaiserschmarren* (Emperor's Pancakes) and *Rindsgulasch* (beef goulash) are available.

Afternoon
After lunch, travel to **Schönbrunn Palace and Gardens** *(see pp172–5)*, the former summer residence of the Habsburgs. Take the "Imperial Tour" of the palace, which will guide you through 22 of the palace's state rooms, aided by a free explanatory audio guide. You will be impressed by the palace's grandeur. If you still have time after the tour, wander out into the park and visit the garden's **maze** *(see p172)* and labyrinth for a unique outdoor adventure as well as some picturesque scenery.

One of several statues in the gardens of the Schönbrunn Palace

GREEN VIENNA

- **Tour a Butterfly House**
- **Dine in a 1794 café**
- **Take a stroll on a man-made island**
- **Climb a 252-m (827-ft) tower**

TWO ADULTS allow at least 100 euros

Morning
Start the day with a trip to **Burggarten** *(see p102)*, a park in central Vienna that was created by the Habsburgs on land around the Hofburg. Here you can wander among the trees and view statues of Goethe, Mozart and Emperor Franz I. The park is also well-known for its greenhouses, designed by the Jugendstil architect Friedrich Ohmann. Among them is the Butterfly House *(Schmetterlinghaus)*, home to over 150 different species which fly around in a recreated rainforest environment. Next, take a lunch break at the nearby **Café Mozart** *(see p219)*, on Albertinaplatz. In this historic and elegant café, which has been in existence since 1794, you can dine on gourmet vegetarian or traditional Austrian dishes and enjoy some pastries for dessert.

Afternoon
After lunch, pay a visit to **Danube Park** *(see p161)*, which was created in 1964 and is the second largest park in Vienna. Here you can go for a leisurely stroll or jog, or a ride along the cycle paths. For a relaxing moment, sit down by Lake Iris, which is an artificial lake

Gustav Klimt's Beethoven Frieze on display in the Secession Building

in the centre. A must-see while in the park is the **Danube Tower** *(see p161)*, which is 252 m (827 ft) high and has a revolving restaurant, a café and an observation deck. An elevator will take you to the top of the tower where you can view the whole Vienna metropolitan area. On a clear day, the view stretches to beyond the city.

The elegant interior of the historic and popular Café Mozart

ART AND ARCHITECTURE

- Tour an art museum designed in Jugendstil
- Dine on classic Greek food
- View an imperial art history museum

TWO ADULTS allow at least 100 euros

Morning
Begin your day with a visit to the **Secession Building** *(see p138)*, which was designed in Jugendstil style and is now used as an exhibition hall for displays of contemporary art. Exhibitions have included Oswald Oberhuber and Maja Vukoje. The building is also home to Gustav Klimt's famous Beethoven Frieze. After viewing the art, try nearby **Kostas** *(see p215)* for a classic Greek lunch of moussaka.

Afternoon
Having eaten, head for the **MuseumsQuartier** *(see pp118–21)* and, for an unforgettable experience, visit the **Kunsthistorisches Museum** (Museum of the History of Art) *(see pp122–3)*. Here you can spend an afternoon viewing magnificent works of art and antiquities, many of which are from imperial Habsburg collections. The Picture Gallery on the first floor is especially impressive and features paintings from the artists Giovanni Bellini, Titian, Pieter Bruegel and Diego Velázquez among others. After a day of browsing, stop off at the **Lux-Gasthaus-Café-Bar** *(see p214)*, just west of the MuseumsQuartier, for a glass of wine or some juice.

A FAMILY DAY

- Explore the Volksprater Funfair in the Prater
- Lunch at the Prater's Schweizerhaus restaurant
- Ride a rickshaw along the Hauptallee

FAMILY OF 4 allow at least 300 euros

Morning
This day starts with a trip to the **Volksprater Funfair** *(see p162)*, the oldest amusement park in the world. Take a spin on the famous Ferris wheel built in 1897. Older kids might then like to ride on the daring Volare roller coaster, while parents with smaller children might enjoy the carousel, or the 4-km (2.5-mile) miniature railway. For lunch, visit the **Schweizerhaus restaurant** *(see p216)* inside the park and sample some hearty fare, such as beef stew and fried chicken.

Afternoon
After lunch, families can rent a rickshaw (or, perhaps, a mountain bike, tandem or children's bike) from the Bicycle Rental Hochschaubahn stand near the Hochschaubahn roller coaster. Go for a two-hour ride down the **Hauptallee** *(see p163)* in the Prater's green area, which is a boulevard famous for jogging and cycling, or just enjoying a pleasant stroll. Return to one of the funfair's fast-food stands for an ice-cream cone or soft drink.

VolksPrater Funfair with its famous landmark, the Ferris wheel.

Putting Vienna on the Map

Vienna has a population of just over 1.6 million and covers an area of 415 sq km (160 sq miles). The River Danube flows through it and the Danube Canal flows through the city centre. It is the capital of the Republic of Austria, of which it is also a federal state, and is the country's political, economic, cultural and administrative centre. At the heart of Central Europe, it makes a good base from which to explore cities such as Bratislava, Prague, Budapest, Zagreb, Salzburg and Munich, as well as many Austrian towns.

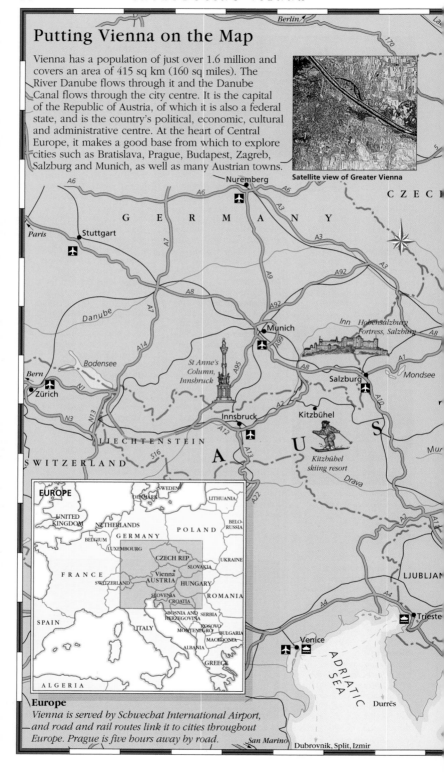

Satellite view of Greater Vienna

Europe

Vienna is served by Schwechat International Airport, and road and rail routes link it to cities throughout Europe. Prague is five hours away by road.

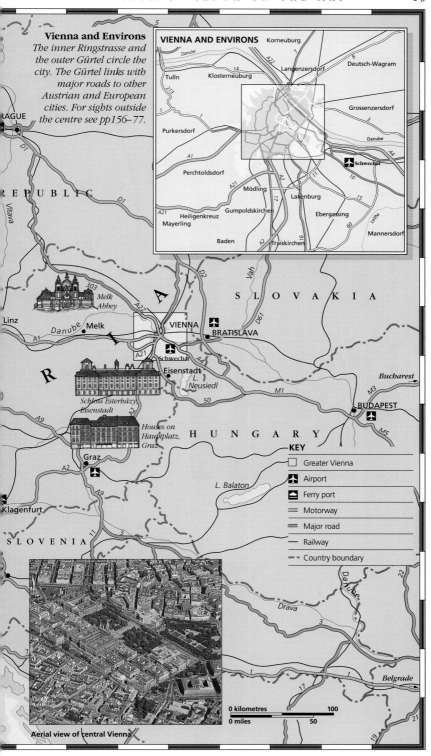

Vienna and Environs
The inner Ringstrasse and the outer Gürtel circle the city. The Gürtel links with major roads to other Austrian and European cities. For sights outside the centre see pp156–77.

VIENNA AND ENVIRONS

Danube
Korneuburg
Tulln
Klosterneuburg
Langenzersdorf
Deutsch-Wagram
Grossenzersdorf
Purkersdorf
Danube
Schwechat
Perchtoldsdorf
Mödling
Laxenburg
Heiligenkreuz
Gumpoldskirchen
Mayerling
Ebergassing
Mannersdorf
Baden
Traiskirchen

REPUBLIC
Vltava
PRAGUE

Melk
Abbey
303
SLOVAKIA
Linz
Danube
Melk
VIENNA
BRATISLAVA
Schwechat
Eisenstadt
L. Neusiedl
Bucharest
Schloss Esterházy
Eisenstadt
M1
BUDAPEST
Houses on
Hauptplatz,
Graz
HUNGARY
Graz
L. Balaton
Klagenfurt
SLOVENIA

KEY

☐	Greater Vienna
✈	Airport
⚓	Ferry port
═	Motorway
═	Major road
—	Railway
- - -	Country boundary

Drava
Danube
Belgrade

0 kilometres   100
0 miles   50

Aerial view of central Vienna

Central Vienna

This book divides Vienna into six areas in the centre of town, and has further sections for sights on the outskirts of the city, suggested walks and day trips, as well as practical information. Each of the six main areas has its own chapter, and contains a selection of sights that convey some of that area's history and distinctive character, such as the Stephansdom in the Stephansdom Quarter and the imperial buildings in the Hofburg Quarter. Most of the city's famous sights are in or close to the city centre and are easy to reach on foot or by public transport.

Detail on the door of the Pallavicini Palace (1784) in Josefsplatz

Bars in Sterngasse
Sterngasse, in the Jewish Quarter (see p84), is packed with lively bars like these spilling out into the street (see Restaurants, Cafés and Bars on p218).

KEY

	Major sight
U	U-Bahn station
	Badner Bahn stop
P	Parking
	Tourist information office
	Police station
	Church

0 metres 500
0 yards 500

View over the Rooftops from Am Hof
Am Hof, the largest enclosed square in Vienna, is circled by a number of interesting houses, some with statuary on their roofs and pediments (see p87).

Rathauskeller Façade
The city has plenty of wine cellars – many associated with old vineyards – where wine, beer and simple food is served. This one is located beneath the city hall (see p130).

Pallas Athene Fountain
The figure of Pallas Athene by Karl Kundmann was placed on the fountain in front of the Parliament building in 1902 (see p121).

THE HISTORY OF VIENNA

Vienna was originally a Celtic settlement on the site of the present-day city. Under the Romans it became the garrison of Vindobona, supporting the nearby town of Carnuntum. Its location on the edge of the Hungarian plains, however, made it vulnerable to attack, and Barbarian invasions reduced the town to ruins by the early 5th century. In the 10th century, the German Babenberg dynasty acquired Vienna, and during their reign of almost three centuries the city became a major trading centre. Later, in the 13th century, Vienna came under the control of the Habsburgs. In the 16th century, Turkish invasions threatened Vienna and devastated its outskirts. Only in 1683 were the Turks finally defeated, allowing Vienna to flourish. Immense palaces were built around the court within the city, and in the

Maximilian I shield

liberated outskirts, and by the 18th century Vienna was a major imperial and cultural centre. Napoleon's occupation of Vienna in 1809 shook the Habsburgs' confidence, as did the revolution of 1848 – the year Franz Joseph came to the throne. By 1914, Vienna's population had expanded to two million, as people from all over the Habsburg Empire flocked to this vibrant centre. After World War I, the Habsburg Empire collapsed and Vienna's role as the Imperial capital ended. In the following years a strong municipal government – "Red Vienna"– tried to solve the social problems of the city. Austria was annexed by Nazi Germany in the Anschluss of 1938 and then, following Hitler's defeat in 1945, came under Allied control. Vienna regained its independence in 1955, when Austria became a sovereign state.

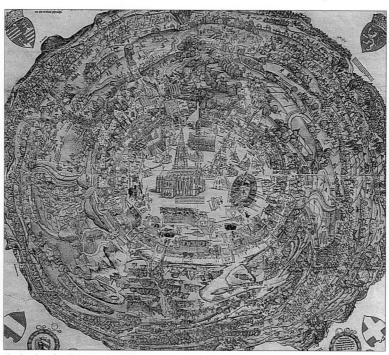

Circular plan of Turkish siege, from 1529

◁ Detail from *The Marriage of Joseph II to Isabella of Parma* (1760) by the Martin van Meytens School

Vienna's Rulers

Vienna emerged from the Dark Ages as a German outpost controlled by Babenberg dukes, who brought great prosperity to the city by the 12th century. There followed a period of social disorder, and intermittent Bohemian rule known as the Interregnum. Vienna fell into Habsburg hands in the 13th century and remained the cornerstone of their domains until the dynasty's downfall in 1918. From 1452 until 1806, Habsburg rulers were almost invariably elected as Holy Roman Emperor, enabling Vienna to develop as an Imperial capital on the grandest scale.

Duke Friedrich II with falconer

1278–82 Rudolf I of Germany is regent of Austria.

1246–50 Interregnum under Margrave Hermann of Baden after death of Duke Friedrich II

900	1000	1100	1200	1300	1400
BABENBERG RULERS				HABSBURG RULERS	
900	1000	1100	1200	1300	1400

976 Leopold of Babenberg

1198–1230 Duke Leopold VI

1177–1194 Duke Leopold V

1358–65 Duke Rudolf IV

1141–77 Duke Heinrich II Jasomirgott

1251–76 Interregnum under Przemysl Ottakar II

Emperor Franz Joseph I

1637–57 Emperor Ferdinand III

1452–93 Friedrich V (crowned as Holy Roman Emperor Friedrich III)

1485–90 King Matthias Corvinus of Hungary occupies Vienna

1493–1519 Emperor Maximilian I

1612–19 Emperor Matthias

1657–1705 Emperor Leopold I

1835–48 Emperor Ferdinand I of Austria

1576–1612 Emperor Rudolf II

1705–11 Emperor Joseph I

1848–1916 Emperor Franz Joseph I

1711–40 Emperor Karl VI

1500	1600	1700	1800	1900

1500	1600	1700	1800	1900

1619–37 Emperor Ferdinand II

1792–1835 Emperor Franz II (becomes Franz I of Austria in 1806)

1918 Habsburgs exiled

1564–76 Emperor Maximilian II

1916–18 Emperor Karl I

1556–64 Emperor Ferdinand I

1790–92 Emperor Leopold II

1780–90 Emperor Joseph II

1519–1556 Emperor Karl V

1740–80 Empress Maria Theresa

Early Vienna

The region around Vienna was first inhabited in the late Stone Age, and Vienna itself was founded as a Bronze Age settlement in about 800 BC. Settled by Celts from about 400 BC, the Romans incorporated it into the province of Pannonia in 15 BC, establishing the garrison of Vindobona by the 1st century AD. Later overrun by Barbarian tribes, Vindobona diminished in importance until the 8th century, when the Frankish Emperor Charlemagne made it part of his Eastern March and part of the Holy Roman Empire.

Roman urn

EXTENT OF THE CITY

☐ *150 AD*   ☐ *Today*

Hallstatt Idol
The Iron-Age Hallstatt culture flourished around Vienna from 750 to 400 BC.

Main defensive wall

VINDOBONA
Established around 100 AD, the garrison of Vindobona was allied to the town of Carnuntum.

Vindobona   Carnuntum

Venus of Willendorf
Now in the Natural History Museum (see p126), this late Stone Age figurine was found at Willendorf, close to Vienna, in 1906.

Roman Map
This map of Pannonia shows the position of Roman towns and forts along the Danube.

TIMELINE

2000 BC Indo-Germanic settlements on northwest wooded slopes

800 BC Bronze Age settlements on what is now Hoher Markt

750 BC Hallstatt culture

400 BC Celtic culture

Marcus Aurelius

180 Roman Emperor Marcus Aurelius dies in Vindobona

280 Roman Emperor Probus authorizes wine growing in the Danube area

5000	2000	800	0	100	200

5000 BC Late Stone Age culture

Preserved shoe from the Hallstatt culture

15 BC Celtic region of Noricum occupied by Romans

250 Vindobona, developed as a garrison town, has a population of 20,000

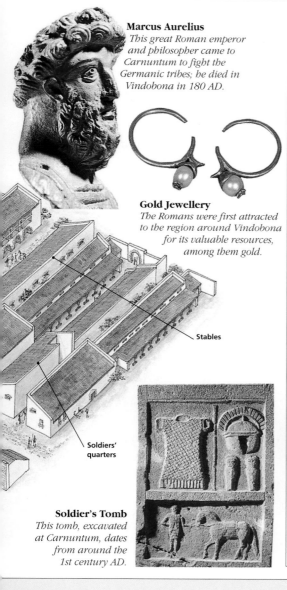

Marcus Aurelius
This great Roman emperor and philosopher came to Carnuntum to fight the Germanic tribes; he died in Vindobona in 180 AD.

Gold Jewellery
The Romans were first attracted to the region around Vindobona for its valuable resources, among them gold.

Stables

Soldiers' quarters

Soldier's Tomb
This tomb, excavated at Carnuntum, dates from around the 1st century AD.

WHERE TO SEE EARLY VIENNA

Many of the Roman walls and ditches have left their mark on the layout of Vienna, but excavations have not been numerous. The most impressive are at Hoher Markt (*see p84*), at No. 10 Am Hof (*p87*), and in the Michaelerplatz (*p92*). The most extensive remains are not in Vienna itself but at Carnuntum, about 25 miles (40 km) east of Vienna, where two amphitheatres and other ruins survive.

The Hoher Markt, *in the very heart of Vienna, is the site of excavations of the Roman garrison of Vindobona.*

This Gorgon's Head, *a large Roman relief of the mythical Medusa, is from Hoher Markt.*

395 First Barbarian invasions approach Vindobona

405 Romans withdraw from Vindobona

500–650 Repeated invasions by Langobards, Goths, Avars and Slav tribes

300	400	500	600	700	800

433 Vindobona destroyed by Huns

Barbarian horseman

883 First mention of Wenia (Vienna) on the borders of the Eastern March founded by Charlemagne

Medieval Vienna

In 955 the Holy Roman Emperor Otto I expelled Hungarian tribes from the Eastern March *(see p20)*. In 976 he made a gift of Vienna to the German Babenbergs, who, despite further incursions by the Hungarians, restored the city's importance as a centre of trade and culture. Following Friedrich II's death in 1246 and the ensuing Interregnum *(see p18)*, the Habsburgs began centuries of rule over Austria. Vienna became a major European city and hub of the Holy Roman Empire.

EXTENT OF THE CITY

☐ *1400*   ☐ *Today*

St Ruprecht
St Ruprecht was the patron saint of salt merchants, who brought this precious commodity along the Danube from salt mines in western Austria. Today his statue overlooks the Danube canal.

DEATH OF FRIEDRICH II

Duke Friedrich II was the last of the Babenbergs to rule Vienna. He died in battle against invading Hungarian forces in 1246.

Stephansdom

The Nobility
Often elected as Holy Roman Emperors, the Habsburgs attracted nobility from all over their huge empire.

Duke Friedrich II

Coronation Robe
This magnificent medieval robe (1133), originally from Palermo, formed part of the Habsburg's imperial regalia.

TIMELINE

955 Otto I of Germany defeats the Hungarians, restoring Christianity and re-establishing the Eastern March ("Ostmark", later renamed Ostarrichi)	**1030** The Hungarians besiege Vienna	**1147** Stephansdom consecrated
		1136 Death of Margave Leopold III
900	**1000**	**1100**
909 Eastern March invaded by Hungarian forces	**976** Otto I makes Leopold of Babenberg Margrave of the Eastern March, initiating Babenberg rule	**1137** Vienna becomes a fortified city
		1156 Heinrich II Jasomirgott moves his court to Vienna; builds Am Hof *(see p87)*

Richard the Lionheart

In 1192, Richard I of England, returning from the crusades in the Holy Land, was captured and held to ransom by Duke Leopold V.

WHERE TO SEE MEDIEVAL VIENNA

Gothic churches include the Stephansdom (see pp76–9), Maria am Gestade (p85), the Burgkapelle, Minoritenkirche (p103), Ruprechtskirche (p81) and Augustinerkirche (p102). The Michaelerkirche (p92) includes some Gothic sculptures and the Schotten-kirche medieval art (p110). Surviving medieval houses include the Basiliskenhaus in Schönlaterngasse (p74).

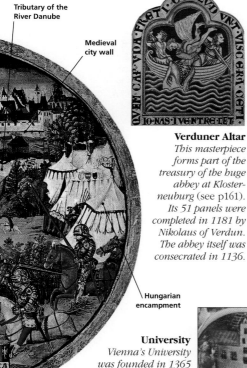

Tributary of the River Danube

Medieval city wall

Hungarian encampment

Verduner Altar

This masterpiece forms part of the treasury of the huge abbey at Kloster-neuburg (see p161). Its 51 panels were completed in 1181 by Nikolaus of Verdun. The abbey itself was consecrated in 1136.

Stained glass *(about 1340) in the Cathedral Museum (p74).*

University

Vienna's University was founded in 1365 by Duke Rudolf IV. This miniature (about 1400) shows the medieval university building and some of the tutors and their students.

Seal of Přzemysl Ottakar II

1278–82 Rudolf I becomes ruler of Austria after defeating Ottakar II; 640 years of Habsburg rule follow

1288 Viennese uprising against Habsburgs crushed

1359 Rudolf IV lays foundation stone of the Stephansdom tower

1365 University founded

1477 Friedrich III's son Maximilian I marries Mary of Burgundy, heiress to the Low Countries

1200 — **1300** — **1400**

1246 Death of Friedrich II followed by Interregnum, during which Přzemysl Ottakar II rules Vienna

1273 Count Rudolf of Habsburg crowned Rudolf I of Germany

1278 Vienna granted a city charter

1330 The first Gothic section of Maria am Gestade built

1438 Albrecht V elected Holy Roman Emperor; Vienna made seat of Empire

1452 Friedrich V crowned as Holy Roman Emperor Friedrich III

1485 Vienna occupied by King Matthias Corvinus of Hungary

Renaissance Vienna

Under Maximilian I, Vienna was transformed into a centre for the arts. The Habsburgs were invariably elected Holy Roman Emperor, and by the 16th century their mighty empire had expanded into Spain, Holland, Burgundy, Bohemia and Hungary. But it was under constant threat: from Turkish attacks, the plague, and disputes between Protestants and Catholics that destabilized the city until 1576, when the Jesuits spearheaded the Counter-Reformation.

EXTENT OF THE CITY

▨ 1600   ☐ Today

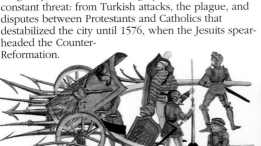

Book Illustration
This Renaissance war wagon (1512) is from Maximilian I's collection of books of engravings and illustrations.

Viennese Enamel Casket
This ornate enamel and crystal casket is typical of the skilful craftsmanship practised in Vienna in the 16th century.

Maximilian I married Mary of Burgundy in 1477 and acquired the Burgundian domains.

Imperial Crown
This beautiful crown was made by Bohemian craftsmen in 1610 for Rudolf II and can now be seen in the Hofburg Treasuries (see pp100–1).

Ferdinand I married Anna of Bohemia and Hungary, and inherited Bohemia in 1526. It was a Habsburg domain until 1918.

TIMELINE

1516 Maximilian's grandson, Karl V, inherits Spain

1519 Karl V inherits Burgundy titles and is elected Holy Roman Emperor; his brother Ferdinand I becomes Austria's archduke

1533 Ferdinand I moves his court to the Hofburg in Vienna

1556 Karl V's son, Philip II, inherits Spain; Ferdinand I takes Bohemia, Austria, Hungary, and imperial title

1571 Protestant Maximilian II allows religious freedom; 80% of city is Protestant

1500	1520	1540	1560	1580

1498 Emperor Maximilian I founds Vienna Boys' Choir

Suleiman the Magnificent

1541 Plague

1572 Spanish Riding School founded

1493 Maximilian I expels Hungarians from Vienna

1529 Graf Niklas Salm vanquishes Turkish army besieging Vienna

1551 Jesuits start Counter-Reformation

1577 Protestant services forbidden by Rudolf II

Triumphal Arch of Maximilian I

The German artist Albrecht Dürer (1471–1528) paid homage to Maximilian I in a famous volume of engravings, which included this design for a triumphal arch.

Philip I married Juana of Castile and Aragon in 1496 and acquired Spain.

THE FAMILY OF MAXIMILIAN I

Painted by Bernhard Strigel (around 1520), this portrait can be read as a document of how, by marrying into prominent European families, the Habsburg family was able to gain control of almost half of Europe.

Mary of Burgundy was married to Maximilian I and was Duchess of the Burgundian domains.

Karl V inherited Spain from his mother, Juana of Castile and Aragon, in 1516.

WHERE TO SEE RENAISSANCE VIENNA

The Schweizertor *(see p97)* in the Hofburg is the most colourful surviving remnant of Renaissance Vienna, though the Salvatorkapelle portal *(p85)* surpasses it in elegance. Also in the Hofburg is the Renaissance Stallburg *(p93)*. Some courtyards, such as those at No. 7 Bäckerstrasse *(p75)* and the Mollard-Clary Palace *(p94)*, preserve a few Renaissance features.

The Schweizertor, *built in the 16th century, forms the entrance to the Schweizerhof of the Hofburg (p97).*

Alte Burg

The medieval core of the Hofburg was constantly being rebuilt. This engraving shows its appearance in the late 15th century, before Ferdinand I had it rebuilt in the 1550s.

edallion ommemorating ximilian II

1618 Bohemian rebellion starts Thirty Year's War

1629 Plague claims 30,000 lives

1643 Swedish forces threaten Vienna

1673–9 War with France over the Low Countries

1600	1620	1640	1660

1598–1618 Protestantism is banned

1620 Ferdinand II defeats Protestant Bohemian aristocracy; Counter-Reformation spreads throughout Habsburg domains

1621 Jews expelled from Inner City

17th-century French infantry

Baroque Vienna

J B Fischer v on Erlach

The Turkish threat to Vienna ended in 1683 when Kara Mustapha's forces were repelled. Under Karl VI the city expanded and the Karlskirche and the Belvedere palaces were constructed. Around the Hofburg, mansions for noble families sprang up, built by architects such as Johann Bernhard Fischer von Erlach *(see p149)* and Johann Lukas von Hildebrandt *(see p152)*. Vienna was transformed into a resplendent Imperial capital.

EXTENT OF THE CITY

☐ *1700*   ☐ *Today*

WINTER PALACE OF PRINCE EUGENE

J B Fischer von Erlach and Johann Lukas von Hildebrandt designed the Winter Palace *(see p80)* for Prince Eugene, hero of the Turkish campaign.

Plague
This lithograph depicts the plague of 1679, which killed around 30,000 Viennese.

Turkish Bed
Ornamented with martial emblems, this bed was designed for Prince Eugene in 1707.

Coffee Houses
The first coffee houses opened in Vienna in the mid-17th century and they have been a prized institution ever since.

Baroque Architecture
Baroque architecture was at its most prolific in Vienna in the early 18th century. **Trautson Palace (see p117)**

TIMELINE

1683 Turkish siege of Vienna by 200,000 soldiers, under Kara Mustapha, from 14 July to 12 September

1700–14 The war of the Spanish Succession

1680	1690	1700

1679 Plague in Vienna

1683–1736 Prince Eugene of Savoy wins more victories over Turks and French, restoring Austria's fortunes

Kara Mustapha

The war of the Spanish Succession: Battle of Blenheim

Turkish Siege

The defeat of the Turks in 1683 was crucial, not only for Vienna, but for Central Europe, which was spared the prospect of Ottoman rule.

WHERE TO SEE BAROQUE VIENNA

The Baroque is everywhere in Vienna. Hardly a street in the old city or inner suburbs is without a Baroque mansion or church. Fine examples of Baroque architecture include the Belvedere Palaces (*see pp152–57*), the Prunksaal (*p102*), the Karlskirche (*pp148–9*), the Leopoldinischer Trakt in the Hofburg (*pp96–7*), the Winter Riding School (*pp98–9*) and the Bohemian Court Chancery (*p84–5*). Beautiful Baroque houses line many streets, including Naglergasse (*p94*) and Kurrentgasse (*p86*).

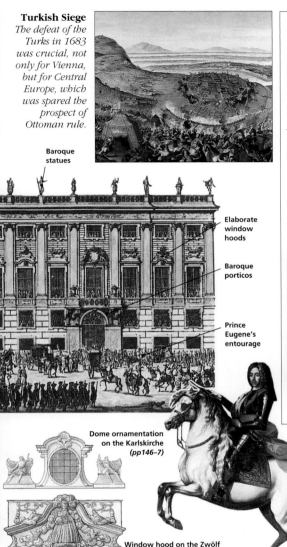

Baroque statues

Elaborate window hoods

Baroque porticos

Prince Eugene's entourage

The Prunksaal *(1721–6) was built by J B Fischer von Erlach.*

Dome ornamentation on the Karlskirche *(pp146–7)*

Window hood on the Zwölf Apostelkeller *(p74)*

Prince Eugene

Best remembered for his role in defeating the Turks, Prince Eugene showed great military prowess in the ensuing decades, and died in 1736 laden with honours.

1713 Karl VI proclaims Pragmatic Sanction, allowing succession through the female line

1719 Karlskirche begun

Statue of Maria Theresa holding Pragmatic Sanction

1720

1730

1716 Lower Belvedere completed

1724–6 Prunksaal and Upper Belvedere completed

Upper Belvedere

1722 Vienna becomes an archbishopric

1713–14 Last plague in Vienna

Vienna under Maria Theresa

The long reign of Maria Theresa was a time of serenity, wealth and sensible administration, despite a background of frequent wars. The vast palace of Schönbrunn was completed by the Empress, who also presided over Vienna's development as the musical capital of Europe. She was succeeded by Joseph II, who introduced many reforms, including religious freedom and public health measures. However, these reforms made him unpopular with his subjects, including the nobility who were angered by the way he handed out titles to bankers and industrialists.

Empress Maria Theresa

EXTENT OF THE CITY

| ☐ 1775 | ☐ Today |

Rococo Table
Wilhelm Martitz designed this Rococo table in 1769 for Maria Theresa, who employed artists committed to the elaborate Rococo style.

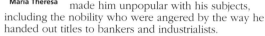

Karlskirche   Stephansdom

Young Mozart
Mozart often performed for the Habsburgs, who were highly receptive to his genius.

Burgtheater Programme
This programme was printed for the first performance of Mozart's The Marriage of Figaro in 1786, which took place in the original Burgtheater on Michaelerplatz.

TIMELINE

Christoph von Gluck

1744–9 Schönbrunn Palace is extensively altered by Maria Theresa's court architect, Nikolaus Pacassi

1754 Vienna's first census records a population of 175,000

1740	1750	1760

1740 Maria Theresa comes to the throne; war of the Austrian Succession

Schönbrunn Palace

1762 First performance of Christoph von Gluck's *(see p38) Orpheus and Eurydice* in the Burgtheater

1766 Prater, formerly an imperial game reserve, opened to the public by Joseph II

Damenkarussell

This painting by Martin van Meytens depicts the Damen-karussell (1743), which was held at the Winter Riding School (see pp98–9) to celebrate the defeat of the French army at Prague.

WHERE TO SEE MARIA THERESA'S VIENNA

Schönbrunn Palace (see pp174–5) and the Theresianum (p151) date from the reign of Maria Theresa. Joseph II later commissioned the Josephinum (p111) and the Narrenturm (p111), and opened the Augarten (p164) and Prater (pp162–63) to the public. A Rococo organ is in the Michaelerkirche (p92), and some of Maria Theresa's tableware is in the Hofburg Treasuries (pp100–1).

Schönbrunn Palace *is filled with Rococo interiors commissioned by Maria Theresa.*

VIEW FROM THE BELVEDERE

Under Maria Theresa, the Viennese were able to enjoy a prosperous city. This townscape by Bernardo Bellotto (1759–61) shows them sauntering through the gardens of the Belvedere, with the palaces and churches of the city in the distance.

Belvedere Gardens

The Rococo high altar *which is in the Michaelerkirche dates from around 1750.*

The Pope

In 1782 Pope Pius VI came to Vienna in an attempt to undo the religious reforms of Joseph II.

1781 Joseph II's Edict of Toleration

Allgemeine Krankenhaus

1784 Joseph II founds the Allgemeine Krankenhaus and Narrenturm (see p111)

770 | 1780 | 1790

1775 Augarten opened to the public by Joseph II

1782 Pope Pius VI in Vienna

1786 First performance of Mozart's *The Marriage of Figaro* in the Burgtheater

1790–2 Emperor Leopold II

1791 First performance of Mozart's *The Magic Flute*

Biedermeier Vienna

Napoleon's defeat of Austria was a humiliation for Emperor Franz I. The French conqueror briefly occupied Schönbrunn Palace, demolished part of the city walls, and married Franz I's daughter. After the Congress of Vienna, Franz I and his minister, Prince Metternich, imposed autocratic rule in Austria. The middle classes, excluded from political life, retreated into the artistic and domestic pursuits that characterized the Biedermeier age.

Early 19th-century dress

Revolution in 1848 drove Metternich from power but led to a new period of conservative rule under Franz Joseph.

EXTENT OF THE CITY

■ 1830   □ Today

Prince Metternich
The architect of the Congress of Vienna, Metternich gained political supremacy of Austria over four decades. In 1848 revolutionary mobs drove him from Vienna.

THE CONGRESS OF VIENNA

After the defeat of Napoleon in 1814, the victorious European powers gathered in Vienna to restore the established order that had been severely disrupted by the French emperor. The crowned heads and elected rulers of Europe spent a year in the city, where the court and nobility entertained them with a succession of balls and other diversions. The outcome was the restoration of reactionary rule across Europe that, although repressive in many countries, managed to maintain the peace until a series of revolutions swept across Europe in 1848.

The singer Michael Vogl

Franz Schubert playing the piano

TIMELINE

1800 Vienna's population 232,000

1806 The Holy Roman Empire ends after Franz II abdicates and becomes Emperor Franz I of Austria

1805 First performance of Beethoven's Eroica Symphony and *Fidelio* in Theater an der Wien. Napoleon wins victory at Austerlitz

Napoleon Bonaparte

1800

1809 Napoleon moves into Schönbrunn Palace and marries Franz I's daughter Maria-Louisa

1811 Austria suffers economic collapse and state bankruptcy

1812–14 Napoleon defeated by Russia, Prussia, England and Austria

1810

1815–48 Period of political suppression known as the Vormärz

1814–15 Congress of Vienna held under Presidency of Metternich; Austria loses Belgium but gains parts of Northern Italy

Franz Grillparzer

1820

1825 Johann Strauss the Elder forms first waltz orchestra

The 1848 Revolution
This painting from 1848 by Anton Ziegler shows the revolution in Vienna, when the middle classes and workers fought together against Metternich.

SCHUBERTIADE
Franz Schubert *(see p38)* wrote over 600 songs. These were often performed at musical evenings such as the one shown in this painting, *An Evening at Baron von Spaun's*, by Moritz von Schwind (1804–71).

Biedermeier Chair
This style of furniture characterized the domestic aspirations of Vienna's middle classes in the 1820s.

WHERE TO SEE BIEDERMEIER VIENNA

Napoleon's partial demolition of the city walls led to the creation of the Burggarten *(p102)* and the Volksgarten *(p104)*. Domestic architecture flourished – Biedermeier houses include the Geymüller Schlössl *(p160)* and the Dreimäderlhaus *(p131)* – as did the applied arts *(pp82-3)*.

The Geymüller Schlössl,
dating from 1802, is home to Vienna's Biedermeier museum.

The Grand Gallop
Waltzes, popularized by Johann Strauss I (the Elder) (see p38), were extremely popular in the 1820s.

1827 Death of Beethoven	**1830** Vienna's population reaches 318,000	**1837** First railway constructed	**1846** Johann Strauss the Younger becomes music director of the court balls until 1870	**1850** City population reaches 431,000
	1831–2 Cholera epidemic			

1830

1840

1828 Death of Schubert

1831 The dramatist Franz Grillparzer completes *Des Meeres und der Liebe Wellen*

1845 Gas lighting introduced

1848 Revolution in Vienna; Metternich forced from office, and Emperor Ferdinand I abdicates to be replaced by Franz Joseph

Ringstrasse Vienna

The Emperor Franz Joseph ushered in a new age of grandeur, despite the dwindling power of the Habsburgs. The city's defences were demolished and a circular boulevard, the Ringstrasse, was built, linking new cultural and political institutions. Vienna attracted gifted men and women from all over the empire, as well as traders from Eastern Europe. However, the resulting ethnic brew often resulted in overcrowding and social tension.

Franz Joseph

EXTENT OF THE CITY

▨ 1885	☐ Today

Votivkirche (1856–79) *p111*
Heinrich Ferstel

Neues Rathaus (1872–83) *p130*
Friedrich von Schmidt

Parliament (1874–84) *p121*
Theophil Hansen

The Natural History Museum (1871–1890) *pp128–9, Gottfried Semper*

Kunsthistorisches Museum (1871–1890) *pp122–7*
Gottfried Semper

THE SUICIDE OF ARCHDUKE RUDOLF AT MAYERLING

In 1889 the 30-year-old heir to the throne was found dead with his mistress Mary Vetsera. The Archduke's suicide was more than a social scandal. It was a blow to the Habsburg regime, since he was a progressive and intelligent man. His despair may have been aggravated by court protocol that offered no outlet for his ideas.

Theophil Hansen
This Danish-born architect (1813–91) studied in Athens before settling in Vienna. The Greek influence is most evident in his Parliament building on the Ringstrasse.

TIMELINE

Excavation for the Ringstrasse

1867 First performance of *The Blue Danube* by Strauss in Vienna. Hungary granted autonomy, leading to Dual Monarchy with separate governments

1850	1855	1860	1865

Anton Bruckner

1868 Anton Bruckner *(see p39)* moves from Linz to Vienna

1869 Johannes Brahms settles in Vienna as conductor of the Gesellschaft der Musikfreunde. Opera House opens on Ringstrasse

1857–65 Demolition of fortifications and the building of the Ringstrasse

The Danube
The River Danube often flooded its banks, so its course was altered and regulated in the 1890s by a system of canals and locks.

Vienna Café Society
In the 19th century, Vienna's cafés became the haunts of literary and political cliques.

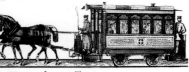

Museum of Applied Arts (1867–71)
pp82–3, Heinrich Ferstel

Horse-drawn Trams
Trams appeared on the Ringstrasse in the 1860s. Horseless trams ran along it by the end of the 19th century.

Stadtpark

Opera House (1861–69) *pp140–1*
Eduard van der Null and August Siccardsburg

RINGSTRASSE
This great boulevard, built on the orders of Franz Joseph, separates the Stephansdom and Hofburg Quarters from the suburbs. Completed in the 1880s, the Ringstrasse is as grand now as it was then.

The Opening of the Stadtpark
Laid out on either side of the River Wien, the Stadtpark was inaugurated in 1862.

1874 First performance of Strauss's *Die Fledermaus* at the Theater an der Wien. Opening of Central Cemetery

1889 Suicide of Archduke Rudolf at Mayerling

70   **1875**   **1880**   **1885**

1873 Stock market crash

1872 Death of Austrian poet and dramatist Franz Grillparzer

1879 Lavish historical parade along the Ringstrasse celebrates Franz Joseph's silver wedding

1890 The suburbs are incorporated into the city

Vienna in the 1900s

The turn of the century was a time of intellectual ferment in Vienna. This was the age of Freud, of the writers Karl Kraus and Arthur Schnitzler, and of the Secession and Jugendstil *(see pp54–7)*. At this time artists such as Gustav Klimt and the architects Otto Wagner and Adolf Loos *(see p92)* created revolutionary new styles. This was all set against a decaying Habsburg empire, which Karl I's abdication in 1918 brought to an end. After World War I Austria became a republic.

Engel Apotheke sign

EXTENT OF THE CITY

◼ *1912* ☐ *Today*

Wiener Werkstätte
Josef Hoffmann (see p56), designer of this chair, was the principal artist and founder of this Viennese arts workshop (see p83).

KIRCHE AM STEINHOF
This stupendous church was designed by Otto Wagner and decorated by Kolo Moser *(see p57)*.

Loos Haus
The restrained elegance of this former tailoring firm is typical of Loos's style (see p92).

The Secession
This poster by Kolo Moser (see p57) was used to publicize the Secession's exhibitions.

Angels by Othmar Schimkowitz

TIMELINE

1899 First issue of Karl Kraus's periodical *Die Fackel*

1903 Wiener Werkstätte founded

1906 Arnold Schönberg's *Chamber Symphony* and works by Anton von Webern and Alban Berg performed at the Musikverein, provoking a riot

1895

1900

1905

1897 Secession established when 19 painters and architects break with the Künstlerhaus. Karl Lueger becomes mayor

1902 Gustav Klimt paints the *Beethoven Frieze*. Tramways are electrified

Gustav Klimt

1905 Franz Lehar's operetta *The Merry Widow* first performed. Anti-Semitic riots at the university

1896 Death of the composer Anton Bruckner

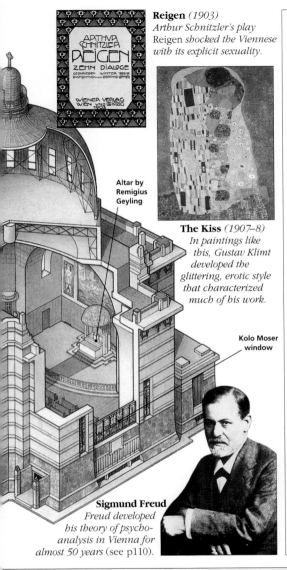

Reigen *(1903)*
Arthur Schnitzler's play
Reigen *shocked the Viennese
with its explicit sexuality.*

The Kiss *(1907–8)
In paintings like
this, Gustav Klimt
developed the
glittering, erotic style
that characterized
much of his work.*

Altar by
Remigius
Geyling

Kolo Moser
window

Sigmund Freud
*Freud developed
his theory of psycho-
analysis in Vienna for
almost 50 years (see p110).*

WHERE TO SEE 1900S VIENNA

Otto Wagner designed the
Karlsplatz Pavilions
(see p146), the Wagner
Apartments *(p139)*, and the
Kirche am Steinhof *(p160)*.
Adolf Loos *(p92)* designed
Loos Haus *(p92)* and the
American Bar *(p105)*. Subur-
ban architecture includes
the Wagner Villas *(p160)*.
Paintings by Klimt, Schiele,
and Kokoschka are displayed
at the Upper Belvedere
(pp154–5) and the Museum of
Modern Art *(p120)*.

The Secession Building *is
where Gustav Klimt's Beethoven Frieze is exhibited (p55).*

The Wagner Apartments *are
decorated with Jugendstil motifs
(p56) by Kolo Moser (p57).*

1907 Gustav Mahler
resigns as director
of Court Opera.
Hitler studies art in
Vienna

1911 Death of
Gustav Mahler

1914 Archduke
Ferdinand assassi-
nated in Sarajevo;
international crisis
follows resulting in
World War I

1910

1915

1910 Death of Karl Lueger

1916 Death of
Franz Joseph

1908 *The Kiss* by Klimt
is first exhibited

1918 Declaration of Austrian Republic
after abdication of Emperor Karl I.
Austria shrinks from an empire of
50 million to a state of 6.5 million

Modern Vienna

Two decades of struggle between the left and
right political parties followed World War I, ending
with the union of Austria with Germany – the
Anschluss – in 1938. After World War II Vienna
was split among the Allies until 1955, when Austria
regained its independence.

1929 Ludwig
Wittgenstein,
a prominent
member of the
Vienna circle,
leaves Vienna
for England

1955 On 15 May the
Austrian State Treaty
brings to an end the
Allied occupation.
Austria granted
independence and
declares itself to be
permanently neutral

1927 Workers, angered
by deaths of bystanders
during political
violence, storm the
Palace of Justice

1922 Karl Kraus
publishes his
immense drama
*The Last Days
of Mankind*

1951 The
First
Festival of
Vienna

1944 Allied bombing of
Vienna begins

1967 UN Industrial
Development
Organization (UNIDO)
comes to Vienna

1920	1930	1940	1950	1960

1920	1930	1940	1950	1960

1922 Death in Madeira of
exiled Karl I, last
Habsburg emperor

1939 Death
of novelist
Joseph Roth

1945 World War II
ends. The second
Austrian republic is
declared, but Vienna
remains divided
between the four
Allied powers

1920–34 Socialism prevails
in so-called "Red Vienna",
despite conservative
Catholic rule in Austria

1918–20 Severe food shortages
and an influenza epidemic
afflict the Viennese

1955
Reopening
of Opera
House and
Burgtheater

1933 Chancellor Dollfuss
dissolves Parliament and forms a
fascist regime, but refuses to
accommodate Hitler

1961 John F
Kennedy
meets Nikita
Khrushchev at
East-West sum-
mit in Vienna

1934 Street fighting in Vienna
between socialists and government
troops; socialists banned. Murder of
Chancellor Dollfuss by the Nazis

1938 Chancellor Schuschnigg
resigns. Hitler enters Vienna and
pronounces Anschluss

1956 Atomic Energy
Agency located in Vienna

1959 Ernst Fuchs and Arik Brauer
establish the school of fantastic realism

1988 Irmgard Seefried, star of the Vienna Opera House, dies

1986 The controversial Kurt Waldheim elected president; Franz Vranitzky elected Chancellor

1989 Death of Empress Zita, the last Habsburg to have ruled Austria

1979 East-West summit held between Leonid Brezhnev and Jimmy Carter

1983 Pope John Paul visits Vienna

1978 U-Bahn system opened

70–83 cialist Bruno eisky is ancellor

1992 Fire in the Hofburg Palace

2008 Football European Cup

| 70 | 1980 | 1990 | 2000 | 2010 | 2020 |

| 70 | 1980 | 1990 | 2000 | 2010 | 2020 |

2006 Mozart year commemorated; 250 years since Mozart's birth

2009 Haydn Year

2008 Jörg Haider dies in car crash

1985 Hundertwasser Haus by Friedensreich Hundertwasser completed

1995 Austria joins the European Union

1989 Velvet Revolution in Czechoslovakia heralds Austria's growing economic influence in the new democratic central Europe. Completion of Hans Hollein's Haas Haus in Stephansplatz

1979 UNO city opened

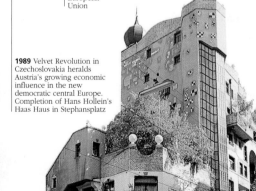

Music in Vienna

From the late 18th to the mid 19th centuries Vienna was the music capital of Europe. At first the Habsburg family and the aristocracy were the city's musical paymasters, but with the rise of the middle classes during the Biedermeier period *(see pp30–31)* music became an important part of bourgeois life. Popular music also flourished as migration from all parts of the Habsburg Empire brought in richly diverse styles of music and dance.

The Waltz became popular following the Congress of Vienna in 1814

a state occasion. The music of Franz Schubert (1797–1828) was little known in his short lifetime. He mostly performed chamber works, piano music and songs at Biedermeier *Schubertiaden* – evenings of music with friends. His music became more popular following his death. After this, "serious" music went through a

CLASSICISM

In the 18th century, Vienna's musical life was dominated by the Imperial Court. Christoph Willibald Gluck (1714–87) was Court *Kapellmeister* (in charge of the court orchestra) to Maria Theresa until 1770, and wrote 10 operas specially for Vienna, including *Orpheus and Eurydice* (1762). His contemporary Wolfgang Amadeus Mozart (1756–91) later built on these foundations. Joseph Haydn (1732–1809) moved to Vienna in the 1790s from Prince Esterházy's palace in Eisenstadt *(see pp176–7)*, and wrote masterpieces such as *The Creation*.

Performance of The Creation (1808) on Haydn's birthday

ROMANTICISM

With the arrival of Ludwig van Beethoven (1770–1827) in Vienna in the mid-1790s, the age of the composer as romantic hero was born. Beethoven was a controversial figure in his time, and many of his most innovative works were only successful outside Vienna. His funeral, however, attended by more than 10,000 people, was

Biedermeier *Schubertiade* evening

fallow period in Vienna, but Johann Strauss I (1804–49) and Joseph Lanner (1801–43) began creating dance music, centred on the waltz.

Performance of The Magic Flute (1791) by Mozart

TIMELINE

					1797–1828 Franz Schubert	Johannes Brahms
1714–1787 Christoph Willibald Gluck	1732–1809 Joseph Haydn		Joseph Haydn	Ludwig van Beethoven		1833–97 Johannes Brahms
1700	**1725**		**1750**	**1775**	**1800**	**1825**
	Christoph Willibald Gluck	1756–91 Wolfgang Amadeus Mozart		1770–1827 Ludwig van Beethoven	1804–49 Johann Strauss I	1825–99 Johann Strauss II
					1801–43 Joseph Lanner	1824–96 Anton Bruckner

AGE OF FRANZ JOSEPH

A new era of high musical art began in the 1860s. Johannes Brahms (1833–97) came to Vienna in 1862, and incorporated popular musical styles into works such as his Liebeslieder waltzes and Hungarian Dances. The Romantic composer Anton Bruckner (1824–96) came to the city from Upper Austria in 1868. Johann Strauss II (1825–99) rose to the status of civic hero, composing nearly 400 waltzes, including his famous operetta *Die Fledermaus*. One popular offshoot of the period was *Schrammel* music, named after Joseph Schrammel

Jugendstil poster (1901) for the Waltz depicting Johann Strauss II

(1850– 93) and characterized by an ensemble of guitars, violins and accordion. Popular music also influenced Gustav Mahler (1860–1911), director of the Vienna Opera for 10 years.

THE MODERNS

The early years of the 20th century saw the rise of the Second Viennese School: Alban Berg (1885–1935), Arnold Schönberg (1874–1951) and Anton von Webern (1883–1945). These composers were not well received in Vienna, and Schönberg found he had to start his own society to get his works, and those of his colleagues, heard. In 1933 he emigrated to the USA. Since World War II no composers of comparable stature have arisen, though Kurt Schwertsik (born 1935) and H K Gruber (born 1943) now attract international attention. However, the Vienna Philharmonic, established in 1842, is still one of the finest orchestras in the world. The State Opera continues to enjoy a strong reputation, and Vienna has an abundance of fine orchestras, opera and operetta venues, chamber ensembles and choirs.

The Johann Strauss II orchestra at a Court ball

Concert poster (1913) for Arnold Schönberg

1860–1911 Gustav Mahler	1874–1951 Arnold Schönberg		
	1875		
	1883–1945 Anton von Webern	1885–1935 Alban Berg	
850–93 oseph chrammel			

VIENNA BOYS' CHOIR

The world-famous Vienna Boys' Choir, the Wiener Sängerknaben, was founded in 1498 by that great patron of the arts, Maximilian I. Today the boys perform masses by Mozart, Schubert or Haydn on Sundays and church holidays at the Burgkapelle *(see p103)*. To obtain a seat you need to book at least eight weeks in advance.

VIENNA AT A GLANCE

Vienna is a compact city and most of its sights are contained within a small area. However, the city boasts an astonishing array of monuments, palaces, parks and museums, which themselves house an impressive array of art and artefacts from all over the world and from all periods of history. Nearly 150 sights are listed in the *Area by Area* section of this book, but to help make the most of your stay, the next 20 pages offer a guide to the very best that Vienna has to offer. As well as churches, palaces, museums and galleries, there are sections on Jugendstil art and coffee houses. Many of the sights listed have a cross-reference to their own full entry. To start with, some of Vienna's top tourist attractions are listed below.

VIENNA'S TOP TOURIST ATTRACTIONS

Opera House
See pp140–41.

Burgtheater
See pp132–33.

Prater
See pp162–63.

Karlskirche
See pp148–49.

Schönbrunn *See pp172–75.*

Spanish Riding School
See pp98–9.

Kunsthistorisches Museum
See pp122–27.

Stephansdom *See pp76–9.*

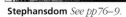

Belvedere
See pp152–57.

Café Central
See p61.

MuseumsQuartier
See p118–20.

◁ The façade of Otto Wagner's Majolikahaus *(see p139)* on the Linke Wienzeile

Vienna's Best: Historic Houses and Palaces

Baroque mansions dominate the streets of the Stephansdom Quarter, while outside the centre of Vienna are the grand summer palaces where the Habsburg emperors and aristocracy lived during warm Middle European summers. The interiors of several of the houses can be visited, while others can only be admired from the outside or from their inner courtyards and staircases. Further details can be found on pages 44–5.

Sigmund Freud's House
This waiting room in the house on Berggasse, where Sigmund Freud lived from 1891 to 1938, has been lovingly restored.

Schottenring and Alsergrund

Kinsky Palace
This mansion (1713–16) by Johann Lukas von Hildebrandt (see p152), was built for the Daun family, and is sometimes called the Daun Kinsky Palace. Wirch Philip Daun was commander of the city garrison, and his son Leopold Joseph Daun was Maria Theresa's field marshal.

Museum and Townhall Quarter

Hofburg
The apartments here are made up of over 20 rooms; among them are ceremonial halls and living quarters which were once occupied by Franz Joseph (see pp32–3) and the Empress Elisabeth.

```
0 kilometres    0.5

0 miles       0.25
```

Opera and Naschmarkt

Schönbrunn Palace
This palace, by J B Fischer von Erlach, was built on a scale to rival the palace of Versailles outside Paris. Parts of it were later redesigned by Maria Theresa's architect Nikolaus Pacassi (see p172).

Neidhart Fresco House
Frescoes dating from 1400, depicting the songs of the medieval minnesinger Neidhart van Reuenthal, decorate the dining room of this former house of a wealthy clockmaker.

Mozarthaus Vienna
Mozart lived in this Baroque building for three years between 1784 and 1787, and composed one of his most famous works, The Marriage of Figaro, *here.*

Winter Palace of Prince Eugene
J B Fischer von Erlach and Johann Lukas von Hildebrandt designed this Baroque palace, with its spectacular staircase, for the war hero Prince Eugene (see pp26–7).

Zum Blauen Karpfen
A stucco relief of a blue carp and a frieze of putti *adorn the façade of this 17th-century house on Annagasse.*

Belvedere
Designed by Johann Lukas von Hildebrandt, Prince Eugene's summer palaces were built on what were originally the southern outskirts of Vienna. The Upper Belvedere now houses the Museum of Austrian Art.

Exploring Vienna's Historic Houses and Palaces

A stroll around Vienna's streets offers the visitor an unparalleled choice of beautifully-preserved historic buildings, from former imperial residences to humbler burgher's dwellings. The majority date from the 17th and 18th centuries, and illustrate the various phases of Baroque architecture. In most cases their original function as residences of the rich and famous has been superseded; a number have now been turned into museums, and their interiors are open to the public.

Façade of the Schönborn-Batthyány Palace

Frescoed ceiling of the Liechtenstein Museum

TOWN PALACES

The most extensive town palace is the **Hofburg**, with its museums and imperial apartments. The staircase of the magnificent **Winter Palace of Prince Eugene** is on view to the public, and the 19th-century Neo-Gothic **Ferstel Palace** (1860) houses the Café Central *(see p58)*. The **Obizzi Palace** is home to the Clock Museum *(see p86)*. Town palaces which can be admired from the outside only are the **Kinsky Palace** (1713–16), **Trautson Palace**, **Schönborn-Batthyány Palace**, **Lobkowitz Palace**, and **Liechtenstein Palace** (1694–1706), the winter home of the Liechtenstein family.

GARDEN PALACES

Although it seems strange that palaces within the city limits should be termed garden palaces, when they were built they were outside the city boundaries, and offered a cool refuge during the hot summer months for the inhabitants. The most famous example is **Schönbrunn Palace**, where the state apartments can be seen as part of a guided tour. The **Belvedere**, to the south of the city, houses the Museum of Austrian Art, and many of the rooms retain their original splendid decoration. The **Hermes Villa** (1884), a cross between a hunting lodge and a Viennese villa, was commissioned by Franz Joseph for his wife Elisabeth. The interior of the Neo-Classical **Rasumofsky Palace** (1806–7), occupied by the Imperial Geological Institute, can sometimes be seen on special occasions. The **Liechtenstein Museum** houses the private art collection of the Liechtenstein family *(see p111)*.

SUBURBAN VILLAS

The Döbling regional museum is housed in the Biedermeier **Villa Wertheimstein** (1834–5), where the interior is furnished in its original flamboyant and overcrowded manner. By contrast, the **Geymüller Schlössl**, containing the Sobek Collection of clocks and watches, is a model of taste and restraint. In Hietzing, the **Villa Primavesi** (1913–15) is a small Jugendstil masterpiece designed by Josef Hoffmann *(see p56)* for the banker Robert Primavesi.

BURGHERS' HOUSES

On Tuchlauben, the **Neidhart Fresco House** is decorated with secular frescoes from around 1400. Charming Baroque houses of modest dimensions can be seen on **Naglergasse** and **Kurrentgasse** and in inner districts such as **Spittelberg** and **Josefstadt**. A particularly fine example of external decoration can be seen on the Baroque inn **Zum Blauen Karpfen** in Annagasse *(see p80)*. The **Dreimäderlhaus** in Schreyvogelgasse, built in an intermediate style between Rococo and Neo-Classicism, is also worth visiting.

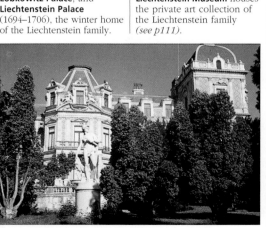
Façade and gardens of the Hermes Villa

MEMORIAL HOUSES

Vienna abounds in the former residences of famous composers. They are not all of great architectural merit, and their interest resides mainly in the exhibits they contain. The **Pasqualati Haus** was one of Beethoven's many Viennese residences – it was here that he composed the opera *Fidelio* – and it now houses portraits and other mementoes of the great composer. The **Heiligenstadt Testament House** (at No. 6 Probusgasse, Heiligenstadt), where Beethoven stayed in an attempt to cure his deafness, is now a memorial. The first-floor apartment of the **Haydn Museum** in Haydngasse is pleasantly

Courtyard of the Heiligenstadt Testament House

furnished and filled with letters, manuscripts, personal possessions and the composer's two pianos. Mozart and his family lived from 1784–7 in the **Mozarthaus Vienna**. This is where Mozart wrote *The Marriage of Figaro*. The **Freud Museum** houses furnishings, documents and photographs, and the waiting room is as it looked when Freud used to see his patients. It is also a study centre.

DECORATIVE DETAILS

Many of the historic houses and palaces of Vienna were built during a period corresponding to the Baroque and late Baroque styles of architecture. Details such as window hoods and pediments over doorways were often extremely ornate.

Caryatid on the doorway of the Liechtenstein Palace

Decorative window hood on the façade of the Trautson Palace

Decorative urns on the Lobkowitz Palace

Decorative pediment with shield on the Schönborn-Batthyány Palace.

Stucco *putti* on the façade of Zum Blauen Karpfen

FINDING THE PALACES AND HOUSES

Vienna's Best: Museums and Galleries

Vienna boasts an astonishing number of museums, and many of the collections are housed in elegant former palaces or handsome buildings specially commissioned for the purpose. Some of the museums are of international importance, while others are of more local or specialist interest. Further details can be found on pages 48–9.

Natural History Museum
This museum has displays of fossils, ethnography, mineralogy and a much-visited dinosaur hall.

Sacred and Secular Treasuries
The Ainkurn sword (around 1450) can be seen in the Imperial Treasuries in the former imperial palace of the Hofburg.

Schottenring and Alsergrund

Museum and Townhall Quarter

Hofburg Quarter

Kunsthistorisches Museum
Hans Holbein's portrait of Jane Seymour (1536) is one of hundreds of Old Master paintings displayed in this fine art museum.

Opera and Naschmarkt

MuseumsQuartier
This vast cultural centre contains the largest Egon Schiele collection in the world, including this Self-portrait with Lowered Head *(1912).*

Albertina
This museum houses temporary exhibitions mainly based on the Albertina's celebrated collection of prints and drawings (here, Albrecht Dürer's The Hare *dated 1502).*

Wien Museum Karlsplatz

Stained-glass windows from the Stephansdom (around 1390) are among the many items here documenting Vienna's history.

Cathedral Museum

This St Andrew's cross reliquary (about 1440) is one of many medieval religious treasures on display here.

Austrian Museum of Applied Arts

The applied arts of Vienna, such as this early 19th-century beaker and Wiener Werkstätte furniture (see pp54–7), are among the varied artefacts on display in this museum.

Stephansdom Quarter

The Belvedere

The Upper Belvedere displays art from the Middle Ages onwards, including medieval painting and sculpture and Renaissance and Baroque works. Ferdinand Waldmüller's Roses in the Window, *shown here, is displayed on the upper floor, along with Gustav Klimt's* The Kiss. *The Lower Belvedere and Orangery house temporary exhibitions.*

Belvedere Quarter

Heeresgeschichtliches Museum

Paintings of battles and military commanders, such as Sigmund L'Allemand's portrait of Field Marshal Gideon-Ernst Freiherr von Laudon (1878), are part of this museum's collection.

0 kilometres   0.5

0 miles   0.25

Exploring Vienna's Museums and Galleries

Vienna's museums exhibit an amazing variety of fine, decorative and ethnic art from all periods of history and from different regions of the world. The visitor can see artefacts from all over the ancient world as well as more recent collections, from medieval religious art to 19th- and 20th-century paintings. Silverware is displayed in the city's imperial collections, and Vienna is also unrivalled for its turn-of-the-century exhibits.

Interior of Friedensreich Hundert-wasser's Kunsthaus Wien

ANCIENT AND MEDIEVAL ART

Vienna has marvellous collections of medieval art. The **Neidhart Fresco House** contains medieval secular frescoes, while a number of superb Gothic altarpieces can be seen in the historic Palace Stables at the **Belvedere**. Displayed in the **Cathedral Museum** are outstanding Gothic sculptures as well as masterpieces of applied art; the highlight is a 9th-century Carolingian Gospel. The **Sacred and Secular Treasuries** in the Hofburg are awash with precious medieval objects, including the insignia and crown of the Holy Roman Empire, and a unique collection of medieval objects and Gothic paintings is on display in the treasury of the **Deutschordenskirche**. The splendours of the Verduner Altar at **Klosterneuberg** await

those prepared to make a short journey out of the centre of Vienna. The **Ephesos Museum** of the Hofburg houses ancient Roman and Greek antiquities unearthed at the turn of the century.

OLD MASTERS

The picture gallery in the **Kunsthistorisches Museum** has one of the best collections of Old Masters in the world, reflecting the tastes of the many generations of Habsburg collectors who formed it. There are works by Flemish and Venetian artists, and the best collection of Bruegels on display in any art gallery, as well as Giuseppe Arcimboldo's (1527–93) curious portraits composed of fruit and vegetables. The **Academy of Fine Arts** houses some fine examples of Dutch and Flemish works, its prize exhibit being Hieronymos Bosch's triptych of the *Last Judgement*, which contains some

of the most horrifying images in Christan art. There are also paintings by Johannes Vermeer (1632–75) and Peter Paul Rubens (1577–1640). The ground floor of the Upper Belvedere focuses on Austrian paintings and sculptures from the 17th and 18th centuries. The Belvedere itself is a masterpiece of Baroque architecture.

19TH- AND 20TH-CENTURY ART

A permanent display of 19th- and 20th-century Austrian art is housed in the Upper Belvedere. The most famous exhibits are by Gustav Klimt, and his newly-restored *Beethoven Frieze* can be seen in the **Secession Building**.

The **Museum of Modern Art**, which is located in the MuseumsQuartier *(see p120)*, contains exhibits by 20th-century European artists. They include including recent works by the Viennese avant garde.

The **Leopold Museum** has an enormous Egon Schiele collection, as well as Expressionist and Austrian inter-war paintings. The work of Friedensreich Hundertwasser, perhaps Vienna's best-known modern artist, is on show at his gallery, the **Kunsthaus Wien**. Prints, drawings and photographs are housed in the **Albertina**.

Parthian monument (around AD 170) in the Ephesos Museum

THE APPLIED ARTS AND INTERIORS

Glass by Josef Hoffmann in the Lobmeyr Museum

On display in the **Austrian Museum of Applied Arts** is a rich collection of the decorative arts, including Oriental carpets, medieval ecclesiastical garments, Biedermeier and Jugendstil furniture, and the archives of the Wiener Werkstätte. The **Wien Museum Karlsplatz** houses a reconstructed version of the poet Franz Grillparzer's apartment as well as Adolf Loos's *(see p92)* drawing room. In the **Silberkammer** of the Hofburg is a dazzling array of dinner services collected by the Habsburgs. The **Lobmeyr Museum** exhibits glassware designed by Josef Hoffmann.

Picture clock in the Clock Museum

SPECIALIST MUSEUMS

Clock enthusiasts can visit the **Clock Museum** and the Sobek Clock and Watch Collection at the **Geymüller Schlössl**. Music is celebrated at the **Sammlung Alter Musikinstrumente**, while the darker side of life can be seen at the **Kriminalmuseum**, and at the **Bestattungsmuseum**, which houses exhibits to do with Viennese funeral rites. The **Heeresgeschichtliches Museum** houses reminders of Austria's military past. The **Hofjagd und Rüstkammer** exhibits historical weaponry. Other specialist museums include the **Österreichisches Filmmuseum** and the **Haus der Musik**.

NATURAL HISTORY AND SCIENCE

Still occupying the building constructed for it in the 19th century is the **Natural History Museum**, which has displays of mineralogy, dinosaur skeletons and zoology. The **Josephinum** houses a range of wax anatomical models, while the **Technical Museum** documents the contribution Austria has made to developments in technology, ranging from home-made items such as an amateur wooden typewriter, to the invention of the car.

ETHNOLOGY AND FOLKLORE

Vienna's Museum of Ethnology in the Hofburg, the **Völkerkundemuseum**, contains objects from all over the world. There are artefacts from Mexico and a collection of musical instruments, masks and textiles from the Far East. The Benin collection from Africa is now back on display in the museum *(see p95)*. There is also a section on Eskimo culture. The **Museum für Volks kunde** in Josefstadt houses fascinating exhibits on Austrian folklore and rural life over the centuries.

Benin carving in the Völkerkundemuseum

FINDING THE MUSEUMS

Vienna's Best: Churches

Vienna's most potent symbol is its cathedral – the Stephansdom – a masterpiece of Gothic architecture which stands out in a city where the overwhelming emphasis is on the Baroque. After the defeat of the Turks in 1683 *(see pp26–7)*, many churches were built or remodelled in the Baroque style, although it is often possible to detect the vestiges of older buildings beneath later additions. Many church interiors are lavishly furnished, and several have fine frescoes. Churches are generally open during the day except when mass is being held. Stage concerts or organ recitals are given in the evenings in some churches. A more detailed overview of Vienna's churches is on pages 52–3.

Peterskirche
The tall dome of this late Baroque church dominates the view as you approach from the Graben.

Michaelerkirche
This church has one of the most impressive medieval interiors in Vienna. The Neo-Classical façade and this cascade of Baroque stucco angels over the high altar were later additions.

Schottenring and Alsergrund

Museum and Townhall Quarter

Hofburg Quarter

Maria Treu Kirche
A statue of Mary Immaculate graces the square in front of this Baroque church (1716). Its façade dates from 1860.

Opera and Naschmarkt

| 0 kilometres | 0.5 |
| 0 miles | 0.25 |

Augustinerkirche
Antonio Canova's (1753–1822) tomb for Archduchess Maria Christina is in the Gothic Augustinerkirche, which once served as the Habsburgs' parish church.

Ruprechtskirche
Vienna's oldest church has a Romanesque nave and bell tower, a Gothic aisle and choir, and stained-glass windows which date back to the turn of the 14th century.

Maria am Gestade
Dating from the 14th century, this church was restored in the 19th century. This 15th-century Gothic panel, shows The Annunciation.

Stephansdom
The richly-carved Wiener Neustädter Altar from 1447 was a gift from Friedrich III (see p19).

Stephansdom Quarter

Jesuitenkirche
A series of twisted columns rise up to support the vault of the Jesuitenkirche (1623–31), which also features a trompe l'oeil dome.

Belvedere Quarter

Karlskirche
J B Fischer von Erlach's eclectic Baroque masterpiece (1714–39) boasts a dome, minarets and two Chinese-inspired lateral pavilions.

Franziskanerkirche
The dramatic high altar (1707) by Andrea Pozzo features a Bohemian statue of the Virgin Mary as its centrepiece.

Exploring Vienna's Churches

Many of Vienna's Churches have undergone modifications over the centuries, and they often present a fascinating mixture of styles, ranging from Romanesque to Baroque. The great era for church building in the city was in the 17th and 18th centuries, when the triumphant Catholic church, in a spate of Counter-Reformation fervour, remodelled several early churches and built new ones. A number of churches were also constructed after the Turks were defeated in 1683 *(see pp26–7)*, and the city as a whole was able to spread out beyond its earlier confines.

MEDIEVAL CHURCHES

At the heart of the city is the **Stephansdom**. Parts date from Romanesque times but most of the cathedral is Gothic; it contains a collection of Gothic sculpture, including a pulpit by Anton Pilgram *(see p78)*. Vienna's oldest church is the **Ruprechtskirche**, which stands in its own square in the Bermuda Triangle *(see p84)*; its plain façade contrasts with the delicate Gothic tracery of **Maria am Gestade**, which has a filigree spire and a lofty, vaulted interior. The early interior of the **Deutschordenskirche** contains a number of heraldic blazons. A late Romanesque basilica with Gothic modifications lurks behind the façade of the **Michaelerkirche**. The 14th-century

Madonna and Child in the Minoritenkirche

Augustinerkirche contains the hearts of the Habsburg families *(see pp24–5)* down the centuries as well as Antonio Canova's tomb for Maria Christina *(see p102)*. Behind the façade of the **Minoritenkirche** is a newly-restored Gothic interior; the same is true of the **Burgkapelle**.

17TH-CENTURY CHURCHES

There is little Renaissance architecture in Vienna, but a number of churches built before the Turkish siege survive. The **Franziskanerkirche**, with its gabled façade and theatrical high altar, and the **Jesuitenkirche** are fine examples of the architecture inspired by the Counter-Reformation *(see p24)*. The **Ursulinenkirche**, built between 1665 and 1675, has a high-galleried interior and **Annakirche** is notable for its beautiful Baroque tower. The **Dominikanerkirche** has a majestic early Baroque façade built in the 1630s by Antonio Caneval. Although it dates back to Romanesque

times, the bulk of the rather squat **Schottenkirche** was built between 1638 and 1648. In the middle of the Baroque square of Am Hof is the impressive façade of the **Kirche am Hof**. It was founded by the Carmelites and is also known as "Church of the Nine Choir Angels".

Carving of St Anne (about 1505) in Annakirche, attributed to Veit Stoss

LATE BAROQUE AND NEO-CLASSICAL CHURCHES

After the Turkish defeat *(see pp26–7)*, a number of Viennese High Baroque churches were built. The most exotic is the **Karlskirche**, and just off the Graben is the great **Peterskirche**. The tiny, ornate **Stanislaus-Kostka Chapel** was once the home of a Polish saint. Two graceful 18th-century churches are to be found on the edge of the inner city: the majestic **Maria Treu Kirche** and the **Ulrichskirche**. Joseph Kornhäusel's **Stadttempel** has a Neo-Classical interior.

TOWERS, DOMES AND SPIRES

Vienna's skyline is punctuated by the domes, spires and towers of its fine churches. Topping **Maria am Gestade** is a delicate openwork lantern, while the **Ruprechtskirche** tower is characteristically squat. The towers of the **Jesuitenkirche** are Baroque and bulbous, and **Karlskirche** has freestanding columns. **Peterskirche** has an oval dome and small towers.

Ruprechts-kirche

Maria am Gestade

Jesuitenkirche

The frescoed interior of the late Baroque Stanislaus-Kostka Chapel

19TH-CENTURY CHURCHES

During the 19th century the prevailing mood of Viennese architecture was one of Romantic historicism. Elements of past styles were adopted and re-created, for churches and for many other municipal buildings, specifically on the Ringstrasse (see pp32–3). The **Griechische Kirche** on Fleischmarkt, took its inspiration from Byzantine architecture, and the inside is replete with iconostases and

frescoes. The **Votivkirche**, built just off the Ringstrasse as an expression of gratitude for Franz Joseph's escape from assassination, is based on French Gothic architecture; its richly-coloured interior contains the marble tomb of Count Niklas Salm, who defended Vienna from the Turks during the siege of 1529 (see p24). On Lerchenfelder Strasse the red-brick **Altlerchenfelder Kirche** is a 19th-century architectural hodge-podge of Gothic and Italian Renaissance styles.

20TH-CENTURY CHURCHES

A masterpiece of early 20th-century church architecture is Otto Wagner's (see p57) massive **Kirche am Steinhof**, built to serve a psychiatric hospital. The interior has a slightly clinical air, since it is tiled in white, but the austerity is relieved by Kolo Moser's (see p57) stained-glass windows and mosaics.

The haphazard, sculpted blocks of the modern Wotruba Kirche.

The **Dr-Karl-Lueger- Kirche**, located in the Central Cemetery, was built by a protégé of Otto Wagner, Max Hegele, and has the same monumental feel about it. For true devotees of the modern, there is the **Wotruba Kirche** on Georgsgasse in the suburb of Mauer, designed by the sculptor Fritz Wotruba. Not universally liked, this looks as if it is a haphazard assembly of concrete blocks.

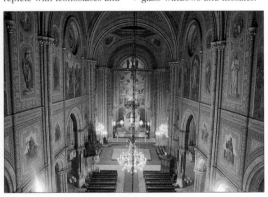

19th-century interior of the Altlerchenfelder Kirche

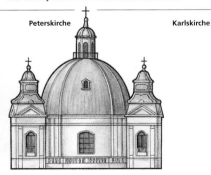

Peterskirche

Karlskirche

Vienna's Best: Jugendstil

A stroll around Vienna's streets will reveal the richness of the city's turn-of-the-century architecture. Some of the buildings are well known and instantly recognizable, and a few of the public ones, such as the Secession building, can be seen inside. However, it can be just as rewarding to discover the lesser-known buildings and monuments of the period and to savour the variety of finely-crafted architectural details. Further details can be found on pages 56–7.

Strudelhof Steps
The setting for a famous novel of the same name by Heimato von Doderer (1896–1966), these magnificent steps were built by Theodore Jäger in 1910.

Schotten and Alsergru

Museum a Townhal Quarter

Kirche am Steinhof
Commissioned for the grounds of a lunatic asylum on the outskirts of the city, this church with its grand copper dome was designed by Otto Wagner in 1905. The stained-glass windows are by Kolo Moser.

Opera and Naschmarkt

Wagner Apartments
Otto Wagner's two apartment blocks (1899) overlook the River Wien. No. 40, the Majolikahaus, is covered with ceramic decoration. No. 38 has gold Jugendstil motifs.

Otto-Wagner-Hofpavillon
Otto Wagner's imperial station pavilion (1899) was built as a showcase for his work.

Anker Clock
This clock, created by the artist Franz Matsch in 1911, sits on a bridge spanning two buildings on the Hoher Markt. Every hour, on the hour, moving figures parade across the clock face.

Postsparkasse
One of Otto Wagner's masterpieces, this post office savings bank exhibits the finest workmanship outside, and inside. Even the interior ventilator shafts are by Wagner.

Stadtpark Portals
The city's municipal park is adorned with magnificent portals (1903–7), designed by Friedrich Ohmann as part of a project to regulate the flow of the River Wien.

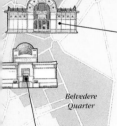

Stephansdom Quarter

fburg arter

Karlsplatz Pavilions
Two recently-restored pavilions standing in Karlsplatz were built as part of Otto Wagner's scheme for Vienna's turn-of-the-century underground system.

Belvedere Quarter

0 kilometres 1

0 miles 0.5

Secession Building
Nicknamed the Golden Cabbage because of its golden filigree dome, the Secession Building was designed at the turn of the century by Joseph Maria Olbrich for exhibitions of avant-garde art. In the basement is Gustav Klimt's Beethoven Frieze.

Exploring Viennese Jugendstil

The turn of the century saw a flowering of the visual arts in Vienna. A new generation of avant-garde artists formed the Secession in 1896 and, together with architects and designers, forged close ties between the fine and decorative arts, and created new architectural styles.

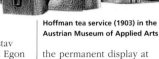

PAINTING AND DRAWING

Viennese art at the turn of the century did not conform to one particular style, but there were common elements. These included an obsession with line and rich surface pattern, as well as themes such as the *femme fatale*, love, sex and death. The finest collection of paintings from this period is in the **Belvedere** where pictures by Gustav Klimt (1862–1918) and Egon Schiele (1890–1918) feature prominently. Paintings by both artists and their contemporaries also form part of

Hoffman tea service (1903) in the Austrian Museum of Applied Arts

the permanent display at the **Wien Museum Karlsplatz**. Further examples are at the **Museum of Modern Art** in the MuseumsQuartier. The **Albertina** sometimes shows Schiele drawings. Klimt's *Beethoven Frieze* is in the **Secession Building**, and the decorative schemes he produced for the **Burgtheater** and **Kunsthistorisches Museum** are still in situ.

APPLIED ARTS

The Wiener Werkstätte – an arts and crafts studio – was founded by Josef Hoffmann (1870–1956) in 1903, and produced jewellery, fabrics, ceramics, metalwork, cutlery, bookbinding and fashion accessories with the same artistic consideration normally given to painting or sculpture. An outstanding collection is in the **Austrian Museum of Applied Arts**, which also houses a document archive open to researchers. Glass designed by Hoffmann for the Viennese firm of Lobmeyr is displayed in the **Lobmeyr Museum**.

Decoration (1891) by Gustav Klimt in the Kunsthistorisches Museum

FAVOURITE JUGENDSTIL MOTIFS

Jugendstil motifs were similar to those employed by the French Art Nouveau movement, but were generally made up of a more rigorous, geometric framework. Decorations based on organic plant forms such as sunflowers were very popular, as were female figures, heads and masks. Abstract designs made up of squares and triangles were also used to great effect.

Sunflower motif from the Karlsplatz Pavilions by Otto Wagner

Postcard designed by Joseph Maria Olbrich from *Ver Sacrum*

FURNITURE

The leading Secession designers, such as Hoffmann and Kolo Moser (1868–1918), wanted interior design to return to the simple lines of Biedermeier style *(see pp30–1)* after the excesses of the Ringstrasse era. The **Austrian Museum of Applied Arts** has several interesting displays of their work, as well as that of the Thonet firm, which made the bentwood furniture admired by the Wiener Werkstätte. Furniture was often conceived as just one element of interior design. Unfortunately, many interiors have disappeared or are not open to the public, but the **Wien Museum Karlsplatz**, which also has some pieces of Jugendstil furniture, has a recreation of Adolf Loos's *(see p92)* living room. This is a rare example of a progressive Viennese interior from the turn of the century, created before the architect finally broke with the Secession.

Writing desk and chair by Kolo Moser (1903) in the Austrian Museum of Applied Arts

Altar in the Kirche am Steinhof (1905–7)

ARCHITECTURE

Anyone walking around Vienna will notice several buildings with charming Jugendstil details. By the 1890s young architects were beginning to react against buildings of the Ringstrasse era, many of which were pastiches of earlier historical styles. The leading architects at this time were Otto Wagner (1841–1918) and Joseph Maria Olbrich (1867–1908), who collaborated on a number of projects, notably the design and installation of a new city railway and its stations, the most famous examples of which are the **Otto-Wagner-Hofpavillon** at Hietzing and the **Karlsplatz Pavilions**, as well as the **Wagner Apartments** on the Linke Wienzeile. Working independently, Wagner produced the extraordinary **Kirche am Steinhof** as well as the **Postsparkasse**, while Olbrich designed the

Secession Building as an exhibition space for radical artists and designers. Hoffmann created a number of houses for Secession artists in **Steinfeldgasse**. There are also some Jugendstil houses in **Hietzing**, while the **Anker Clock** by Franz Matsch (1861–1942) is an example of the late flowering of the style. Other examples of street architecture are the **Strudelhof Steps** (1910) by Theodore Jäger and the **Stadtpark Portals** by Friedrich Ohmann (1858–1927) and Joseph Hackhofer (1868–1917).

Postcard design by Joseph Maria Olbrich from *Ver Sacrum*

Gold leaf detail from the Wagner Apartments

Lettering by Alfred Roller from *Ver Sacrum*

Abstract fabric design by Josef Hoffmann

Vienna's Best: Coffee Houses

Coffee houses have been an essential part of Viennese life for centuries. The coffee house is more than just a place to go to drink coffee. It is a meeting place, somewhere to linger over a snack or a light lunch, and a refuge from city life. Each coffee house attracts its own particular clientele and has its own unique atmosphere. Most of them also serve alcohol. Further details of what coffee houses have to offer can be found on pages 60–61.

Landtmann
This comfortable and formal coffee house used to be frequented by Sigmund Freud. Today it is visited by theatregoers and actors from the nearby Burgtheater, and by journalists and politicians.

Central
Once the meeting place of writers and free thinkers, the most splendid of all the coffee houses in Vienna has now been restored to its former grandeur.

Schottenring and Alsergrund

Museum and Townhall Quarter

Hofburg Quarter

Sperl
Just outside the city centre, the Sperl has a faithful clientele, including many young people who come here for the billiard tables and hot strudels.

Eiles
Its location near various government offices has made the Eiles a favourite haunt of officials and lawyers.

Opera and Naschmarkt

Café Museum
The Café Museum was built in 1899 to designs by Adolf Loos (see p92), but was remodelled in the 1930s. It has now been restored in accordance with Loos's original design.

Hawelka
This famous coffee house has long cultivated its bohemian image. The atmosphere is warm and theatrical, and no visit to Vienna is complete without a late-night cup of coffee or a drink here.

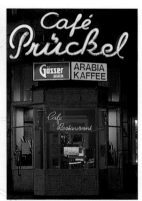

| 0 kilometres | 0.5 |
| 0 miles | 0.25 |

Prückel
The Prückel has been shabby and run down for as long as anyone can remember, but it has become a mecca for bridge players and locals who crowd into its back room.

Kleines
One of the smallest, quaintest coffee houses in Vienna, the Kleines still attracts a loyal clientele of actors.

Frauenhuber
The oldest coffee house in Vienna, this is where Mozart once performed. Its location off Kärntner Strasse makes it handy for shoppers and for tourists visiting the nearby Stephansdom.

Exploring Vienna's Coffee Houses

The Viennese coffee house serves many functions and to make the best of the institution it helps to understand the many roles it plays in the lives of local people. In a coffee house you can read the newspapers, share a simple lunch with a friend, or in some play a game of bridge or billiards. Most places serve wines, beers and spirits as well as coffee. The coffee house is a priceless urban resource and, though no longer unique to Vienna, it is here that it has flourished in its most satisfying form. Vienna also has many *Café-Konditoreien (see p203)*.

Waiter at the Dommayer café

THE HISTORY OF THE COFFEE HOUSE

Legend maintains that the first coffee house opened its doors after the defeat of the Turks in 1683 *(see p26)*. However, historians insist that coffee was known in the city long before this date. Coffee houses took the form we know today in the late 18th century. They reached their heyday in the late 19th century, when they were patronized by cliques of like-minded politicians, artists, writers, composers, doctors or civil servants. In 1890, for instance, the controversial literary

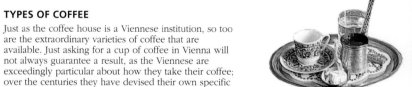
18th-century Viennese girl holding a coffee grinder

group Jung Wien met regularly at the **Griensteidl**, while the essayist Peter Altenberg was reputed to have never been seen outside his favourite café, the **Central**.

Today, as in the past, the **Ministerium**, **Museum**, **Frauenhuber**, **Raimund**, **Eiles**, **Schwarzenberg** and **Zartl** continue to attract their own specific clientele.

COFFEE HOUSE ETIQUETTE

There is a simple but formal etiquette attached to a coffee house. A waiter, almost certainly dressed in a tuxedo, however shabby the coffee house, will take your order, which will often be served with a plain glass of water. Once

you have ordered you are free to occupy your table for as long as you like. A cup of coffee is not cheap, but entitles you to linger for an hour or two and to read the newspapers which are freely available. The grander coffee houses, such as the **Landtmann** and **Central**, will also have a selection of foreign newspapers and periodicals.

WHAT COFFEE HOUSES HAVE TO OFFER

Coffee houses often function as local clubhouses. At the **Sperl** you can play billiards, at the **Prückel** there are bridge tables, and at

TYPES OF COFFEE

Just as the coffee house is a Viennese institution, so too are the extraordinary varieties of coffee that are available. Just asking for a cup of coffee in Vienna will not always guarantee a result, as the Viennese are exceedingly particular about how they take their coffee; over the centuries they have devised their own specific vocabulary to convey to the waiter precisely how they like their beverage served. The list that follows will cover most variations of the Viennese cup of coffee, although you may well find local ones.

Türkischer: plain, strong black Turkish coffee served in the traditional manner.

Brauner:
coffee with milk (small or large).

Melange:
a blend of coffee and hot milk.

Kurz:
extra strong.

Obers:
with cream.

Mokka:
strong black coffee.

Kapuziner:
black coffee with a dash of milk, usually frothed.

Schwarzer:
black coffee (small or large).

Konsul:
black coffee with a dash of cream.

Kaffeinfreier Kaffee:
decaffeinated coffee.

Espresso: strong black coffee made by machine. Ask for it *gestreckt* for a weak one.

the **Dommayer** you can attend literary readings. The **Central** and **Bräunerhof** both offer live piano music with your coffee. The **Kleines** is, as its name suggests, too tiny to offer entertainment, but still draws a regular crowd. The **Imperial** is part of the hotel of the same name. Coffee houses outside the city centre include the excellent **Westend**.

Coffee house sign

WHAT TO EAT

Most coffee houses offer snack foods throughout the day, simple lunches and occasional specialities, such as pastries, which are served at particular times. The **Hawelka** serves hot jam-filled buns (*Buchteln*) late at night, and the **Sperl** often has fresh strudel late morning. Larger coffee houses, such as **Diglas** and **Landtmann**, offer extensive lunchtime menus as well as a range of excellent pastries made on the premises.

Old Viennese coffee machine in Diglas

COFFEE PLAIN AND SIMPLE

There are times when you quite simply want a good cup of coffee – when newspapers or a table of your own are luxuries you can dispense with. On such occasions you should keep an eye out for an Espresso bar, where you can lean informally against a counter and order coffee at a half or a third of the price you would normally expect to pay at a coffee house. The *Café-Konditoreien* belonging to the Aida chain, apart from serving delicious cakes and pastries, also function as Espresso bars.

Pharisäer: strong black, with whipped cream on top, served with a small liqueur glass of rum.

Schlagobers: strong black coffee served with either plain or whipped cream.

Einspänner: large glass of coffee with whipped cream on top.

Kaisermelange: black coffee with an egg yolk and brandy.

VIENNA THROUGH THE YEAR

Spring often arrives unexpectedly, with a few days of sunshine and warmth. The climax of spring is the Wiener Festwochen in May. Summers are long and hot, and ideal for swimming and for river trips on the Danube *(see pp178–9)* during July and August, when some venues officially close. Vienna comes alive again in September when the most important theatres reopen. More often than not,

there is an Indian summer at this time, and it is still warm enough to sit in the Stadtpark. As autumn turns to winter, the streets fill with stalls selling chestnuts and by the feast of St Nicholas on 6 December, snow has often fallen. Christmas is a family occasion, but the New Year is celebrated in style as it heralds the start of the carnival season. The Wiener Tourismusverband *(see p239)* has details of important events.

SPRING

Vienna is beautiful in spring and is the time for the **Wiener Festwochen** *(see May)*. It is also a season that brings a few days of balmy weather, and when beautiful colours appear in the parks and the Prater woods *(see pp162–63)*. This is the best time of the year to visit the Stadtpark *(see p98)* with its open-air bandstand and much-photographed resident peacock. The Volksgarten, Burggarten and the great parks of the Belvedere and Schönbrunn also come into their own and there are some splendid views of the city from the Stephansdom tower.

A collection of life-sized dolls on display during the Wiener Festwochen

MARCH

Easter Market *(two weeks before Easter)*, held at the Freyung. Items on sale include arts, crafts and traditional food.
Schönbrunner Schlosskonzerte *(until end Oct)*, at the Orangery, Schönbrunn Palace *(see p172)*. Performances of popular melodies of Johann Strauss.

Runners taking part in the annual Spring Marathon

APRIL

Volksprater Funfair *(1 Apr–31 Oct)*, held in the Prater woods *(pp162–63)*.
Spring Marathon starts from Schönbrunn Palace *(see pp172–3)*, passing the Hofburg, Ringstrasse and Opera House, and ends at the Neues Rathaus (Town Hall).
Frühlingsfestival *(2nd week Apr to mid-May)*. Classical music festival alternating between the Musikverein *(p146)* and the Konzerthaus *(p229)*.
Spanish Riding School *(until Jun)*. Lipizzaner horses' performances in the Winter Riding School *(pp98–9)*.
Hofburg Orchestra *(until Oct)*. Concerts at Musikverein *(p146)* and Hofburg *(pp96–7)*.
Kursalon *(until end Oct)*. Open-air concerts *(p229)*. Indoor concerts all year.

MAY

Tag der Arbeit *(1 May)*. Public holiday. Every year, Labour Day is celebrated with parades on Rathausplatz and Ringstrasse.
Maifest *(1 May)*, in the Prater *(pp162–63)* with music and children's programmes.
Vienna Music Festival *(6 May–21 Jun)*, part of the Wiener Festwochen programme, which begins a few days earlier at the Wiener Konzerthaus *(p229)* and MuseumsQuartier *(p120)*.
Dancing on the *Vindobona* *(15 May to end Sep)*. Board the boat at Schwedenplatz for a cruise on the Danube.
Wiener Festwochen *(mid-May to mid-Jun)*. Vienna's greatest festival features operas, plays and performing arts.

AVERAGE DAILY HOURS OF SUNSHINE

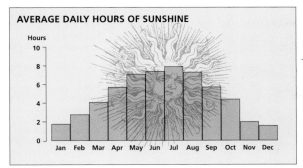

Hours

10
8
6
4
2
0

Jan Feb Mar Apr May Jun Jul Aug Sep Oct Nov Dec

Sunshine Chart
*June, July and August
are the hottest months
in Vienna, with between
six and eight hours of
sunshine each day, but
summer can also be
quite damp and humid.
Although the city cools
down in September, Indi-
an summers are quite
common.*

SUMMER

Summer can be both the
busiest and most relaxing time
in Vienna. The great theatres
may be officially closed, but
the Jazz Festival is on at the
Opera House and the Volkstheater in July. The Danube
beaches are ideal for sunbath-
ing, swimming and other
watersports on sunny days. In
the evenings, people relax at
the Heuriger wine taverns
on the outskirts of the city.

Summer outside the Votivkirche

JUNE

Corpus Christi *(2 Jun)*. Public
holiday. Catholic festival held
in honour of the Eucharist.
Vinova *(2nd week Jun)*, wine
fair in the Prater *(pp162–63)*.

The Concordia Ball
(2nd Fri in Jun) takes place at
the Neues Rathaus *(p130)*.
Ball der Universität
(18 Jun) held at the University
(p130).
Donauinselfest *(last weekend
in Jun)*, three-day pop concert
on Danube island.

JULY

**Outdoor films, operas and
concerts** *(until Sep)* shown
on a giant screen in
Rathausplatz. Seating is
provided free.
Theater an der Wien
(Jul–Aug). While the State
Opera and Volksoper are
closed in July and August,
opera performances and
concerts continue at this
theatre *(see p138)*.
Oper Klosterneuburg
(Jul) Performances are in the
Kaiserhof courtyard of the
palatial religious foundation,
Klosterneuberg, a short way
north of Vienna *(see p129)*.
Jazzfest *(1st two weeks Jul)*,
part of Klangbogen Wien
music festival. Venues
include the Opera House
(pp140–41), the Volkstheater
(p230) and the arcaded
courtyard of the Neues
Rathaus *(p130)*.

Bathing beside the Danube

International Dance Weeks
(mid-Jul to 3rd week Aug)
at the Universitäts
Sportzentrum, Schmelz;
Volkstheater *(p230)*.
**Summer Dance Festival
(Im Puls)** *(end-Jul to 3rd week
Aug)* is held at the
Volkstheater *(p230)* and
Universitäts Sportzentrum at
Schmelz.
Seefestspiele Mörbisch
(Thu–Sun mid-Jul to end Aug).
An operetta festival which
takes place in Mörbisch, some
40 km (25 miles) away.

AUGUST

Maria Himmelfahrt
(15 Aug), public holiday. A
Catholic festival which
celebrates the assumption of
the Madonna.

Seefestspiele Mörbisch, an annual operetta festival performed against the backdrop of Lake Neusiedl

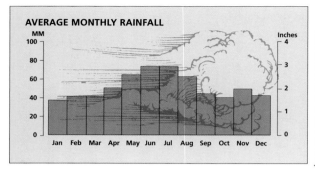

AVERAGE MONTHLY RAINFALL

Rainfall Chart
The summer months are not only the hottest but also the wettest, helping to keep the city cool. During spring and autumn, days can be mild, with some drizzle, until November, which can be very wet. Around 600 mm (23 inches) of rain falls annually.

AUTUMN

In Vienna, autumn means a new start. The theatres, and particularly Vienna's great opera houses, reopen once again. Shops get ready to tempt buyers with their range of autumn fashions. Then, almost overnight, all the shop windows seem to be filled with figures of St Nicholas and his wicked companion Krampus. This cute little furry devil appears everywhere. It is only after 6 December that the shop windows are finally cleared for Christmas displays.

SEPTEMBER

Spanish Riding School performances *(until end Oct)* and training sessions of the Lipizzaner horses *(pp98–9)*.
Vienna Boys' Choir *(mid-Sep to Dec)* perform at Mass at the Burgkapelle *(p103)* on Sundays.
Trotting in the Krieau *(until Jun)*. Trotting races at the Prater *(pp162–63)*.

OCTOBER

National Holiday *(26 Oct)*. Celebrations to mark the passing of the Neutrality

Krampus, the wicked furry devil who accompanies St Nicholas

The Vienna Boys' Choir performing at the Konzerthaus

Act in 1955, which was followed by the withdrawal of the Allied troops stationed in Austria since 1945.
Viennale *(end Oct)*, film festival at Gartenbau, Parkring 12; Metro, Johannesgasse 4; Künstlerhaus, Akademiestrasse 13; and Stadtkino, Schwarzenbergplatz 7–8.
Wien Modern *(until end Nov)*. Modern music festival at the Konzerthaus *(p229)*.

NOVEMBER

Allerheiligen *(1 Nov)*. Public holiday. Catholic festival celebrating All Saints' Day.

Antik-Aktuell *(2nd week Nov)*, art and antiques fair held at the Hofburg.
Schubertiade *(3rd week Nov)* at the Musikverein *(p146)*.
Krippenschau *(until mid-Dec)*, display of historic mangers at Peterskirche *(p87)*.
Christkindlmarkt *(2nd Sat Nov to end Dec)*, Christmas market and children's workshop by the Rathaus *(p130)*.
Christmas markets *(from last Sat Nov)* held at the Freyung, Heiligenkreuzerhof, Schönbrunn, Karlsplatz and Spittelberg.
International choirs *(last Sat Nov)* at the Town Hall, or Rathaus *(p130)*.

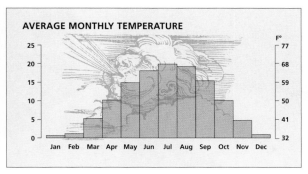

AVERAGE MONTHLY TEMPERATURE

Temperature Chart
The chart shows the average temperatures each month. Top temperatures in July and August can reach 25° C (77° F) although May and September are also quite warm. Winters are icy, and temperatures can be as low as -1.4° C (29.5° F) in January.

WINTER

Roasting chestnuts over hot coals is a regular winter sight on Vienna's streets. As Christmas draws near, stalls offer mulled wine and hot snacks and shops enter into the festive spirit putting up lights and decorations.

The Viennese celebrate Christmas Eve with a traditional meal consisting of *Fischbeuschelsuppe*, a creamy fish soup, followed by fresh fried carp. The usual dish which is eaten on Christmas Day is goose, although turkey is becoming more popular.

New Year also marks the start of Fasching, Vienna's famous Carnival season.

DECEMBER

Christmas markets (*continue from November*).

PUBLIC HOLIDAYS

New Year's Day (1 Jan)
Epiphany (6 Jan)
Easter Sunday
Easter Monday
Tag der Arbeit (1 May)
Ascension Day (6th Thu after Easter)
Whit Monday (6th Mon after Easter)
Corpus Christi (2 Jun)
Maria Himmelfahrt (15 Aug)
National Holiday (26 Oct)
Allerheiligen (1 Nov)
Maria Empfängnis (8 Dec)
Christmas Day (25 Dec)
Stefanitag (26 Dec)

Chestnut-roasting in winter

Maria Empfängnis (*8 Dec*). Public holiday. Catholic festival celebrating the Immaculate Conception.
Midnight Mass (*Christmas Eve*) held in the Stephansdom (*pp76–7*). No tickets needed but arrive early for seats.
Stefanitag (*26 Dec*). Public holiday for Boxing Day.
New Year's Eve performance of Die Fledermaus (*31 Dec*) at the Opera House (*pp140–41*) and Volksoper (*p229*). The performance is shown on a large screen in Stephansplatz (*p70*).
New Year's Eve concerts at the Konzerthaus (*p229*) and Musikvereinsaal (*p146*).
Kaiserball (*31 Dec*) at the Hofburg (*pp96–7*).
New Year's Eve in the city centre: a street party with snacks and drink. Marquees provide music and cabaret.

JANUARY

New Year's Concert (*31 Dec & 1 Jan*) by the great Vienna Philharmonic at the Musikverein (*p146*). Requests for tickets for next year's concert must arrive on 2 Jan (*p228*).

Beethoven's Ninth Symphony (*31 Dec & 1 Jan*) is performed at the Konzerthaus (*p229*).
Fasching (*6 Jan to Ash Wed*), the Vienna Carnival includes the **Heringschmaus** (*Ash Wed*), a hot and cold buffet.
Holiday on Ice (*mid- to end Jan*). This is held at the Stadthalle, Vogelweidplatz.
Resonanzen (*2nd to 3rd week Jan*). Festival of ancient music at the Konzerthaus (*p229*).
Vienna Ice Dream (*mid-Jan to end Feb*). Ice-skating in front of City Hall (*p130*).

FEBRUARY

Opera Ball (*last Thu before Shrove Tue*), one of the grandest balls of Fasching (*p141*).
Wintertanzwoche (*5–13 Feb*). Part of the Dance Festival (*see below*). Events are held in the MuseumsQuartier (*p118*).
Dance Festival (*17 Feb to 27 Mar*), includes classic and jazz dance at the Universitäts Sportzentrum at Schmelz.
Haydn Tage (*3rd week Feb to 1st week Mar*). Haydn's music at the Konzerthaus (*see p229*).

The Christkindlmarkt, in front of the Neues Rathaus

Johann Strauss II statue in the Stadtpark ▷

VIENNA AREA
BY AREA

STEPHANSDOM QUARTER

The winding streets and spacious squares of this area form the ancient core of Vienna. Following World War II, subterranean excavations uncovered the remains of a Roman garrison from 2,000 years ago, and every succeeding age is represented here, from the Romanesque

Plaque on No. 19 Sonnenfelsgasse, once part of the university

arches of the Ruprechts-kirche to the steel and glass of the spectacular Haas Haus in Stephansplatz. Many of the buildings in the area house government offices, businesses, taverns and stylish shops. Dominating the skyline is the Stephansdom, the focus of the city at its geographical centre.

SIGHTS AT A GLANCE

Streets and Squares
Am Hof ㉟
Annagasse ⑱
Bäckerstrasse ⑭
Blutgasse ③
Domgasse ④
Fleischmarkt ㉓
Griechengasse ㉔
Grünangergasse ⑥
Hoher Markt ㉗
Jewish District ㉖
Judenplatz ㉛
Kurrentgasse ㉝
Schönlaterngasse ⑩
Sonnenfelsgasse ⑫

Historic Buildings
Academy of
   Sciences ⑨
Altes Rathaus ㉙
Bohemian Court
   Chancery ㉘
Haas Haus ⑮
Heiligen-
   kreuzerhof ⑬
Postsparkasse ㉒
Winter Palace of
   Prince Eugene ⑰

Churches and Cathedrals
Annakirche ⑲
Deutschordenskirche ②
Dominikanerkirche ⑦
Franziskanerkirche ⑯
Jesuitenkirche ⑧
Kirche am Hof ㉞
Maria am Gestade ㉚
Peterskirche ㊱
Ruprechtskirche ㉕
Stephansdom pp76–9 ①

Museums and Galleries
*Austrian Museum of Applied
   Arts pp82–3* ㉑
Cathedral Museum ⑪
Clock Museum ㉜
Mozarthaus Vienna ⑤
Haus der Musik ⑳
Museum Judenplatz ㉛

GETTING THERE
This area is served by the Stephansplatz (lines U1, U3), Stubentor (line U3) and Schwedenplatz (lines U1, U4) U-Bahn stations. Trams 1 and 2 go along parts of the Ring-strasse. Buses 1A, 2A and 3A stop at the junction of Hoher Markt and Marc-Aurel-Strasse.

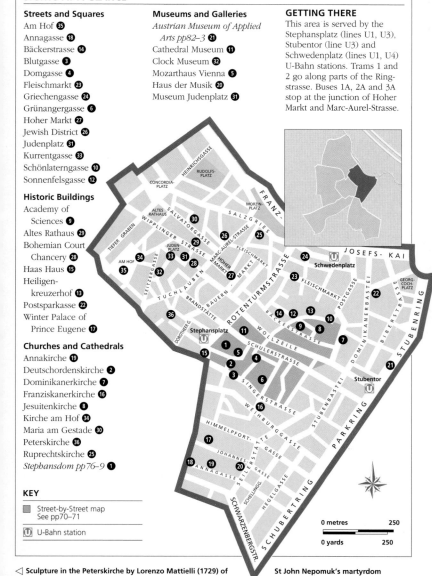

KEY

Street-by-Street map
See pp70–71

🚇 U-Bahn station

◁ **Sculpture in the Peterskirche by Lorenzo Mattielli (1729) of St John Nepomuk's martyrdom**

Street-by-Street: Old Vienna

This part of the inner city retains its medieval layout, offering a complex of lanes, alleys and spacious courtyards. The influence of the church is particularly evident. You can find remains of monastic orders such as the Dominicans and feudal orders such as the Teutonic Knights, as well as ideological orders, for example the Jesuits. Yet there is nothing ossified about the area: at night the bars and restaurants on Bäckerstrasse and Schönlaterngasse are thronged with people until the early hours of the morning. Dominating everything is the 137-m high (450-ft) spire of the Stephansdom cathedral in the very heart of Vienna.

★ Cathedral Museum
Much of this collection was donated by Duke Rudolf IV who is shown here ⓫

★ Stephansdom
The cathedral took centuries to build and is rich in medieval and Renaissance monuments ❶

To Rotenturmstrasse

To Kärntner Strasse   S T E P H A N S P L A T Z

S T R O B E L G A S S E

B L U T G A S S E

Deutschordenskirche
A remarkable Treasury, with objects collected by German aristocrats, lies alongside this Gothic church ❷

The Haas & Haas Tea House is a charming, informal café and tea house.

S I N G E R S T R A S S E

Mozarthaus Vienna
Mozart lived here from 1784 to 1787. He had a suite of rooms where he wrote many of his great works ❺

Domgasse
This pretty street includes a bookshop at No. 8, Buchhandlung 777 ❹

Blutgasse
Courtyards like this are typical of the tenement houses on Blutgasse ❸

**Dominikaner-
kirche**
*Originally consec-
rated on this site
in 1237, the
present Baroque
church dates from
the 1630s* 7

LOCATOR MAP
See Street Finder, maps 2 & 6

STEPHANSDOM
QUARTER

HOFBURG
QUARTER

OPERA &
NASCH-
MARKT

Schönlaterngasse
*The lantern at No. 6
gave this charming
street its name* 10

SCHÖNLATERNGASSE

BÄCKERSTRASSE

DR-IGNAZ-
SEIPEL-PLATZ

POSTGASSE

WOLLZEILE

SCHULERSTRASSE

KUMPFGASSE

Jesuitenkirche
*This pulpit detail of the
apostle Matthew is from the
Baroque Jesuitenkirche.
One of Vienna's most ornate
churches, it was built by
the Jesuits in the 1620s* 8

★ Academy of Sciences
*The great hall (Aula) of the
Academy is one of the
noblest salons in Vienna* 9

**Grünanger-
gasse**
*This quiet lane is
full of bookshops
and art galleries* 6

RIEMERGASSE

KEY

– – – Suggested route

0 metres   50

0 yards   50

STAR SIGHTS

★ Stephansdom

★ Cathedral Museum

★ Academy of Sciences

Stephansdom ●

See pp76–9.

Deutschordens-kirche ●

Singerstrasse 7. **Map** 2 E5 & 6 D3. *Tel*
5121065. Ⓤ *Stephansplatz.* **Church**
◯ *7am–6pm daily.* ◙ *Treasury*
◯ *10am–noon Mon & Thu, 3–5pm*
Wed & Fri, 10am–noon & 3–5pm Sat.
◉ *Tue & Sun, public hols.* ◪

This church belongs to the
Order of Teutonic Knights,
a chivalric order which was
established in the 12th century.
It is 14th-century Gothic, but
was restored in the 1720s by
Anton Erhard Martinelli.
Numerous coats of arms of
teutonic knights and memorial
slabs are displayed on the
walls. The altarpiece from
1520 is Flemish and
incorporates panel paintings
and carvings of scenes from
the Passion beneath some very
delicate traceried canopies.

The Order's Treasury
is situated off the church's
courtyard and now serves as
a museum, displaying various
collections acquired by its
Grand Masters over the
centuries. The starting point is
a room which houses a large
collection of coins, medals and
a 13th-century enthronement
ring. This leads into the second
room which contains chalices
and Mass vessels worked
with silver filigree. Following
this is a display of
maces, daggers
and ceremonial

Inner courtyard of No. 9 Blutgasse, the Fähnrichshof

garb. The final exhibits show
some Gothic paintings and a
Carinthian carving of *St George
and the Dragon* (1457).

Blutgasse ●

Map 2 E5 & 6 D3. Ⓤ *Stephansplatz.*

A local legend relates that
this street acquired its
gruesome name – Blood Lane
– after a massacre in 1312
of the Knights Templar (a
military and religious order)
in a skirmish so violent that
the streets flowed with blood.
But there is no evidence to
support this story and the
street's name belies its charm.

Its tall apartment buildings
date mostly from the 18th
century. Walk into No. 3 and
see how the city's restorers
have linked up the buildings
and their courtyards. No. 9,
the Fähnrichshof,
is particularly
impressive.

Winged altar-
piece in the
Deutschordens-
kirche (1520)

Domgasse ●

Map 2 E5 & 6 D3. Ⓤ *Stephansplatz.*

In addition to the Figarohaus,
Domgasse boasts some
interesting buildings, including
the Trienter Hof, with its airy
courtyard. No. 6 is a house of
medieval origin called the
Kleiner Bischofshof or small
bishop's house: it has a 1761
Matthias Gerl façade. Next
door is the site of the house
where Franz Georg Kolschitzky
lived and, in 1694, died. It is
said that he claimed some
Turkish coffee beans as a
reward for his bravery in the
1683 Turkish siege, and later
opened Vienna's first coffee
house. The truth of this story,
however, is doubtful.

Mozarthaus Vienna ●

Domgasse 5. **Map** 2 E5 & 6 D3.
Tel 5121791. Ⓤ *Stephansplatz.*
◯ *10am–7pm daily.* ◪ ◙
www. mozarthausvienna.at

Mozart and his family
occupied a flat on the first
floor of this building from
1784 to 1787. Of Mozart's 11
Viennese residences, this is
the one where he is said to
have been happiest. It is also
where he composed a
significant number of his
masterworks: the exquisite
Haydn quartets, a handful of
piano concerti, and *The
Marriage of Figaro*. Restored
for the anniversary year 2006,
the Mozarthaus now has
exhibitions on two upper floors
as well as the first-floor flat.

Elaborate nave of the Dominikanerkirche

Grünangergasse ❻

Map 4 E1 & 6 D3. Ⓤ *Stephansplatz.*

This quiet lane takes its name from the creperie Zum Grünen Anker at No. 10, a tavern frequented by Franz Schubert in the 19th century.

No. 8's portal has crude carvings of rolls, croissants and pretzels. It is known as the Kipferlhaus after a Viennese crescent-shaped roll. The former Fürstenberg Palace, from 1720, has a Baroque portal with carved hounds racing to the top of the keystone.

Dominikaner-kirche ❼

Postgasse 4. **Map** 2 E5 & 6 E3.
Tel 5129174. Ⓤ *Stephansplatz, Schwedenplatz.* ◯ *7am–7pm Mon–Sat, 7am–9pm Sun.* 📷

The Dominican order of monks came to Vienna in 1226, and by 1237 they had consecrated a church here. In the 1630s Antonio Canevale

designed their present church, which boasts a majestic and really rather handsome Baroque façade. The interior is equally imposing. The central chapel on the right has swirling Rococo grilles and candelabra, and there is a very beautiful gilt organ above the west door. Its casing dates from the mid-18th century. The frescoes by Tencala and Rauchmiller are especially noteworthy, as is the high altar.

Jesuitenkirche ❽

Dr-Ignaz-Seipel-Platz 1. **Map** 2 E5 & 6 E3. **Tel** 5125232. Ⓤ *Stubentor, Stephansplatz, Schwedenplatz.* ◯ *7am–6:30pm daily.* 📷

Andrea Pozzo, an Italian architect, redesigned the Jesuitenkirche between 1703 and 1705 and its broad, high façade dominates the Dr-Ignaz-Seipel-Platz. In the 1620s the Jesuits decided to move their headquarters here in order to be near the Old University, which they controlled. The

Jesuit order was the dominant force behind the Counter-Reformation. The Jesuits were not afraid of making a statement, and the church's grand design and high façade reflects this dominance.

The interior is gaudy, with plump marble columns screening the side chapels. Pozzo's ceiling frescoes are cleverly executed using a *trompe l'oeil* effect and the pews are richly carved.

Academy of Sciences ❾

Dr-Ignaz-Seipel-Platz 2. **Map** 2 E5 & 6 E3. Ⓤ *Schwedenplatz, Stubentor.* **Tel** 515810. ◯ *8am–5pm Mon–Fri.*

Once the centrepiece of the Old University, the Akademie der Wissenschaften has an impressive Baroque façade. Designed in 1753 by Jean Nicolas Jadot de Ville-Issey as the *Aula*, or great hall, it has recently been restored. A double staircase leads up to a huge salon that, despite its reconstruction after a fire in 1961, is still one of the great rooms of Vienna.

Elaborate frescoes adorn the ceilings of the Ceremonial Hall and the walls are composed of marble embellished with Rococo plasterwork. Haydn's *Creation* was performed here in 1808 in the presence of the composer: it was the eve of his 76th birthday and his last public appearance.

Fountain by Salomon Kleiner on the Academy of Sciences (about 1755)

The Baroque Bernhardskapelle *(left)*, seen from Schönlaterngasse

Schönlaterngasse ⑩

Map 2 E5 & 6 E3. Ⓤ *Stephansplatz, Schwedenplatz*. **Alte Schmiede** *Schwedenplatz*. ⬛ *Tel 5128329*. ⬜ *10am–3pm Mon–Fri*.

The attractive curving lane derives its name (Pretty Lantern Lane) from the handsome wrought-iron lantern which is clamped to No. 6. This is a copy of the 1610 original which is now in the Wien Museum Karlsplatz *(see p146)*. At No. 4, a solid early 17th-century house guards the curve of the street. No. 7, the Basilisken-haus, which is of medieval origin, displays on its façade an artist's impression of a mythical serpent, dating from 1740. A serpent is reputed to have been discovered in 1212 in a well by the house.

The composer Robert Schumann lived at No. 7a from 1838 to 1839. No. 9 is the Alte Schmiede – the large smithy from which it takes its name has been reassembled in the basement. This complex also contains an art gallery and a hall used for poetry readings and musical workshops.

Cathedral Museum ⑪

Stephansplatz 6. **Map** 2 E5 & 6 D3. ⬛ *Tel 515523560*. Ⓤ *Stephansplatz*. ⬜ *10am–5pm Tue–Sat*. ⬛ *24 & 31 Dec, Maundy Thu & Easter Mon*. 🖼 🅿 ⓞ ♿

Known in German as the Dom und Diözesanmuseum, its exhibits include 18th-century religious paintings by important Austrian artists such as Franz Anton Maulbertsch, and some 16th- and 17th-century rustic carvings. There are also works by the Dutch painter Jan van Hemessen. Not to be missed is the display of medieval carvings, many of which are of the Madonna and Child.

The Treasury is spectacular as many of the items were the personal gift of Duke Rudolf IV to the Cathedral. His shroud is housed here as well as a famous portrait of him by a Bohemian master dating from the 1360s *(see p70)*. Other items include the St Leopold reliquary from 1592, which is encrusted with figures of saints and coats of arms, and some outstanding enamels from the 12th-century.

Sonnenfelsgasse ⑫

Map 2 E5 & 6 E3. Ⓤ *Stephansplatz, Schwedenplatz*.

Fine houses line this pleasant street. Though by no means uniform in style, most of the dwellings on the north side of the street are solid merchant and patrician houses dating from the late 16th century. No. 19, which was built in 1628 and renovated in 1721, was once part of the Old University *(see p73)*. No. 11 has an impressive courtyard. Many of the balconies overlooking the courtyard have been glassed in to their full height so as to provide extra living space. No. 3 has the most elaborate façade, and contains a *Stadtheuriger* called the Zwölf Apostelkeller *(see p218)*. This is an urban equivalent of the *Heurige*, the wine growers' inns found in the villages outside Vienna *(see p219)*. The street was named after a soldier called Joseph von Sonnenfels. He became Maria Theresa's legal adviser and under his guidance, she totally reformed the penal code and abolished torture.

Gothic Madonna (1325) in the Cathedral Museum

Heiligen-kreuzerhof ⓭

Schönlaterngasse 5. **Map** 2 E5 & 6 E3.
Tel 5125896. ⓤ Schwedenplatz.
⬜ 6am–9pm Mon–Sat. ⬤ Sun.
◳ ♿ **Bernhardskapelle**
⬜ on request

In the Middle Ages, the rural-monasteries expanded by establishing a presence in the cities. Secularization in the 1780s diminished such holdings, but this one, belonging to the abbey of Heiligenkreuz (see p176), survived.

The buildings around the courtyard housing the city's Applied Arts College present a serene 18th-century face. On the south side of the courtyard is the Bernhardskapelle. Dating from 1662, but altered in the 1730s, the chapel is a Baroque gem. Across from the chapel a patch of wall from Babenberg times (see pp22–3) has been exposed to remind you that, as so often in Vienna, the building is much older in origin than it at first appears.

Fresco at No. 12 Bäckerstrasse

Bäckerstrasse ⓮

Map 2 E5 & 6 D3. ⓤ Stephansplatz.

Nowadays people visit this street, which used to house the city's bakers in medieval times, to sample its nightlife rather than its bread. The architecture is also of considerable interest: No. 2 sits beneath a 17th-century tower, and has a pretty courtyard. Opposite, at No. 1, is the site of the Alte Regensburgerhof, the outpost of Bavarian merchants who were given incentives to work in Vienna in the 15th century. No. 8 is the former palace of Count Seilern dating from 1722, and No. 7 is famous for its arcaded Renaissance courtyard and

stables, which is the only surviving example in Vienna. Two other houses of Renaissance origin are located at Nos. 12 and 14.

Haas Haus ⓯

Stephansplatz 12. **Map** 2 E5 & 6 D3.
Tel 5356083. ⓤ Stephansplatz.
⬜ 8am–2am daily. ◳ ♿

Commissioning a modern-building directly opposite the Stephansdom was a sensitive task, and the city entrusted its design to one of Austria's leading architects, Hans Hollein. The result is the 1990 Haas Haus, a shining structure of glass and blue-green marble that curves elegantly round right into the Graben. The building has a very pleasing asymmetrical appearance, with decorative elements such as lopsided cubes of marble attached to the façade, a protruding structure high up resembling a diving board and a Japanese bridge inside. The atrium within is surrounded by cafés, shops, a restaurant, Do & Co (see p214) and offices.

Franziskaner-kirche ⓰

Franziskanerplatz 4. **Map** 4 E1 & 6 D4.
Tel 5124578. ⓤ Stephansplatz.
⬜ 6:30am–noon & 2–5:30pm
Mon–Sat, 7am–5:30pm Sun. ◳ ♿

The Franciscans were fairly late arrivals in Vienna and one of their first tasks was to build a church on the site of a former medieval convent. Dating from 1603, the church totally dominates the Franziskanerplatz.

The façade is in South German Renaissance style, and is topped by an elaborate scrolled gable with obelisks.

Detail from Andrea Pozzo's altar (1707) in the Franziskanerkirche

The Moses Fountain in front of the church was designed by the Neo-Classicist Johann Martin Fischer in 1798.

The interior is in full-blown Baroque style and includes a finely-modelled pulpit dating from 1726, and richly-carved pews. A dramatic high altar by Andrea Pozzo rises to the full height of the church. Only the front part of the structure is three-dimensional – the rest is trompe l'oeil. Look out for a 1725 Crucifixion by Carlo Carlone among the paintings in the side altars.

You usually have to ask a passing monk for permission to see the church organ. It is worth being persistent, as this is the oldest organ in Vienna (1642), designed by Johann Wöckerl. It has statues of angel musicians and beautifully painted doors on religious themes.

Gleaming façade of Haas Haus (1990)

Stephansdom ●

Situated in the centre of Vienna, the Stephansdom is the soul of the city itself; it is no mere coincidence that the urns containing the entrails of some of the Habsburgs lie in a vault beneath its main altar. A church has stood on the site for over 800 years, but all that remains of the original 13th-century Romanesque church are the Giants' Doorway and Heathen Towers. The Gothic nave, choir and side chapels are the result of a rebuilding programme in the 14th and 15th centuries, while some of the outbuildings, such as the Lower Vestry, are Baroque additions.

Carving of Rudolf IV

★ Giants' Doorway and Heathen Towers
The entrance and twin towers apparently stand on the site of an earlier heathen shrine.

The North Tower, according to legend, was never completed because its master builder, Hans Puchs-baum, broke a pact he had made with the devil, by pronouncing a holy name. The devil then caused him to fall to his death.

Entrance to the catacombs

Pilgram's Pulpit *(see p78)*

STAR FEATURES

★ Giants' Doorway and Heathen Towers

★ *Steffl* or Spire

★ Tiled Roof

★ Singer Gate

The symbolic number "O5" of the Austrian Resistance Movement was carved here in 1945.

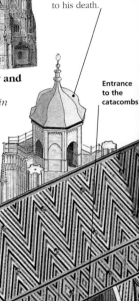

Main entrance

★ Singer Gate
This was once the entrance for male visitors. A sculpted relief above the door depicts scenes from the life of St Paul.

Lower Vestry

★ Steffl or Spire
The 137-m high (450-ft) Gothic spire is a famous landmark. From the Sexton's Lodge (see p79), visitors can climb the stairs as far as a viewing platform.

VISITORS' CHECKLIST

Stephansplatz 3, A-1010.
Map 2 E5 & 6 D3. *Tel*
515523526. Stephansplatz.
1A. 6am–10pm daily.
High Mass: 10:15am Sun & hols;
Jul & Aug 9:30am. Guided tours
in English: Apr–Oct 3:45pm
daily; Pummerin Bell (elevator)
8:30am–5:30pm daily; catacomb
tours daily.
organ concerts May–Nov:
Wed. **www**.stephansdom.at

★ Tiled Roof
Almost a quarter of a million glazed tiles cover the roof; they were meticulously restored after the damage caused in the last days of World War II.

JOHANNES CAPISTRANO

On the exterior north-eastern wall of the choir is a pulpit built after the victory over the Turks at Belgrade in 1456. It was from here that the Italian Franciscan, Johannes Capistrano, (1386–1456) is said to have preached against the Turkish invasion in 1451. The 18th-century Baroque statue above it depicts the triumphant saint trampling on a defeated Turkish invader.

South-eastern entrance

TIMELINE

1147 The first Romanesque building on the site consecrated by the Bishop of Passau		**1304** Duke Rudolf IV initiates work on High Gothic Albertine Choir		**1515** Anton Pilgram carves his pulpit		**1711** Pummerin bell cast from remains of guns left by Turks on their retreat from Vienna		**1948** Reconstruction and restoration carried out	
1100	**1200**	**1300**	**1400**	**1500**	**1600**	**1700**	**1800**	**1900**	**2000**
1230 Second Romanesque building erected on the same ground		**1359–1440** Main aisle, southern arches and southern tower built	**1515** Double wedding of grandchildren of Maximilian with children of the King of Hungary takes place		**1556** North Tower is roofed over — **1783** Stephansdom churchyard closed after plague		**1916** Emperor Franz Joseph's funeral	**1945** Cathedral catches fire during bombing	

Inside the Stephansdom

The lofty vaulted interior of the Stephansdom contains an impressive collection of works of art spanning several centuries. Masterpieces of Gothic sculpture include the fabulously intricate pulpit, several of the figures of saints adorning the piers, and the canopies or baldachins over many of the side altars. To the left of the High Altar is the early 15th-century winged Wiener Neustädter Altar bearing the painted images of 72 saints. The altar panels open out to reveal delicate sculpture groups. The most spectacular Renaissance work is the tomb of Friedrich III, while the High Altar adds a flamboyant Baroque note.

The Catacombs
A flight of steps leads down to the catacombs, which extend under the cathedral square.

Portrait of Pilgram
Master craftsman Anton Pilgram left a portrait of himself, holding a square and compass, below the corbel of the original organ.

Christ with Toothache (1420) is the irreverent name of this figure; an old legend has it that Christ afflicts mockers with toothache.

Lift to the Pummerin Bell

Bishop's Gate

The Tirna Chapel houses the grave of the military hero Prince Eugene.

The Statue of Crucified Christ above the altar has, according to legend, a beard of human hair that is still growing.

Main entrance

★ **Pilgram's Pulpit**
Pilgram's intricate Gothic pulpit is decorated with portraits of the Four Fathers of the Church (theologians representing four physiognomic temperaments), while Pilgram himself looks out from a "window" below.

Organ Gallery and Case
In 1960 this modern organ was installed in the loft above the entrance. A more recent organ is in the south choir area.

The Canopy with Pötschen Madonna is a 16th-century canopy that shelters a 1697 icon of the Madonna, to which Prince Eugene's victory over the Turks at Zenta was attributed. It comes from Pecs, a village in Hungary.

★ Wiener Neustädter Altar
Friedrich III commissioned the elaborate altarpiece in 1447. Painted panels open out to reveal an earlier carved interior showing scenes from the life of the Virgin Mary and Christ. This panel portrays the Adoration of the Magi (1420).

Albertine Choir

Exit from crypt

Emperor Friedrich III's tomb is made from ornate red marble and has a lid bearing a lifelike carved portrait of the Emperor. It dates from the 15th century.

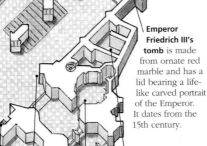

The Sexton's Lodge houses the stairs that lead up the steeple.

★ High Altar
Tobias Pock's altarpiece shows the martyrdom of St Stephen. The sculptures were fashioned by Johann Jakob Pock in 1647.

Chapel of St Catherine

The Madonna of the Servants

The Füchsel Baldachin is a fine Gothic canopy.

The Trinity Altar probably dates from around 1740.

THE PUMMERIN BELL

The bell that hangs in the North Tower, known as the *Pummerin* or "Boomer", is a potent symbol for the city reflecting Vienna's turbulent past. The original bell was made from melted-down cannons abandoned when the Turks fled Vienna in 1683. The bell crashed down through the roof in 1945 when fire swept through the Stephansdom, so a new and even larger bell was cast using the remains of the old.

STAR SIGHTS

★ Pilgram's Pulpit

★ Wiener Neustädter Altar

★ High Altar

Statuary in the hall of the Winter Palace of Prince Eugene

Winter Palace of Prince Eugene **⑰**

Himmelpfortgasse 4–8. **Map** 4 E1 & 6 D4. **Tel** 51433. Ⓤ *Stephansplatz.* **Vestibule** ◯ *8am–4pm Mon–Fri.* ⊙

The Winter Palace was commissioned in 1694 by Prince Eugene of Savoy (*see p27*), hero of the 1683 Turkish siege. It was begun by Johann Bernhard Fischer von Erlach (*see p149*) and taken over by Johann Lukas von Hildebrandt (*see p152*) in 1702. The result is an imposing town mansion, considered one of the most magnificent Baroque edifices in Vienna. Maria Theresa bought it for the state in 1752. Access is limited, but you can view the Baroque staircase (*see p43*) and glance into the courtyard with its lovely Rococo fountain.

Annagasse **⑱**

Map 4 E1 & 6 D4. Ⓤ *Stephansplatz.* **Zum Blauen Karpfen** ● *to the public.*

Now splendidly Baroque, Annagasse dates from medieval times. It is pedestrianized and a pleasant place to browse in the bookshops.

Of note are the luxurious Mailberger Hof and the stucco-decorated Römischer Kaiser hotels (*see p196*). No. 14's lintel has a Baroque carving of babes making merry, while above this is a relief of the blue carp that gives the house, once a pub, its name: Zum Blauen Karpfen. No. 2 is the 17th-century Esterházy Palace, which is now a casino. Until a few years ago you could see the Countess Esterházy sweeping her front doorstep!

Annakirche **⑲**

Annagasse 3b. **Map** 4 E1 & 6 D4. **Tel** 5124797. Ⓤ *Stephansplatz.* ◯ *7am–7pm daily.* ⊙

There has been a chapel in Annagasse since 1320, but the present Annakirche dates from 1629 to 1634, and it was renovated by the Jesuits during the early 18th century. Devotion to St Anne has deep roots in Vienna and this very intimate church is often full of quiet worshippers.

The finest exterior feature of the church is the moulded copper cupola over the tower. Daniel Gran's ceiling frescoes are now fading and his richly-coloured painting glorifying St Anne on the High Altar is more striking. Gran, together with Franz Anton Maulbertsch, was a leading painter of the Austrian Baroque period. The first chapel on the left houses a copy of a carving of St Anne from about 1505 – the original is in the cathedral museum (*see p74*). St Anne is portrayed as a powerfully maternal figure and shown with her daughter, the Virgin Mary, who in turn has the baby Jesus on her knee. The carving is attributed to the sculptor Veit Stoss.

Haus der Musik **⑳**

Seilerstätte 30. **Map** 4 E1. **Tel** 51648. Ⓤ *Stephansplatz, Stubenring.* ◯ *10am–10pm daily.* ⊙ ⊙ *on request.* ⊡ ⊡ **www**.hdm.at

The House of Music opened in 2000 and makes the most of the latest audio-visual and interactive technologies to explain and demonstrate all aspects of music. Visitors move through "experience zones" such as the Instrumentarium, with its giant instruments, and the Polyphonium, which is a collection of different sounds.

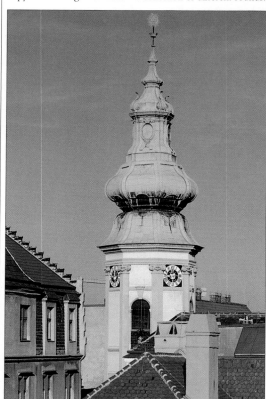

Moulded copper cupola over the tower of the Annakirche

Detail on the façade of the Griech-ische Kirche on Griechengasse

Austrian Museum of Applied Arts ㉑

See pp82–3.

Postsparkasse ㉒

Georg-Coch-Platz 2. **Map** 2 F5 & 6 F3. *Tel* 514000. Ⓤ *Schwedenplatz*. ◯ *8am–3pm Mon–Wed & Fri, 8am–5:30pm Thu.* ◎

This building is the Austrian Post Office Savings Bank and is a wonderful example of Secession architecture *(see pp54–57)*. Designed between 1904 and 1906 by Otto Wagner, it still looks unashamedly modern. The building features the architect's characteristic overhanging eaves, spindly aluminium columns supporting a canopy, heroic sculptures of angels and ornament-like nailheads protruding from the surface of the building.

Wagner was a pioneer in incorporating many functional elements into his decorative schemes. Inside the banking hall the metal columns are clad in aluminium, and tubular heating ducts encircle the hall.

Fleischmarkt ㉓

Map 2 E5 & 6 D2–E3. Ⓤ *Schwedenplatz*. *Griechische Kirche*. *Tel* 5122133. ◯ *9am–4pm Mon–Fri*.

Fleischmarkt, the former meat market, dates from 1220. The small cosy inn called the Griechenbeisl *(see p213)* is its best-known landmark. On its façade is a woodcarving of a bagpiper known as *Der liebe Augustin* (Dear old Augustin). Rumour has it that during the 1679 plague, this bagpiper slumped drunk into the gutter one night and, taken for dead, was put in the plague pit. He woke, attracted attention by playing his pipes and was rescued. Miraculously, he did not catch the plague.

Next to the Griechenbeisl is the Neo-Byzantine Griechische Kirche (Greek church of the Holy Trinity). The versatile architect Theophil Hansen *(see p32)* created its rich, gilt appearance in the 1850s.

A passage links the Griechen-beisl to Griechengasse.

Griechengasse ㉔

Map 2 E5 & 6 E2. Ⓤ *Schwedenplatz*. *Griechische Kirche*. *Tel* 5122133. ◯ *by appt, 9am–4pm Mon–Fri, 10am–1pm for mass only Sat & Sun.*

This street name refers to the Greek merchants who settled here in the 18th century and it leads up from Rotenturm-strasse. The house on the right dates from 1611 but has since been altered. Opposite is the Griechische Kirche (St George's), not to be confused with the Griechische Kirche in Fleischmarkt. This one was built in 1803 but the gable was added later, in 1898. No. 7 is a 17th-century house. The façade was rebuilt in the late 18th century.

Ruprechtskirche ㉕

Ruprechtsplatz. **Map** 2 E5 & 6 D2. *Tel* 5356003. Ⓤ *Schwedenplatz*. ◯ *9:30–11:30am Mon–Fri & for mass 5pm Sat & 10:30am Sun; Jul–Aug: for mass 6pm Sat only.* ◎ ♿ *Donation expected.*

Ivy-clad façade of Ruprechtskirche

St Ruprecht *(see p22)* was the patron saint of Vienna's salt merchants and the church that takes his name overlooks the merchants' landing stage on the Danube canal. There is a statue of the saint holding a tub of salt at the foot of the Romanesque tower. Salt was a valuable commodity in the Middle Ages, and evidence suggests that the church dates back to the 11th century, making it the oldest church in Vienna. The interior is less interesting, having been restored at various times, but the chancel has two panes of Romanesque stained glass. The choir is 13th century, the vault-ed south aisle 15th century.

Carving of the bagpiper on the façade of the Griechenbeisl, Fleischmarkt

Austrian Museum of Applied Arts ㉑

The renovated MAK (Museum für angewandte Kunst) acts both as a showcase for Austrian decorative arts and as a repository for fine objects from around the world. Originally founded in 1864 as a museum for art and industry, it expanded and diversified over the years to include objects representing new artistic movements. The museum has a fine collection of furniture, including some classical works of the German cabinet-maker David Roentgen, textiles, glass, Islamic and East Asian art and fine Renaissance jewellery. In 1993 the museum was completely renovated and each room was re-designed by a different leading artist. The result is a series of displays that lend the exhibits a unique, unusual flavour.

★ Wiener Werkstätte Collection
Kolo Moser created this brass vase, inlaid with citrines (false topaz), for the Wiener Werkstätte in 1903.

Stairs to second floor

First floor

First floor mezzanine

★ Dubsky Porcelain Room
A reassembly of a room (around 1724) in the Dubsky Palace at Brno, Czech Republic.

Romanesque, Gothic and Renaissance Room
Blue walls set off the furniture and ceramics in display cases designed by Matthias Esterházy in 1993.

Entrance to MAK Café (see p213)

Entrance hall

Stubenring entrance

Basement

MUSEUM GUIDE
The basement houses the individual collections, and the extension is used for special exhibitions. Most of the permanent collection is displayed in the ground-floor galleries, although the Wiener Werkstätte collection plus 20th- and 21st-century architecture is on the first floor. Stairs in the west wing lead to the contemporary design rooms.

KEY
- ☐ Romanesque, Gothic, Renaissance
- ☐ Baroque, Rococo
- ☐ Wiener Werkstätte
- ☐ Art Nouveau, Art Deco
- ☐ Islamic Art
- ☐ Biedermeier
- ☐ 20th-century design
- ☐ Individual collections
- ☐ Temporary exhibition space
- ☐ Non-exhibition space

Monk of the Nichiren Sect
This Japanese wooden sculpture of a praying monk dates from the Muromachi Period (around 1500).

THE WIENER WERKSTATTE

In 1903 Josef Hoffman (pictured) and Kolo Moser founded a co-operative arts and crafts workshop, the Wiener Werkstätte. This promoted all aspects of design from postage stamps and book illustrations to fabric, furniture, jewellery and interiors. The museum houses its archives, which include sketches, fabric patterns and fine pieces.

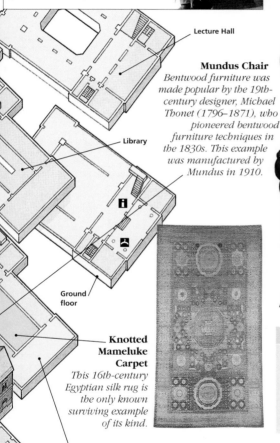

Lecture Hall

Mundus Chair
Bentwood furniture was made popular by the 19th-century designer, Michael Thonet (1796–1871), who pioneered bentwood furniture techniques in the 1830s. This example was manufactured by Mundus in 1910.

Library

Ground floor

Knotted Mameluke Carpet
This 16th-century Egyptian silk rug is the only known surviving example of its kind.

STAR FEATURES

★ Dubsky Porcelain Room

★ Wiener Werkstätte Collection

★ Biedermeier Room

★ Biedermeier Room
This cherrywood sofa (1825–30), designed and manufactured by Danhauser'sche Möbelfabrik, is an out-standing example of Viennese Empire-style Biedermeier design (see pp30–31). The original upholstery has been reproduced.

Jewish District 🈯

Map 2 F5 & 6 D2. 🚇 *Schwedenplatz.*
***Stadttempel Tel** 531040.* ⭕ *Mon
& Thu for tours at 11:30am and 2pm
(take identification).*

Vienna's Jewish District is
more famous today for its
area of bars and discos called
the Bermuda Triangle than
for its Jewish community.
Judengasse is now a bustling
lane lined with clothes shops
and bars. There are some
solid Biedermeier apartment
blocks and on Ruprechts-
platz, in the former town
hall, a kosher restaurant, the
Arche Noah. Behind it is a
jutting tower, the Korn-
häuselturm. Named after Josef
Kornhäusel, an architect from
the Biedermeier period *(see
pp30–31)*, it was apparently
built as a refuge from his wife.

Close to Arche Noah is
Sterngasse. This street has an
English-language bookshop
called Shakespeare & Co *(see
p225)* and the Neustädter-Hof,
a Baroque palace built by
Anton Ospel in 1734. A
Turkish cannonball, fired in
1683, is embedded in its façade.

Vienna's oldest surviving
synagogue, the Stadttempel,
designed by Kornhäusel in
the 1820s, is on Seitenstetten-
gasse. On the same street is
the headquarters of Vienna's

The Anker Clock in Hoher Markt

Jewish community. It used to
house the Jewish museum,
which is now located in
Dorotheergasse *(see p93)*.

Hoher Markt 🈯

Map 2 E5 & 6 D2. 🚇 *Stephansplatz,
Schwedenplatz.* **Roman Museum
Tel** 5058747-85/ 80. ⭕ *9am–6pm,
Tue–Sun & hols.* 🖼

Hoher Markt is the oldest-
square in Vienna. In
medieval times fish and cloth
markets were held here, and

so were executions. Today it
is possible to view the subterranean ruins of a former
Roman garrison beneath it *(see
p21)*. Discovered after World
War II, the ancient foundations
show groups of houses bisect-
ed by straight roads leading
to the town gates. It seems
probable that they were 2nd-
and 3rd-century officers'
houses. The excavations are
well laid out and exhibits of
pottery, reliefs and tiles supplement the ruins.

In the centre of the square is
the Vermählungsbrunnen
(Nuptial Fountain), or Josefs-
brunnen. Emperor Leopold I
vowed to commemorate the
safe return of his son Joseph
from the Siege of Landau
and commissioned Johann
Bernhard Fischer von Erlach
to design this monument,
which was built by von
Erlach's son Joseph Emanuel
between 1729 and 1732. The
fountain celebrates the
betrothal of Joseph and Mary
and bears figures of the high
priest and the couple, with gilt
urns, statues of angels, and
fluted columns supporting an
elaborate canopy.

Linking two office buildings
on the square is the bronze
and copper sculptural clock,
known as the Anker Clock.
Commissioned by the Anker
Insurance Company and
designed by Franz Matsch, it
was completed in 1914. Every
hour a procession of cut-out
historical figures, ranging from
the Emperor Marcus Aurelius
and Duke Rudolf IV to Joseph
Haydn, glide from one side of
the clock to the other to the
sound of organ music. Noon
is the best time to see it, as all
the figures are on display then.

Bohemian Court
Chancery 🈯

Judenplatz 11. **Map** 2 D5 & 5 C2.
Tel 53122. 🚇 *Stephansplatz.*
⭕ *8am–3:30pm Mon–Fri.*

Habsburg rulers were also
kings of Bohemia, which was
governed from this mag-
nificent palace (1709–14). Its
architect was the finest of the
day: Johann Bernhard Fischer
von Erlach *(see p148)*.

VIENNA'S JEWS – PAST AND PRESENT

A Jewish community has thrived in Vienna since at least the
12th century, with Judenplatz and, later, the Stadttempel at its
core. Unfortunately, the Jews' commercial success caused
envy and in 1421, after a charge of ritual murder, almost the
entire Jewish population was burnt to death, forcibly baptised
or expelled. Thereafter Jewish fortunes fluctuated, with periods of prosperity alternating with expulsions. The 1781 Edict
of Tolerance lifted legal constraints that had applied to Jews
and by the late 19th century the city's cultural and intellectual
life was dominated by Jews. Anti-Semitism spread in the
early 20th century and burgeoning Nazism forced many Jews
to leave. Of those who remained, 65,000 were murdered. In

1938 170,000
Jews lived in the
city; 50 years later
there were 7,000.
Now Eastern
European Jews
are adding to the
number.

**The interior of
the Stadttempel**

Matthias Gerl enlarged the Chancery between 1751 and 1754 to accommodate the Ministry of the Interior. Its glory is the huge Baroque portals, yet the building is as subtle as it is powerful. The elegantly-curved window frames on the first floor are particularly noteworthy.

The building's interior, now a courthouse, and its two courtyards, are less impressive, partly due to reconstruction undertaken after serious bomb damage in World War II.

Altes Rathaus ㉙

Wipplinger Strasse 8. **Map** 2 D5 & 6 D2. Ⓤ Schwedenplatz. **Salvatorkapelle Tel** 5337133. ☐ 9am–5pm Mon–Thu, or by appointment. **Austrian Resistance Archive Tel** 2289469 319. ☐ 9am–5pm Mon–Wed, Fri; 9am–7pm Thu. **www**.doew.at

After the German brothers Otto and Haymo of Neuburg conspired to overthrow the Habsburgs (see p22) in 1309,

Ironwork at the Rathaus entrance

their property was confiscated and donated to the city. Over the centuries the site was expanded to form the complex of buildings that until 1883 served as the city hall or *Rathaus*.

The entrance of the Altes Rathaus is festooned with ornamental ironwork. The building is now occupied by offices and shops. The District Museum, which deals with the first municipal district of Vienna (roughly covering the area within the Ring), is also here. Of much greater interest is the Austrian Resistance Archive on

Portal figure by Lorenzo Mattielli in the Bohemian Court Chancery

the first floor, where Austrian Resistance to Nazism is documented. Although many Austrians welcomed Hitler's takeover in 1938, a distinguished minority fiercely resisted it, and this exhibition pays tribute to them.

In one corner of the Altes Rathaus is the Andromeda Fountain. Located in the main courtyard, it was the last work by sculptor Georg Raphael Donner who designed it in 1741. The relief shows Perseus rescuing Andromeda.

At No. 5 Salvatorplatz is a late 13th-century chapel, the Salvatorkapelle, the only surviving building of the original medieval town house. It has since been enlarged and renovated, but retains its fine Gothic vaults. The walls are lined with old marble tomb slabs, some from the 15th century. Its pretty organ dates from around 1740 and is sometimes used for recitals in the chapel. On the outside wall on Salvatorgasse is an exquisite Renaissance portal dating from 1520 to 1530 – a rare example of Italianate Renaissance style.

Maria am Gestade ㉚

Salvatorgasse 12. **Map** 2 D5 & 5 C2. **Tel** 5339594. Ⓤ Schwedenplatz, Stephansplatz. ☐ 7:30am–6pm daily & inside at rear by appointment only. ☐

One of the city's oldest sights is this lofty, Gothic church with its 56-m high (180-ft) steeple and immense choir windows. Mentioned as early as 1158, the present building dates from the late 14th century. It was restored in the 19th century. The church has had a chequered history and during the occupation of Vienna by Napoleon in 1809 his troops used it as an arsenal.

Inside, the nave piers are enlivened with Gothic canopies sheltering statues from various periods: medieval, Baroque and modern. The choir contains two High Gothic panels (1460): they depict the Annunciation, the Crucifixion and the Coronation of the Virgin. Behind the high altar the windows contain medieval stained glass, which is patched with surviving fragments. Tucked away on the north side of the choir is a chapel with a beautiful painted stone altar from 1520. The main parts of the interior are visible from the front entrance, but to walk around inside you need to make an appointment.

Gothic canopies in the Maria am Gestade church

Holocaust memorial in Judenplatz

Judenplatz ③

Map 2 D5 & 5 C2. Ⓤ *Stephansplatz, Herrengasse.* **Museum Judenplatz Tel** 53504310. ☐ *10am–6pm Sun–Thu, 10am–2pm Fri.* ● *on main Jewish holidays.* ◐ & *except to synagogue.* ◎ *free, 2pm & 5pm Thu & Sun. Take identification.* **www**.jmw.at

Judenplatz was the site of the Jewish ghetto in medieval times. In the centre of the square stands a statue of the German playwright and critic Ephraim Lessing by Siegfried Charoux. The Nazis did not like a tribute to a writer whose works plead for toleration towards Jews, and they destroyed it in 1939. It was later redesigned by the same sculptor and reinstated in the square in 1982.

In 1996 British artist Rachel Whiteread was the controversial winner of a competition to design a monument for the Jewish victims of the Nazi regime, to be unveiled in the square on 9 November 1999, the anniversary of Kristal Nacht. A heated public debate ensued and following many changes, including the repositioning of the monument by one metre, Judenplatz was reopened on 25 October 2000 as a place of remembrance. It now contains

Whiteread's memorial, the new Museum Judenplatz at No. 8, and the excavated remains of the medieval synagogue that lie beneath the square. The museum celebrates the vibrant Jewish quarter that was centred on the square until the expulsion of the Jews in 1421, an event gleefully recorded in an inscription, *Zum Grossen Jordan*, on the façade of No. 2. The museum also houses a public database of the 65,000 Austrian Jews killed by the Nazis and, in the basement, the excavated synagogue.

Clock Museum ③

Schulhof 2. **Map** 2 D5 & 5 C2. **Tel** 5332265. Ⓤ *Stephansplatz.* ☐ *10am–6pm Tue–Sun.* ● *1 Jan, 1 May, 25 Dec.* ◎ **www**.wienmuseum.at

You don't have to be a clock fanatic to enjoy a visit to this wonderful and fascinating museum. Located in the beautiful former Obizzi Palace (1690), the museum contains a fine collection of clocks, some of which were accumulated by an earlier curator, Rudolf Kaftan. Others belonged to the novelist Marie von Ebner-Eschenbach.

Lavish specimen in the Clock Museum

The first floor displays the mechanisms of tower clocks from the 16th century

onwards, painted clocks, grandfather clocks and pocket watches. On the other floors are huge astronomical clocks and a wide range of novelty ones.

There are more than 3,000 exhibits. A major highlight is the astronomical clock by David Cajetano, dating from the 18th century. It has over 30 readings and dials that show, among other things, the dates of solar and lunar eclipses. Many other exhibits date from the Biedermeier and *belle époque* periods.

At every full hour the three floors of the museum resound to the incredible sound of numerous clocks striking, chiming and playing. All are carefully maintained to keep the correct time.

The museum gives its visitors a comprehensive account of the history of chronometry through the ages, and of clock technology from the 15th century through to the present day.

Kurrentgasse ③

Map 2 D5 & 5 C2. Ⓤ *Stephansplatz.* **Grimm bakery** ☐ *7am–6:30pm Mon–Fri, 7am–noon Sat.*

This narrow street is shaded by elegant tall Baroque houses, their lower floors filled with cosy bars and pricey Italian restaurants. It's a pleasant place to while away an afternoon. The Grimm bakery at No. 10 is one of the best in Vienna and offers an astonishing variety of breads. No. 12, a house dating from 1730, has an attractive pink cobbled courtyard filled with numerous plants and trees.

One of the many fascinating showrooms in the Clock Museum

Statue on top of No. 10 Am Hof

Kirche am Hof **34**

Schulhof 1. **Map** 2 D5 & 5 C2.
Tel *5338394.* Herrengasse.
7am–noon, 4–6pm daily.

This Catholic church, which is picturesquely dedicated to the Nine Choirs of Angels, was founded by Carmelite friars in the late 14th century. The façade, at present being renovated, was redesigned by the Italian architect Carlo Carlone in 1662 to provide space for a large balustraded balcony. The church is now used for services by Vienna's large Croatian community.

It is also worth taking a walk behind the church into Schulhofplatz to look at the tiny restored shops which snuggle happily between the buttresses of the Gothic choir.

Am Hof **35**

Map 2 D5 & 5 C2.
Stephansplatz, Schottentor.

This is the largest enclosed square in Vienna. The Romans established a garrison here and, later, the Babenberg ruler Duke Heinrich II Jasomirgott built his castle close to where No. 2 Am Hof stands. In the centre of the square you can see the Marien-säule (Column of Our Lady), a monument that commemorates the end

of the threat of Swedish invasion during the Thirty Years War *(see p25)*. Dating from 1667, it was designed by Carlo Carlone and Carlo Canevale.

There are a number of interesting houses around the square. Opposite the church is the palatial Märkleinisches Haus which was designed by Johann Lukas von Hildebrandt *(see p152)* in 1727. Its elegant façade was wrecked by the insertion of a fire station on the ground floor in 1935. The 16th-century red house next door is the headquarters of Johann Kattus, a producer of sparkling wine. No. 10, designed by Anton Ospel, is the Bürgerliche Zeughaus, the citizens' armoury, where the city's fire services are now permanently based. The façade is dominated by the Habsburg coat of arms and military emblems. The allegorical statues above are by Lorenzo Mattielli.

At No. 12 the bay-windowed Urbanihaus dates from the 1730s, and its iron inn sign dates from the same period. Next door is the Collalto Palace – it was here, in 1762, that Mozart made his first public appearance aged just six *(see p38)*.

Peterskirche **36**

Petersplatz 6. **Map** 2 D5 & 5 C3.
Tel *5336433.* Stephansplatz.
7am–6pm daily.

A church has stood here since the 12th century, but the oval structure you see today dates from the early 18th century. It was modelled on St Peter's in Rome and a number of architects collaborated on the design, notably Gabriele Montani. The interior is amazingly lavish, and there's an exuberant, eye-catching pulpit (1716) by the sculptor Matthias Steindl. The richly-clothed skeletons on the right and beneath the altar are the remains of early Christian martyrs originally deposited in the catacombs in Rome. The frescoes inside the huge dome, depicting the Assumption of the Virgin, are by J M Rottmayr.

In 1729 Lorenzo Mattielli designed the sculpture of St John Nepomuk to the right of the choir. This priest earned his sainthood by being thrown into the River Vltava in Prague in 1393 after he refused to reveal the secrets of the confessional to King Wenceslas IV; his martyrdom by drowning later became a favourite subject of artists.

**18th-century engraving
of Peterskirche**

HOFBURG QUARTER

What began as a modest city fortress has grown over the centuries into a vast palace, the Hofburg. The palace was still expanding up until a few years before the Habsburgs fell from power in 1918. The presence of the court had a profound effect on the surrounding area. The former gardens of the palace are now

Portal detail in Josefsplatz

the Volksgarten and Burggarten, and some of the buildings are now splendid museums. Streets such as Herrengasse and Bankgasse are lined with the palaces that the nobility built in their eagerness to be as close as possible to the centre of imperial power. This area is bustling with tourists by day, but at night it is almost deserted.

SIGHTS AT A GLANCE

Streets and Squares
Bankgasse **31**
Dorotheergasse **7**
Graben **8**
Herrengasse **13**
Josefsplatz **6**
Kärntner Strasse **36**
Kohlmarkt **10**
Michaelerplatz **1**
Minoritenplatz **29**
Naglergasse **12**
Neuer Markt **35**
Stock-im-Eisen-Platz **38**

Historic Buildings
American Bar **37**
Bundeskanzleramt **28**
Demel Konditorei **11**
Grosses und Kleines
  Michaelerhaus **3**
Hofburg Complex pp96–7 **15**
Lobkowitz Palace **33**
Loos Haus **2**
Mollard-Clary Palace **14**
Prunksaal **24**
Stallburg **5**
*Spanish Riding School
  pp98–9* **26**

Churches and Cathedrals
Augustinerkirche **23**
Burgkapelle **25**
Kapuzinerkirche
  und Kaisergruft **34**
Michaelerkirche **4**
Minoritenkirche **30**

Museums and Galleries
Albertina **22**
Ephesos Museum **17**
Hofjagd und Rüstkammer **19**
Neue Burg **16**
Sammlung Alter
  Musikinstrumente **18**
*State Apartments and
  Treasuries pp100–101* **27**
Völkerkundemuseum **20**

Parks and Gardens
Burggarten **21**
Volksgarten **32**

Monuments
Pestsäule **9**

0 metres 250
0 yards 250

GETTING THERE
This area is served by the Herrengasse (line U3) U-Bahn station. Tram 1 runs along the Burgring and Tram 2 leaves the Ring at Parliament. Buses 2A and 3A run along Herrengasse and bus 1A goes from Stubentor to the Graben.

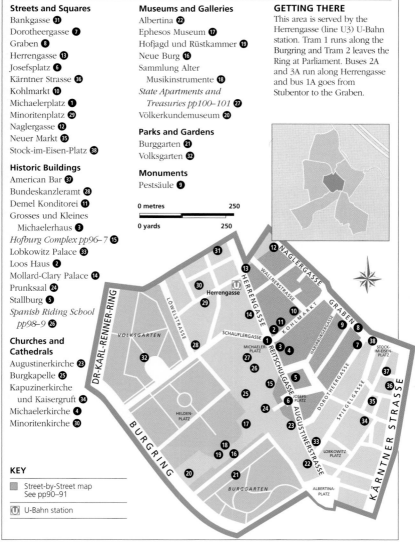

KEY

[colour box] Street-by-Street map
See pp90–91

[U] U-Bahn station

◁ **Detail of Danubius fountain by Johann Meixner (1869) outside the Albertina**

Street-by-Street: Imperial Vienna

The streets around the Hofburg are no longer
filled with the carriages of the nobility. Most of
the palaces have become offices, embassies or
apartments. Yet this district remains the most
fashionable in Vienna, crammed with elegant
shops, art galleries and coffee houses, which
offer enjoyable interludes between visits to the
many museums and churches in the area.

Herrengasse
*This was a prime
site for the palaces
of the nobility* **⑬**

Herrengasse U-Bahn

Demel Konditorei
*This Café-Konditorei
offers delightful décor
and exquisite pastries* **⑪**

**Grosses und
Kleines Michaelerhaus**
*Joseph Haydn (see p38) once
lived in rooms overlooking the
handsome courtyard of the
Grosses Michaelerhaus* **❸**

Mollard-Clary Palace
*This mansion, built at the
end of the 17th-century,
has a façade designed by
J L Hildebrandt* **⑭**

Michaelerplatz
*Roman remains
were recently
excavated
here* **❶**

★ Loos Haus
*Built in 1912, this unadorned
design outraged the conservative
sensibilities of the ornament-
loving Archduke Franz
Ferdinand (see p166)* **❷**

STAR SIGHTS

★ Loos Haus

★ Michaelerkirche

★ Pestsäule

KEY

— — — Suggested route

0 metres	50
0 yards	50

★ Michaelerkirche
*The crypt of this church contains
well-preserved corpses from
the late 18th century* **❹**

Josefsplatz
*An equestrian statue of Joseph II stands at
the centre of this elegant square* **❻**

Naglergasse
This lane has some of the finest Baroque façades in the city ⑫

Graben
The Spar-Casse Bank, with its gilt bee on the pediment, is just one of many fine buildings on the pedestrianized Graben ⑧

LOCATOR MAP
See Street Finder, maps 2 & 5

Kohlmarkt
This street has a number of shops by Hans Hollein, one of Austria's finest architects ⑩

★ Pestsäule
Built after the plague of 1679, this is the most imposing of the Baroque plague columns ⑨

Dorotheergasse
Lining this narrow lane are art galleries and auction houses, and the much-loved Café Hawelka (see p58–61) ⑦

Stallburg
Once a royal residence, the Stallburg now houses the Spanish Riding School stables and the Lipizzaner Museum ⑤

The Palffy Palace
Built in the 16th century, it was a venue for a performance of Mozart's *The Marriage of Figaro.*

The Pallavicini Palace is a late 18th-century aristocrats' palace, strategically located opposite the Hofburg.

Michaelerplatz ❶

Map 2 D5 & 5 C3. Ⓤ *Herrengasse.*

Michaelerplatz faces the grandiose entrance into the Hofburg, the Michaelertor. Opposite are the Michaelerkirche and Loos Haus. On one side of Michaelerplatz is the Michaelertrakt, commissioned by Franz Joseph in 1888 when the new Burgtheater *(see pp132–33)* on the Ringstrasse opened, and the original theatre dating from 1751, which occupied this site, was demolished. An old design by Joseph Emanuel Fischer von Erlach *(see p149)* was used as the basis for a new design by Ferdinand Kirschner (1821–96). It was finished in 1893, complete with gilt-tasselled cupolas and statuary representing Austria's land and sea power.

Recent excavations have uncovered remains of a Roman encampment, as well as some medieval foundations.

Loos Haus ❷

Michaelerplatz 3. **Map** 2 D5 & 5 C3. *Tel* 53173455. Ⓤ *Herrengasse.* ◯ *8am–3pm Mon–Wed & Fri, 8am–5:30pm Thu.* ♿

Erected opposite the Michaelertor in 1910–12, and designed by Adolf Loos, this building so outraged Franz Ferdinand *(see p166)* that he declared he would

---

ADOLF LOOS

Unlike his contemporary Otto Wagner *(see p57)*, Adolf Loos (1870–1933) loathed ornament for its own sake. Instead, he used smooth lines and exquisite interior decoration; his buildings' lack of "eye-brows" (the window hoods on many of Vienna's buildings) scandalized Viennese society. Surviving interiors include Knize *(see p93)*, the American Bar *(see p105)* and the Café Museum *(see p137)*.

---

never use the Michaelertor again. Today it's hard to understand why: the outside is unexceptional but the inside is a lesson in stylish elegance.

Grosses und Kleines Michaelerhaus ❸

Kohlmarkt 11 & Michaelerplatz 6. **Map** 2 D5 & 5 C3. Ⓤ *Herrengasse.* 🚫 *to the public.*

Michaelerplatz fountain

At No. 6 Michaelerplatz a footpath leads to the Baroque Kleines Michaelerhaus (1735). Look out for a vivid painted relief of Christ on the Mount of Olives with a crucifixion in the background (1494) on the side of the Michaelerkirche. The Baroque façade of the Grosses Michaelerhaus is at No. 11 Kohlmarkt. It has a handsome courtyard and coach house. From here there is a fine view of the older parts of the Michaelerkirche. The buildings surrounding the courtyard were erected in about 1720, and the composer Joseph Haydn *(see p38)* is said to have lived in an unheated attic here in 1749.

Michaelerkirche ❹

Michaelerplatz 1. **Map** 2 D5 & 5 C3. *Tel* 5338000. Ⓤ *Herrengasse.* ◯ *6:30am–6pm daily.* 🎵 📷 ♿ 🕐 *May–Oct: 11am, 1pm, 2pm, 3pm, 4pm; Nov–Apr: 11am, 3pm.*

The Michaelerkirche was once the parish church of the court. Its earliest parts were built in the 13th century, and the choir dates from 1327–40. The Neo-Classical façade is from 1792. Its porch is topped by Baroque statues (1724–25) by Lorenzo Mattielli depicting the Fall of the Angels. Inside are Renaissance and 14th-century frescoes, and a glorious, vividly-carved organ from 1714 by Johann David Sieber. The main choir (1782), replete with tumbling cherubs and sunbursts, is by Karl Georg Merville. The altarpiece of the north choir (1755) is by Franz Anton Maulbertsch.

Off the north choir is the crypt entrance. In the 17th and 18th centuries parishioners were frequently buried beneath their church. Corpses clothed in their burial finery, well-preserved due to the constant temperature, can still be seen in open coffins.

Baroque organ (1714) in the Michaelerkirche

Stallburg ❺

Reitschulgasse 2. **Map** 4 D1 & 5 C3.
Ⓤ *Stephansplatz, Herrengasse.*

The Stallburg was built in the mid-16th century for Archduke Maximilian. This former royal residence was later converted to stables for the Hofburg. These are ranged around a large courtyard with arcades on three storeys. The Stallburg today houses the Spanish Riding School (see pp98–9).

For much of the 18th century, the Stallburg was the home of the Imperial art collection. In 1776, the collection was transferred to the Belvedere so that it would be accessible to the public, and in 1891 it was moved to its present home, the Kunsthistoriches Museum.

Josefsplatz ❻

Augustinerstrasse. **Map** 4 D1 & 5 C4. Ⓤ *Stephansplatz, Herrengasse.*

In the centre of the Josefs-platz is an equestrian statue (1807) of Joseph II by Franz Anton Zauner. Despite his reforms, Joseph II was a true monarchist, and during the 1848 revolution (see p31) loyalists used the square as a gathering place.

Facing the Hofburg are two palaces. No. 5 is the Pallavicini Palace (1783–4), a blend of Baroque and Neo-Classical styles by Ferdinand von Hohenberg. No. 6 is the 16th-

century Palffy Palace. On the right of the Prunksaal (see p102) is the Redoutensaal. It was built from 1750–60 and was the venue for masked balls in imperial times. To the left is an extension to the library which was built a few years later. Both are by Nikolaus Pacassi, a favourite architect of Maria Theresa.

Dorotheergasse ❼

Map 4 D1 & 5 C4. Ⓤ *Stephansplatz.*
Jewish Museum Tel 5350431. ⬜
10am–6pm Sun–Fri. **www**.jmw.at

At No. 11 of this street is the Eskeles Palace, now home to the Jewish Museum (Jüdisches Museum) which, along with its new extension in Juden-platz (see p86), chronicles the city's rich Jewish heritage. At No. 27 is the Dorotheum (see pp224–5), from the 17th century. A pawnbrokers and, more importantly, an auction house, it has branches all over Vienna. Halfway along the street is the Evangelical church (1783–4), originally by Gottlieb Nigelli. Towards the top end, close to Graben, are two immensely popular Viennese gathering places, Café Hawelka at No. 6 (see pp58–61), and the Buffet Trzesniewski at No. 1 (see p218). There are many art and antique dealers in this area.

Baroque plague column (Pestsäule)

Graben ❽

Map 2 D5 & 5 C3. Ⓤ *Stephansplatz.*
Neidhart Fresco House ⬜ 9am–12:15pm, 1–4:30pm Tue–Sun.

Facing No. 16 of this pedestrianized street is the Joseph Fountain by Johann Martin Fischer. Further along is his identical Leopold Fountain (both 1804). No. 13, the clothing shop Knize (see p223), is by Adolf Loos. No. 10, the Ankerhaus by Otto Wagner, is topped by a studio used by Wagner himself and, in the 1980s, by Friedensreich Hundertwasser (see p164). No. 21 is Alois Pichl's Spar-Casse Bank from the 1830s. Just off the Graben at No. 19 Tuch-lauben is the Neidhart Fresco House, containing medieval frescoes. (see pp54–7).

Pestsäule ❾

Graben. **Map** 2 D5 & 5 C3.
Ⓤ *Stephansplatz.*

During the plague of 1679, Emperor Leopold I vowed to commemorate Vienna's eventual deliverance. The plague over, he commis-sioned Matthias Rauchmiller, Lodovico Burnacini and the young Johann Bernhard Fischer von Erlach (see p149) to build this Baroque plague column. Devised by the Jesuits, its most striking image shows a saintly figure and an angel supervising the destruc-tion of a hag representing the plague, while above the bewigged Emperor prays.

Statue in Josefsplatz of Joseph II by Franz Anton Zauner (1746–1822)

Exterior of Schullin shop (see p223)

Kohlmarkt ⑩

Map 2 D5 & 5 C3. Ⓤ *Herrengasse.*

Leading directly up to the Imperial Palace, the pedestrianized Kohlmarkt is lined with some of Vienna's most exclusive shops and remarkable shopfronts. No. 9, the Jugendstil Artaria Haus (1901), was the work of Max Fabiani (1865–1962), a protégé of Otto Wagner *(see p57)*. No.16, the bookshop and publishers Manz, boasts a characteristic portal from 1912 by Adolf Loos *(see p92)*. The striking abstract shopfront of jewellers Schullin (1982) was designed by the architect Hans Hollein *(see p91)*.

Demel Konditorei ⑪

Kohlmarkt 14. **Map** 2 D5 & 5 C3. *Tel* 53517170. Ⓤ *Stephansplatz.* ⏰ *10am–7pm daily.* 📷 ♿

This famous pastry shop at No. 14 Kohlmarkt still bears its imperial patent – K.u.k. Hof-Zuckerbäcker – proudly lettered above the shopfront.

The pastry shop was founded in Michaelerplatz in 1785 and acquired by the pâtissier Christoph Demel in 1857, before moving to its present site on Kohlmarkt in 1888. Its many small rooms are in an ornate late 19th-century style.

Naglergasse ⑫

Map 2 D5 & 5 C2. Ⓤ *Herrengasse.*

During the Middle Ages needle-makers had their shops here, which is how the street acquired its name. This narrow lane also follows the line of a wall that used to stand here in Roman times. Today Naglergasse is lined with a succession of gorgeous Baroque houses. The delightful Renaissance bay window of No. 19 is ornamented with carved cherubs. No. 13 dates from the 16th century but has been considerably altered since. No. 21 (1720) is now an inn with a particularly snug and cosy interior.

Herrengasse ⑬

Map 2 D5 & 5 B2. Ⓤ *Herrengasse.*

Flanking the Hofburg, this street was the prime location for the palaces of the Habsburg nobility. In 1843 a visiting writer, J G Kohl, wrote of the street's "silent palaces", and today little has changed.

The base of the provincial government of Lower Austria, the Landhaus, is at No. 13; the façade of the present building dates from the 1830s.

In the courtyard a tablet from 1571 warns visitors not to carry weapons or to fight here. The injunction was famously ignored when the 1848 Revolution *(see p31)* was ignited on this very spot.

The long, low Neo-Classical façade of No. 7 received its present appearance from Ludwig Pichl and Giacomo Quarenghi in 1811. At No. 5 Anton Ospel (1677–1756) gave the Wilczek Palace (built before 1737) an original façade, with angled pilasters lending the central bays an illusion of perspective.

Coat of arms in the courtyard of the Mollard-Clary Palace

Mollard-Clary Palace ⑭

Herrengasse 9. **Map** 2 D5 & 5 B3. *Tel* 53410710. Ⓤ *Herrengasse.* *Globe Museum* ⏰ *10am–2pm Mon, Wed, Fri; 3pm–7pm Thu.*

At No. 9 Herrengasse is the former Mollard-Clary Palace, a mansion constructed by Domenico Martinelli in 1698. The façade was the first commission for Johann Lukas von Hildebrandt *(see p152)*.

From 1923 until 1997 the palace housed the Lower Austrian Provincial Museum, or Landesmuseum. Today the building houses offices and the Globe Museum.

In the courtyard is a 16th-century elaborate wrought-iron well cover and a carved stone coat of arms (1454).

Hofburg Complex ⑮

See pp96–101.

Inside the ornately-decorated Demel Konditorei

Neue Burg

Heldenplatz. **Map** 4 D1 & 5 B4.
Tel 52524484. 🚇 *Volkstheater,
Herrengasse.* 🚊 *1, 2, D.*
🕐 *10am–6pm Mon, Wed–Sun.*
🖼 📷 www.khm.at

The Neue Burg, a massive
curved building situated on
Heldenplatz, was added to the
Hofburg Complex in 1881–
1913. It embodies the last gasp
of the Habsburg Empire as it
strained under aspirations of
independence from its domains,
when the personal prestige of
Emperor Franz Joseph was all
that seemed able to keep it
intact. It was not the perfect
moment to embark on an
extension to the Hofburg, but
the work was undertaken
nevertheless, and the Neue
Burg was built to designs by
the Ringstrasse architects Karl
von Hasenauer (1833–94) and
Gottfried Semper (1803–79).
Five years after its completion,
the Habsburg empire ended.

In 1938, Adolf Hitler stood
on the terraced central bay to
proclaim the Anschluss – the
union of Austria and Germany
– to tens of thousands of
Viennese *(see p36).*

Today the Neue Burg is
home to the reading room of
the National Library, as well
as a number of museums
(see following entries).

Ephesos Museum ⓱

As Neue Burg. **Tel** *525244098.*
🕐 *10am–6pm Mon, Wed–Sun.*
www.khm.at

For decades Austrian
archaeologists
have been
excavating the
Greek and
Roman site of
Ephesus in Turkey.
Since 1978 their discov-
eries have been on display
in the main block of the Neue
Burg. Also on show are finds
from the Greek island of
Samothrace, excavated in
the 1870s. The main exhibits
include a colossal frieze
commemorating Lucius
Verus's victory over the
Parthians in AD 165, and
many architectural fragments.

Armour at Hofjagd und Rüstkammer

Sammlung Alter Musikinstrumente ⓲

As Neue Burg.

Pianos that belonged to
Beethoven, Schubert and
Haydn, among countless
other items, are housed in the
musical instrument museum.
More important, however, is
the collection of Renaissance
instruments, widely believed
to be the finest in the world.
The claviorgan (1596), the
oldest surviving example of
this instrument, is particularly
fascinating, and features stops
used to create special effects
such as birdsong.

**Renaissance cittern
from the Sammlung
Alter Musikinstrumente**

Hofjagd und Rüstkammer ⓳

As Neue Burg.

The Hofburg's weapons
collection is impressive
both for its size and for the
workmanship of its finest
items: ivory and filigree inlay
on weapons, medieval ceremonial saddles and jewelled
Turkish and Syrian maces.
Particularly resplendent are
the 16th-century ceremonial
suits worn by the Habsburgs
for tournaments and military
parades, and the decorative
fighting and hunting weapons.

The museum was based on
the personal armouries of the
Habsburg emperors and, not
surprisingly, houses one of the
finest collections in Europe.

Völkerkunde-museum ⓴

As Neue Burg. **Tel** *525240.*
🕐 *10am–6pm Mon, Wed–Sun.*
www.ethno.museum.ac.at

Ranged around an arcaded
Italian Renaissance-style
courtyard, at the west end of
the Neue Burg, is the ethnological museum. To one side
are the Oriental collections:
lacquer screens, clothes,
furniture, weapons, ceramics,
farm tools, masks and musical
instruments. In a neighbouring
room are African figurines
and masks. The artefacts from
Benin are the highlight of the
African collection. Australasia
and Polynesia dominate the
displays upstairs, with fabrics
from Bali, weapons from
Borneo and many musical
instruments from the Far East.

The large pre-Columbian
collection from Mexico
includes an Aztec feather
headdress. A recent addition
to the permanent collection is
a section on Eskimo culture.

The Hofburg Complex ⑮

The vast Hofburg Complex contains the former imperial apartments, several museums, a chapel, a church, the Austrian National Library, the Winter Riding School and the President of Austria's offices. It was the seat of Austrian power for over six centuries, and successive rulers were all anxious to leave their mark. Seven centuries of architectural development can be seen in the 10 or so buildings, ranging from Gothic to late 19th-century historicism.

Burggarten *(see p102)*

Albertina *(see p102)*

Augustiner-kirche *(see p102)*

★ Prunksaal
The showpiece of the Austrian National Library (1722–35) is the flamboyant, wood-panelled Prunksaal, or Hall of Honour.

Statue of Joseph II (1806) in Josefs-platz *(see p93)*

Burgkapelle *(see p103)*

Alte Burg

Redoute Wing

Stallburg (Stables) *(see p93)*

★ Michaelertrakt *(1893)*
The curved façade of the Michaelertrakt is surmounted by an imposing dome.

Spanish Riding School *(see pp98–9)*

Michaelertor

Reichskanzleitrakt

TIMELINE

Statue of the angel Gabriel in the Burgkapelle

1275 First fort built on site of the Schweizerhof		**1558–65** Stallburg built – a Renaissance palace, later a mews	**1729–35** JE Fischer von Erlach's Winter Riding School built	**1938** Hitler proclaims annexation of Austria from the Neue Burg
		1575–1611 Amalienburg built	**1881–1913** Neue Burg built	
1300	**1500**	**1700**		**1900**
	1547–52 Ferdinand I reconstructs the Alte Burg	**1552–3** Schweizertor built	**1728** Work begun on J E Fischer von Erlach's Reichskanzleitrakt	**1992** The banqueting hall and ball-room in the Redoute Wing destroyed by fire
1447–9 Alterations carried out on the Burgkapelle under Friedrich III		**1660–80** Leopoldinischertrakt built under Leopold I	**1889–93** Construction of Michaelertrakt and Michaelertor	

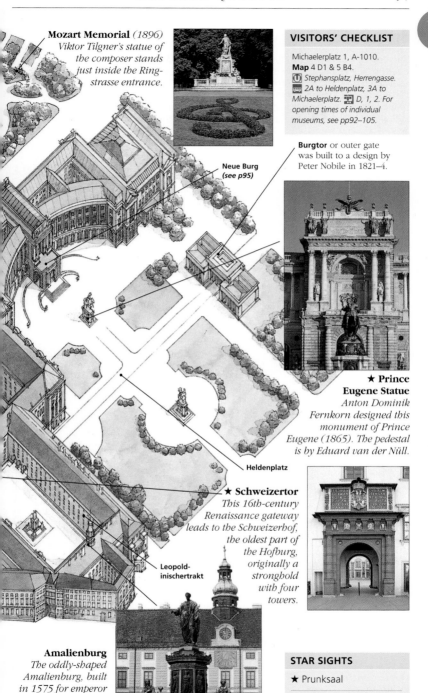

Mozart Memorial (1896)
Viktor Tilgner's statue of the composer stands just inside the Ringstrasse entrance.

VISITORS' CHECKLIST

Michaelerplatz 1, A-1010.
Map 4 D1 & 5 B4.
🅄 Stephansplatz, Herrengasse.
🚌 2A to Heldenplatz, 3A to Michaelerplatz. 🚋 D, 1, 2. For opening times of individual museums, see pp92–105.

Burgtor or outer gate was built to a design by Peter Nobile in 1821–4.

Neue Burg (see p95)

★ **Prince Eugene Statue**
Anton Dominik Fernkorn designed this monument of Prince Eugene (1865). The pedestal is by Eduard van der Nüll.

Heldenplatz

★ **Schweizertor**
This 16th-century Renaissance gateway leads to the Schweizerhof, the oldest part of the Hofburg, originally a stronghold with four towers.

Leopoldinischertrakt

Amalienburg
The oddly-shaped Amalienburg, built in 1575 for emperor Maximilian's son Rudolf, has a Renaissance façade and an attractive Baroque clock tower.

STAR SIGHTS

★ Prunksaal

★ Prince Eugene Statue

★ Schweizertor

★ Michaelertrakt

Spanish Riding School 26

The origins of the Spanish Riding School are obscure, but it is believed to have been founded in 1572 to cultivate the classic skills of *haute école* horsemanship. By breeding and training horses from Spain, the Habsburgs formed the Spanische Reitschule. Today, 80-minute shows take place in the building known as the Winter Riding School. Commissioned by Karl VI, it was built from 1729 to 1735 to a design by Josef Emanuel Fischer von Erlach. There are two entrances to the building – one from door 2, Josefsplatz, the other from the Michaelerkuppel.

Specially-bred Lipizzaner stallions are trained from the age of three.

The black bicorn hat has a gold braid stripe from the upper left to the lower centre.

Jackets are coffee-coloured – waisted, double-breasted and with two rows of brass buttons.

Buckskin jodhpurs are worn.

Pale leather gloves are worn.

Long boots covering the knees are part of the uniform.

Tack
The elegant saddle with embroidered cloth differs from modern versions and complements the historical dress of the riders; the curb rein is generally used.

Stables
The three storey-high Renaissance former palace of the Stallburg is across the road from the Winter Riding School. It now provides stabling for the horses.

THE HORSES' STEPS

The steps made by the horses and riders are part of a carefully orchestrated ballet. Many derive from exercises that were developed during the Renaissance period by cavalry men, who needed agile horses capable of special manoeuvres.

The Croupade: the horse leaps into the air with hind legs and forelegs bent under its belly.

Levade: the horse stands on its hind legs with hocks almost touching the ground.

VISITORS' CHECKLIST

Michaelerplatz 1, A-1010. **Map** 5
C3. **Tel** 5339031. Ⓤ Herrengasse.
🚌 3A to Habsburgasse, 2A to
Michaelerplatz. ☐ for performances. ● 1 Jan, 6 Jan, 1 May,
Ascension Day, Corpus Christi, 15
Aug, 26 Oct, 1 Nov, 8 Dec, 25–
26 Dec (dates do vary). 📷 📮
📷 ♿ some areas. **www**.srs.at

Portrait of Karl VI

*An equestrian portrait of
Emperor Karl VI who
commissioned the building,
hangs in the royal box.
Whenever a rider enters the
hall, he must express his
respect to the founder of the
school by raising his bicorn
hat to the portrait.*

THE LIPIZZANER HORSES

The stallions that perform their athletic feats on the sawdust
of the Winter Riding School take their name from the stud at
Lipizza near Trieste in Slovenia *(see below)*, which was
founded by Archduke Karl in 1580. Today the horses are
bred on the Austrian National Stud Farm at Piber near Graz.
The breed was originally produced by crossing Arab, Berber
and Spanish horses. The horses are renowned for their grace
and stamina. You may be able to obtain a ticket without a
reservation to see them at their morning training session.

Interior of the Winter Riding School

*The gracious interior is lined
with 46 columns and
adorned with elaborate plasterwork, chandeliers and a
coffered ceiling. At the head
of the arena is the court box.
Spectators sit here or watch
from upper galleries.*

Capriole: this is a
leap into the air with
a simultaneous kick
of the hind legs.

The Piaffe: the horse
trots on the spot, often
between two pillars.

State Apartments and Treasuries ㉗

The state apartments in the Reichskanzleitrakt (1723–30) and the Amalienburg (1575) include the rooms occupied by Franz Joseph from 1857 to 1916, Empress Elisabeth's apartments from 1854 to 1898 and the rooms where Tsar Alexander I lived during the Congress of Vienna in 1815. The sacred and secular treasures amassed during centuries of Habsburg rule are displayed in 21 rooms. They include relics of the Holy Roman Empire, the crown jewels and liturgical objects of the imperial court.

Entrance Treasurie

★ **10th-Century Crown**
The insignia of the Holy Roman Empire includes this crown set with enamel plaques and cabochons.

Emperor Maximilian I
(around 1500) This portrait by Bernhard Strigel hangs in the room containing Burgundian treasure. Emperor Maximilian married Mary, Duchess of Burgundy in 1477.

Cradle of the King of Rome
Designed by the French painter Prud'hon, Maria Louisa gave this cradle to her son, the King of Rome (see p175).

Entrance through the Michaelerkuppel to State Apartments and Silberkammer

Crucifix after Giambologna
(around 1590) This type of crucifix, a Cristo Morto, can be traced back to a similar model by Giambologna which is in Florence.

KEY

- ☐ Franz Joseph's State Apartments
- ☐ Elisabeth's State Apartments
- ☐ Alexander's State Apartments
- ☐ Sacred Treasury
- ☐ Secular Treasury
- ☐ Sisi Museum
- ☐ Non-exhibition space

STAR FEATURES

★ 10th-Century Crown

★ Imperial Dining Hall

★ Empress Elisabeth by Franz Xaver Winterhalter

THE SILBERKAMMER

On display in the ground-floor rooms of the court tableware and silver depot is a dazzling array of items – gold, silver and the finest porcelain – that were once used at the Habsburg state banquets. One of the highlights is a 33-m long (100-ft) gilded bronze centrepiece with accompanying candelabra from around 1800. Visitors can also admire the mid-18th-century Sèvres dinner service that was a diplomatic gift from Louis XV to Maria Theresa.

Goblet from the Laxenburg Service (around 1821)

VISITORS' CHECKLIST

Map 4 D1 & 5 B3. *State Apartments (Kaiserappartements), Sisi Museum & Silberkammer* Michaelerkuppel. *Tel* 5337570. 🕐 9am–5pm daily. 📷 Sat & Sun. **www**.hofburg-wien.at *Secular & Sacred Treasuries (Schatzkammer)* Schweizerhof. *Tel* 525240. 🕐 10am–6pm Wed–Mon; 24 Dec: to 1pm; 31 Dec: to 3pm. 1 Jan, 1 May, 25 Dec. 📷 www.khm.at

Elisabeth's Gymnastic Equipment

The Empress was a fitness enthusiast, and the bars at which she exercised are still in place in her dressing room.

Passage to Neue Burg and Heldenplatz

Sisi Museum

Ticket office

Entrance through the Kaisertor to State Apartments and Silberkammer

Exit from apartments

★ Imperial Dining Hall

The table is laid as it used to be in Emperor Franz Joseph's day (see p32–3), in the room where the Imperial family used to dine.

★ Empress Elisabeth

Winterhalter's portrait of the Empress (1865) with stars in her hair hangs in the Sisi Museum.

GUIDE TO TREASURIES

Entering the Secular Treasury, Rooms 1–8 contain items from the Austrian Empire (with Room 5 commemorating Napoleon). Rooms 9–12 exhibit treasures from the Holy Roman Empire, while the Burgundian Inheritance is displayed in Rooms 13–16. Rooms I–V, furthest from the entrance, house the Sacred Treasury.

Greenhouses in the Burggarten by Friedrich Ohmann (1858–1927)

Burggarten ㉑

Burgring/Opernring. **Map** 4 D1 & 5 B4. 🚇 Karlsplatz. 🚃 1, 2, D. 🕐 Apr–Sep: 6am–10pm; Oct–Mar: 6am–8pm daily.

Before leaving Vienna, Napoleon showed his contempt for the Viennese by razing part of the city walls which had proved so ineffective at preventing his entry. Some of the space left around the Hofburg was later transformed by the Habsburgs into a landscaped garden, planted with a variety of trees. It was opened to the public in 1918.

Overlooking the garden are greenhouses (1901–7) by the Jugendstil architect Friedrich Ohmann, and near the Hofburg entrance is a small equestrian statue (1780) of Emperor Franz I by the sculptor Balthasar Moll. Closer to the Ringstrasse is the Mozart Memorial (1896) by Viktor Tilgner.

Albertina ㉒

Augustinerstrasse 1. **Map** 4 D1 & 5 C4. **Tel** 534830. 🚇 Karlsplatz, Stephansplatz. 🕐 10am–6pm daily (to 9pm Wed). 🖼️ ♿ 📷 🎫 🍴 🌐 www.albertina.at

Once hidden away at the Opera end of the Hofburg, the newly restored Albertina is now a distinctive landmark, its raised entrance boasting a controversial freestanding diving-board roof by architect Hans Hollein (see p91). The palace once belonged to Maria Theresa's daughter, Maria Christina, and her husband

Duke Albert of Sachsen-Teschen, after whom the gallery is named. Today the Albertina houses a collection of one million prints, over 65,000 watercolours and drawings, and some 70,000 photographs. The gems of the collections are by Dürer, with Michelangelo and Rubens also well represented. Picasso heads a fine 20th-century section.

Temporary exhibitions feature paintings on loan along with works from the Albertina. The Batliner Collection, which comprises over 500 works of art and is one of the most significant private collections in Europe, is on permanent loan.

The new extension on the Burggarten side houses study facilities and the largest of the three exhibition halls. The recent renovation restored a number of features of the Albertina to their former glory, including the façades and the central courtyard. Most notably, the Habsburg State Rooms are now open to the public for the first time in 200 years. They represent a remarkable example of Neo-Classical architecture and interior decoration, inspired by the Archduchess Maria Christina herself.

Augustinerkirche ㉓

Augustinerstrasse 3. **Map** 4 D1 & 5 C4. **Tel** 5337099. 🚇 Stephansplatz. 🕐 8am–5pm daily. 📷

The Augustinerkirche has one of the best-preserved 14th-century Gothic interiors in Vienna; only the modern chandeliers strike a jarring note. The church also houses the Loreto Chapel, which is currently closed for restoration. The chapel contains the silver urns that preserve the hearts of the Habsburg family (see pp24–5). Here too is one of the most powerful works by the Italian Neo-Classical sculptor Antonio Canova, the

tomb of Maria Christina, favourite daughter of Maria Theresa. Like the tomb of Leopold II, which is also here, Maria Christina's tomb is empty; the royal remains lie in the Kaisergruft (see p104).

The church is also celebrated for its music, including masses by Schubert or Haydn held here on Sundays.

Prunksaal ㉔

Josefsplatz 1. **Map** 4 D1 & 5 C4. **Tel** 534100. 🚇 Herrengasse. 🕐 10am–6pm Tue–Sun, 10am–9pm Thu. 🎫 📷 www.onb.ac.at

Commissioned as the court library by Karl VI, the main hall, or Prunksaal, of the National Library was designed by Johann Bernhard Fischer von Erlach (see p149) in 1719. After his death in 1723, the building was completed by his son. The collection consists of approximately 2.6 million books, and includes the personal library of Prince Eugene (see pp26–7), as well as books that were taken from monastic libraries closed during the religious reforms of Joseph II (see p29).

The Prunksaal is 77 m (252 ft) long and is the largest Baroque library in Europe. Paired marble columns frame the domed main room, and bookcases line the walls. Spanning the vaults are frescoes by the Baroque painter Daniel Gran (1730), which were restored by Franz

Domed interior of the Prunksaal in the National Library building

Anton Maulbertsch (1769). The many fine statues, including the likeness of Karl VI in the centre of the hall, are the work of Paul Strudel (1648–1708) and his brother Peter (1660–1714).

Burgkapelle ㉕

Hofburg, Schweizerhof. **Map** 4 D1 & 5 B4. *Tel* 5339927. Ⓤ *Herrengasse.* ⬜ *11am–3pm Mon–Thu, 11am–1pm Fri by appointment.* ⬛ *1 Nov, 8 Dec, 1 Jan.* ⬛ Ⓧ **Vienna Boys' Choir** ⬜ *Jan–Jun & Sep–Dec: 9:15am Sun (book by fax: 533992775, or email: whmk@chello.at).* ⬛

From the Schweizerhof, steps lead up to the Burgkapelle, or Hofburg Chapel, originally constructed in 1296 but modified 150 years later. On Sundays, visitors can hear the Wiener Sängerknaben, the Vienna Boys' Choir *(see p39)*. The chapel interior has Gothic statuary in canopied niches and Gothic carvings, and boasts a bronze crucifix (1720) by Johann Känischbauer.

Spanish Riding School ㉖

See pp98–9.

State Apartments and Treasuries ㉗

See pp100–1.

Bundeskanzleramt ㉘

Ballhausplatz 2. **Map** 1 C5 & 5 B3. *Tel* 531150. Ⓤ *Herrengasse.* ⬛ *to the public.*

The Bundeskanzleramt (1717–19), the Austrian Chancery and Foreign Ministry, was designed by Johann Lukas von Hildebrandt *(see p152)*. It was expanded to its present size in 1766 by Nikolaus Pacassi. Major events that shaped Austria's history have taken place here, including meetings of the Congress of Vienna *(see p30)* in 1814–15, the final deliberations in 1914 that led to

No. 4 Minoritenplatz

the outbreak of World War I, and the murder of Chancellor Dollfuss by Nazi terrorists in 1934 *(see p36)*.

Minoritenplatz ㉙

Map 2 D5 & 5 B3. Ⓤ *Herrengasse.*

At No. 1 Minoritenplatz is the Baroque-style State Archives building (the archives are no longer housed here), built on to the back of the Bunderskanzleramt in 1902. There are a number of palaces around the square. No. 3 is the former Dietrichstein Palace of 1755, an early building by Franz Hillebrand. It now contains the offices of the Federal Chancellor and the Foreign Office. No. 4 is the side of the Liechtenstein Palace *(see p104)*. The mid-17th-century Starhemberg Palace is at No. 5. Now housing ministry offices, it was the residence of Count Ernst Rüdiger von Starhemberg, a hero of the 1683 Turkish siege *(see p27)* when he led the Austrian forces within the city.

Minoritenkirche ㉚

Minoritenplatz 2. **Map** 1 C5 & 5 B3. *Tel* 5334162. Ⓤ *Herrengasse.* ⬜ *9am–6pm daily.* ⬛

This ancient church was established here by the Minor Friars in around 1224, although the present structure dates from 1339. The tower was given its odd pyramidal

shape during the Turkish siege of 1529, when shells sliced the top off the steeple. In the 1780s the Minoritenkirche was restored to its original Gothic style, when Maria Theresa's son, Joseph II *(see p28)*, made a gift of the church to Vienna's Italian community. The church retains a fine west portal (1340) with statues beneath traceried canopies; the carvings above the doorway are modern.

The interior of the church is unexpectedly bright and large and contains a mosaic copy of Leonardo da Vinci's *Last Supper*. Napoleon Bonaparte commissioned Giacomo Raffaelli to execute this work as he proposed to substitute it for the original in Milan and remove the real painting to Paris. Following Napoleon's downfall at Waterloo in 1815, Raffaelli's version was bought by the Habsburgs. In the south aisle is a painted statue of the Madonna and Child (dating from around 1350), while at the same spot in the north aisle is a faded fragment of a 16th-century fresco of St Francis of Assisi.

Gothic statue (about 1400) of Leopold III in the Burgkapelle

Bankgasse ③

Map 1 C5 & 5 B3. ⓤ *Herrengasse.*

Few streets in Vienna are more crammed with the palaces of the nobility.

At Nos. 4–6 is the former Strattmann-Windischgrätz Palace (1692–1734), which was originally designed by Johann Bernhard Fischer von Erlach *(see p149)*. The present façade (1783–4) was the work of Franz Hillebrand, who considerably increased the size of the building by incorporating the palace next door. Today, it houses the Hungarian Embassy.

Nos. 5–7 are the back of the Starhemberg Palace. No. 9 is the Liechtenstein Palace, built as a town residence for the Liechtenstein family by Domenico Martinelli (1694– 1706). No. 2 is the Schön- born-Batthyány Palace (1695).

Volksgarten ③

Dr-Karl-Renner-Ring. **Map** 1 C5 & 5 A3. **Tel** 5339083. ⓤ *Herrengasse.* ◯ *Apr–Nov: 6am–10pm daily; Dec–Mar: 6:30am–10pm daily.* 📷 ♿

Like the Burggarten land- scaped garden *(see p102)*, the Volksgarten was created after the destruction of the city

Statuary above the portal to the Lobkowitz Palace

walls by Napoleon, and opened up a space previously occupied by fortifications. Unlike the Burggarten, the Volksgarten was opened to the public soon after its com- pletion in 1820. The formal plantations, especially the splendid rose gardens, are matched in grandeur by the garden's ornaments, notably the Temple of Theseus (1823) by Peter von Nobile. It was built to house Canova's statue of the Greek god, which now graces the staircase of the Kunsthistorisches Museum. Other compositions include Karl von Hasenauer's monument to the poet Franz Grillparzer *(see p33)* and the fountain memorial to the assassinated Empress Elisabeth (1907) by Friedrich Ohmann *(see p57)* and the sculptor Hans Bitterlich.

Lobkowitz Palace ③

Lobkowitzplatz 2. **Map** 4 D1 & 5 C4. **Tel** 525243460. ⓤ *Karlsplatz, Stephansplatz.* ◯ *10am–6pm Tue–Sun.* 📷 🖼 ♿ **www**.theatermuseum.at

This large palace was built for Count Dietrichstein in 1685–7 by Giovanni Pietro Tencala and altered by Johann Bernhard Fischer von Erlach *(see p149)* in 1710. In 1753 it was acquired by the Lobkowitz family. Balls were held here during the Congress of Vienna *(see p30)*.

Since 1991 the palace has been the Austrian Theatre Museum, which houses a model of the first Hofburg theatre and the Eroica-Saal (1724–29) – where many first performances of Beethoven's work took place. The main exhibits chronicle Austrian theatre in the 1940s.

Kapuzinerkirche und Kaisergruft ③

Tegetthoffstrasse 2. **Map** 4 D1 & 5 C4. **Tel** 5126852. ⓤ *Stephansplatz.* **Kaisergruft** ◯ *10am–6pm daily.* **Kapuzinerkirche** ◯ *6am–6pm daily.* 🖼

Beneath the Kapuziner-kirche are the vaults of the Kaiser- gruft, the imperial crypt founded in 1619 by the Cath- olic Emperor Matthias. Here lie the remains of 138 Habsburgs, including Maria Theresa and her husband Franz Stephan in a large tomb by Balthasar Moll (1753). The most poignant tomb is that of Franz Joseph, flanked by his assassinated wife Elisabeth and their son Rudolf, who

Formal rose garden in the Volksgarten

Tomb of Karl VI by Balthasar Moll

committed suicide *(see p32)*. The last reigning Habsburg, Empress Zita, died in 1989 and her remains are also buried in the crypt.

Neuer Markt ③⑤

Map 4 D1 & 5 C4. Ⓤ *Stephansplatz.*

Known as the Mehlmarkt or flour market until around 1210, the Neuer Markt was also used as a jousting area. Of these origins nothing is left, though a few 18th-century houses remain. In the middle of the Neuer Markt is a replica of the Donner Fountain (1737–9) by Georg Raphael Donner, a symbolic celebration of the role played by rivers in the economic life of the Habsburg Empire. The four figures denote tributaries of the Danube, while the central figure represents Providence. The original figures are in the Lower Belvedere *(see p157).*

Kärntner Strasse ③⑥

Map 4 D1 & 5 C5.
Ⓤ *Stephansplatz.* **Malteserkirche**
◻ *8am–6pm daily.* **Lobmeyr**
Museum ◻ *9am–6pm Mon–Fri, 10am–5pm Sat.*

This pedestrianized street was the main highway to Carinthia in medieval times. Now it is the old city's principal shopping street. Day and night, it is packed with people shopping, buying fresh fruit juice from stands, pausing in cafés, or listening to the street musicians.

No. 37 is the Malteser-kirche. This church was founded by the Knights of Malta who were invited to Vienna early in the 13th century by Leopold VI. The interior retains lofty Gothic windows and vaults.

At No. 1 is the Lobmeyr Museum, which houses glass designed by Josef Hoffmann *(see p56)*, among others, for the Viennese firm of Lobmeyr.

Around the corner at No. 5 Johannesgasse is the superb Questenberg-Kaunitz Palace which dates from the early 18th century. Its design has been attributed to the architect Johann Lukas von Hildebrandt *(see p152).*

American Bar ③⑦

Kärntner Strasse 10. **Map** 4 D1 & 6 D3. Ⓤ *Stephansplatz.*

Beneath a garish depiction of the Stars and Stripes is this bar designed by Adolf Loos *(see p92)* in 1908. The interior, restored in 1990, is a gem.

The Donner Fountain in Neuer Markt

The bar is tiny, with every detail worked out by Loos, such as the tables lit from below and the exquisite glass cabinets for storing glasses. One of his hallmarks is the use of mahogany panelling, and this bar is no exception. Mirrors give the impression that the interior is larger than it actually is, and onyx and marble panels reflect a soft light.

Façade of the American Bar

Stock-im-Eisen-Platz ③⑧

Map 2 D5 & 5 C3. Ⓤ *Stephansplatz.*

This square is at the intersection of Stephansplatz, Kärntner Strasse and Graben. Opposite Haas Haus *(see p75)* is the Equitable Palace (1891), once headquarters to the Equitable Life Insurance Company. There is also an old tree trunk with nails in it in the square. Passing locksmiths' apprentices would bang in a nail to ensure a safe passage home.

SCHOTTENRING AND ALSERGRUND

This part of the city is dotted with sites of interest, such as the ornate Ferstel Palace and the glass-roofed Ferstel Passage that runs through it. The Schottenring and the Schottentor are named after the Benedictine monks who came here in Babenberg times to found the Schottenkirche Monastery. Later rulers of Austria were responsible for the area's

Relief on the façade of the Schottenkirche

other monuments: Joseph II built a huge public hospital, now the Josephinum, and Franz Joseph founded the Votivkirche as a way of giving thanks after escaping assassination in 1853. To the east, nearer the Danube Canal, quiet residential streets are broken only by the imposing Liechtenstein Museum, one of many summer palaces built beyond the city gates by Vienna's nobility.

SIGHTS AT A GLANCE

Streets and Squares
Freyung ❷
Freyung Passage ❶

Churches and Cathedrals
Schottenkirche ❸
Servitenkirche ❺
Votivkirche ❾

Museums and Galleries
Freud Museum ❹
Josephinum ❼
Liechtenstein Museum ❻
Narrenturm ❽

GETTING THERE
This area is served by the Schottentor (line U2) and Rossauer Lände (line U4) U-Bahn stations. Trams 37, 38, 40, 41 and 42 go along Währinger Strasse. Bus 40A runs the length of Liechtensteinstrasse.

KEY

- Street-by-Street map
  See pp108–109
- 🚇 U-Bahn station

0 metres 250
0 yards 250

◁ **The impressive façade of the 19th-century Votivkirche**

Street-by-Street: Around the Freyung

At the core of this elegant part of the city is the former medieval complex of the Schottenkirche and its courtyards and school. On the other side of the Freyung square are some beautiful Baroque palaces, including Hildebrandt's Kinsky Palace (1713–16), and the Palais Ferstel. The Freyung Passage links the Freyung square with Herrengasse, which is lined with Baroque mansions as well as the city's first skyscraper.

Statue of Turkish soldier, south of the Freyung

Backing onto the Schottenring is the Italianate Börse.

★ **Schottenkirche**
Founded in 1177 and redecorated in the Baroque period, this fine church has a museum and there is a famous school alongside it ❸

Passageway leading from No. 2 Helferstorferstrasse to the Freyung

HELFERSTRFERSTRASSE

SCHOTTENGASSE

★ **Freyung**
This square is overlooked by fine buildings, including the former Schottenkirche priory, originally founded in 1155, then rebuilt in 1744 and, due to its appearance, known by the Viennese as the "chest of drawers house" ❷

★ **Freyung Passage**
The Freyung and Herrengasse are connected by a luxury shopping arcade ❶

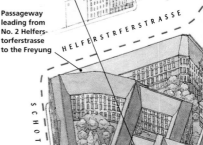

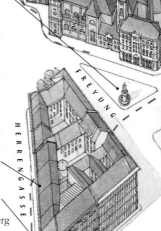

FREYUNG

HERRENGASSE

The Café Central
has a papier-mâché statue of the poet Peter Altenberg next to the main entrance. Altenberg spent a great deal of time in various coffee houses around the city *(see pp58–61)*. **To Herrengasse U-Bahn**

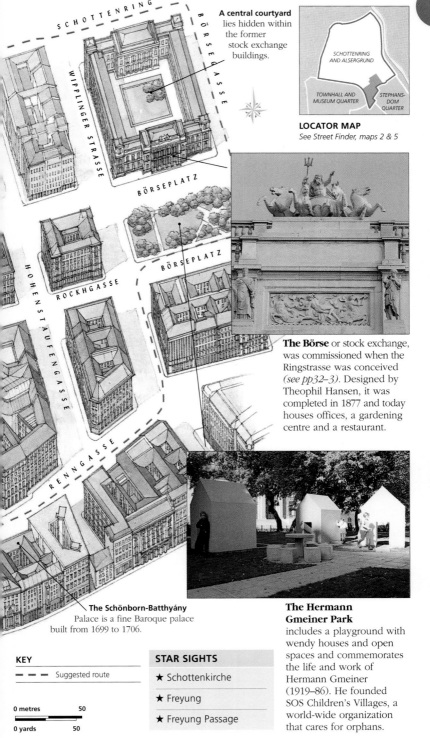

A central courtyard lies hidden within the former stock exchange buildings.

SCHOTTENRING
AND ALSERGRUND

TOWNHALL AND
MUSEUM QUARTER

STEPHANS-
DOM
QUARTER

LOCATOR MAP
See Street Finder, maps 2 & 5

The Börse or stock exchange, was commissioned when the Ringstrasse was conceived *(see pp32–3).* Designed by Theophil Hansen, it was completed in 1877 and today houses offices, a gardening centre and a restaurant.

The Hermann Gmeiner Park includes a playground with wendy houses and open spaces and commemorates the life and work of Hermann Gmeiner (1919–86). He founded SOS Children's Villages, a world-wide organization that cares for orphans.

The Schönborn-Batthyány Palace is a fine Baroque palace built from 1699 to 1706.

KEY

– – – Suggested route

0 metres   50

0 yards   50

STAR SIGHTS

★ Schottenkirche

★ Freyung

★ Freyung Passage

Freyung Passage ❶

Map 2 D5 & 5 B2. Ⓤ *Herrengasse.*

Facing the Freyung is the Italian-style *palazzo* known as the Palais Ferstel, dating from 1860 and taking its name from the architect, Heinrich von Ferstel. Wander in and you will find yourself in the glass-roofed Freyung Passage: lined with elegant shops, it converges on a small courtyard of which the centrepiece is a many-tiered statue portraying the lissom water-sprite of the Danube holding a fish. It then emerges on Herrengasse. As an example of civilized urban amenities, the passage is a great success. It also has an entrance into one of Vienna's grandest coffee houses, the Café Central *(see pp59–61).*

Danube Mermaid's Fountain (1861) in Freyung Passage

Freyung ❷

Map 2 D5 & 5 B2. Ⓤ *Herrengasse.* **Kinsky Palace** ◯ *10am–5pm Mon–Fri.*

The Freyung is a curiously shaped "square". Its name derives from the right of sanctuary granted to the monks of the Schottenkirche that lasted until Maria Theresa abolished it. Fugitives from persecution who entered the area were safe from arrest. No. 4 is the Kinsky Palace (1713–16), by Johann Lukas von Hildebrandt *(see p152).* Next door is the Porcia Palace of 1546, one of the oldest in Vienna, though much altered. At No. 3 is the Harrach

Façade of the Schottenkirche

Palace; the interior has some fine Rococo doors. Opposite is the Austria Fountain: its four figures symbolize the major rivers of the Habsburgs' lands. Behind is the former Schotten-kirche priory, unkindly known as the chest-of-drawers house.

Schottenkirche ❸

Schottenstift, Freyung 6. **Map** 2 D5 & 5 B2. **Tel** 53498600. Ⓤ *Schottentor. Museum* ◯ *11am–5pm Thu–Sat,* ● *Sun & hols.* 🎫 🚫

Despite its name (Scottish church) this 1177 monastic foundation was established by Irish Benedictines. The adjoining buildings have a fine medieval art collection that includes the famous Schotten altarpiece (1475).

The church has been altered repeatedly and has recently undergone extensive renovation. Today it presents a rather drab Neo-Classical façade, with a rich Baroque interior.

Freud Museum ❹

Berggasse 19. **Map** 1 C3. **Tel** 3191596. Ⓤ *Schottentor.* ◯ *9am–5pm daily (to 6pm Jul–Sep).* 🎫 📷 www.freud-museum.at

No. 19 Berggasse differs little from any other 19th-century apartment in Vienna, yet it is now one of the city's most famous addresses. The father of psychoanalysis, Sigmund Freud, lived, worked and received patients here from 1891 until his departure from Vienna in 1938.

The flat housed Freud's family as well as his practice. The catalogue lists 420 items of memorabilia on display, including letters and books, furnishings, photographs documenting Freud's long life, and various antiquities.

Although quickly abandoned when the Nazis forced Freud to leave the city where he had lived almost all his life, the flat still preserves an intimate domestic atmosphere. Even his hat and cane are on show.

Servitenkirche ❺

Servitengasse 9. **Map** 1 C3. **Tel** 317 6195. Ⓤ *Rossauer Lände.* ◯ *7–9am, 6–7pm Mon–Fri, 7–9am, 5–8pm Sat, 7am–noon, 5–8pm Sun.* 🎫 ♿

Although off the beaten track, this Baroque church (1651–77) is well worth a visit. Inside, a riot of Baroque decoration includes elaborate stucco ornamentation, a fine wrought-iron screen near the entrance, and an exuberant pulpit (1739), partly by Balthasar Moll.

FREUD'S THEORIES

Sigmund Freud (1856–1939) was not only the founder of the techniques of psychoanalysis, but a theorist who wrote many essays and books expounding his contentious ideas. Modern concepts such as subconscious, ego, sublimation and Oedipus complex, evolved from Freudian theories. Freud posited different structural systems within the human psyche that, if seriously out of balance, result in emotional or mental disturbance.

Liechtenstein Museum ⑥

Fürstengasse 1. **Map** 1 C2.
Tel 3195767252. Ⓣ Friedensbrücke.
🚌 40A. 🚆 D. ◯ 10am–5pm Fri–
Tue. **www**.liechtensteinmuseum.at

Designed by Domenico
Martinelli and completed in
1692, the Liechtenstein Palace
was the summer home of the
Liechtenstein family and now
houses the art collection of
Prince Hans-Adam II von und
zu Liechtenstein. Behind the
imposing Palladian exterior,
notable features include the
Neo-Classical library, and the
Hercules Hall and grand staircase with their magnificent
frescoes. The art collection
centres on the Baroque, with
a special focus on Rubens,
and numerous paintings and
sculptures by German, Dutch
and Italian masters from the
Renaissance through to the
19th century. The palace
stands in an extensive English-
style garden, designed in the
19th century.

Josephinum ⑦

Währinger Strasse 25/1. **Map** 1 C4.
Tel 4016026000. Ⓣ Schottentor.
🚆 37, 38, 40, 41, 42. ◯ 9am–4pm
Mon, Tue; 10am–6pm Thu–Sun. ◯
public hols. 🌀 🚻

The ardent reformer Joseph II
(see p28) established this military surgical institute. Designed
by Isidor Canevale in 1785, it is
now a medical museum. Some
rooms contain memorabilia
from the 19th century, when
Vienna was a leading centre for
medical research, but the main
attraction is the unusual collection of wax anatomical models
commissioned by the emperor
from Tuscan artists.

Narrenturm ⑧

Spitalgasse 2. **Map** 1 B3. **Tel** 4068672.
Ⓣ Schottentor. 🚆 5, 33, 43, 44.
◯ 3–6pm Wed, 8–11am Thu, 10am–
1pm 1st Sat of month. 🌀

What used to be the
Allgemeines Krankenhaus,
founded by Joseph II (see

Detail on the Votivkirche façade

p28) in 1784, has been
renovated and now houses
various faculties of the
University of Vienna. At the
far end of the complex is the
Narrenturm Tower, a former
lunatic asylum designed by
Isidor Canevale. The tower
now houses the Museum for
Pathological Anatomy, which
includes a reconstruction of
an apothecary's shop and wax
models. The few ground-floor
rooms open to the public
only show a small part of the
collection, but serious students
can enrol on a guided tour of
the corridors upstairs.

Votivkirche ⑨

Rooseveltplatz 8. **Map** 1 C4 & 5 A1.
Tel 4061192. Ⓣ Schottentor.
◯ 9am–1pm, 4–6:30pm Tue–Sat,
9am–1pm Sun. 🌀 🚻 side entrance.

After a deranged tailor tried
but failed to assassinate
Emperor Franz Joseph on 18
February 1853, a collection
was made to pay for a new
church to be built opposite
the Mölker-Bastei, where the
attempt had been made. The
architect was Heinrich von
Ferstel, who began the church
in 1856 though it was not
dedicated until 1879. The lacy
steeples and spire are very
attractive. Many of the church's
chapels are dedicated to
Austrian regiments and
military heroes. The finest
monument is the Renaissance
sarcophagus tomb of Niklas
Salm in the chapel just west
of the north transept. Salm
commanded Austria's forces
during the 1529 Turkish siege.

Wooden pietà in Gothic style (1470) in the Servitenkirche

MUSEUM AND TOWNHALL QUARTER

The Emperor Franz Joseph commissioned the major institutional buildings of the Habsburg empire, and the city, along the Ringstrasse in the mid-19th century *(see pp32–3)*. Today these buildings remain a successful and imposing example of good urban planning. The districts to the west of the Ring-strasse are untouched, including

Der liebe Augustin,
Sankt-Ulrichs-Platz

Josefstadt, which still retains an 18th-century atmosphere with its picturesque streets, modest palaces and Baroque churches. The area's cultural institutions are vibrant: the brilliant productions of the Burgtheater and the wide-ranging exhibits of the Natural History Museum and the Kunsthistorisches Museum are all popular today.

SIGHTS AT A GLANCE

Streets and Squares
Mölker-Bastei ⑰
Sankt-Ulrichs-Platz ⑥
Spittelberg Pedestrian Area ⑦

Historic Buildings
Alte Backstube ②
Burgtheater pp132–33 ⑲
Café Landtmann ⑮
Dreimäderlhaus ⑯
Josefstadt Theater ④
Neues Rathaus ⑫
Parliament ⑨
Pasqualati Haus ⑱
Trautson Palace ⑤
University ⑭

Churches and Cathedrals
Dreifaltigkeitskirche ⑬
Maria Treu Kirche ③

Museums and Galleries
Kunsthistorisches Museum
pp122–27 ⑩
Museum für Volkskunde ①
MuseumsQuartier ⑧
Natural History Museum
pp128–9 ⑪

GETTING THERE
This area is served by the Rathaus (line U2) and Volkstheater (lines U2, U3) U-Bahn stations. Tram 5 runs from Josef-städter Strasse to Lange Gasse, and 46 goes down Lerchenfelder Strasse. Bus 2A runs from Schwedenplatz to Volkstheater. 13A runs along Piaristengasse, and 48A along Burggasse.

KEY

■ Street-by-Street map
See pp114–115

Ⓤ U-Bahn station

0 metres   250
0 yards   250

◁ **Neues Rathaus façade by night**

Street-by-Street: Josefstadt

Tucked behind the grand museums of the Ringstrasse is the 18th-century district known as Josefstadt, named after Emperor Joseph II. Although outside the Inner City, Josefstadt has a vibrant cultural life of its own, with a popular theatre, many good restaurants, and handsome churches and museums. Students from the university and lawyers from the courthouses provide a constantly changing clientele for the district's varied establishments.

★ Maria Treu Kirche
Founded by the fathers of the Piarist order, this church was built from 1716 ❸

Josefstadt Theater
Founded in 1788, Vienna's oldest theatre has kept its doors open continuously since it was rebuilt by Josef Kornhäusel (see p84) in 1822 ❹

No. 29 Lange Gasse
Originally built for servants and workers in the 18th century, the cottages lining this courtyard have changed little over the years.

KEY

━ ━ ━ Suggested route

To Lerchen-felder Strasse

The Plag
Column h
commemora
an epidemic t
occurred in 17

STAR SIGHTS

★ Maria Treu
Kirche

★ Museum für
Volkskunde

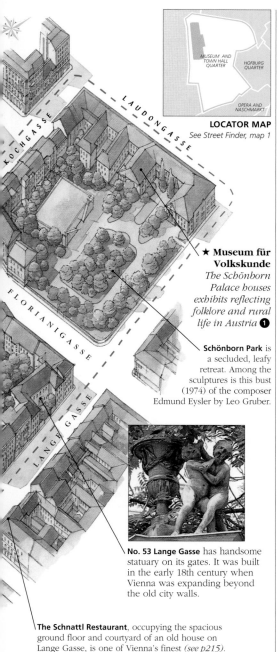

LAUDONGASSE

KOCHGASSE

FLORIANIGASSE

LANGE GASSE

LOCATOR MAP
See Street Finder, map 1

MUSEUM AND
TOWN HALL
QUARTER

HOFBURG
QUARTER

OPERA AND
NASCHMARKT

★ **Museum für
Volkskunde**
*The Schönborn
Palace houses
exhibits reflecting
folklore and rural
life in Austria* ❶

Schönborn Park is
a secluded, leafy
retreat. Among the
sculptures is this bust
(1974) of the composer
Edmund Eysler by Leo Gruber.

No. 53 Lange Gasse has handsome
statuary on its gates. It was built
in the early 18th century when
Vienna was expanding beyond
the old city walls.

The Schnattl Restaurant, occupying the spacious
ground floor and courtyard of an old house on
Lange Gasse, is one of Vienna's finest *(see p215)*.

Alte Backstube
*A working bakery from 1701 to 1963, since
1965 it has been a museum and restaurant* ❷

0 metres   50
0 yards   50

Museum für Volkskunde ❶

Laudongasse 15–19. **Map** 1 B4.
Tel 4068905. ⓤ *Rathaus.* ⬭ *10am–
5pm Tue–Sun.* ⬤ *1 Jan, Easter Mon,
1 May, 1 Nov, 25 Dec.* 🖼 📷 ♿
www.volkskundemuseum.at

The charming Museum of
Austrian Folklore is a
reminder that Vienna is not
only full of imperial grandeur.
Here you will find artifacts
reflecting the culture of
people in Austria and
neighbouring countries.
Exhibits include objects
dating from the 17th to 19th
centuries. The museum is
housed in the 18th-century
Schönborn Palace, designed
by Johann Lukas von
Hildebrandt as a homely
two-storey mansion and
altered in 1760 by Isidor
Canevale. Today it has a
rather imposing façade
with statuary running along
its top. There is a pleasant
park behind the palace.

Alte Backstube ❷

Lange Gasse 34. **Map** 1 B5.
ⓤ *Rathaus.* **Tel** *4061101.*
⬭ *11am–midnight Mon–Sat,
5pm–midnight Sun.* ⬤ *mid-Jul–
mid-Aug and public hols.* 📷 ♿

One of the finest middle-
class houses in Vienna was
built at No. 34 Lange Gasse in
1697 by the jeweller Hans
Bernhard Leopold. The
sandstone sculpture that is
positioned above the doorway
symbolizes the Holy Trinity.
Inside is an old bakery, the
Alte Backstube, that was in
continuous use from 1701 to
1963. The baking ovens were
never removed, and today the
rooms have been sympatheti-
cally restored and incorporated
into a traditional restaurant
and café. They also contain a
museum dedicated to the art
of baking where 300-year-old
equipment is on display.
   A few doors away, at No. 29,
it's worth glancing into the
courtyard to see the rows of
single-storey houses facing
each other – a rare example of
working-class Vienna that is
probably about 200 years old.

Maria Treu Kirche ❸

Jodok-Fink-Platz. **Map** 1 B5.
Tel 4061453. Ⓣ Rathaus. ☐ for
services and by appointment. ▣

Overlooking Jodok-Fink-
Platz and flanked by monastic
buildings stands the Church
of Maria Treu. It was founded
in 1698 by the fathers of the
Piarist order.

This outstanding church was
originally designed by Johann
Lukas von Hildebrandt in 1716
and altered by Matthias Gerl
in the 1750s. The elegant twin
towers were not completed
until 1854. Inside, there is a
splendid Baroque frescoed
ceiling in vibrant colours from
1752–3 by the great Austrian
painter Franz Anton Maul-
bertsch. A chapel immediately
to the left of the choir contains
an altarpiece of the Crucifixion
dating from about 1774, also
painted by Maulbertsch.

Directly in front of the
church and rising up from the
square is a fine Baroque pillar
topped with a statue of the
Madonna, attended beneath
by statues of saints and angels.
Like many such columns in
Vienna, it was erected to
commemorate an outbreak
of plague, in this case the
epidemic of 1713.

**Ceiling frescoes above the altar in
the Maria Treu Kirche**

Josefstadt Theater ❹

Josefstädter Strasse 26. **Map** 1 B5.
Tel 427000. Ⓣ Rathaus. ☐ for
performances. **www**.josefstadt.org

This intimate theatre (see
p230), one of the oldest still
standing in Vienna, has
enjoyed a glorious history.

The façade of the glorious Josefstadt Theater

Founded in 1788, it was
rebuilt by Joseph Kornhäusel
(see p84) in 1822, and has
been in operation ever since,
accommodating ballet, opera
and theatre performances.
Beethoven composed and
conducted his overture *The
Consecration of the House*
for the reopening of the
theatre in 1822 after its renovation. The director Max
Reinhardt supervised the
restoration of this attractive
theatre in 1924. Today, it
puts on mostly light plays
and comedies.

Trautson Palace ❺

Museumstrasse 7. **Map** 3 B1.
Ⓣ Volkstheater. ◉ to the public.

Set back from the street next
to the Volkstheater is this
elegant Baroque palace,
designed in 1710 by Johann
Bernhard Fischer von Erlach
(see p149). Most Viennese
palaces have flat fronts but on
this one the central bays of
the façade jut out with real
panache. Nor is there
anything restrained about the
ornamentation: above the
cornice and pediment is one
of the largest collections of
statuary atop any palace in
the whole of Vienna. This
includes a large statue of
Apollo playing the lyre.
Passing beneath the tall portal
you will see on the left an
immense staircase, with
carvings of bearded giants
bearing its weight, by the
Italian sculptor Giovanni
Giuliani. This leads to the
ceremonial hall.

Originally built for Count
Johann Leopold Donat
Trautson who was in the
service of Joseph I, the palace
was acquired in 1760 by
Maria Theresa (see pp28–9).
She donated it to the Royal
Hungarian Bodyguard that
she had founded. It has
housed the Ministry of Justice
since 1961, so there is no
public access to the interior.

Sankt-Ulrichs-
Platz ❻

Between Neustiftgasse and Burggasse.
Map 3 B1. Ⓣ Volkstheater. **Café
Nepomuk Tel** 06766124003. ☐
8am–11pm Mon–Fri, 8am–11pm Sat
& Sun. **Ulrichskirche Tel** 5231246.
☐ on request or for services only.

This tiny sloping square is an
exquisite survival of early
Vienna. The dainty Baroque
house at No. 27 is now the
Café Nepomuk, and adjoining
it is a Renaissance house that
escaped destruction by the
Turks during the sieges of the
city, most probably because
the Turkish commander Kara
Mustafa pitched his own tent
nearby.

The house partly obscures
the façade of the Baroque
Ulrichskirche, built by Josef
Reymund from 1721–4.
Handsome patrician houses
encircle it, of which the
prettiest is No. 2, the
Schulhaus. Elaborately
decorated, it dates from the
mid-18th century. In the
church the composer Gluck
was married and Johann
Strauss the Younger was
christened.

Spittelberg Pedestrian Area ❼

Map 3 B1. Ⓤ *Volkstheater.* **Amerling-
haus** ◯ *2–10pm Mon–Fri.* **Market**
◯ *Apr–Jun & Sep–Nov: 10am–6pm
Sat; Jul & Aug: 2–9pm Sat.* 📷 ♿

A group of streets – the
pedestrianized Spittelberggasse, Gutenberggasse and
Schrankgasse – has been well
restored to present a pretty
group of 18th- and 19th-
century houses.
Traditionally the area
was lower class and
very lively, home
to the actors,
artists and strolling
players of the day.
The houses were
mostly tenements,
without gardens or courtyards.

The charm of the district was
rediscovered in the 1970s and
the city authorities set about
restoring the buildings. Today,
it is a district of restaurants, cafés

**Façade detail at No. 20
Spittelberggasse**

and boutiques. It hosts
a Christmas and an
Easter market, as well
as a regular arts and
crafts market from
April to November.
The Amerlinghaus
theatre at No. 8
Stiftgasse is the area's
cultural centre and provides a
venue for exhibitions and events.
The Spittelberg is a great success,
and café life keeps the cobbled
streets buzzing into the early
hours of the morning.

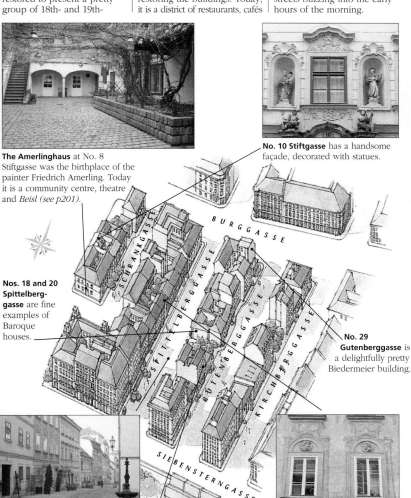

The Amerlinghaus at No. 8
Stiftgasse was the birthplace of the
painter Friedrich Amerling. Today
it is a community centre, theatre
and *Beisl (see p201).*

No. 10 Stiftgasse has a handsome
façade, decorated with statues.

**Nos. 18 and 20
Spittelberg-
gasse** are fine
examples of
Baroque
houses.

**No. 29
Gutenberggasse** is
a delightfully pretty
Biedermeier building.

Spittelberggasse acts as the venue
for an arts and crafts market that is
held on every Saturday from April
to November, and daily during
Easter and Christmas.

The Witwe Bolte restaurant
used to be an inn in the 18th
century; legend has it that
Emperor Joseph II was
thrown out of here in 1778.

No. 9 Spittelberggasse is a
beautifully-decorated house,
with skilfully-painted *trompe
l'oeil* windows, dating from
the 18th century.

MuseumsQuartier Wien ⓮

Once home to the Imperial stables and carriage houses, the MuseumsQuartier Wien is one of the largest cultural centres in the world. It houses a diverse range of facilities from classical art museums to venues for film, theatre, architecture, dance, new media and a children's creativity centre, as well as a variety of shops, cafés and restaurants. Blending the Baroque architecture of the imperial stables with bold modern buildings, such as the white limestone façade of the Leopold Museum and the dark grey basalt of the Museum of Modern Art Ludwig Foundation Vienna, this impressive and diverse complex aims to provide an almost unprecedented experience.

★ **Leopold Museum**
Self-portrait with Chinese Lantern (1912) by Egon Schiele is part of the world's largest collection of Schiele's works, housed in this museum.

★ **ZOOM Kindermuseum**
Providing an exciting place to learn, children are encouraged to explore in the ZOOM Lab, play in ZOOM Ocean, be creative in ZOOM Atelier and have fun exploring the ZOOM exhibitions.

math.space

Tanzquartier Wien

STAR SIGHTS

★ ZOOM Kindermuseum

★ Leopold Museum

★ Museum of Modern Art Ludwig Foundation Vienna (MUMOK)

quartier21
As Vienna's centre for contemporary applied art, quartier21 provides a range of frequently changing exhibitions for the public, as well as numerous fashion, design, book and music shops.

Halls E + G
This foyer leads to the former Winter Riding Hall, now Halls E + G showing a variety of concert, theatre and dance performances. The foyer is also the entrance to the Kunsthalle Wien which exhibits international modern art.

VISITORS' CHECKLIST

Museumsplatz 1. **Map** 3 C1.
Tel *523 58 81/1730.*
🚇 *MuseumsQuartier,*
Volkstheater. 🚌 *2a to the*
MuseumsQuartier, 48a to
Volkstheater. 🚊 *49 to*
Volkstheater. **Visitor Centre** ⬜
10am–7pm daily. **Ticket Centre**
⬜ *10am–7pm daily.* 🖼 📷 ✒
in English by arrangement. ♿
🍴 💻 🛍 🚻 🅿
6am–midnight daily.
www.mqw.at

Architekturzentrum
Wien

quartier21
(alternate entrance)

Main entrance in the Fischer
von Erlach Wing

Main Courtyard
Often called the largest open-air festival hall in Vienna, from here the diverse architecture of the complex can be appreciated.

★ Museum of Modern Art Ludwig Foundation Vienna
Homme accroupi *(1907) by Andre Derain, is part of the collection of European contemporary and modern art in this museum, otherwise known as MUMOK.*

Exploring the MuseumsQuartier Wien

Over 20 different cultural institutions are gathered together in the MuseumsQuartier Wien, together with a wide variety of restaurants, cafés and shops. The sight is an ideal starting point for any trip to Vienna, as many other attractions are nearby. It is advisable to begin your visit by going to the Visitor Centre in the Fischer von Erlach Wing, to obtain a programme detailing the events and the exhibitions happening in the complex.

Die Quelle (1923), Leopold Museum

Architekturzentrum Wien

Tel 522311530. ◯ *10am–9pm daily.* 🔟 www.azw.at

The permanent exhibition at this venue is concerned with thematic and structural diversity in 20th-century architecture. Committed to providing access to architecture, the venue introduces new architectural work to the public. The four to six temporary exhibitions a year aim to complement this by linking modern architecture with architectural history.

Museum of Modern Art Ludwig Foundation Vienna (MUMOK)

Tel 52500. ◯ *10am–6pm Tue–Sun (to 9pm Thu).* www.mumok.at

This museum contains one of the largest European collections of modern and contemporary art. MUMOK comprises of a variety of genres ranging from American Pop Art, Photo Realism, Fluxus and Nouveau Réalism to Viennese Actionism, Arte Povera, Conceptual and Minimal Art, as well as other contemporary art from Central and Eastern Europe. The galleries are split historically and chronologically over five levels, two underground.

quartier21

Tel 0820 600600. ◯ *10am–8pm daily, except special events.*

Over 40 different groups have turned quartier21 into Vienna's centre for contemporary applied art. The attractions for the public, which are on the ground floor, include fashion, design, book and music shops, an exhibition space for art schools, and large event halls.

Leopold Museum

Tel 525700. ◯ *10am–6pm daily (10am–9pm Thu).* www.leopoldmuseum.org

Home to over 5,000 works of art, the Leopold Collection of Austrian art was compiled over five decades by Rudolf Leopold. The exhibition space spans five floors. One of the highlights is the world's largest Egon Schiele collection (on the second floor) along with Expressionist paintings and Austrian inter-war paintings.

Paintings after 1945 and works by Albin Egger-Lienz, including *Die Quelle,* are on the first floor, while an exhibition on Secessionism and Art Nouveau is on the ground level, with major works by Gustav Klimt, Richard Gerstl

and Oskar Kokoschka. The lower two levels include art from other 19th- and early 20th-century Austrian artists.

Tanzquartier Wien

Tel 581359160. www.tqw.at

The Tanzquartier Wien offers facilities and training to dancers and presents dance and other performances to the public.

ZOOM Kindermuseum

Tel 5247908. ◯ *8:30am–5pm Mon–Fri; 10am–5:30pm Sat, Sun, school hols, public hols. Visits must be pre-booked.* www.kindermuseum.at

This lively centre offers an unconventional approach to the world of the museum for children from babies to the age of 12. The aim is to encourage learning about exhibition subjects through play and exploration, such as the ZOOM Lab for older children, while younger ones can have a dip in the ZOOM Ocean with their parents.

KUNSTHALLE wien

Tel 5218933. ◯ *10am–7pm daily (to 10pm Thu).* www.kunsthallewien.at

This striking red brick building is a home for innovation and creativity, showing exhibitions of international and contemporary art. The exhibitions emphasize cross-genre and cross-border trends in the arts. Highlights range from experimental architecture, video, photography and film, to new media.

math.space

Tel 5235881/1730. ◯ *varies, phone to check.* http://math.space.or.at

Linking maths to the arts, this centre for the popularization of maths is aimed at people of all ages, with interactive workshops for children and many programmes for adults.

The Red Horseman (1974) by Roy Lichtenstein in MUMOK

Parliament  ❾

Dr-Karl-Renner-Ring 3. **Map** 1 C5 & 5 A3. **Tel** 401102400. Ⓤ *Volkstheater.* ☐ for 📷 except when parliament is in session: *mid-Sep–mid-Jul: 11am, 2pm, 3pm, 4pm Mon–Thu; 11am, 1pm, 2pm, 3pm, 4pm Fri; 11am, noon, 1pm, 2pm, 3pm, 4pm Sat; mid-Jul–mid-Sep: 11am, noon, 1pm, 2pm, 3pm, 4pm Mon–Sat.* ♿ **www**.parlament.gv.at

The architect Theophil Hansen *(see p32)* chose a strict Neo-Classical style when he designed the Parliament building (and the neighbouring Palais Epstein). The building was originally constructed as part of the Ringstrasse development to act as the *Reichsrat* building (the Parliament of the Austrian part of the Habsburg empire). Construction began in 1874 and finished in 1884.

The Parliament's entrance is raised above street level and approached up a broad ramp. At the foot of the ramp are the the bronze Horse Tamers (1901) by sculptor Josef Lax; the ramp itself is decorated with marble figures of Greek and Roman historians. On the roof there are chariots and impressive statues of ancient scholars and statesmen.

In front of the central portico is the Athenebrunnen,

Façade of the Parliament building and the Athenebrunnen fountain

a fountain dominated by the figure of Pallas Athene, the goddess of Wisdom. It was designed by Karl Kundmann and was placed here in 1902. In this splendid, if chilly, setting on 11 November 1918 after the collapse of the Habsburg empire, the parliamentary deputies proclaimed the formation of the republic of

Deutsch-Österreich. It was renamed the Republic of Austria in 1919.

During World War II, half of the Parliament building was completely destroyed. Reconstruction was eventually completed by June 1956, but the restoration of some of the damaged artwork, only began in the 1990s.

THE AUSTRIAN PARLIAMENT

The Austrian parliament is composed of two houses – the Lower House, or *Nationalrat,* and the Upper House, or *Bundesrat.* The Lower House has 183 seats and its members are elected for a four-year term by proportional representation. It comprises the governing party and the opposition. The Upper House is composed of elected representatives from Austria's nine provinces, and its function is to approve legislation passed by the Lower House. Bills may also be presented to parliament by the general public or by the Chambers of Labour (representing consumers and employees) and the Chambers of the Economy (representing employers and industry). The federal President is elected for a six-year term and is largely a figurehead. Theoretically, he or she has the power to veto bills and dissolve parliament, though this has never occurred.

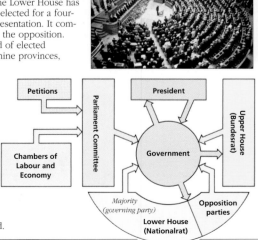

Petitions

Parliament Committee

President

Upper House (Bundesrat)

Chambers of Labour and Economy

Government

Majority (governing party)

Opposition parties

Lower House (Nationalrat)

Kunsthistorisches Museum ⑩

More than one and a half million people visit the
Museum of the History of Art every year. Its collections
are based largely on those built up over the centuries by
generations of Habsburg monarchs. Originally the works
of art were housed in the Hofburg and the Belvedere,
but when the Ringstrasse was built *(see pp32–3)*
two magnificent buildings were erected to house
the collections of imperial art and natural
history. The former are on display in this
museum where lavish internal
decoration complements the exhibits.

Second floor

Coin collection

★ **Hunters in the Snow** *(1565)*
*The last painting in Pieter Bruegel the
Elder's series of the seasons shows hunters
returning to the village on a winter's day.*

First floor

★ **The Artist's Studio**
*In this 1665 allegory of art,
Johannes Vermeer shows an
artist in decorative dress
painting a model posing as
Clio, the Muse of History.*

★ **Salt Cellar** *(1540–3)*
*Benvenuto Cellini's sumptuous
gold Saliera shows the sea and
earth united, represented by a
female earth goddess and
the sea god
Neptune.*

KEY

- ☐ Egyptian and Near Eastern collection
- ☐ Collection of Greek and Roman Antiquities
- ☐ Collection of Sculpture and Decorative Arts
- ☐ Picture gallery
- ☐ Coin cabinets
- ☐ Non-exhibition space

Portrait of the Infanta Margarita Teresa *(1659)*

Diego Velázquez captures the fragility of the eight-year-old Spanish princess in all her finery in this official portrait.

MUSEUM GUIDE

The ground floor, housing sculpture and the applied arts, is due to reopen in 2011. Until then, parts of this collection are on display in the picture gallery, on the first floor. Three rooms on the second floor house the impressive coin collection.

Gemma Augustea
The Emperor Augustus dressed as Jupiter sits next to Roma, the personification of Rome, in this Roman cameo carved from onyx.

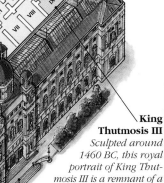

Ground floor

Rooms 1-7

King Thutmosis III
Sculpted around 1460 BC, this royal portrait of King Thutmosis III is a remnant of a standing or kneeling figure.

Main entrance from Maria-Theresia-Platz

Rotunda

STAR EXHIBITS

★ Hunters in the Snow by Bruegel

★ The Artist's Studio by Vermeer

★ Salt Cellar by Cellini

THE APOTHEOSIS OF THE RENAISSANCE

Many prominent artists were employed to decorate the museum's interior. As part of an extravagant decorative scheme, the Hungarian painter Michael Munkácsy contributed a fabulous *trompe l'oeil* ceiling painting for the main staircase depicting *The Apotheosis of the Renaissance* (1890). It features Leonardo, Raphael, Veronese, Michelangelo and Titian and their models, presided over by Pope Julius II.

Exploring the Kunsthistorisches' Picture Collection

The collection focuses on Old Masters from the 15th to the 18th centuries, and largely reflects the personal tastes of its Habsburg founders. Venetian and 17th-century Flemish paintings are particularly well represented, and there is an excellent display of works by earlier Netherlandish and German artists. Broadly speaking, the pictures are hung following regional schools or styles of painting, although there is considerable overlap between the various categories.

Large Self-Portrait (1652) by Rembrandt van Rijn

The Fur (around 1635–40) by Peter Paul Rubens

Three rooms, XIII, XIV and XX, are devoted to Rubens and include large-scale religious works such as the *Ildefonso Altarpiece* (1630–32) and *The Fur*, an intimate portrait of his wife. Rubens' collaborator and pupil, Anthony Van Dyck, is also represented here by some outstanding works in which his sensitivity to human emotion is fully portrayed.

FLEMISH PAINTING

Because of the historic links between the Habsburg monarchy and the Netherlands, there are several works from this part of Europe (present-day Belgium). The works of the early Flemish masters, who pioneered the development of oil painting, are characterized by their luminous colours and close attention to detail. This can be seen in the triptychs by Rogier van der Weyden and Hans Memling, and Jan van Eyck's *Cardinal Niccolo Albergati* (1435). The highlight for many is Room X, in which about half of all Pieter Bruegel the Elder's surviving works are displayed, including his *Tower of Babel* and most of the cycle of *The Seasons*, all from the mid-16th century.

DUTCH PAINTING

Protestant Holland's newly-rich merchants of the 17th century delighted in pictures that reflected their own world rather than the hereafter. The Dutch genre scenes include works of great domestic charm such as Pieter de Hooch's lovely *Woman with Child at her Breast* (1663–5) and Gerard ter Borch's *Woman Peeling Apples* (1661) while Jacob van Ruisdael's *Great Forest* (1655–60) shows the advances made by Dutch painters in their observations of the natural world. All the

Rembrandts on show in Room XV are portraits; there is the picture of his mother as the prophetess Hannah (1639) and, in contrast to earlier works, the *Large Self-Portrait* shows the artist wearing a plain smock, with the emphasis on his face. The only painting by Johannes Vermeer is the enigmatic *The Artist's Studio* (Room 24). It is a complicated work with layers of symbolism; whether it is a self portrait or not has never been resolved.

ITALIAN PAINTING

The Italian galleries have a strong collection of 16th-century paintings from Venice and the Veneto. In Room I the broad chronological and stylistic sweep of Titian's work, from his early *Gypsy Madonna*

Susanna and the Elders (1555) by Tintoretto

(1510) to the late *Nymph and Shepherd* (1570–5), can be seen. Other Venetian highlights include Giovanni Bellini's graceful *Young Woman at her Toilette* (1515) and Tintoretto's *Susanna and the Elders*. This is considered to be one of the major works of Venetian Mannerism. Giuseppe Arcimboldo's series of allegorical portrait heads representing the elements and the seasons are usually on show in Room 19, together with other works commissioned by Emperor Rudolf II. Italian Baroque painting includes works by Annibale Carracci and Michelangelo Merisi da Caravaggio, including the huge *Madonna of the Rosary*. Painted between 1606 and 1607, it depicts an intensely realistic Madonna advising St Dominic to distribute rosaries.

FRENCH PAINTING

Although the number of French paintings on show is relatively small, there are some minor masterpieces. The minutely detailed and highly original portrait of *The Court Jester Gonella* (1440–45), is thought to be the work of Jean Fouquet. It depicts a wily old man, seemingly squeezed into the picture, believed to be a famous court jester of the time. A more formal court portrait from 1569 is that of the youthful Charles IX of France by François Clouet. *The Destruction of the Temple in Jerusalem*, a monumental work painted by Nicolas Poussin in 1638, depicts the Emperor Titus watching the Old Testament prophecy of the destruction of the Temple of Solomon come true. It combines agitated movement with thorough archaeological research. Joseph Duplessis' *Christopher Willibald Ritter von Gluck at the Spinet* shows the famous composer gazing into the heavens for inspiration.

Summer (1563) by Giuseppe Arcimboldo

BRITISH AND GERMAN PAINTING

There are few British works. Perhaps the most appealing is the *Landscape of Suffolk* (around 1750) by Thomas Gainsborough. There are also portraits by Gainsborough, Reynolds and Lawrence.

The German collection is rich in 16th-century paintings. There are several Albrecht Dürer works, including his

Madonna with the Pear (1512). Other works include the *Stag Hunt of Elector Friedrich the Wise* (1529) by Lucas Cranach the Elder and seven portraits by Hans Holbein the Younger.

SPANISH PAINTING

Room 10 houses several fine portraits of the Spanish royal family by the artist Diego Velázquez. He lived from 1599 to 1660 and was the court painter to Philip IV. His works include three portraits of Philip IV's daughter, the Infanta Margarita Teresa (in one aged three, another aged five and in a third aged eight), as well as a portrait of her sickly infant brother, Philip Prosper. Other Spanish works include paintings by Alonso Sánchez Coello and Antonio de Pereda.

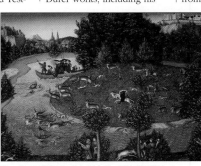

Stag Hunt of Elector Friedrich the Wise (1529), by Lucas Cranach the Elder, in the German Collection

Exploring the Kunsthistorisches' Other Collections

Apart from the picture gallery, the Kunsthistorisches-Museum houses several distinct collections of three-dimensional art and objects. Most of the European sculpture and decorative art is from approximately the same period as the paintings (from the 15th to the 18th centuries), but there is also a fine display of medieval objects, while exhibits on show in the Egyptian, Greek and Roman rooms provide an intriguing record of the world's earliest civilizations.

sculptures on display were made to contain deceased souls. Other rooms house mummified animals, Egyptian scripts and artifacts such as pots, clothing and jewellery.

Also shown are a glazed brick relief of a lion from Babylon, and items from Arabia.

ORIENTAL AND EGYPTIAN ANTIQUITIES

Four specially decorated rooms adorned with Egyptian friezes and motifs provide the perfect setting for the bulk of the museum's collection of Egyptian and Near Eastern antiquities. The

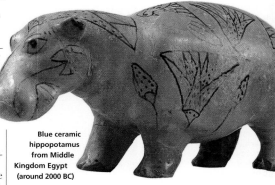

Blue ceramic hippopotamus from Middle Kingdom Egypt (around 2000 BC)

nucleus of the collection was formed under the earlier Habsburg monarchs. Most of the items were either bought in the 19th century, after Napoleon's Egyptian expedition had increased interest in the area, or added early this century, when Austrian archaeologists excavated at Giza; an outstanding example is the so-called *Reserve Head* (around 26th century BC). The entire 5th-dynasty Tomb Chapel of Ka-Ni-Nisut, from the Pyramid district of Giza, and its well-preserved hieroglyphics (from around 2400BC) are on display in Room II.

The remarkable collection of objects and sculpture spans a wide chronological period from the Pre-Dynastic era until Roman times. There is a bust of King Thutmosis III *(see p123)* as well as portraits of Egyptian gods and goddesses. In Rooms I and V, where the decorative scheme incorporates Egyptian columns from Aswan, there are items associated with the mortuary cult in Ancient Egypt, including sarcophagi, canopic jars (which used to contain the entrails of mummified corpses), scarabs, mummy cases and papyrus books of the dead. In Room VIII there is a small blue ceramic statue of a hippopotamus. These were often found in Middle Kingdom tombs, as hippopotamus hunting was a royal privilege given to citizens who had won the king's favour. Many of the small-scale

GREEK AND ROMAN ANTIQUITIES

Only part of the museum's Greek and Roman collection is housed in the main building; the finds from Ephesus and Samothrace are displayed in the Neue Burg *(see p95)* in the Hofburg.

If you approach the collection from the Egyptian galleries, the first room you come to (Room X) is devoted to early Greek sculpture. Rooms 6–7 house the Austria Romana collection which includes a statue of the *Youth from Magdalensberg*, a 16th-century cast of a lost Roman statue, found buried in an Austrian field. The main gallery (Room XI), decorated in the style of an imperial Roman villa, includes a mosaic of Theseus and the Minotaur, a Roman marble statue of Isis, Greek sculpture and a sarcophagus with fine relief decoration. Rooms XII and XIII house numerous portrait heads.

The collection also boasts figurines and bronzes from Greece and Rome, vases from Tanagra (a town in Ancient Greece) and a large collection of Roman cameos, jewellery,

Room I from the Egyptian galleries, with papyrus stalk columns from Aswan (around 1410 BC)

busts of Roman Emperors and Roman glass. Etruscan and Cypriot art are in rooms 1–3. Coptic, Byzantine and Germanic items are shown in the rest of the rooms, where pride of place goes to the Treasure of Nagyszentmiklós, a late 9th-century collection of golden vessels found in Romania in 1799.

Medal of Ulrich II Molitor (1581)

SCULPTURE AND DECORATIVE ARTS

The collection consists of many treasures bought or commissioned by Habsburg connoisseurs, particularly Rudolf II and Archduke Leopold William, for their Kunstkammern, or chambers of art and marvels housed in their Habsburg residences. In addition to sculpture, these princely treasuries contained precious items of high craftsmanship, exotic, highly unusual novelties, and scientific instruments. Among the most intriguing are some intricate automata, including a musical box in the form of a ship, and a moving clock. Some of the royal patrons worked in the studio themselves; on display is some glass blown by the Archduke Ferdinand II and embroidery sewn by Maria Theresa.

As in the Picture Gallery, the main emphasis is on the Renaissance and Baroque, although there is a great display of medieval items. These include fine, late Gothic religious carved statues by artists such as Tilman Riemenschneider, some medieval ivories, drinking horns and communion vessels. The

Virgin with Child (about 1495) by Tilman Riemen- schneider

highlights of the Italian Renaissance rooms are a marble bust of a laughing boy by Desiderio da Settignano, a marble relief of Bacchus and Ariadne and a fine bronze and gilt figurine called Venus Felix after an antique marble statue. Included in the large German Renaissance collection are early playing cards and a table centrepiece, incorporating "vipers' tongues" (in fact, fossilized sharks' teeth), said to ward off poison. Other gems include Benvenuto Cellini's Salt Cellar *(see p122)*, made for the French king François I, and some statuettes by Giambologna. This section is due to reopen in 2011 but the Italian Renaissance items can be seen in the Italian Renaissance paintings rooms (on the first floor).

Youth from Magdalensberg, 16th century, cast after a Roman original

COINS AND MEDALS

Tucked away on the second floor is one of the most extensive coin and medal collections in the world. For those with a special interest in the area it is exceptional. Once again, the nucleus of the collection came from the former possessions of the Habsburgs, but it has been added to by modern curators and now includes many 20th-century items. Only a fraction of the museum's 500,000 pieces can be seen in the three exhibition rooms.

Room I gives an overview of the development of money. It includes coins from Ancient Greece and Rome, examples of Egyptian, Celtic and Byzantine money, and medieval, Renaissance and European coins, as well as the whole range of Austrian currency.

Also on display is a collection of primitive forms of money such as stone currency from Yap Island in Micronesia.

Rooms II and III house an extensive collection of 19th- and 20th-century medals. The portrait medallions are often miniature works of art in themselves. Particularly noteworthy are the unusual silver and gilt medals belonging to Ulrich Molitor, the Abbot of Heiligenkreuz, and the silver medallion which was engraved by Bertrand Andrieu and minted to commemorate the baptism of Napoleon's son. This shows the emperor as a proud father, lifting aloft his baby, the King of Rome *(see p175)*.

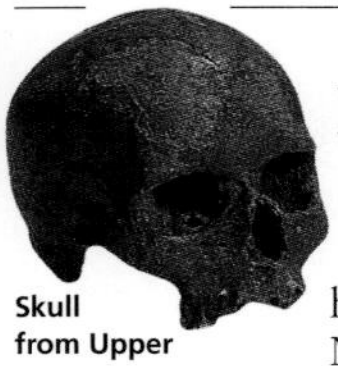

Natural History Museum ⑪

Skull from Upper Paleolithic period

Almost the mirror image of the Kunsthistorisches Museum, the Natural History Museum was designed by the same architects, and opened in 1889. Its carefully devised interior decoration reflects the nature of the collections. These are quite wide ranging and include archaeological, anthropological, mineralogical, zoological and geological displays. There are casts of dinosaur skeletons, the world's largest display of skulls illustrating the history of man, one of Europe's most comprehensive collections of gems, prehistoric sculpture, Bronze Age items, and extinct birds and mammals.

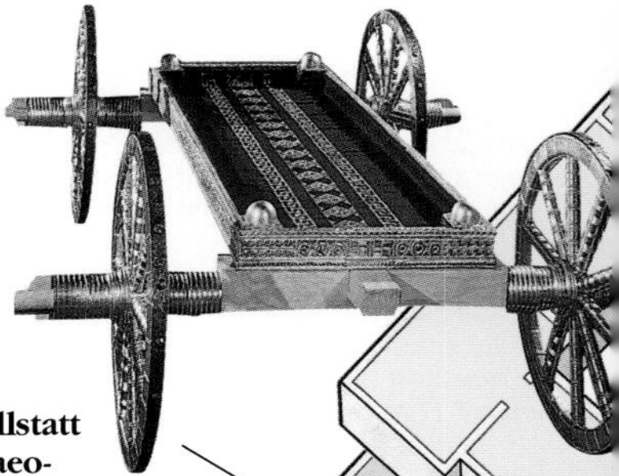

★ Hallstatt Archaeological Finds
This reconstructed chariot from the Bycis Kala cave in Moravia dates from the early Iron Age.

★ Venus of Willendorf
This ancient fertility figure (see p20) found in Lower Austria is around 24,000 years old.

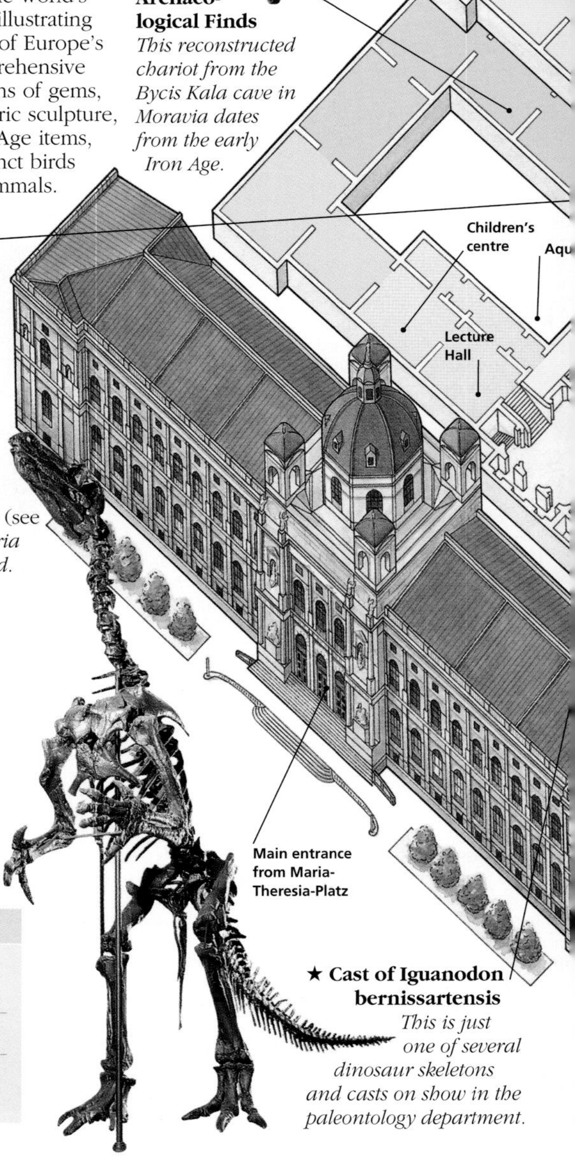

Children's centre   Aqu

Lecture Hall

KEY

- Mineralogy
- Geology, Paleontology
- Archaeology
- Anthropology
- Zoology
- Temporary exhibition space
- Non-exhibition space

Main entrance from Maria-Theresia-Platz

STAR EXHIBITS

- ★ Hallstatt Archaeological Finds
- ★ Venus of Willendorf
- ★ Cast of *Iguanodon bernissartensis*

★ Cast of Iguanodon bernissartensis
This is just one of several dinosaur skeletons and casts on show in the paleontology department.

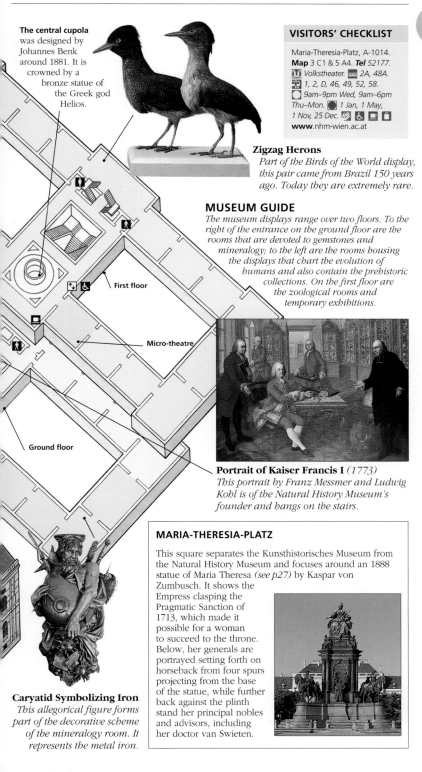

The central cupola was designed by Johannes Benk around 1881. It is crowned by a bronze statue of the Greek god Helios.

Zigzag Herons
Part of the Birds of the World display, this pair came from Brazil 150 years ago. Today they are extremely rare.

VISITORS' CHECKLIST

Maria-Theresia-Platz, A-1014.
Map 3 C1 & 5 A4. *Tel 52177.*
🇺 *Volkstheater.* 🚌 *2A, 48A.*
🚋 *1, 2, D, 46, 49, 52, 58.*
⏺ *9am–9pm Wed, 9am–6pm*
Thu–Mon. ⬤ *1 Jan, 1 May,*
1 Nov, 25 Dec. 🎟 ♿ 📷 📱
www.nhm-wien.ac.at

MUSEUM GUIDE

The museum displays range over two floors. To the right of the entrance on the ground floor are the rooms that are devoted to gemstones and mineralogy; to the left are the rooms housing the displays that chart the evolution of humans and also contain the prehistoric collections. On the first floor are the zoological rooms and temporary exhibitions.

First floor

Micro-theatre

Ground floor

Portrait of Kaiser Francis I *(1773)*
This portrait by Franz Messmer and Ludwig Kohl is of the Natural History Museum's founder and hangs on the stairs.

MARIA-THERESIA-PLATZ

This square separates the Kunsthistorisches Museum from the Natural History Museum and focuses around an 1888 statue of Maria Theresa *(see p27)* by Kaspar von Zumbusch. It shows the Empress clasping the Pragmatic Sanction of 1713, which made it possible for a woman to succeed to the throne. Below, her generals are portrayed setting forth on horseback from four spurs projecting from the base of the statue, while further back against the plinth stand her principal nobles and advisors, including her doctor van Swieten.

Caryatid Symbolizing Iron
This allegorical figure forms part of the decorative scheme of the mineralogy room. It represents the metal iron.

Neues Rathaus ⑫

Friedrich-Schmidt-Platz 1. **Map** 1 B5 & 5 A2. **Tel** 52550. ⓤ *Rathaus.* ⬜ for ⬜ 1pm Mon, Wed & Fri & through phone bookings for groups. ⬜

The new town hall is the seat of the Vienna City and Provincial Assembly. Built from 1872 to 1883 to replace the Altes Rathaus *(see p85)*, it is unashamedly Neo-Gothic in style. The architect, Friedrich von Schmidt, was chosen by the authorities in a competition for the best design.

A huge central tower, 100 m (325 ft) high and topped by the 3-m (11-ft) statue of a knight in armour with a lance, dominates the front façade. Known affectionately as the Rathausmann, it was designed by Franz Gastell and made by the wrought-iron craftsman Alexander Nehr. The most attractive feature of the façade is the lofty loggia with its delicate tracery and curved balconies. The building has seven court-yards and summer concerts are held in the Arkadenhof court-yard. At the top of the first of the two grand staircases is the *Festsaal*, a ceremonial hall that stretches the length of the building. Round all four sides are Neo-Gothic arcades and statues of Austrian worthies, including prominent Habsburgs. In front of the building is the wide Rathausplatz Park.

Dreifaltigkeits-kirche ⑬

Alser Strasse 17. **Map** 1 B4. **Tel** 4057225. ⓤ *Rathaus.* ⬜ 8–11:30am Mon–Sat, 8am–noon Sun. ⬜ ♿ entrance on Schlösselgasse for services.

Built between 1685 and 1727, the church of the Holy Trinity contains an altarpiece (1708) in the north aisle by the

16th-century crucifix by Veit Stoss, in the Dreifaltigkeitskirche

painter Martino Altomonte, and a graphic crucifix in the south aisle from the workshop of Veit Stoss. It was to this church that Beethoven's body was brought after he died in 1827. Following the funeral service which was attended by many of his contemporaries, including Schubert and the poet Franz Grillparzer, the cortege bore his coffin to the cemetery at Währing on the city outskirts.

University ⑭

Dr-Karl-Lueger-Ring 1. **Map** 1 C4 & 5 A2. **Tel** 42770. ⓤ *Schottentor.* ⬜ 6:30am–8:30pm Mon–Fri, 8am–1pm Sat. ⬜ ♿

Founded in 1365 by Duke Rudolf IV, the University of Vienna now has approximately 50,000 students. The versatile architect Heinrich Ferstel designed its present home in 1883, adopting an Italian Renaissance style.

From the entrance hall, huge staircases lead up to the university's ceremonial halls. In 1895 Gustav Klimt was commissioned to decorate the hall with frescoes, but the degree of nudity portrayed in some panels proved unacceptable to the authorities. Eventually, when no agreement could be reached, Klimt returned his fee to the government and took back the paintings; they were destroyed during World War II.

Front elevation of the Neues Rathaus showing the Rathausmann on his tower some 98 m (320 ft) above the ground

A spacious arcaded court-yard, lined with busts of the university's most distinguished professors, is located in the centre of the building. Among the figures on display include the founder of psycho-analysis, Sigmund Freud *(see p110)*, and the philosopher Franz Brentano. Nearby are the smoke-filled and poster-daubed corridors of today's university students.

Café Landtmann ⓯

Dr-Karl-Lueger-Ring 4. **Map** 1 C5 & 5 B2. **Tel** 24100. Ⓤ *Schottentor, Volkstheater.* 🚃 1, D. 🕐 8am–midnight daily. 📷 🔽

If the Café Central *(see p58)* was, and perhaps still is, the coffee house of Vienna's intelligentsia, this café *(see p58)* is undoubtedly the coffee house of the affluent middle classes. With mirrors and elegant panelling, it is an exceedingly comfortable place. Established in 1873 by coffee-maker Franz Landtmann, it is still a popular café. It was Sigmund Freud's *(see p110)* favourite coffee house.

The attractive Dreimäderlhaus (left) on Schreyvogelgasse

Dreimäderlhaus ⓰

Schreyvogelgasse 10. **Map** 1 C5 & 5 B2. Ⓤ *Schottentor.* 📷

A delightful remnant of Biedermeier Vienna is found in the houses on one side of the cobbled Schreyvogelgasse. The prettiest is the Dreimäderlhaus (1803). There is a legend that Schubert had three sweethearts *(drei Mäderl)* ensconced here, but it is more likely that the house was named after the 1920s' operetta, *Dreimäderl-haus*, which uses his melodies.

One of the arcades surrounding the University courtyard

Mölker-Bastei ⓱

Map 1 C5 & 5 B2. Ⓤ *Schottentor.*

A few paces away from the bustling Schottentor, a quiet street has been built on to a former bastion of the city walls. It boasts some beautiful late 18th-century houses. Beethoven lived here, and the Emperor Franz Joseph nearly met his death on the bastion in 1853 when a tailor attempted to assassinate him. No. 10 is the house where the Belgian Prince Charles de Ligne lived during the Congress of Vienna in 1815 *(see p30)* . De Ligne, an elderly aristocrat, wrote a number of cynical commentaries on the various activities of the crowned heads of Europe who came to Vienna at that time. A ladies' man, he caught a fatal chill while waiting for an assignation on the bastion.

Plaque on the front of the Pasqualati Haus

Pasqualati Haus ⓲

Mölker-Bastei 8. **Map** 1 C5 & 5 B2. **Tel** 5358905. Ⓤ *Schottentor.* **Museum** 🕐 9am–12:15pm & 1–4:30pm Tue–Sun. 📷

The Pasqualati Haus is no different in appearance from any of the other houses along this lane, but it is the most famous of more than 30 places where Ludwig van Beethoven resided in Vienna. Named after its original owner, Baron Johann von Pasqualati, it was Beethoven's home between 1804 and 1808, and 1810 and 1815. He composed many of his best-loved works here, including the Symphonies 4, 5, 7 and 8, the opera *Fidelio*, the Piano Concerto No. 4, and string quartets. Today, the rooms on the fourth floor which the composer occupied house a small museum. Various memorabilia, such as a lock of Beethoven's hair, a photograph of his grave at Währing cemetery, a deathbed engraving and early editions of his scores are on display. The museum also contains busts and paintings of Beethoven and his patron Prince Rasumofsky, the Russian ambassador to Vienna.

Liebenberg monument (1890) below the Mölker-Bastei

The Burgtheater ⑲

The Burgtheater is the most prestigious stage in the German-
speaking world *(see also p230)*. The original theatre built in
Maria Theresa's reign was replaced in 1888 by today's Italian
Renaissance-style building by Karl von Hasenauer and Gottfried
Semper. It closed for refurbishment in 1897 after
the discovery that the auditorium had several
seats with no view of the stage. Forty-eight
years later a bomb devastated the building,
leaving only the side wings containing the Grand
Staircases intact. Subsequent restoration was so
successful that today its extent is hard to assess.

**Two statues of the
muses** of music and
dramatic art adorn
the roof.

Busts of playwrights
*Lining the walls of the Grand
Staircases are busts of playwrights whose works are
still performed here, including this one of Johann
Nestroy by Hans Knesl.*

JOHANN
NESTROY
1801 – 1892

Ceiling frescoes by
the Klimt brothers
and Franz Matsch
cover the
north and
south wings.

Entrance for tours

Candelabra
lining the
staircase

**★ Grand Staircases in
North and South Wings**
*Two imposing gala stair-
cases lead up from the side
entrances to the foyer. Each is
a mirror image of the other.*

Main
entrance
on Dr Karl-
Lueger-Ring

STAR FEATURES

- ★ Grand Staircases in
  North and South Wings

- ★ Der Thespiskarren by
  Gustav Klimt

Foyer
*The 60-m long
(200-ft) curving
foyer serves as a
waiting area
during intervals.
Portraits of famous
actors and actresses
line its walls.*

Auditorium
The central part of the Burgtheater was rebuilt in 1952–5 after war damage, but the auditorium is still decorated in the imperial colours of cream, red and gold.

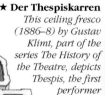

★ **Der Thespiskarren**
This ceiling fresco (1886–8) by Gustav Klimt, part of the series The History of the Theatre, depicts Thespis, the first performer of a Greek tragedy.

Sculpted cherubs on the balustrade (1880– 83)

Front Façade
A statue of Apollo (about 1883) seated between Melpomene and Thalia presides over a frieze of Bacchus and Ariadne by Rudolf Weyr.

TIMELINE

1741 Maria Theresa founds the Burgtheater in an empty ballroom at the Hofburg

1776 Joseph II reorganizes the theatre and promotes it to the status of a national theatre

The Old Burgtheater in the mid-18th century

1874 Work on the present building begins

1850

1888 The Burgtheater opens on 14 October in the presence of the Emperor Franz Joseph and his family

1897 The auditorium is adapted

1900

1945 World War II fire destroys the auditorium

1955 Theatre reopens with Grillparzer's King Ottokar

1950

1750

OPERA AND NASCHMARKT

his is an area of huge contrasts, ranging from the stateliness of the Opera House and the opulence of the Opernring shops to the raucous modernity of Mariahilfer Strasse. This long street is lined with cinemas and department stores, drawing shoppers not just from Vienna but from much of eastern Europe. The other major thoroughfare in our area is the Linke Wienzeile, which runs parallel to the Rechte Wienzeile. Both roads stretch from

Relief on the façade of the Secession Building

just beyond the Ringstrasse to the city outskirts, following the curving and sometimes subterranean River Wien. Between these roads is the bustling Naschmarkt, which is overlooked by Otto Wagner's Jugendstil apartments on the Linke Wienzeile. Visitors wanting to escape the crowds should visit the celebrated Café Museum, located near the three great cultural institutions of the area – the Academy of Fine Arts, the Opera House and the Secession Building.

SIGHTS AT A GLANCE

Streets and Squares
Mariahilfer Strasse ⑧

Historic Buildings
Hotel Sacher ②
Opera House pp140–1 ①
Theater an der Wien ⑤
Wagner Apartments ⑦

Museums and Galleries
Academy of Fine Arts ③
Haydn Museum ⑩
Kaiserliches Hofmobilien-
   depot ⑨
Secession Building ④

Markets
Naschmarkt ⑥

GETTING THERE
This area is served by
Zieglergasse (line U3),
Neubaugasse (line U3) and
MuseumsQuartier (line U2)
U-Bahn stations. Bus 13A
runs from Josefstädter Strasse
to Mariahilfer Strasse and
to the southern end of the
Linke Wienzeile. Bus 57A
travels the length of
Gumpendorfer Strasse.

KEY

Street-by-Street map
See pp136–7

Ⓤ U-Bahn station

0 metres 250
0 yards 250

◁ **Main staircase and hallway at the Opera House**

Street-by-Street: Opernring

Between the Opera House and the Karl-skirche, two of the great landmarks of Vienna, lies an area that typifies the varied cultural vitality of the city as a whole. Here are an 18th-century theatre, a 19th-century art academy, and the Secession Building. Mixed in with these cultural monuments are emblems of the Viennese devotion to good living: the Hotel Sacher, as sumptuous today as it was a century ago; the Café Museum (see p58), still as popular as it was in the 1900s; and the hurly-burly of the colourful Naschmarkt, where you can buy everything from oysters and exotic fruits to second-hand clothes.

★ **Academy of Fine Arts**
This Italianate building is home to one of the best collections of old masters in Vienna ❸

The Goethe Statue was designed by Edmund Hellmer in 1890.

The Schiller Statue dominates the park in front of the Academy of Fine Arts.

★ **Secession Building**
This delightful structure, built in 1898 as a showroom for the Secession artists, houses Gustav Klimt's (see p56) Beethoven Frieze ❹

Theater an der Wien
Today this 18th-century theatre is used as an opera house. It has been the venue for many premieres, among them Beethoven's Fidelio ❺

SCHILLERPLATZ

MAKARTGASSE

GETREIDEMARKT

MILLÖCKERGASSE

LINKE WIENZEILE

Naschmarkt
This market sells everything from fresh farm produce to bric-a-brac. It is liveliest on Saturday mornings ❻

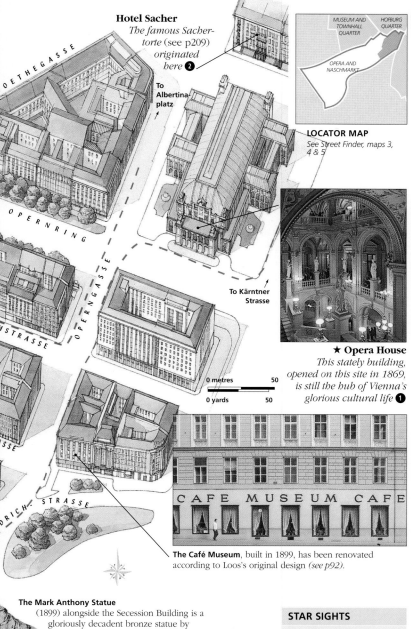

Hotel Sacher
The famous Sacher-torte (see p209) originated here ❷

To Albertina-platz

LOCATOR MAP
See Street Finder, maps 3, 4 & 5

MUSEUM AND TOWNHALL QUARTER

HOFBURG QUARTER

OPERA AND NASCHMARKT

To Kärntner Strasse

★ **Opera House**
This stately building, opened on this site in 1869, is still the hub of Vienna's glorious cultural life ❶

0 metres 50
0 yards 50

The Café Museum, built in 1899, has been renovated according to Loos's original design *(see p92)*.

The Mark Anthony Statue
(1899) alongside the Secession Building is a gloriously decadent bronze statue by Arthur Strasser.

STAR SIGHTS

★ Secession Building

★ Academy of Fine Arts

★ Opera House

KEY

– – – Suggested route

Opera House ❶

See pp140–141.

Hotel Sacher ❷

Philharmonikerstrasse 4. **Map** 4 D1 & 5 C5. **Tel** 514560. Ⓤ *Karlsplatz.* ◯ *6:30am–midnight daily.* 📷 ♿ **www**.sacher.com

Founded by the son of Franz Sacher, who, according to some, was the creator of the *Sachertorte* in 1840 *(see p209)*, this hotel *(see p200)* came into its own under Anna Sacher. The cigar-smoking daughter-in-law of the founder ran the hotel from 1892 until her death in 1930. During her time the Sacher became a venue for the extra-marital affairs of the rich and noble. It is still a discreetly sumptuous hotel.

Academy of Fine Arts ❸

Schillerplatz 3. **Map** 4 D2 & 5 B5. **Tel** 58816225. Ⓤ *Karlsplatz.* ◯ *10am–6pm Tue–Sun & public hols.* ● *1 Jan, 1 May, Corpus Christi and following Fri, 1 & 2 Nov, 24, 25 & 31 Dec.* 🎦 📷 ♿ **www**.akademiegalerie.at

Theophil Hansen built the Academy of Fine Arts in Italian Renaissance style from 1872 to 1876. In 1907 Adolf Hitler was barred from entrance

Columned entrance to the Theater an der Wien

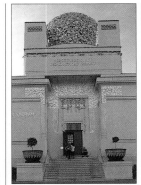
Façade of the Secession Building

on the grounds that he lacked talent. Today the Academy acts as an arts college and has a gallery showing changing exhibitions. These include late Gothic and early Renaissance works, some Rubens' pieces, 17th-century Dutch and Flemish landscapes, as well as a 19th-century Austrian collection.

Secession Building ❹

Friedrichstrasse 12. **Map** 4 D2. **Tel** 5875307. Ⓤ *Karlsplatz.* ◯ *10am–6pm Tue, Wed, Fri–Sun, 10am–8pm Thu.* 🎦 📷 ♿ **www**.secession.at

Joseph Maria Olbrich designed the unusual Secession Building in Jugendstil style *(see pp54–7)* as a showcase for the Secession movement's artists *(see p34)*. The almost windowless building, with its filigree globe of entwined laurel leaves on the roof, is a squat cube with four towers. The motto of the founders, emblazoned in gold on the façade, states, *"Der Zeit ihre Kunst, der Kunst ihre Freiheit"*, which translates as: "To every Age its Art, to Art its Freedom". Alongside the building stands the marvellous statue of Mark Anthony in his chariot being

drawn by lions (1899), by Arthur Strasser. Gustav Klimt's *Beethoven Frieze* is the Secession's best-known exhibit. Designed in 1902 as a decorative painting, it covers three walls and is 34 m (110 ft) long. It shows interrelated groups of figures and is thought to be a commentary on Beethoven's Ninth Symphony *(see also p35)*.

Theater an der Wien ❺

Linke Wienzeile 6. **Map** 3 C2. **Tel** 58885. Ⓤ *Kettenbrückengasse.* ◯ *for performances.* **www**.theater-wien.at

Emanuel Schikaneder founded this theatre *(see p226)* in 1801; a statue above the entrance shows him playing Papageno in Mozart's *The Magic Flute.* The premiere of Beethoven's *Fidelio* was staged here in 1805, and it is currently used for opera performances.

Typical stall at the Naschmarkt

Naschmarkt ❻

Map 3 C2–C3. Ⓤ *Kettenbrückengasse.* **Market** ◯ *6am–6:30pm Mon–Fri, 6am–6pm Sat.* **Schubert Museum** ◯ *2–6pm Fri–Sun & hols.*

The Naschmarkt is Vienna's liveliest market. It has many well-established shops and some of the best snack bars in Vienna *(see pp217–19).* As you walk west it gradually becomes less formal, with flower vendors', wine producers' and farmers' stalls spilling out onto the street and offering meats, breads and so on. This area in turn leads into the flea market – a chaos of makeshift stalls.

It's also worth going to No. 6 Kettenbrückengasse, by the U-Bahn, to see the simple flat where Franz Schubert died in 1828. It displays facsimiles, prints and a family piano.

The Majolikahaus, one of the Wagner Apartments

Wagner Apartments **7**

Linke Wienzeile 38 & 40. **Map** 3 C2.
Ⓤ *Kettenbrückengasse.*

Looking onto the Nasch-
markt are two remarkable
apartment buildings. Designed
by Otto Wagner in 1899, they
represent the apex of Jugendstil style *(see pp54–7)*. No. 38
has sparkling gilt ornament,
mostly by Kolo Moser. The
façade of No. 40 has subtle
flower patterns in pink, blue
and green. Even the sills are
moulded and decorated.
No. 40, which is called the
Majolikahaus after the glazed
pottery used for the weather-
resistant surface decoration, is
the more striking. No. 42 next
door, in historicist style *(see
pp32–3)*, shows what
Secession architects were
reacting against.

Mariahilfer Strasse **8**

Map 3 A3 & 5 A5. Ⓤ *Zieglergasse,
Neubaugasse.* **Stiftkirche** ☐
*7:30am–6pm Mon–Fri, 7am–11pm
Sat, 8:30am– 9:30pm Sun.*
Mariahilfer Kirche ☐ *8am–7pm
Mon–Sat, 8:30am–7pm Sun.*

This is one of Vienna's
busiest shopping streets.
On the corner of Stiftgasse is
the Stiftkirche. The architect is

unknown, but the church
dates from 1739. The façade is
an austere pyramidal structure,
rising to a bulbous steeple. Of
particular interest, there are
some lively Rococo reliefs set
into the walls.
  Across the street at No. 45 is
the house where the playwright
Ferdinand Raimund was born
in 1790. Its cobbled courtyard
is lined with shops.
  Mariahilfer Kirche is named
after a 16th-century cult of the
Virgin Mary which was
founded at the pilgrimage of
Mariahilfer Kirche at Passau.
The Viennese church is in
the Baroque style and is
dominated by two towers with
bulbous steeples.

Kaiserliches Hof-mobiliendepot **9**

Andreasgasse 7. **Map** 3 A2.
Tel 52433570. Ⓤ *Zieglergasse.*
☐ *10am–6pm Tue–Sun.* 🖼
www.hofmobiliendepot.at

The Imperial furniture
collection, founded
by Maria Theresa in
1747, gives an intimate
portrait of the Habsburg
way of life, as well as a
detailed historical record of
Viennese interior decoration
and cabinet-making in the 18th
and 19th centuries. Also
included in the collection are

pieces created by artists and
designers of the early 20th
century. Room after room
is filled with outstanding
furnishings and royal domestic
objects, ranging from a faithful
re-creation of Empress
Elisabeth's Schönbrunn Palace
apartments to a simple folding
throne that was used while
travelling. The exhibits, which
range from the mundane to
the priceless and often
eccentric, provide a fascinating
and evocative insight into
the everyday lives of the
imperial family.

Haydn Museum **10**

Haydngasse 19. **Map** 3 A3.
Tel 5961307. Ⓤ *Zieglergasse.* ☐
9am–6pm Tue–Sun & hols. ●
1 Jan, 1 May, 25 Dec. 🖼 📷

As with many of the museums
dedicated to composers,
the Haydn Museum does not
have a very comprehensive
collection of exhibits: only a
few copies of documents and
scores, a piano and clavichord.
  Haydn built this house in
what was then a new suburb
of Vienna with money he had
earned from his successful
visits to London which had
taken place between 1791 and
1795. He lived in the house
from 1797 until his death in
1809 and it was here that he
composed many of his major
works, including *The Creation*
and *The Seasons*. There is also
a room that contains some
furniture and
mementos
belonging to
Johannes
Brahms.

**Antique wheelchair in the
Kaiserliches Hofmobiliendepot.**

The Opera House ①

Vienna's state Opera House, or Staatsoper, was the first of the grand Ringstrasse buildings to be completed *(see pp32–3)*; it opened on 25 May 1869 to the strains of Mozart's *Don Giovanni*. Built in Neo-Renaissance style, it initially failed to impress the Vien-nese. Yet when it was hit by a bomb in 1945 and largely destroyed, the event was seen as a symbolic blow to the city. With a brand new auditorium and stage incorporating the latest technology, the Opera House reopened on 5 November 1955 with a performance of Beethoven's *Fidelio*.

Gustav Mahler by Rodin

Reliefs of Opera and Ballet *(1861–9)*
Painted allegorical lunettes by Johann Preleuthner represent ballet, tragic opera and comic opera. The one here depicts comic opera.

The Auditorium

★ Grand Staircase
A superb marble staircase sweeps up from the main entrance to the first floor. It is embellished with statues by Josef Gasser of the seven liberal arts (such as Music and Dancing) and reliefs of opera and ballet.

★ Schwind Foyer
The foyer is decorated with scenes from operas painted by Moritz von Schwind. Among the busts of famous composers and conductors is Rodin's bronze bust of Mahler (1909).

Main entrance

One of the five bronze statues
by Ernst Julius Hähnel, depicting Heroism, Drama, Fantasy, Humour and Love, standing under the arches of the loggia.

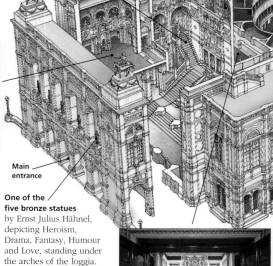

★ Tea Room
Franz Joseph and his entourage used to spend the intervals in this graceful room, which is decorated with silk hangings bearing the Emperor's initials.

STAR FEATURES

★ Grand Staircase

★ Schwind Foyer

★ Tea Room

THE VIENNA OPERA BALL

On the last Thursday of the Vienna Carnival *(see p65)* the stage is extended to cover the seats in the auditorium to create space for the Opera Ball *(see p231)*. This is an expensive society event which opens when the cream of the *jeunesse dorée* – well-to-do girls clad in white and their escorts – take to the floor.

VISITORS' CHECKLIST

Opernring 2, A-1010. **Map** 4 D1 & 5 C5. **Tel** 514447810. Ⓤ Karl-splatz. 🚊 1, 2, D. ☐ for performances. ☐ call 514442606/ 2421 for details. 🏷 📷 ♿ 🖥 🎵 **www**.wiener-staatsoper.at

The Architects
The architects of the Opera House were August Siccardsburg (right) and Eduard van der Nüll (left).

Fountain
On either side of the Opera House stand two graceful fountains. Designed by Hans Gasser, this one depicts the legendary siren Lorelei supported by figures representing Grief, Love and Vengeance.

The Magic Flute Tapestries
One of the two side salons, the Gustav Mahler Saal, is hung with modern tapestries by Rudolf Eisenmenger illustrating scenes from The Magic Flute.

BELVEDERE QUARTER

The Belvedere Quarter is a grandiose and extravagant district. From the Karlsplatz, with its gardens and statues, there is a lovely view of Johann Bernhard Fischer von Erlach's Baroque Karlskirche. East of this great church, visitors can see more delights, including the two palaces of the Belvedere, now public galleries, and the Schwarzenberg Palace. These huge palaces and beautiful gardens were designed by Johann Lukas

Statue of Leonardo da Vinci in the Künstlerhaus

von Hildebrandt, following the crucial defeat of the Turks in 1683. Only after the Turkish threat had been removed was it possible for Vienna to expand. The turbulent history of the city is excellently documented in the Wien Museum Karlsplatz. Just a few paces away is the Musikverein, home to the Vienna Philharmonic. There is also the Bestattungsmuseum (undertakers' museum), that chronicles the importance the Viennese attach to pomp and death.

SIGHTS AT A GLANCE

Streets and Squares
Rennweg **9**
Schwarzenbergplatz **7**

Historic Buildings
Imperial Hotel **6**
Karlsplatz Pavilions **4**
Musikverein **3**
Schwarzenberg Palace **8**
Theresianum **13**

Museums and Galleries
Bestattungsmuseum **12**
Wien Museum
  Karlsplatz **2**
Künstlerhaus **5**
*Palaces and Gardens
  of the Belvedere
  pp152–57* **10**

Parks and Gardens
Botanical Gardens **11**

Churches
Karlskirche pp148–49 **1**

GETTING THERE
This area is served by the Karlsplatz (lines U1, U2, U4) and Taubstummengasse (line U1) U-Bahn stations. Tram 71 runs along Rennweg and Bus 4A goes from Wittelsbachstrasse to Karlsplatz.

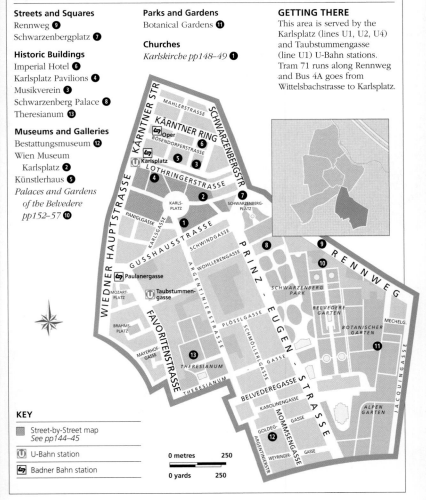

KEY

▢ Street-by-Street map
  See pp144–45

Ⓤ U-Bahn station

🚆 Badner Bahn station

0 metres   250
0 yards   250

◁ **Botanical Gardens**

Street-by-Street: Karlsplatz

This part of the city became ripe for development once the threat of Turkish invasion had receded for good in 1683 (*see pp26–7*). The Ressel Park, at the front of the Karlskirche, gives an unobstructed view of this grandiose church, built on the orders of Karl VI. The park itself is lined with a variety of cultural institutions, notably the Wien Museum Karlsplatz and, across the road, the Musikverein.

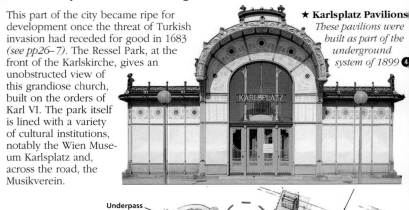

★ **Karlsplatz Pavilions**
These pavilions were built as part of the underground system of 1899 ④

KARLSPLATZ

Underpass

To Karlsplatz U-Bahn

Ressel Park café

KARL

The Technical University with its Neo-Classical façade (1816) fronts on to Ressel Park, which contains busts and statues of famous 19th-century Austrian scientists and engineers.

Ressel Statue

STAR SIGHTS

★ Karlsplatz Pavilions

★ Wien Museum Karlsplatz

★ Karlskirche

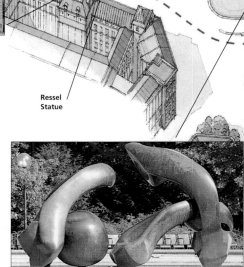

Henry Moore's Hill Arches were presented to the City of Vienna by the artist himself in 1978.

Musikverein
This Ringstrasse-style (see p146) concert hall, home of the Vienna Phil-harmonic Orchestra, is renowned for its superb acoustics ❸

LOCATOR MAP
See Street Finder, map 4

★ **Wien Museum Karlsplatz**
This museum houses relics of Roman Vienna, stained glass from the Stephansdom and the reconstructed rooms of celebrated Viennese such as Adolf Loos (see p92) ❷

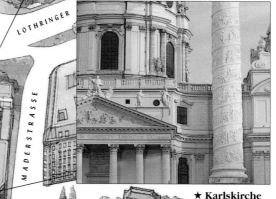

★ **Karlskirche**
Promised to the people during the 1713 plague, this is Vienna's finest Baroque church ❶

French Embassy

THE ART NOUVEAU FRENCH EMBASSY

Built in 1904–12 by the French architect Georges Chédanne, the Embassy is typical of French Art Nouveau, resembling houses along Rue Victor Hugo in Paris. Unaccustomed to this foreign style, some thought the building was oriental, giving rise to a rumour that its plans had been mixed up with those of the French Embassy in Istanbul.

Art Nouveau façade of the French Embassy

0 metres   50

0 yards   50

Y

− − Suggested route

Karlskirche ❶

See pp148–9.

Wien Museum Karlsplatz ❷

Karlsplatz. **Map** 4 E2. **Tel** 5058747.
Ⓤ *Karlsplatz.* ◯ *9am–6pm
Tue–Sun.* 📷 ♿ 🖼 **www.**
wienmuseum.at

The Wien Museum Karlsplatz
moved to its current location
in 1959. The ground floor
usually has Roman and
pre-Roman items, as well as
exhibits from the Gothic
period. These include 14th-
and 15th-century gargoyles
and figures, and stained glass
from the Stephansdom, and
carved portraits of early rulers
of Vienna. These displays are
sometimes moved to make
space for visiting exhibitions.

The first-floor 16th- and
17th-century exhibits include
prints depicting Turkish sieges
from 1529 onwards, as well as
a portrait of the Turkish commander Kara Mustafa, captured
banners and weapons, and
prints of the celebrations after
Austria's victory. Here too are
Johann Bernhard Fischer
von Erlach's original plans
for the Schönbrunn Palace
(see pp172–5), and the
original lantern from No. 6
Schönlaterngasse *(see p74)*.

The monumental, historicist-style façade of the Musikverein

On the second floor are a
reconstructed 1798 room from
the Caprara-Geymüller Palace
in Wallnerstrasse, panelled
with painted silks, and the
apartment of Austria's most
famous poet, Franz Grillparzer.
There are displays chronicling
the popularity of ballet,
theatre and operetta.

Exhibits from the 20th
century include Richard
Gerstl's portrait of Arnold
Schönberg *(see p39)* and
portraits by Egon Schiele and
Gustav Klimt. There is a room
(1903) from Adolf Loos's
house *(see p92)* in Bösendorferstrasse, silver- and
glassware by Josef Hoffmann,
designs from the Wiener
Werkstätte *(see p56)* and
pictures of Vienna over the
past hundred years.

Musikverein ❸

Bösendorferstrasse 12. **Map** 4 E2.
Tel 5058190. Ⓤ *Karlsplatz.* ◯ *for
concerts only.* 🚫 ♿ **www.**
musikverein.at

The Musikverein building –
the headquarters of the
Society of the Friends of
Music – was designed from
1867 to 1869 by Theophil
Hansen, in a mixture of styles
employing terracotta statues,
capitals and balustrades. It is
the home of the great Vienna
Philharmonic Orchestra *(see
p229)*, which gives regular
performances here, and forms
the orchestra of the Opera
House. The concert hall seats
almost 2,000. Tickets are sold
on a subscription basis to
Viennese music lovers, but
some are also available on
the day of the performance.
The most famous annual
event here is the New Year's
Day concert *(see p65)*.

Karlsplatz Pavilions ❹

Karlsplatz. **Map** 4 D2. **Tel** 5058747-
85177. Ⓤ *Karlsplatz.* ◯ *Apr–Oct:
9am–6pm Tue–Sun.* 📷

Otto Wagner *(see pp54–57)*
was responsible for designing
and engineering many
aspects of the early
underground system in the
late 19th century. Some of
these bridges and tunnels are
remarkable in themselves, but
cannot match his stylish pair
of underground railway exit
pavilions (1898–9) alongside

Sunflower motifs on the façade of the Karlsplatz Pavilions

The enormous Hochstrahlbrunnen in Schwarzenbergplatz

Imperial Hotel ❻

Kärntner Ring 16. **Map** 4 E2 & 6 D5.
Tel 50110. Ⓤ *Karlsplatz.* 🅾 &
www.luxurycollection.com

Along with the Hotel Sacher
(*see p138*), this is the best
known of the 19th-century
hotels. You can sip tea to the
sound of a pianist playing in
the background or stay in the
same room Richard Wagner
occupied. Adolf Hitler made
the hotel his headquarters
after the Anschluss (*see p36*).

Schwarzenberg-platz ❼

Map 4 E2. Ⓤ *Karlsplatz.* **Arnold
Schönberg Center** *Tel* 7121888.

At the centre of this grand
square is the equestrian statue
(1867) of Prince Schwarzenberg, who led the Austrian
and allied armies against Napoleon at the Battle of Leipzig
(1813). The square combines
huge office blocks, the Ringstrasse and the Baroque
splendours of the Schwarzenberg and Belvedere palaces.
Behind the fountain of Hochstrahlbrunnen (1873), at the
intersection of Prinz-Eugen-
Strasse and Gusshausstrasse, is
the monument commemorating
the Red Army's liberation of
the city. It is none too popular
with older Viennese, who still
recall the brutalities endured
in the Russian zone until 1955.

The Arnold Schönberg
Center, at the eastern end of
the square, houses recordings,
scores and memorabilia from
the famous Viennese composer.

the Karlsplatz, which are
among his best-known
buildings. The green copper
colour of the roofs and the
ornamentation complement
the Karlskirche beyond. Gilt
patterns are stamped onto the
white marble cladding and
eaves, with repetitions of
Wagner's beloved sunflower
motif. But the greatest impact
is made by the buildings'
elegantly curving rooflines.
The two pavilions face each
other: one is now a café, the
other is used for exhibitions.

Künstlerhaus ❺

Karlsplatz 5. **Map** 4 D2 & 6 D5.
Tel 5879663. Ⓤ *Karlsplatz.*
⬜ *10am–6pm Fri–Wed; 10am–9pm
Thu.* 🚫 & **www**.k-haus.at

Commissioned by the Vienna
Artists' Society as an exhi-
bition hall for its members, the
Künstlerhaus was built in 1868.
The society favoured grand,

academic styles of painting in
tune with the historicist Ringstrasse architecture. The
Künstlerhaus itself is typical of
this style, which is named
after the Vienna boulevard
where the look is most preva-
lent (*see pp32–3*). Designed
by August Weber (1836–1903)
in a Renaissance palazzo style,
the Künstlerhaus is now used
for temporary art exhibitions.

Palazzo-style façade of the Künstlerhaus (1868)

Karlskirche ●

During Vienna's plague epidemic in 1713, Emperor Karl VI vowed that as soon as the city was delivered from its plight he would build a church dedicated to St Charles Borromeo (1538–84), a former Archbishop of Milan and a patron saint of the plague. The following year he announced a competition to design the church, which was won by the architect Johann Bernhard Fischer von Erlach. The result was a richly eclectic Baroque masterpiece: the gigantic dome and portico are borrowed from the architecture of ancient Greece and Rome, while there are Oriental echoes in the gatehouses and minaret-like columns. Building took almost 25 years, and the interior was richly embellished with carvings and altarpieces by the foremost artists of the day, including Daniel Gran and Martino Altomonte.

Angel representing the New Testament

The Pulpit
Two putti surmount the canopy of the richly-gilded pulpit, decorated with rocailles and flower garlands.

Stairway (closed to public)

★ High Altar
The high altar features a stucco relief by Albert Camesina showing St Charles Borromeo being assumed into heaven on a cloud laden with angels and putti.

The two gatehouses leading into the side entrances of the church are reminiscent of Chinese pavilions.

STAR FEATURES

★ High Altar

★ Frescoes in the Cupola

★ The Two Columns

Pediment reliefs by Giovanni Stanetti show the suffering of the Viennese during the 1713 plague.

Angel representing the Old Testament

Main entrance

Cupola
Cross

★ **Frescoes in the Cupola**
*Johann Michael Rottmayr's
fresco, painted between 1725
and 1730, depicts the
Apotheosis of St Charles
Borromeo. It was the
painter's last
commission.*

**JOHANN BERNHARD
FISCHER VON ERLACH**

Many of Vienna's finest buildings, including the Trautson
and Schönbrunn Palaces,
were designed by Fischer
von Erlach (1656–1723).
He died before he finished
the Karlskirche and his son
completed it in 1737.

★ **The Two Columns**
*Inspired by Trajan's Column
in Rome, they are decorated
with spiralling scenes of
St Charles Borromeo's life.
Qualities of Steadfastness
are illustrated on the left,
and Courage on the right.*

**Visitors
entrance and
tickets**

St Charles Borromeo
*Lorenzo Mattielli's
statue of the patron
saint crowns the
pediment.*

**Angel
representing
the New
Testament**

Schwarzenberg Palace and Joseph Fischer von Ehrlach's fountain

Schwarzenberg Palace ⑧

Schwarzenbergplatz 9. **Map** 4 E2.

The Palais Schwarzenberg was built by Johann Lukas von Hildebrandt *(see p152)* in 1697 and then altered by the Fischer von Erlachs *(see p149)* in the 1720s. The main salon has a domed hall with a magnificent chandelier. Behind the palace are the lawns and shady paths of the park, focused around a pool and fountain designed by Joseph Emanuel Fischer von Erlach. In the past the main reception rooms were used as a venue for concerts and balls, and there are plans to turn part of the building into a luxury hotel.

One wing is occupied by the Swiss embassy. The present head of the Schwarzenberg family served as an advisor to President Havel after the Velvet Revolution in Czechoslovakia in 1989 and became Czech foreign minister in 2007.

Rennweg ⑨

Map 4 E2. 🚇 *Karlsplatz.*
Gardekirche ◯ *8am–8pm daily.*

Rennweg runs from the Schwarzenbergplatz along the edges of the Belvedere palaces. At No. 3, a house built by Otto Wagner *(see p57)* in 1890 is now the (former) Yugoslav Embassy. Though the façade is in shabby condition, the house remains an interesting example of Wagner's work

just as he was making the transition from Ringstrasse pomp to his later Jugendstil style of architecture.

Next door at No. 5 is where Gustav Mahler *(see p39)* lived from 1898 to 1909. No. 5a is the Gardekirche (1755–63) by Nikolaus Pacassi (1716–99), Maria Theresa's court architect. It was originally built as the church of the Imperial Hospital and since 1897 has been Vienna's Polish church. A huge dome covers the entire interior, which adds to its spaciousness. One feature of interest is the gilt Rococo embellishment over the side chapels and between the ribs of the dome. Just beyond the Belvedere palace gates at No. 6a stands a Baroque mansion, while the forecourt at No. 8 has formed part of the Hoch-

schule für Musik since 1988. At No. 10, behind splendid wrought-iron gates, stands the Salesianerinnenkirche of 1717–30. The Baroque façade is flanked by monastic buildings in the same style. The upper storey has scrolled projections that serve as the base for statues. Like the Gardekirche, this church is domed, its design partly attributed to Joseph Emanuel Fischer von Erlach *(see p149)*. Apart from the pulpit, the interior is of little interest.

At No. 27, the present-day Italian Embassy is the palace where Prince Metternich *(see p30)* lived until he was forced to flee the city in 1848.

Palaces and Gardens of the Belvedere ⑩

See pp152–57.

Botanical Gardens ⑪

Rennweg 14. **Map** 4 F3. *Tel 4277 54190.* 🚊 *71.* ◯ *Easter–mid-Oct: 9am–dusk daily; also open in winter (weather permitting.)* 📷 ♿

The main entrance to the Botanical Gardens is on the corner of Prätoriusgasse and Mechelgasse. Other entrances

Detail of the façade of the Salesianerinnenkirche in Rennweg

are on Jacquingasse, and via a small gate at the rear of the Upper Belvedere which leads to the Alpine Garden and the Botanical Gardens. The latter contains more than 9,000 plant species. The Botanical Gardens were created in 1754 by Maria Theresa and her physician van Swieten for cultivating medicinal herbs. Expanded to their present shape in the 19th century, they remain a centre for the study of plant sciences as part of the University of Vienna's Institute of Botany. Of equal interest to amateurs, the gardens offer a quiet spot to sit and relax after sightseeing.

The Botanical Gardens created by Maria Theresa in 1754

Bestattungs-museum ⓬

Goldeggasse 19. **Map** 4 E4. **Tel** 501954227. Ⓤ *Südtiroler Platz.* 🚊 *D, O, 18.* 🕐 *Mon–Fri (by appt only).* 📷

In Vienna, death and pomp have always been allied with one another, and even today the Viennese like to be buried in style. For the clearest insight into this fascinating feature of Viennese life, it's worth making a visit to this undertakers' museum.

One of the more eerie items, shown immediately after you enter, is the wrought-iron grille (1784) that formed the entrance to the Catholic cemetery at Matzlein-dorf. Its motif is of a crowned skeleton. You can see the various lanterns and staffs and liveries that were part of the pall-bearers' equipment from the 17th century onwards, as well as the special livery decked around the horses that pulled the hearse. In the 19th century, Viennese specialist couturiers provided widow's mourning attire complete with black handbag and black jewellery. Also in the 19th century a bell was often attached to a rope within the coffin, allowing the recently deceased, should he or she unex-pectedly reawaken, to signal the alarm. This device became unnecessary if you requested in your

will to be stabbed in the heart before the coffin lid was nailed down, and the stiletto used for this practice is on display. Other displays show how corpses were dressed up and seated on a chair for one last photograph.

The custodian of the museum will also show you one of Joseph II's *(see p28)* more eccentric innovations from the late 18th century: the economy-model coffin with a trapdoor in the bottom which allowed the shrouded corpse to be dumped into the grave and the coffin to be reused. This story partly illustrates why the tireless reformer was not universally loved by his subjects. His attempts at reform were often perceived as doing more harm than good, or as unnecessary. The emperor was forced to abandon this unpopular idea.

Theresianum ⓭

Favoritenstrasse 15. **Map** 4 E3. Ⓤ *Taubstummengasse.* ⬤ *to public.*

The original buildings of this former imperial summer palace date from the early 17th century, but were

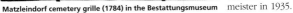

Matzleindorf cemetery grille (1784) in the Bestattungsmuseum

essentially rebuilt after the Turkish siege of 1683 in a Baroque style by the architect and theatre designer Lodovico Burnacini (1636–1707) and others. Known at that time as the Favorita, it became a favourite residence of emperors Leopold I,

Façade of the Theresianum

Joseph I and Karl VI. In 1746 Maria Theresa, who had moved into Schönbrunn *(see pp172–75)*, her summer palace, handed it over to the Jesuits. They established a college here for the education of children from less well-off aristocratic families – the sons of these families were trained to be officials.

Today, the Theresianum is still a school and, since 1964, has also been a college for diplomats and civil servants. In the Theresianum park on Argentinierstrasse stands Radio House. It has a beautiful entrance hall, which was designed by Clemens Holz-meister in 1935.

Palaces and Gardens of the Belvedere ➓

Statuary on a gate of Lower Belvedere

The Belvedere was built by Johann Lukas von Hildebrandt as the summer residence of Prince Eugene of Savoy, the brilliant military commander whose strategies helped vanquish the Turks in 1683. Situated on a gently sloping hill, the Belvedere consists of two palaces linked by a formal garden laid out in the French style by Dominique Girard. The garden is sited on three levels, each conveying a complicated programme of Classical allusions: the lower part of the garden represents the domain of the Four Elements, the centre is Parnassus and the upper section is Olympus.

★ Upper Cascade
Water flows from the upper basin over five shallow steps into the pool below.

Putti on the Steps *(1852)*
Children and cherubs representing the 12 months adorn the steps to the left and right in the middle area of the gardens.

JOHANN LUKAS VON HILDEBRANDT
Hildebrandt became the court architect in Vienna in 1700 and was one of J B Fischer von Erlach's greatest rivals. In addition to the Belvedere, he designed the Schönborn Palace *(see p110)*, the Kinsky Palace *(see p110)* and the Maria Treu Kirche *(see p116)*.

Coloured etching of the Upper Belvedere and Gardens by Karl Schütz (1784)

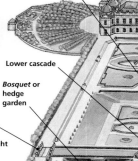

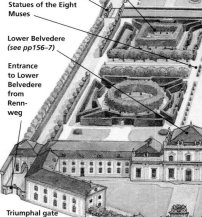

Lower cascade

Bosquet or hedge garden

Statues of the Eight Muses

Lower Belvedere *(see pp156–7)*

Entrance to Lower Belvedere from Rennweg

Triumphal gate to Lower Belvedere

TIMELINE

	1717–19 Dominique Girard landscapes the gardens	1765 Lower Belvedere becomes the barracks for the military guard	1897 Archduke Franz Ferdinand, heir to the throne, moves to the Upper Belvedere	1953 Museum of Medieval Austrian Art opens to the public	
	1720 Orangery built	1781–1891 Belvedere houses the Imperial Picture Gallery, which opens to the public			
1750		**1800**	**1850**	**1900**	**1950**
1721–3 Upper Belvedere built	1752 Habsburgs acquire the Belvedere		1923–9 The Baroque Museum, the 19th-century Gallery and the 20th-century Gallery open to the public	1955 The Austrian State Treaty signed in the Marble Hall	
1714–16 Lower Belvedere built	1779 Belvedere gardens open to the public				

Detail on Upper Cascade

★ **Main Gate of the Upper Belvedere**
The Baroque iron gate (1728) by Arnold and Konrad Küffner, with an "S" for Savoy and the cross of Savoy, leads to the south façade of the Upper Belvedere.

VISITORS' CHECKLIST

Map 4 F3. *Upper Belvedere see pp154–5.* *Lower Belvedere and Orangery see pp156–7.* **Gardens** ◯ 6:30am–dusk all year round. ◎ ♿

Entrance to Upper Belvedere *(see pp154–5)* **and gardens from Prinz-Eugen-Strasse**

★ **Upper Belvedere Façade**
The lively façade dominates the sweeping entrance to the palace (see pp154–5). The domed copper roofs of the end pavilions resemble the shape of Turkish tents – an allusion to Prince Eugene's victories over the Turks.

Statues of Sphinxes
With their lion bodies and human heads, the imposing sphinx statues represent strength and intelligence.

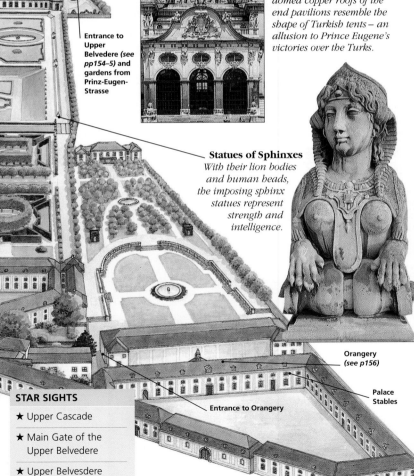

Orangery *(see p156)*

Palace Stables

Entrance to Orangery

STAR SIGHTS

★ Upper Cascade

★ Main Gate of the Upper Belvedere

★ Upper Belvesdere Façade

Upper Belvedere

Standing at the highest point of the garden, the Upper Belvedere has a more elaborate façade than the Lower Belvedere: it was intended to be a symbolic reflection of Prince Eugene's glory. In addition to the impressive interiors of the Sala Terrena with its sweeping staircase, the chapel and the Marble Hall, the building now houses an Austrian art collection with works ranging from the Middle Ages to the present day.

★ Chapel
The centrepiece of this brown, white and gold interior is an altarpiece, The Resurrection, by Francesco Solimena (1723), set among statues of angels. Prince Eugene could enter the chapel from his apartments.

Viewing balcony for chapel

Laughing Self-Portrait (1908)
This picture is by Richard Gerstl, the Viennese artist who was developing his own Expressionist style when he killed himself in his twenties.

KEY

▢	Neo-Classicism-Romanticism
▢	Biedermeier
▢	Early 20th-century art
▢	Historicism-Realism-Impressionism
▨	Masterpieces of baroque and medieval art
▢	Non-exhibition space

GALLERY GUIDE

The ground floor houses masterpieces of baroque and medieval art. Art from around 1900 and the late 19th century is on the ground floor. Early 19th-century art is on the second floor, along with a Biedermeier collection.

Main entrance from gardens

★ Sala Terrena
Four Herculean figures by Lorenzo Mattielli support the ceiling vault of the Sala Terrena, while white stuccowork by Santino Bussi covers the walls and ceiling.

★ Gustav Klimt Collection

This marvellous Jugend-stil collection by Gustav Klimt is considered by some to be the Belvedere's highlight. In the work here, Judith I *(1901), Klimt depicts the Old Testament heroine as a Viennese* femme fatale.

VISITORS' CHECKLIST

Prinz-Eugen-Strasse 27, A-1030.
Map 4 F4. **Tel** 01796570.
13A to Prinz-Eugen-Strasse.
Südbahnhof. 0, 18, D, 71.
10am–6pm daily.
www.belvedere.at

The Tiger Lion *(1926)*
This savage beast from the 20th-century collection was painted by Oskar Kokoschka, a leading figure in Austrian Expressionism.

Second floor

Marble Hall

The Plain of Auvers *(1890)*
Van Gogh's airy landscape from the 20th-century collection.

First floor

STAR SIGHTS

★ Chapel

★ Gustav Klimt Collection

★ Sala Terrena

Stairs to

Ground floor

Corpus Christi Morning *(1857)*
This bright genre scene is typical of the Austrian Biedermeier painter Ferdinand Georg Waldmüller.

Lower Belvedere and Orangery

The architect Johann Lucas von Hildebrandt (1668–1745) was commissioned by Prince Eugene of Savoy to build the Lower Belvedere in 1714, and it was completed in 1716. It previously housed the Museum of Austrian Baroque Art but now displays temporary exhibitions only. Attractions include the Marble Hall, the state bedroom of Prince Eugene of Savoy, the Hall of Grotesques and the Marble Gallery. The Lower Belvedere also incorporates the Orangery and the palace stables.

Exit to Orangery and stables

Prince Eugene's former bedroom

★ **Hall of Mirrors**
A statue of Prince Eugene (1721) by Balthasar Permoser stands in this room, whose walls are covered with huge gilt-framed mirrors.

Hall of Grotesques
The hall is decorated with paintings of grotesques inspired by ancient Roman frescoes of fantastical creatures. They were created by the German painter Jonas Drentwett.

THE ORANGERY

Next door to the Lower Belvedere is the handsome Orangery building, originally used to shelter tender garden plants in winter and now transformed into an exhibition hall retaining its original character. It previously housed the Museum of Austrian Medieval Art but now has regularly-changing temporary exhibitions. Neighbouring the "White Cube", a unique exhibition space, the southern side gallery corridor offers a spectacular view of the Privy Garden and the Upper Belvedere.

The Orangery and gardens in winter

The Palace Stables
Collected here are some 150 items of medieval art, including masterpieces of panel painting and sculpture.

St Jacob's Victory over the Saracens *(1764)*
Franz Anton Maulbertsch's painting portrays St Jacob's victory at the Battle of Clavigo.

VISITORS' CHECKLIST

Rennweg 6a, A-1037. **Map** 4
E3. *Tel* 01796570. 71, D.
10am–6pm daily (to 9pm Wed).
Palace Stables 10am–noon
daily.
www.belvedere.at

★ The Marble Hall
The only two-storey section of the palace, the Marble Hall is clad on all sides with reddish-brown and stucco marble. The magnificent soaring ceiling is dedicated to the sun god Apollo.

Christ on the Mount of Olives *(around 1750)*
Marrying Italian and Austrian painting traditions, Paul Troger's artwork shows Christ deep in prayer on the Mount of Olives after the Last Supper. This detail depicts him being comforted by an angel.

GALLERY GUIDE

The Museum of Austrian Baroque Art displays large works of sculpture in the Marble Hall and the Hall of Grotesques, while smaller exhibits are on show in other rooms.

e Marble
Hall

Library

Main
entrance

KEY

Museum of Baroque Art

Temporary Exhibitions

To gardens

STAR SIGHTS

★ Hall of Mirrors

★ Figures from the
Providentia Fountain
by G R Donner

★ The Marble Hall

★ Figures from the Providentia Fountain *(1739)*
The original lead figures that Georg Raphael Donner made for the Providentia Fountain in the Neuer Markt (see p105) are displayed in the Marble Hall. This central statue represents Providence.

FURTHER AFIELD

For a city of over two million inhabitants, Vienna is suprisingly compact. Nonetheless, some of the most interesting sights are a fair distance from the city centre. At Schönbrunn sprawls the immense palace and gardens so loved by Maria Theresa,

Detail on riding school (1882–6) next to Hermes Villa

and the monastery at Klosterneuburg houses some of Austria's great ecclesiastical art treasures. Many parks and gardens, including the Prater, the Augarten and the Lainzer Tiergarten, all former private Habsburg domaines, are now open to the public.

SIGHTS AT A GLANCE

Historic Buildings
Amalienbad ⑯
Augarten Palace and Park ⑨
Favoriten Water Tower ⑮
Hundertwasser Haus ⑪
Karl Marx Hof ⑦
Otto-Wagner-Hofpavilion Hietzing⑳
Schönbrunn Palace and Gardens pp172–75 ⑲
Wagner Villas ①
Werkbundsiedlung ㉑

Churches and Monasteries
Kirche am Steinhof ②
Klosterneuburg ⑥
Wotruba Kirche ㉓

Museums andGalleries
Geymüller Schlössl ③
Heeresgeschichtliches Museum pp166– 7 ⑬
Kriminalmuseum ⑩
Technical Museum ⑱

Parks and Gardens
Danube Park ⑧
Lainzer Tiergarten ㉒
Prater pp162–63 ⑫

Historic Districts
Grinzing ④
Kahlenberg ⑤

Monuments
Spinnerin am Kreuz ⑰

Cemeteries
Central Cemetery pp168–9 ⑭

10 kilometres = 6 miles

KEY

▨	Central Vienna
▨	Greater Vienvna
▤	Main line railway station
▨	Coach and bus station
▬	Motorway
⋯	Motorway tunnel
▬	Major road
═	Minor road

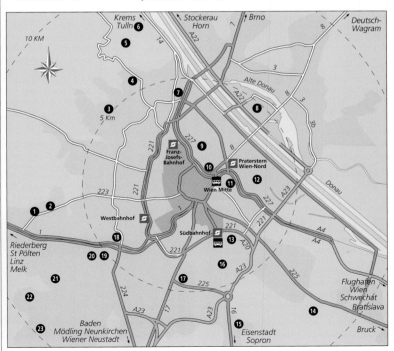

◁ **Part of the façade of the Hundertwasser Haus, built in 1985**

Detail of Ernst Fuchs' Brunnenhaus, next to Wagner Villas

Wagner Villas ❶

Hüttelbergstrasse 26, Penzing.
Tel 9148575. Ⓤ Hütteldorf. 🚌 148, 152. ⓄＯ 10am–4pm Mon–Fri. 📷 ⓞ
www.ernstfuchszentrum.com

The Villa Otto Wagner, designed by Wagner from 1886 to 1888 as his own residence, is stylistically midway between his earlier Ringstrasse architecture and the decorative elements of Jugendstil (*see pp54–7*). The house is built on a grand scale and incorporates classical elements such as Ionic columns, and seems more suited to a north Italian hillside than to Austria. The present owner, the painter Ernst Fuchs (*see p36*), has imposed his own personality on the villa, adding a fertility statue and garish colours.

The simpler villa next door was built more than 20 years later. Completed in 1913, the house is of steel and concrete rather than brick. It is very lightly decorated in a severe geometrical style with deep blue panels and nailhead ornament. The glass ornament is by Kolo Moser (*see p57*).

Kirche am Steinhof ❷

Baumgartner Höhe 1, Penzing.
Tel 9106011204. 🚌 48A. ⓄＯ 4–5pm Sat. 📷 by appointment. 📷 ⓞ

Completed in 1907, this astonishing church was Otto Wagner's (*see pp54–7*) last commission. It is set within the grounds of the Psychiatrisches Krankenhaus, a large mental hospital. The exterior is marble clad with nailhead ornament and has spindly screw-shaped pillars, topped by wreaths, supporting the porch. Four stone columns along the façade are adorned with angels by Othmar Schimkowitz (1864–1947). The statues at each corner of the façade are of St Leopold and St Severin to the left and right respectively. They were designed by Richard Luksch and are seated in chairs by Josef Hoffmann (*see pp56–7*).

The interior is a single space with shallow side chapels. The main decoration consists of gold and white friezes and square roof panels ornamented with gilt nailhead. Illumination is provided by daylight shining through lovely blue glass windows by Kolo Moser (*see p57*).

Geymüller Schlössl ❸

Khevenhüllerstrasse 2, Währing.
Tel 711360. 🚌 41A. 🚋 41.
ⓄＯ May–Nov: 11am–4pm Sun. 📷 ⓞ

The Geymüller Schlössl in Pötzleinsdorf, northwest of the city, is a temple to Biedermeier style (*see pp30–31*). Dating from 1808, the house was built for Johann Heinrich von Geymüller, a rich banker. Now a branch of the Austrian Museum of Applied Arts (*see pp82–3*), it has a collection of intricate Biedermeier and Empire furniture, such as an apparently simple desk that combines a writing desk with a water-colour cabinet. Gadgets abound: spittoons, still-lifes painted on porcelain, bowls, and 200 clocks dating from 1780 to about 1850, the heyday of Viennese clock manufacture.

Jugendstil angels by Othmar Schimkowitz adorning the façade of the Kirche am Steinhof

Grinzing ❹

Heiligenstadt. 38A. 38.

Grinzing is the most famous
Heuriger village *(see
pp186–7)*, but it is also the
least authentic, as many of
the inns here cater to very
large groups of tourists. It is
nonetheless very pretty.

It is divided into the
Oberer Ort and Unterer Ort
(upper and lower towns), the
lower town being where you
will find more authentic
Heurige along such lanes as
Sandgasse.

Grinzing was repeatedly
destroyed by Turkish troops
during the many sieges of
Vienna *(see p26–7)*, and
was again damaged by
Napoleon's forces in 1809
(see p30).

Kahlenberg ❺

38A.

Kahlenberg, at 484 m
(1,585 ft) *(see pp182–3)*,
is the highest point of the
Vienna Woods. It has a
television mast at the top, as
well as a church, an
observation terrace and a
restaurant. The views over the
vineyards below and the city
beyond are fabulous, with the
Danube bridges to the left
and the Vienna Woods to the
right. The Kahlenberg played
a crucial part in the city's
history, in 1683 when the
Polish king, Jan Sobieski, led
his troops down from this
spot to the rescue of
Viennese forces who were
fighting for the city.

Klosterneuburg ❻

*Stift Klosterneuburg. Tel 02243-
411/212. Heiligenstadt.
Franz-Josefs-Bahnhof to
Klosterneuburg-Kierling. 237,
238, 239. 9am–5pm daily.
Daily tours include the Monastery
Museum and Imperial Apartments.
www.stift-klosterneuburg.at*

Above the Danube, 13 km
(8 miles) north of Vienna,
stands the vast monastery and
fortress of Klosterneuburg.

The peach- and salmon-coloured façade of the Karl Marx Hof

Dating originally from the 12th
century, it houses the astonishing Verduner Altar, whose 51
panels were completed
in 1181 *(see p23)*. In the
18th century it was
expanded by Karl VI,
who intended to
build a complex on
the same grand scale
as the Escorial palace
near Madrid. The work
was halted after his
death in 1740.

Statue in Grinzing

Karl Marx Hof ❼

*Heiligenstädterstrasse 82–92,
Döbling. Heiligenstadt. D.
to the public.*

The Karl Marx Hof, dating
from 1927 to 1930, is
an immense council block
which contains 1,382 flats. It
is the most celebrated of the
municipal housing developments built during the period

of Red Vienna *(see p36)*,
when 63,000 new dwellings
went up across the city
between 1919 and 1934. The
architect of the Karl Marx Hof
was Karl Ehn, a pupil of Otto
Wagner *(see p54–7)*.

Danube Park ❽

*Alte Donau. 20B. 24 hrs
daily. Danube Tower Tel 26335720.
10am–midnight daily.*

Adjoining Uno-city *(see
p37)*, the complex of
United Nations agencies, is the
Danube Park. Laid out in 1964,
the park has cycle paths, cafés
and other amenities. Rising
252 m (827 ft) above the park
is the Danube Tower, with
two revolving restaurants and
an observation platform. The
park and surrounding area
have been redeveloped as
the Danube City housing
project, encompassing the
Millennium Tower.

View of the Klosterneuburg monastery with its Baroque dome

Prater ⑫

Originally an Imperial hunting ground, these woods and meadows between the Danube and its canal were opened to the public by Joseph II in 1766. The central avenue, or Hauptallee, was for a long time the preserve of the nobility and their footmen. During the 19th century the western end of the Prater became a massive funfair with booths, sideshows, beer gardens and *Wurst* stands catering for the Viennese workers.

The Miniature Railway
The Liliputbahn travels a 4-km (21/2-mile) circuit.

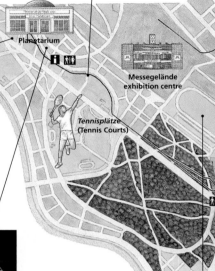

To Praterstern station

Planetarium

Messegelände exhibition centre

Tennisplätze (Tennis Courts)

★ **Ferris Wheel**
The huge wheel circulates very slowly at a speed of about 75 cm (21/2 ft) per second, allowing riders spectacular views over the park and funfair.

★ **Volksprater Funfair**
An amusement park has existed here since the last century. Today the enormous funfair is full of high-tech rides ranging from dodgem cars to ghost trains.

The Trotting Stadium
Built in 1913, the Krieau Stadium is the scene of exciting regional and international trotting races from September to June (see p231).

STAR SIGHTS

★ Hauptallee

★ Volksprater Funfair

★ Ferris Wheel

THE HISTORY OF THE FERRIS WHEEL

One of Vienna's most famous landmarks, the giant Ferris Wheel was immortalized in the film of Graham Greene's *The Third Man*. It was built in 1896 by the English engineer Walter Basset, but it has only half the original number of cabins as fire destroyed many of them in 1945.

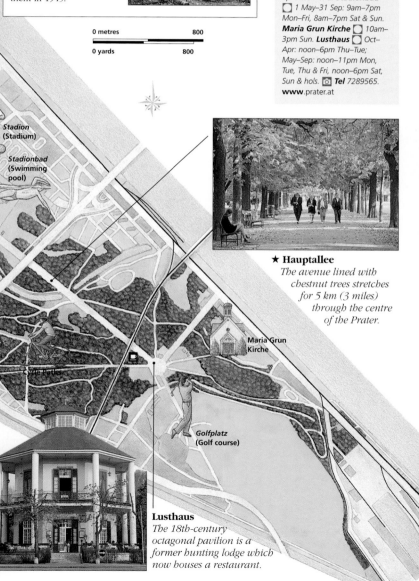

| 0 metres | 800 |
| 0 yards | 800 |

Stadion (Stadium)

Stadionbad (Swimming pool)

Cycle Paths

★ Hauptallee
The avenue lined with chestnut trees stretches for 5 km (3 miles) through the centre of the Prater.

Maria Grun Kirche

Golfplatz (Golf course)

Lusthaus
The 18th-century octagonal pavilion is a former hunting lodge which now houses a restaurant.

Baroque façade of the Augarten Palace set amid 18th-century parkland

Augarten Palace and Park ❾

Obere Augartenstrasse 1. **Map** 2 E2.
🚌 5A. Ⓤ *Praterstern.* 🚃 *31, 32.*
⭕ *6am–dusk daily.* **Porcelain
Museum** ⭕ *9:30am–5pm Mon–Fri.*
Augarten Contemporary ⭕
11am–7pm Thu–Sun. 📷 ♿

There has been a palace on
this site since the days of
Leopold I, when it was
known as the Alte Favorita,
but it was destroyed by the
Turks in 1683 and then rebuilt
around 1700 to a design
attributed to Johann Bernhard
Fischer von Erlach *(see p149).*
Since 1948 it has been the
home of the Vienna Boys'
Choir *(see p39)* and consequently it is inaccessible to
the public.
  The park was planted in
the second half of the 17th
century, renewed in 1712, and
opened to the public in 1775
by Joseph II. The handsome

gates by which the public
now enters the gardens were
designed by Isidor Canevale
in 1775. Mozart, Beethoven,
and Johann Strauss I all gave
concerts in the park pavilion.
The Augarten was also used
for royal receptions and
gatherings while the Congress
of Vienna *(see p30)* was
taking place in 1815. The
pavilion used to be the
imperial porcelain factory,
founded in the 18th century,
but has been run since the
1920s by the municipal
authorities. Its showroom has
displays showing the history
of Augarten porcelain. Behind
the pavilion is the studio of
the early 20th-century
sculptor Gustinus Ambrosi,
open to the public as the
Augarten Contemporary.
  The Augarten has the oldest
Baroque garden in Vienna,
with topiary lining long paths
shaded by walls of foliage. In
the distance, you can see two
of the huge and terrifying

flakturms that the Viennese
are unable to rid themselves
of. Built by German forces
in 1942 as defense towers
and anti-aircraft batteries,
these enormous concrete
monoliths could house
thousands of troops. So thick
are their walls that any
explosives powerful enough
to destroy them would have
a similar effect on the
surrounding residential areas.
There are four other such
flakturms still standing in
other parts of the city.

Kriminalmuseum ❿

Grosse Sperlgasse 24. **Map** 6 E1.
Tel *2144678.* Ⓤ *Nestroyplatz.*
🚌 5A. 🚃 1. ⭕ *10am–5pm
Thu–Sun.* 📷

Since 1991, this house of
medieval origin has been the
home of Vienna's museum of
crime. Once known as the
Seifensiederhaus (the soap

Hundertwasser Haus ⓫

Löwengasse/ Kegelgasse.
Ⓤ *Landstrasse.* 🚌 *4A.* 🚃 *O,
Hetzgasse.* 📷 *to the public.*

The Hundertwasser Haus is a
municipal apartment block
created in 1985 by the artist
Friedensreich Hundertwasser
(see p37), who wished to strike
a blow against what he saw as
soulless modern architecture.
The resulting building, with its
irregular bands of colour and
onion dome cupolas, has been
controversial since its construction. While it is loved by some,
others think it is more like a
stage set than a block of flats.

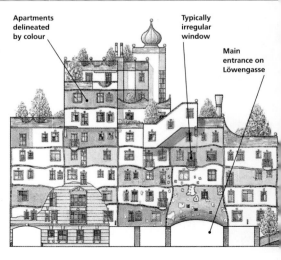

Apartments
delineated
by colour

Typically
irregular
window

Main
entrance on
Löwengasse

boiler's house), this museum's 20 rooms mostly chronicle violent crime, charting the murderous impulses of Vienna's citizenry from the Middle Ages to the 20th century, and the history of the judicial system.

Many of the exhibits come from the archives of the Viennese police force and are distinctly gruesome; there is a wide selection of murder weapons, mummified heads of executed criminals, death masks and case histories

Painting depicting a 1782 robbery

illustrated with photographs and prints. Many of the more unsettling exhibits give a notion of how the Viennese poor of earlier centuries were involved in crime. Political crimes, such as the lynching of a government minister during the revolution of 1848 *(see p30)*, are also covered.

This interesting museum provides a blend of documentary social history and a chamber of horrors which portrays the darker side of Viennese life with gusto.

Prater ⑫

See pp162–63.

Heeresgeschicht-liches Museum ⑬

See pp166–7.

Central Cemetery ⑭

See pp168–9.

Favoriten Water Tower ⑮

Windtenstrasse 3, Favoriten. **Tel** 5995931006. ⓤ *Reumannplatz.* 🚌 *15A.* 🚋 *65, 65A, 7A, 15A.* ⃝ *for guided tours (phone to arrange).*

A complex known the Favoriten pumping station was constructed in 1889 by Franz Borkowitz as part of a municipal scheme for the transportation of drinking water from the Alpine foothills to the rapidly-growing city. By 1910 the construction of other installations around Vienna meant that the operations of the complex had to be scaled down, and of the seven original buildings only the highly decorative yellow-and-red-brick

water tower remains. The fascinating feature of this incongruous-looking tower that soars 67 m (220 ft) into the sky is the original pumping equipment which is still in place. Its utilitarian appearance provides a stark contrast to the ornate turrets, pinnacles and tiles of the building's superstructure. In recent years the interior has been restored and guided tours are available to the public. Nearby is the small children's funfair, the Böhmische Prater *(see p234).*

Favoriten Water Tower

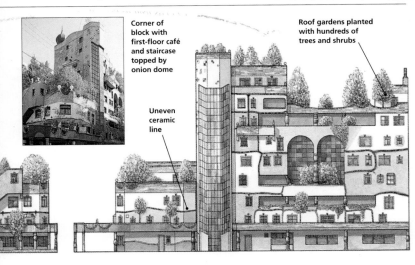

Corner of block with first-floor café and staircase topped by onion dome

Uneven ceramic line

Roof gardens planted with hundreds of trees and shrubs

Heeresgeschichtliches Museum ⑬

This impressive museum of army history is housed in a single block of the military complex known as the Arsenal. It was completed in fortress style in 1856. Theophil Hansen designed the museum itself *(see façade, right)*, which chronicles Austria's military prowess from the 16th century onwards. Exhibits relate to the Turkish siege of 1683, the French Revolution and the Napoleonic wars. Visitors should not miss seeing the car in which Archduke Franz Ferdinand was assassinated, or the modern armaments used in the war that the murder precipitated.

STAR SIGHTS

★ Hall of the Commanders

★ Turkish Standard

★ To the Unknown Soldier by A E Lienz

KEY

☐ Tank park

☐ 16th–19th centuries

☐ 19th and 20th centuries

☐ Non-exhibition space

Ground floor

Sea Power Austria

Republic and Dictatorship 1918–1945

Tank Park
Situated behind the museum are the armoured vehicles used in the Austrian army from 1955 as well as those that belonged to the German army that occupied Austria.

Main entrance from Ghegastrasse

THE ASSASSINATION OF FRANZ FERDINAND

On 28 June 1914 the heir to the throne, Archduke Franz Ferdinand, and his wife Sophie von Hohenberg paid a visit to Sarajevo. Gavrilo Princip, a Serbian nationalist, assassinated the couple, provoking an international crisis that later resulted in World War I. The museum houses the car in which the couple were killed.

MUSEUM GUIDE

The museum is housed on two floors. To view it in chronological order, begin on the first floor on the left, where exhibits relating to the Turkish siege are displayed. Other rooms chronicle the various 18th-century wars and Napoleon's victory over Austria. The 19th and 20th centuries, including heavy artillery used in World War I, are covered on the ground floor. There is also a tank park.

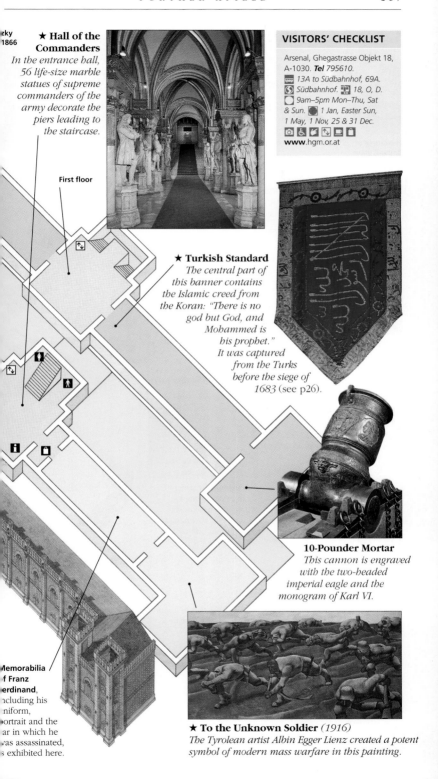

zky
1866

★ **Hall of the Commanders**
In the entrance hall, 56 life-size marble statues of supreme commanders of the army decorate the piers leading to the staircase.

First floor

VISITORS' CHECKLIST

Arsenal, Ghegastrasse Objekt 18, A-1030. **Tel** 795610.
🚌 13A to Südbahnhof, 69A.
Ⓢ *Südbahnhof.* 🚊 18, O, D.
🕐 9am–5pm Mon–Thu, Sat & Sun. ⬤ 1 Jan, Easter Sun, 1 May, 1 Nov, 25 & 31 Dec.
📷 ♿ 🅿 ↑ 🛒 🚻
www.hgm.or.at

★ **Turkish Standard**
The central part of this banner contains the Islamic creed from the Koran: "There is no god but God, and Mohammed is his prophet." It was captured from the Turks before the siege of 1683 (see p26).

10-Pounder Mortar
This cannon is engraved with the two-headed imperial eagle and the monogram of Karl VI.

Memorabilia of Franz Ferdinand, including his uniform, portrait and the car in which he was assassinated, is exhibited here.

★ **To the Unknown Soldier** *(1916)*
The Tyrolean artist Albin Egger Lienz created a potent symbol of modern mass warfare in this painting.

Central Cemetery ⑭

★ Dr-Karl-Lueger-Kirche
Max Hegele, a pupil of Otto Wagner, designed this church dedicated to Vienna's mayor in 1907–10.

Headstone of Brahms' grave

Austria's largest burial ground, containing two and a half million graves, was opened in 1874 on the city's southern outskirts. The central section includes graves of artists, composers, architects, writers and local politicians. Funerals are usually quite lavish affairs, as the Viennese like to be buried in style, with the pomp appropriate to their station in life. The cemetery contains a vast array of funerary monuments varying from the humble to the bombastic, paying tribute to the city's enduring obsession with death.

Presidential Vault
This contains the remains of Dr Karl Renner, the first President of the Austrian Republic after World War II.

Arcades around the Dr-Karl-Lueger-Kirche

Fritz Wotruba's grave (see p171)

CEMETERY LAYOUT

The cemetery is divided into specific numbered sections: apart from the central garden of honour where VIPs are buried, there are old and new Jewish cemeteries; a Protestant cemetery; a Russian Orthodox section and various war graves and memorials. It is easier to take the circulating bus that covers the whole area than to walk.

The Monument to the Dead of World War I is a powerful depiction of a mother lamenting by Anton Hanak.

Old Jewish cemetery

Islamic area

Protestant area

New Jewish cemetery

Arnold Schönberg's Cube
The grave of the modernist Viennese composer Arnold Schönberg is marked with this bold cube by Fritz Wotruba.

STAR SIGHTS
★ Musicians' Graves
★ Dr-Karl-Lueger-Kirche

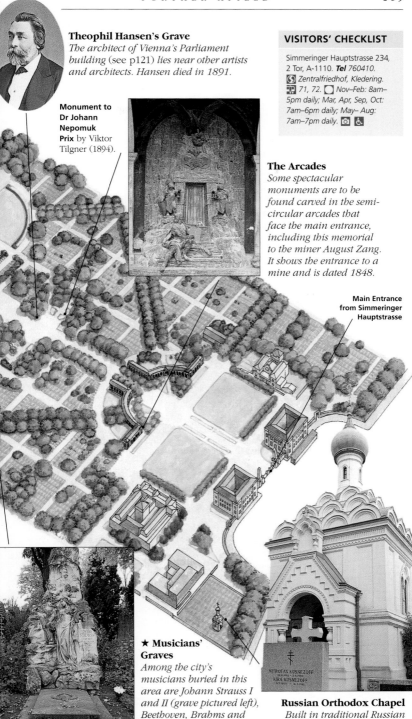

Theophil Hansen's Grave
The architect of Vienna's Parliament building (see p121) lies near other artists and architects. Hansen died in 1891.

Monument to Dr Johann Nepomuk Prix by Viktor Tilgner (1894).

VISITORS' CHECKLIST

Simmeringer Hauptstrasse 234, 2 Tor, A-1110. *Tel* 760410. Zentralfriedhof, Kledering. 71, 72. Nov–Feb: 8am–5pm daily; Mar, Apr, Sep, Oct: 7am–6pm daily; May– Aug: 7am–7pm daily.

The Arcades
Some spectacular monuments are to be found carved in the semi-circular arcades that face the main entrance, including this memorial to the miner August Zang. It shows the entrance to a mine and is dated 1848.

Main Entrance from Simmeringer Hauptstrasse

★ Musicians' Graves
Among the city's musicians buried in this area are Johann Strauss I and II (grave pictured left), Beethoven, Brahms and Schubert. There is a monument to Mozart, who was buried in St Marx cemetery.

Russian Orthodox Chapel
Built in traditional Russian Orthodox style and completed in 1894, this chapel is used by Vienna's Russian community.

Amalienbad ⑯

Reumannplatz 23, Favoriten.
Tel 6074747. Ⓤ *Reumannplatz.* 🚌
7A, 14A, 66A, 67A, 68A. 🚊 *6, 67.*
Swimming pool ◯ *9am–6pm Tue,*
9am–9:30pm Wed & Fri, 7am–9:30pm
Thu, 7am–8pm Sat, 7am–6pm Sun.
Sauna ◯ *1–9:30pm Tue, 9am–*
9:30pm Wed–Fri, 7am–8pm Sat,
7am–6pm Sun. 🚻

Public baths may not seem
like an obvious tourist
destination, but the Jugendstil
Amalienbad (1923–6) shows
how the municipal administration in the 1920s not only
provided essential public
facilities, but did so with
stylistic vigour and conviction.
The two designers, Otto
Nadel and Karl Schmalhofer,
were employees of the city's
architectural department.

The magnificent main pool
is covered by a glass roof that
can be opened in minutes and
is surrounded by galleries overlooking the pool. Elsewhere
in the building are saunas
and smaller baths and pools
used for therapeutic purposes.
When first opened, the baths
were one of the largest of
their kind in Europe, designed
to accommodate 1,300 people.
The interior is enlivened by
imaginative mosaic and tile
decoration, which is practical
as well as colourful. The
baths were damaged in World
War II but were impeccably
restored in 1986.

Spinnerin am Kreuz

Spinnerin am Kreuz ⑰

Triesterstrasse 10, Meidling.
Ⓤ *Meidling.* 🚌 *15A, 65A, 7A.* 🚊 *65.*

A medieval column marks the
southernmost boundary
of Vienna's inner suburbs.
Built in 1452 and carved on
all sides, it stands on the spot
where, according to legend, a
woman sat spinning for years
awaiting her husband's return
from the Crusades. Known as
the Spinner at the Cross, it was
designed by Hans Puchsbaum.
Pinnacled canopies shelter
groups of statuary, including a
crucifixion and a grotesque
figure placing the crown of
thorns on the head of Christ.

Technical Museum ⑱

Mariahilfer Strasse 212, Penzing.
Tel 899986000. 🚊 *52, 58.* ◯ *9am–*
6pm Mon–Fri, 10am–6pm Sat, Sun &
public hols. 🖼 🅾 🚻
www.tmw.ac.at

Franz Joseph founded the
Technisches Museum Wien
in 1908, using the Habsburgs'
personal collections as core
material; it opened its doors
10 years later. It documents all
aspects of technical progress,
from domestic appliances to
large turbines, and includes
exhibitions on heavy industry,
energy, physics and musical
instruments.

A major new section of the
museum opened in June 1999,
featuring displays on computer
technology and oil and gas
drilling and refining, as well as
a reconstruction of a coal mine.

The Railway Museum forms
an integral part of the
Technical Museum. It houses
an extensive collection of
imperial railway carriages
and engines. One of the prize
exhibits is the imperial
carriage that was used by
Franz Joseph's wife, the
Empress Elisabeth.

Schönbrunn Palace and Gardens ⑲

See pp172–75.

Decorative, geometrically-patterned tiling from the 1920s in the Amalienbad

Otto-Wagner-Hofpavillon Hietzing ⓴

Schönbrunner Schlosstrasse 13, Hietzing. *Tel* 8771571. Ⓤ *Hietzing.* ⬛ *51A, 56B, 58B, 156B.* 🚋 *10, 60, 62.* ⬜ *10:30am–12:30pm Sun.* 📷

Otto Wagner (*see p57*) designed and built this railway station for the imperial family and royal guests in 1899. This lovely building is in the shape of a white cube with green iron-work and a copper dome. Its waiting room is panelled with wood and glass, and adorned with a peach and russet asymmetrical carpet and a marble and brass fireplace. The cupola is decorated with glass and gilt flower and leaf motifs.

Wagner built the pavilion without a commission from the emperor in an attempt to showcase his work. Unfortunately, Franz Joseph used the station only twice.

The Hofpavillon Hietzing

Werkbund-siedlung ⓶⓵

Jagdschlossgasse, Veitingergasse and Woinovichgasse, Hietzing. ⬛ *54B, 55B.* 🚋 *60.*

In the 13th district you can find the 30 or so fascinating "model" houses of the *Werkbundsiedlung* (housing estate) built in the early 1930s for the municipality by some of Europe's leading architects. They are neither beautiful nor lavish, since the idea was to produce a formula for cheap housing, with two bedrooms,

Hermes Villa in the grounds of the Lainzer Tiergarten

that was plain and functional. No. 19 Woinovichgasse is by Adolf Loos (*see p92*), and Nos. 83–5 Veitingergasse are by Josef Hoffmann (*see p56*). Each architect had to design a single building, placed side by side with the rest in order to evaluate the different qualities of each. Although intended to be temporary, they have luckily survived.

Lainzer Tiergarten ⓶⓶

Lainzer Tiergarten, Hietzing. **Tiergarten** *Tel* 8041315. ⬛ *60B.* ⬜ *mid-Feb–mid-Nov: 8am–dusk daily.* 📷 **Hermes Villa and Garden** *Tel* 8041324. ⬜ *for exhibitions 9am–6pm (Apr–Sep), 9am–4:30pm (Oct–Mar) Tue–Sun & public hols.* 💳 📷

The Lainzer Tiergarten is a former Habsburg hunting ground which has been converted into an immense nature reserve in the Vienna Woods (*see p176*). The Tiergarten was opened to the public in 1923 and is still encircled by its 24-km (15-mile) stone wall, protecting its herds of deer and wild boar. From the entrance, a 15-minute walk along paths through woods and meadows brings you to the Hermes Villa, built by Karl von Hasenauer in 1884. It became a retreat for the imperial family, notably the Empress

Elisabeth and her husband Franz Joseph, who had a suite of rooms on the first floor. Inside are murals of scenes from *A Midsummer Night's Dream*, as well as art and historical exhibitions.

Wotruba Kirche ⓶⓷

Georgsgasse/Rysergasse, Mauer. *Tel* 8885003. ⬛ *60A.* ⬜ *2–8pm Sat, 9am–4:30pm Sun & hols or Tel* 8885003 *for appointment to see the church.* 📷

Built between 1965 and 1976 in uncompromisingly modern style, this church stands on a hillside very close to the Vienna Woods. It forms a pile of uneven rectangular concrete slabs and glass panels, some of the latter rising to the height of the church. They provide its principal lighting and views for the congregation out on to the woods and hills. The building is raw in style, but powerful and compact. Designed by the sculptor Fritz Wotruba (1907–75), the church looks different from every angle and has a strong sculptural quality. It accommodates a congregation of up to 250.

The exterior of the Wotruba Kirche by Fritz Wotruba, not unlike a modern sculpture

Schönbrunn Palace and Gardens ⑲

The former summer residence of the imperial family takes its name from a beautiful spring that was found on this site. An earlier hunting lodge was destroyed by the Turks, so Leopold I asked Johann Bernhard Fischer von Erlach to design a grand Baroque residence here in 1695. However, it was not until Maria Theresa employed Nikolaus Pacassi that the project was completed in the mid-18th century. The strict symmetry of the architecture is complemented by the gardens with fountains and statues framed by trees and alleyways.

Public swimming pool

Obelisk Cascade

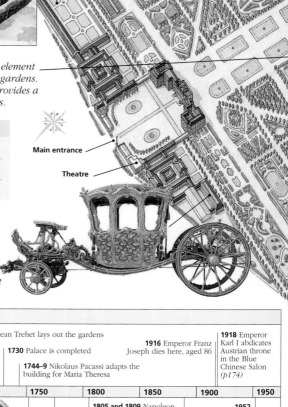

Orangery

Maze
The maze was a favourite element of many European stately gardens. This one at Schönbrunn provides a puzzling detour for visitors.

STAR SIGHTS

★ Gloriette

★ Palm House

★ Coach Museum

Main entrance

Theatre

★ Coach Museum
The former Winter Riding School houses the coaches, sleighs and sedan chairs that were used to transport the imperial family.

TIMELINE

1683 First hunting lodge on site destroyed during the Turkish siege	**1705** Jean Trehet lays out the gardens **1730** Palace is completed **1744–9** Nikolaus Pacassi adapts the building for Maria Theresa	**1916** Emperor Franz Joseph dies here, aged 86	**1918** Emperor Karl I abdicates Austrian throne in the Blue Chinese Salon *(p174)*	
1650	**1700**	**1750**	**1800**	**1850**	**1900**	**1950**
1696 Leopold I commissions J B Fischer von Erlach to design a new palace *Emperor Leopold I*		**1805 and 1809** Napoleon uses palace as headquarters **1775** Gloriette is built **1752** Maria Theresa's husband, Franz Stephan, founds a menagerie, now the zoo		**1952** Reconstruction is completed after war damage **1882** Palm House is built		

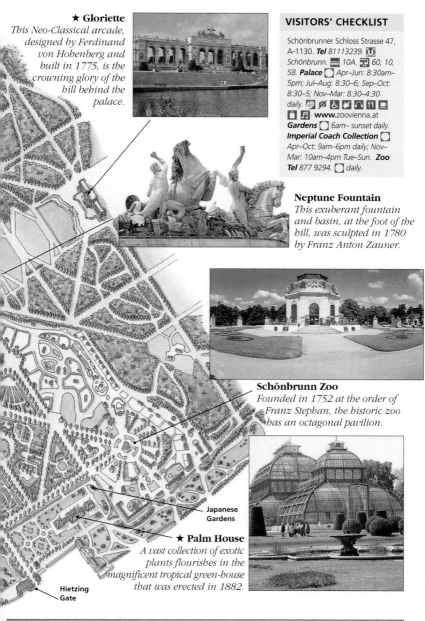

★ Gloriette
This Neo-Classical arcade, designed by Ferdinand von Hohenberg and built in 1775, is the crowning glory of the hill behind the palace.

VISITORS' CHECKLIST

Schönbrunner Schloss Strasse 47, A-1130. **Tel** *81113239*. Ⓤ *Schönbrunn*. 🚌 *10A*. 🚆 *60, 10, 58*. **Palace** ☐ *Apr–Jun: 8:30am–5pm; Jul–Aug: 8:30–6; Sep–Oct: 8:30–5; Nov–Mar: 8:30–4:30 daily*. 🎫 🅿 ♿ 🔒 ♿ 🛗 🍽 🍴 🔲 🔳 🎵 **www.zoovienna.at** **Gardens** ☐ *6am– sunset daily*. **Imperial Coach Collection** ☐ *Apr–Oct: 9am–6pm daily; Nov–Mar: 10am–4pm Tue–Sun*. **Zoo Tel** *877 9294*. ☐ *daily*.

Neptune Fountain
This exuberant fountain and basin, at the foot of the hill, was sculpted in 1780 by Franz Anton Zauner.

Schönbrunn Zoo
Founded in 1752 at the order of Franz Stephan, the historic zoo has an octagonal pavilion.

Japanese Gardens

★ Palm House
A vast collection of exotic plants flourishes in the magnificent tropical green-house that was erected in 1882.

Hietzing Gate

Façade of Schönbrunn Palace seen from the gardens

Inside Schönbrunn Palace

The Rococo decorative schemes devised by Nikolaus Pacassi dominate the Schönbrunn state rooms, where white panelling, often adorned with gilded ornamental framework, tends to prevail. The rooms vary from extremely sumptuous – such as the Millionen-Zimmer, panelled with fig wood inlaid with Persian miniatures – to the quite plain apartments occupied by Franz Joseph and Empress Elisabeth.

★ Round Chinese Cabinet
Maria Theresa used this room for private discussions with her State Chancellor. The walls are adorned with lacquered panels and vases.

★ Great Gallery
Once the venue for imperial banquets, the gallery was used for state receptions as recently as 1994.

Hidden staircase which leads to the apartment of the State Chancellor on the floor above and was used for access to secret conferences.

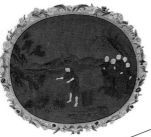

Blue Chinese Salon
The room where Karl I abdicated in 1918 has hand-painted wallpaper with blue insets showing Chinese scenes.

Napoleon Room

Millionen-Zimmer

Memorial Room

First Floor

★ Vieux-Lacque Room
During her widowhood, Maria Theresa lived in this room, which is decorated with exquisite oriental lacquered

Main entrance

Large Rosa Room
...ndscape scenes of Switzerland ...northern Italy by Joseph Rosa give this room its name. The paintings are surrounded by Rococo gilded panels.

Breakfast Room
The imperial family's breakfast room has white wood panelling inlaid with appliqué floral designs worked by Maria Theresa and her daughters.

STAR SIGHTS

★ Round Chinese Cabinet

★ Great Gallery

★ Vieux-Lacque Room

The Blue Staircase (so called due to its original decorative scheme) leads to the entrance for guided tours of state rooms.

ROOM GUIDE

The state rooms open to the public are on the first floor. The suite of rooms to the right of the Blue Staircase were occupied by Franz Joseph and Elisabeth. Two galleries divide these from rooms in the east wing, which include Maria Theresa's bedroom and rooms used by Grand Duke Karl. Two guided tours, the Imperial and the Grand Tour, cover several rooms.

KEY

☐ Franz Joseph's apartments

☐ Empress Elisabeth's apartments

☐ Ceremonial and reception rooms

☐ Maria Theresa's rooms

☐ Grand Duke Karl's rooms

☐ Non-exhibition space

Portrait of Napoleon

Portrait of Maria Louisa

MARIA LOUISA AND THE KING OF ROME

After Napoleon's fall from power, his young son by his Austrian wife Maria Louisa was kept a virtual prisoner in Schönbrunn Palace. In 1832 at the age of 21, after a lonely childhood, he died of consumption in what is known as the Napoleon Room. He was called the Duke of Reichstadt, or the King of Rome, and the Memorial Room contains his portrait as a five-year-old and his effigy. There is also a crested larch under a glass dome; the unhappy boy claimed that he never had a single friend in the palace apart from this bird.

Day Trips from Vienna

Within an hour or two's journey from Vienna there is an astonishing range of countryside from Hungarian-style plains to alpine mountains, majestic rivers and idyllic lakes. Vienna is at the centre of Austria's wine-growing country and is surrounded by historic castles and churches, among which nestle picturesque wine-producing towns and villages. All the sights are accessible by bus or train and trips such as Baden and Mayerling can easily be combined.

Among the trees of Vienna Woods, a popular recreation area

Mayerling and the Vienna Woods **1**

Vienna Sightseeing organizes trips (see p238). 🚌 *365 from Südtiroler Platz to Mayerling and Heiligenkreuz, or 265 to Heiligenkreuz.* **Mayerling Chapel Tel** *02258 2275.* ⏰ *Summer: 9am–6pm; Winter: 9am–5pm Mon–Sat, 10am–5pm Sun & hols.* 🔒 *1 Jan, Good Friday, 25 Dec.* **Heiligenkreuz Abbey Tel** *02258 8703167. Phone to check opening hours.* 📷 *obligatory.*

The Vienna Woods extend from within the western bounds of the city and make excellent walking country. A turn around the Lainzer Tiergarten *(see p171)* makes a convenient half- or full-day outing from Vienna. Further on, where the Vienna Woods stretch out towards the lower slopes of the Alps, there are several interesting sights.

The Mayerling hunting lodge, now the chapel, was the scene in 1889 of the double suicide of Crown Prince Rudolf *(see p32)*, heir to the throne, and his 17-year-old lover Mary Vetsera, daughter of the diplomat Baron Albin Vetsera. Their tragic deaths shook the entire Austro-Hungarian empire. After his son's death, the distraught

Emperor Franz Joseph gave the hunting lodge to a Carmelite convent and it was completely rebuilt. Some of Prince Rudolf's furniture remains in the chapel.

A few miles north of Mayerling is the medieval Cistercian abbey of Heiligenkreuz. Much of the abbey was rebuilt in the Baroque period, having been largely destroyed by the Turks in 1529 and 1683. Inside is a 12th-century nave and a 13th-century chapter house. Fine Baroque features include the bell tower and Trinity Column. The abbey houses the tombs of 13 of the Babenbergs who ruled in Austria during the medieval period *(see pp22–3)*.

Baden **2**

🚌 *552, 360W or 1134 (Mariazell) from Wien Mitte.* Ⓢ *or* 🚆 *from Südbahnhof.* 🚋 *Badner Bahn (WLB) from Karlsplatz/Oper.* **Tel** *02252 22600600.*

To the south of Vienna are several spas and wine-growing towns in the hills of the southern Vienna Woods. The most famous is Baden, a spa with curative hot springs dating back to Roman times. As well as bathing in sulphurous water and mud to treat rheumatism, you can enjoy hot pools of 36°C (97°F).

In the early 19th century Baden was popular with the Imperial Court of Vienna. Then many elegant Biedermeier villas, baths, town houses and a square were built, and the gardens of the Kurpark laid out. The park extends from the town centre to the Vienna Woods and has a rose garden and a memorial museum to Beethoven and Mozart. Today you can sample local wines in Baden's restaurants.

Schloss Hof **3**

🚌 *Shuttle bus operated by Blaguss-Reisen May–Oct: Sat, Sun & hols. Book by phone or online.* **Tel** *7982900.* **www**.blaguss.com ⏰ *Apr–Oct: 10am–6pm daily.* **Tel** *02285 200000.* **www**.schlosshof.at

After extensive restoration, Schloss Hof is an appealing destination. In 1725 Prince Eugene made it his principal country seat and laid out the present formal garden. Extended a generation later under Empress Maria Theresa, the palace contains private and state rooms from both periods.

Schloss Esterházy, the 17th-century residence of the Esterházy princes

SIGHTS AT A GLANCE

Day Trips

KEY

▨	City centre
▨	Greater Vienna
✈	Airport
═	Motorway
═	Major road
═	Minor road

25 kilometres = 15 miles

Eisenstadt ④

566 or 766 from Wien Mitte to
Eisenstadt Domplatz. from Süd-
bahnhof; change at Bruck an der
Leitha. 02682 63384. **Schloss
Esterházy Tel** 02682 7193000.
Apr–Jun, Oct & Nov: 9am–5pm daily;
Jul–Sep: 9am–6pm daily. only.
Haydn Museum Tel 02682
7193900. Mar–Nov: 9am–5pm
daily, Nov–Mar: by appt only. **Jewish
Museum Tel** 02682 65145. May–
Oct: 10am–5pm Tue–Sun; Nov–Apr: by
appt only (groups only).

To the southeast of Vienna,
in Eisenstadt, is Schloss
Esterházy, built for Prince Paul
Esterházy in 1663–73. It contains the Haydnsaal, a great
hall of state in which Joseph
Haydn (see pp38–9) conducted
the prince's orchestra. He lived
nearby on Haydngasse and his
house is now a museum. Also
nearby is a Jewish Museum.

Rust and Lake Neusiedl ⑤

566 or 766 from Eisenstadt; 666
from Wien Mitte. 02685 502.

Lake Neusiedl, part of which
is in Hungary, is surrounded
by reeds, the home of dozens
of species of wild birds. The
reeds are used locally for folk
crafts from thatching to
basketwork. Around the lake
are several wine villages and
resorts, of which the prettiest
is the town of Rust. It is
known for the storks which
nest on its roofs and towers.

Mariazell ⑥

552 via Baden or 1150 from Wien
Mitte. from Westbahnhof,
change at St Pölten to Mariazell
alpine railway. 03882 2366.
Basilica 6am–8pm daily. **Tel**
0388 22595 for tours. **Steam tram
Tel** 0388 23014. Jul–Sep:
10:30am–4:30pm Sat, Sun & hols.

The journey to Mariazell
from St Pölten is by the
Mariazell alpine railway. The
town has long been the main
Catholic pilgrim site of Central
Europe, and a Gothic and
Baroque basilica testifies to its
religious significance. Inside
the basilica, which was
enlarged in the 17th century,
there is a wealth of Baroque
stucco, painting and
decoration. The treasury also
forms part of the church.

A cable car up the mountain
leaves every 20 minutes from
the town centre. An additional
attraction is the world's oldest
steam tram, built in 1884 and
running between Mariazell railway station and a nearby lake.

River Trip from Krems to Melk ⑦

See pp178–9.

View of Mariazell, an important Marian shrine since 1377

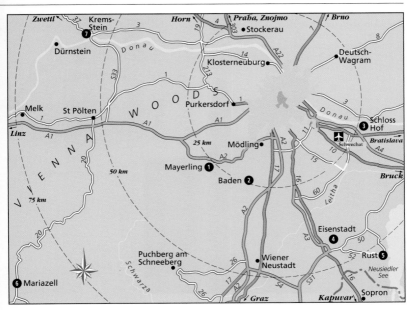

River Trip from Krems to Melk ❼

Some 80 km (50 miles) west of Vienna is one of the most magnificent stretches of river scenery in Europe. Castles, churches and wine-producing villages rise up on either side of the Danube valley and breathtaking views unfold. Redolent with history (it has been settled for over 30,000 years), this stretch from Krems to Melk is called the Wachau. A river trip is the best way to take in the landmarks, either with one of the tours organized by Cityrama, Vienna Line, Vienna Sightseeing or DDSG Shipping *(see p238)*, or independently *(see box)*.

The perfectly-preserved medieval town of Dürnstein ④

Krems to Dürnstein

The beautiful Renaissance town of Stein has in modern times merged into one with Krems, which has a medieval centre ①. At the end of Steinerstrasse is the house of the Baroque artist Kremser Schmidt. Climb one of the narrow hillside streets and look across the Danube for a fine view of Göttweig Abbey ②, an excellent example of Austrian Baroque, and in the 17th century a centre of the Counter-Reformation. You can also see the small town of Mautern ③, which

developed from a 1st-century Roman fortification, and now boasts the gourmet restaurant Bacher in Südtirolerplatz.

Once on board, after about 8 km (5 miles) you will pass the perfectly-preserved medieval town of Dürnstein ④, with a Baroque church overlooked by the ruins of a castle. From 1192 to 1193, after his return from the Third Crusade, England's King Richard the Lionheart was held prisoner in the castle by Duke Leopold V of Babenberg *(see p23)*. He was released only on payment of a huge ransom. Dürnstein has conserved much of its medieval and Baroque character and has splendid river views and side streets leading to charming river walks. A separate visit is advisable if you want to see the town at leisure.

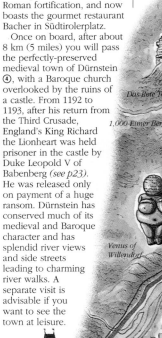

The church at Weissenkirchen which was fortified to hold off the Turks ⑦

Wine-producing towns from Rossatz to Wösendorf

On the opposite bank to Dürnstein lies Rossatz ⑤, which has been making wine for centuries and was once a busy port. Findings of Neolithic and Roman remains testify to early settlement. In the 10th century it belonged to a Bavarian convent, but passed to the Babenbergs and became part of their

Vineyards at Weissenkirchen

Das Rote Tor

1,000-Eimer Berg

Venus of Willendorf

Schönbühel Castle

0 km		5
0 miles		3

KEY

🚢	River boat boarding point
🚉	Railway station
—	Railway line
〰	River
▬	Major road
▭	Minor road

Austrian domain. The Renaissance castle and Gothic church were transformed to Baroque around 1700.

At Weissenkirchen ⑥ the church dates mainly from the 15th and 16th centuries. The town is also renowned for its wine, as are Joching ⑦ and Wösendorf ⑧.

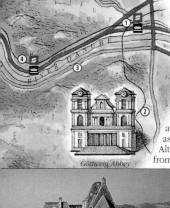

Göttweig Abbey

The Benedictine abbey of Melk dominates the river and town ⑳

Churches and ruins

Clearly visible on top of a hill, the fortified Church of St Michael ⑨ was built between 1500 and 1523. An unusual architectural detail is the stone hares on its tower. Local folklore tells how, once, so much snow fell here that hares were able to leap onto the roof.

On the same side of the river is a ruined arch on a hill, Das Rote Tor ⑩, a fragment of a 14th-century gate through which the Swedes walked on their way to Spitz in 1645 during the 30 Years War *(see p25)*. The town of Mitterarnsdorf ⑪ has Roman remains.

Spitz to Aggsbachdorf

Spitz ⑫ is another pretty wine town and was also a Protestant stronghold during the Reformation. It lies at the foot of the 1,000-Eimer Berg (1,000-Bucket Mountain), so called because it is claimed that in a good year the vine-clad hills can produce enough wine to fill 1,000 buckets.

Further on is a wall-like rocky precipice jutting out from the bank, the Teufelsmauer or Devil's Wall ⑬. It has given rise to a number of legends. One tells how the devil's grandmother wanted to stop pilgrims and crusaders by creating a dam. At Schwallenbach ⑭ the church was rebuilt after the Bohemians devastated the village in 1463. Although you cannot see it from the boat, you will pass very close to the village of Willendorf ⑮, famous for the prehistoric findings made nearby, including the statue and fertility symbol Venus of Willendorf *(see pp20 and 128)*.

Aggstein ⑯ has a ruined castle high above the river. Georg Scheck von Wald, follower of Duke Albrecht I, rebuilt and enlarged the original castle in 1429. Legend has it that he called a rock, placed at the highest point of the castle, his rose garden. He would force his imprisoned enemies to leap to their deaths if the ransom he demanded failed to arrive. Aggsbachdorf ⑰ was settled by the Romans in the 2nd century and owned by the Kuenringer robber-barons during the Middle Ages.

Schönbühel Castle to Melk

The picturesque castle of Schönbühel ⑱ stands on a rocky outcrop overlooking the Danube. Although it has been on record since the 9th century, its present form dates from the early 19th century. Further

on, at the mouth of the 70-km long (43-mile) River Pielach ⑲, 30 Bronze Age tombs and the foundations of a Roman tower have been excavated.

The high point of the trip is the Benedictine abbey of Melk ⑳. The pretty town has Renaissance houses, romantic little streets, old towers and remnants of a city wall built in the Middle Ages. The Baroque abbey, where Umberto Eco's novel *The Name of the Rose* begins and ends, is a treasure trove of paintings, sculptures and decorative art. The great library contains 2,000 volumes from the 9th to the 15th centuries alone. The church has a magnificent organ, and skeletons dressed in luxurious materials inside glass coffins. Some of the Abbey's treasures are not on permanent view.

TIPS FOR INDEPENDENT TRAVELLERS

Starting points: *Krems, Dürnstein, Melk or any river trip boarding point. River trip tickets are on sale at these points.*
Getting there: *Take the national network train from Franz-Josefs- Bahnhof to Krems or Dürnstein. For Melk, depart from Westbahnhof.*
Stopping-off points: *Dürnstein has restaurants, and shops.*
Melk Abbey Tel *02752 555232.*
🕐 *Palm Sunday–1st Sun after All Souls: 9am–5pm (May–Sep: 9am–5:30pm).* 🎧 *in English: 10:55am May–Oct.*
Cycling: *A cycle path runs along the Danube. Hire bikes at Krems, Melk, Spitz and Dürnstein train stations (reduction with train ticket), or from river trip boarding points. Take your passport for identification.* **www**.*stiftmelk.at*

The ruined castle above the river at Aggstein ⑯

THREE GUIDED WALKS

Vienna is a comparatively small city, with several main attractions within easy walking distance of each other. All six sightseeing areas in this guide have a suggested short walk marked on a Street-by-Street map. Yet the city's suburbs are also worth exploring on foot. The following guided walks take you through some of the best walking areas in and around the city, all easily accessible by public transport. The first walk takes you through the town itself. Starting in the Stadtpark, it continues past the Karlskirche to the elegant Wagner Apartments and the colourful Naschmarkt on the Linke Wienzeile. Hietzing, on the western edge of the grounds of Schönbrunn

Makart statue *(p182)*

Palace, is our second walk. The former village's quiet streets are lined with an interesting mix of Biedermeier and Jugendstil villas. Towards the end of the walk is Schönbrunn Palace Park, with an area of woodland and the more formally planted Botanical Garden. The third walk takes you to the old wine village of Grinzing, with its many *Heurige*. The route goes through Heiligenstadt, where there are a number of buildings by well-known 20th-century architects. In addition to these walks, there are signposted routes through the Vienna Woods and the Prater, marked *Stadtwanderwege*. For details of these, phone or write to the Wiener Fremdenverkehrsamt *(see p238)*.

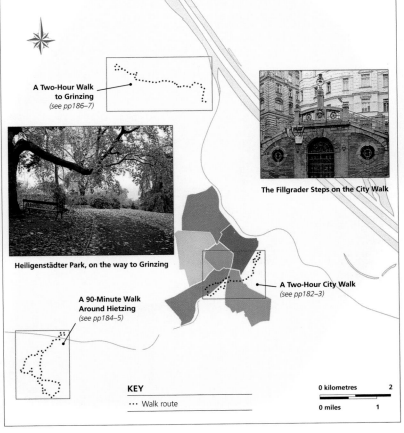

A Two-Hour Walk to Grinzing *(see pp186–7)*

The Fillgrader Steps on the City Walk

Heiligenstädter Park, on the way to Grinzing

A 90-Minute Walk Around Hietzing *(see pp184–5)*

A Two-Hour City Walk *(see pp182–3)*

KEY

··· Walk route

0 kilometres   2

0 miles   1

◁ **Schönbrunn Palace Park** *(see p185)*

A Two-Hour City Walk

This walk skirts the southwestern perimeter of the inner city, following part of the course of the River Wien. It begins with a leisurely stroll through the Stadtpark, which was laid out in English landscape style when the Ringstrasse was built *(see p32)*. Continuing past Schwarzenbergplatz and Karlsplatz through the lively Naschmarkt, it ends with a glance at some masterpieces of Jugendstil architecture on the Linke Wienzeile.

The Stadtpark

Begin at the entrance to the Stadtpark opposite Weihburggasse. Almost facing you is an impressive side entrance ① with sculpted portals which was designed between 1857 and 1862.

On the city side, the park contains many monuments to musicians and artists. The first is the gilded statue of Johann Strauss II *(see p39)* playing his violin (1921) ②. Go left past this monument, and left again, into a paved circular seating area with a fountain dedicated to the Sprite of the Danube ③. Turn right out of this area and you come to an iron bridge across the River Wien, from the middle of which you get a view of the embankments ④.

Walk back to the nearby lake ⑤. On its southern side a statue of the Viennese landscape painter Emil Jakob Schindler (1895) ⑥ sits in the bushes. Follow the path until

No. 38 Linke Wienzeile ㉑

it peters out into a culvert then go left across the bridge. Turn left again until you come to a monument to Franz Schubert (1872) by Karl Kundmann ⑦. Take the path past the lake and turn right at the clock-tower. The painter Hans Makart, who dominated the visual arts in Vienna in the 1870s and 1880s, strikes a rhetorical pose in Viktor Tilgner's 1898 statue ⑧. Walk on past the entrance to the park. On the right is the

Jugendstil portal in the Stadtpark, built in 1903–4 as part of the flood defences along the river ⑪

bust of Franz Lehár, composer of *The Merry Widow* ⑨. Walk towards the Kursalon ⑩, which opened for concerts, balls and waltzes in the 1860s. Continue past the Kursalon, leaving the park through one of the Jugendstil portals *(see p57)* ⑪.

Fillgrader Steps

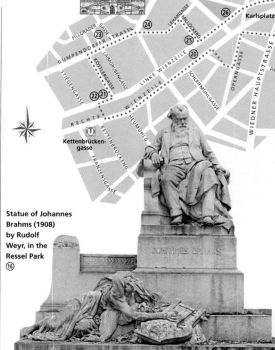

Statue of Johannes Brahms (1908) by Rudolf Weyr, in the Ressel Park ⑯

TIPS FOR WALKERS

Starting point: Weihburggasse Tram 1 or 2 (on Parkring).
Length: 3 km (1½ miles).
Getting there: Trams 1 or 2, which circulate around the Ringstrasse and Franz-Josefs-Kai; or Stubentor U-bahn, then walk.
Stopping-off points: The Kursalon in the Stadtpark serves tea, coffee and cakes on the terrace and has a beer garden to one side. There are also many benches where you can rest. There are cafés in Ressel Park and the Naschmarkt; towards the end of the walk you will find Café Sperl on Gumpendorfer Strasse.

Schwarzenbergplatz

Walk straight ahead, crossing the road into Lothringerstrasse. A monument to Beethoven (1880), showing him surrounded by figures alluding to the Ninth Symphony, stands on the right ⑫. Cross the road to the Konzerthaus (1912–13), home to the Vienna Symphony Orchestra *(see p228)* ⑬.

Cross the busy intersection to get a striking vista of Schwarzenbergplatz to your left, at the end of which is a fountain. It was erected in 1873 to celebrate the city's supply of pure drinking water which comes from the mountains. Behind it is the Memorial to the Red Army which liberated Austria in 1945 ⑭.

The Neo-Renaissance Kursalon ⑩

Ressel Park

Continue along Lothringerstrasse, pass the Wien Museum Karlsplatz *(see p146)* ⑮, into Ressel Park. On the left is a statue of Brahms with his muse at his feet (1908) by Rudolf Weyr ⑯. Look left past Brahms to the Karlskirche *(see pp148–9)* ⑰. Go on, noting Otto Wagner's pavilions *(see p146)* at road level ⑱. Pass the Neo-Classical Technical High School ⑲ to leave the park. Cross Wiedner Hauptstrasse, go straight ahead then left into Operngasse, crossing the road. Walk through Bärenmühlendurchgang passage in the building facing you and cross the road into the Naschmarkt ⑳.

Naschmarkt

A lively food market *(see p138)*, originally held in the Karlsplatz, moved here after this part of the river was paved over in the late 19th century. It is a good vantage point from which to admire the elegant 19th-century buildings along the left bank, or Linke Wienzeile. Leave the

Papageno Gate of the Theater an der Wien ㉕

market and cross the road to look at Otto Wagner's Apartments *(see p139)* with golden medallions by Kolo Moser at No. 38 ㉑, and the Majolikahaus at No. 40, so called because of its floral tiles ㉒. As you turn into Köstlergasse alongside No. 38 it is worth pausing to admire the entrance.

Confession box, Karlskirche ⑰

Gumpendorfer Strasse

Turn right at the end of Köstlergasse and walk up Gumpendorfer Strasse. Look left up Fillgradergasse for a glimpse of the Fillgrader Steps ㉓. Continue on to the historic Café Sperl *(see p58)*, once the haunt of the composer Lehár ㉔. Go on and turn right into Millöckergasse to see the famous Papageno Gate of the Theater an der Wien *(see p138)* ㉕. The sculpture above the entrance shows the theatre's first owner, Emanuel Schikaneder, in the character of Papageno from Mozart's *The Magic Flute*. Continue down Millöckergasse to the Linke Wienzeile. Bear left, passing the Secession Building *(see p138)* ㉖, and go on to Karlsplatz U-Bahn.

KEY

∙∙∙ Walk route

☆ Good viewing point

Ⓤ U-Bahn station

A 90-Minute Walk Around Hietzing

The former village of Hietzing runs along the western edge of the extensive grounds of Schönbrunn Palace (*see p172–75*). In Maria Theresa's time it was a fashionable area where the nobility went to spend their summers; later it became a suburb for the wealthy middle classes. The quiet streets contain a marvellous mix of Biedermeier and Jugendstil villas, while the square around the parish church retains an intimate small-town atmosphere.

Façade of the Park Hotel ⑤

From the station to Am Platz

Take the Hadikgasse exit from Hietzing U-Bahn ① and cross the tram tracks and road to Kennedybrücke. Turn right down Hadikgasse and after a minute you arrive at Otto-Wagner-Hofpavillon Hietzing (*see p171*) ②, a former station designed for the use of the imperial family when they were at Schönbrunn. Retrace

The Kaiserstöckl opposite the Park Hotel, now a post office ⑥

your steps to the U-Bahn and cross the road into Hietzinger Hauptstrasse. Notice the attic of No. 6 with cherubs hugging the columns. The building dates from 1901–2, but the lower storey has been altered to accommodate shops ③. On your left through the railings are long avenues of trees at

the side of Schönbrunn ④. Just across the road is the Park Hotel, its ochre façade echoing that of the palace buildings ⑤. Facing it is the Kaiserstöckl (1770) or Emperor's Pavilion ⑥. Today it is a post office, but it used to be the holiday venue of Maria Theresa's foreign ministers. Continue to Am Platz with its plague column dating from 1730 ⑦. Next door to this is the parish church of Maria Geburt ⑧, originally built in the 13th century, and remodelled in the 17th century. The Baroque interior contains altars by the sculptor Matthias Steindl and ceiling frescoes by Georg Greiner. The church was used by Maria Theresa when she was in residence at Schönbrunn, and her box can be seen in the right-hand wall of the choir. In front of the church stands a statue of Franz Joseph's brother

0 metres 250

0 yards 250

KEY

• • • Walk route

Ⓤ U-Bahn station

TIPS FOR WALKERS

Starting point: Hietzing U-Bahn.
Length: 5 km (3 miles).
Getting there: the U4 and Tram 58 go to Hietzing. **Note:** On Sundays you may need to retrace your steps a short distance if the Maxing Gate is locked.
Stopping-off points: the BAWAG café in Hietzing's Am Platz is a pleasant place to stop for a coffee.
Bezirksmuseum Hietzing
Ⓞ 2–6pm Wed, 2–5pm Sat, 9:30am–noon Sun. ● Jul–Aug.
Schönbrunn Palace and Park (see pp172–75). *Villa Primavesi* ● to public.

Elaborate altar by Matthias Steindl in the Maria Geburt Kirche ⑧

Maximilian, the Emperor of Mexico who was executed in 1867 ⑨. Nearby is a Neo-Classical building housing the Bezirksmuseum Hietzing ⑩, and outside the museum is Vienna's last gas lamp.

Trauttmansdorffgasse and Gloriettegasse

Turn left into Maxingstrasse, named after Maximilian, then right into Altgasse. Almost facing Fasholdgasse is an old *Heuriger*, a Biedermeier building with ochre walls ⑪.

Detail from the majolica façade of the Lebkuchenhaus ⑲

across the road, at No. 27, is the house where the composer Alban Berg *(see p39)* once lived ⑬. Nos. 48 and 50 are contrasting examples of Viennese turn-of-the-century architecture ⑭. More examples of Biedermeier style can be seen at Nos. 54 and 56 ⑮.

At the end of the road, turn left into Gloriette-gasse. On the right at Nos. 14 and 16 is a villa with sculpted figures in the pediments, built in 1913–15 by Josef Hoffmann for the financier Robert Primavesi ⑯. Note the monumental sculpted figures resting in the pediments.

Cross the road to pass a terrace of Biedermeier houses – Nos. 38 and 40 have lunettes above the windows ⑰. No. 21 is the Villa Schopp, designed by Friedrich Ohmann in 1901–2 ⑱. Turn left down Wattmanngasse to see No. 29, the extraordinary Lebkuchen-haus (Gingerbread House) ⑲, so-called because of its dark brown decoration in majolica. It was built in 1914 to designs by a pupil of Otto Wagner *(see pp54–7)*. Turn back into Gloriettegasse. At its southern junction with Wattmann-gasse, at No. 9, is the

house that belonged to Katharina Schratt, the actress and confidante of Emperor Franz Joseph during his later years. It is said that the Emperor was in the habit of arriving here for breakfast ⑳.

Maxing Park and Schönbrunn Park

Walk to the end of Gloriette-gasse, then turn right up Maxingstrasse and cross the road at Maxing Park. If you would like to add another half hour to the walk, Hietzing cemetery, a little further up the hill, contains the graves of Otto Wagner, Gustav Klimt, Kolo Moser and Franz Grillparzer, among others. Alternatively, enter Maxing Park ㉑ and follow the main path upwards towards the right. At the top, go through the gates marked *Zum Tiergarten Schönbrunn*, passing the forestry research institute on your left. Although you are actually in the grounds of Schönbrunn, this heavily wooded area feels very remote from the formal gardens and you may catch a glimpse of deer. At the crossroads in the path turn left, signposted to the Botanical Garden. You soon arrive at a little wooden hut, which was Crown Prince Rudolf's playhouse ㉒.

The path eventually leads to the formally planted Botanical Garden ㉓, which was laid out in 1848 under Emperor Franz I. Take the path through the garden, keeping to the boundary wall with Hietzing. Exit into Maxingstrasse (this gate may be locked on Sundays) and continue north. At No. 18 is the house where Johann Strauss II wrote *Die Fledermaus* in 1874 ㉔. Carry on north along Maxingstrasse and retrace your steps to Hietzing U-Bahn.

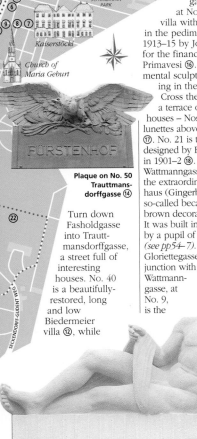

Plaque on No. 50 Trauttmans-dorffgasse ⑭

Turn down Fasholdgasse into Trautt-mansdorffgasse, a street full of interesting houses. No. 40 is a beautifully-restored, long and low Biedermeier villa ⑫, while

Sculpted figure in a pediment of the Villa Primavesi ⑯

A Two-Hour Walk to Grinzing

This walk through part of Vienna's 19th district begins at the site of one of the most important monuments of 20th-century Vienna, the public housing development of the Karl Marx Hof. It then takes you through a pretty 19th-century park to the old wine village of Grinzing. Although the village suffered destruction at the hands of the Turks in 1529 and 1683 and from Napoleon's army in 1809, and is now feeling the effects of modern tourism, its pretty main street preserves its charm.

Façade of the 16th-century
Reinprecht *Heuriger* ⑮

Karl Marx Hof to Heiligenstädter Park

Facing you as you step out of Heiligenstadt station is the long ochre, terracotta and mauve façade of the Karl Marx Hof *(see p161)*, a huge housing project designed by the city architect Karl Ehn and built from 1927 to 1930 during the Red Vienna period ①. It sprawls for 1.2 km (³/₄ mile) and has 1,265 flats.

Cross the road and pass through one of the four arches facing you into 12 Februar Platz to see the main façade from the other side. On the keystone of each arch stands a large figure sculpture by Joseph Riedl (1928) ②. Continue through the square, past a statue (1928)

Figure on the Karl Marx Hof ①

by Otto Hofner of a man sowing seeds ③, and you come to Heiligenstädter Strasse. Turn right, cross the road at the second pedestrian crossing and walk through the square opening in the building facing you. Go up the steps and take the path on the left into Heiligenstädter Park. When you come to a fork, take the left path that winds up a hill, going through woods. Turn right at the top into the formal part of the park ④. From here, you get a good view of the vine-clad slopes of the Kahlenberg ⑤.

Steinfeldgasse

Take the second small path on the right, which descends gradually into Steinfeldgasse, where there is a cluster of houses built by the Secessionist

designer Josef Hoffmann. The first one you come to is the Villa Moser-Moll at Nos. 6–8, designed for Carl Moll and Kolo Moser ⑥. Next to it is the Villa Spitzer ⑦, then the more classical Villa Ast, built in 1909–11 ⑧. Where Steinfeldgasse meets Wollergasse is the Villa Henneberg of 1901 ⑨, and at No. 10 Wollergasse ⑩ is the Moll House II of 1906–7. Its black and white details are charming.

Steinfeldgasse to Grinzinger Strasse

At the point where Steinfeld-gasse and Wollergasse meet, there is a path leading down through some woods. Follow this and descend the steps to the Church of St Michael, Heiligenstadt ⑪, which has striking

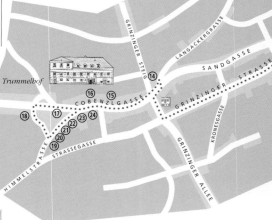

Trummelhof

modern stained-glass windows. Walk past the church, cross Hohe Warte and go up Grinzinger Strasse. You quickly arrive at No. 70, the house where Albert Einstein stayed from 1927 to 1931 ⑫. On the same side of the road is No. 64, the late 18th-century house where Beethoven and the Viennese playwright Franz Grillparzer lodged during the summer of 1808 while Beethoven was composing the Pastoral Symphony ⑬.

Continue up Grinzinger Strasse, passing a number of attractive Biedermeier houses, until you arrive at Grinzinger

Lawns and trees in the Heiligenstädter Park ④

Allee. Turn right past a series of wine gardens and immediately right again to get a quick glimpse of the upper part of Sandgasse, where there are a number of more authentic *Heurige* ⑭.

Grinzing

Turning back on yourself and towards the centre of Grinzing, ascend Cobenzlgasse, the upper fork of Grinzing's main street. The Reinprecht *Heuriger* at No. 22 Cobenzlgasse is a 16th-century house, the façade of

Cobenzlgasse, Grinzing's main street

| 0 metres | 500 |
| 0 yards | 500 |

Karl Marx Hof Ⓤ Ⓢ
Heiligenstadt

Villa Spitzer

No. 64 Grinzinger Strasse

Courtyard at the Passauer Hof, an old wine press house ⑰

TIPS FOR WALKERS

Starting point: *Heiligenstadt station.*

Length: *3.5 km (2 miles).*

Getting there: *Heiligenstadt station is served by U-Bahn lines U4 and U6, trains S40 and S45 and buses 10A, 11A, 38A and 39A. Tram D stops on Heiligen-städter Strasse.*

Stopping-off points: *There are numerous Heurige (usually open from 4pm), coffee shops and restaurants in Grinzing. Avoid the larger Heurige – the smaller ones sell their own wine. Those at the top of Sandgasse are good.*

KEY

• • • Walk route

🌟 Good viewing point

🚉 Tram terminus

Ⓤ U-Bahn station

Ⓢ Schnellbahn station

═══ Railway line

which has a tablet commemorating the composer Robert Stolz ⑮. No. 30 Cobenzlgasse is the Baroque Trummelhof, standing on the site of an 1835 brewery ⑯. Further up on the left, at No. 9, is the Passauer Hof, an old wine press house that contains fragments of a far older, Romanesque building ⑰. On the corner of Cobenzlgasse and Feilergasse is the Altes Presshaus, whose cellar contains an old wine press ⑱.

Turn left into Feilergasse, and you soon come face to face with the impressive white Jugendstil façade of

Nos. 41–3 Himmelstrasse ⑲. Continue down Himmelstrasse to No. 35, another *Heuriger*, Das Alte Haus, which has a charming plaque of the Virgin Mary above its door ⑳. There is a another such painting at No. 31, which shows a holy man carrying various items ㉑. No. 29 ㉒ is another *Heuriger* with a tablet to Sepp Fellner, a *Schrammel* musician *(see p39)* described as "The Schubert of Grinzing". Ironically, at No. 25, a grand building with shields above the doorway, there is a memorial to the real Schubert, described as "The Prince of Song, who loved to tarry in Grinzing" ㉓. Grinzing also has an attractive late Gothic church with a copper cupola and much-restored interior ㉔. Continue down the road to the tram terminus, where the No. 38 tram goes back to town.

Plaque of a holy man on the façade of No. 31 Himmelstrasse ㉑

View down Kohl Markt towards Hofburg ▷

TRAVELLERS' NEEDS

WHERE TO STAY

With more than 500 hotels and pensions, Vienna offers accommodation to suit everyone. From palaces to simple lodgings, it has some of the grandest European city hotels as well as numerous small boarding-houses and self-catering establishments. Hotels are generally larger and better equipped (some also have business facilities), and pensions are always bed and breakfast establishments. Included in this guide is a selection of accommodation to suit all tastes and budgets. Hotels are listed by area and in order of price category. For more details of facilities and for a short description, turn to the listings on pages 194-199. For further types of accommodation available in and on the outskirts of Vienna, see pages 192-193.

Baroque façade of the Mailberger Hof on Annagasse (see p195)

WHERE TO LOOK

One of the thrills of visiting Vienna is that you can stay grandly or cheaply right in the city centre. Almost all of the famous hotels – the Sacher, Bristol, Imperial (see Listings pp194-199) – are on or just off the Ringstrasse, as are most of the large chain hotels. In the city centre lie a number of comfortable hotels and pensions. Most are on fairly quiet side streets. The Townhall and Museum Quarter has some good small hotels and offers affordable lodgings for budget travellers. A few hotels in, or near, wine villages to the north (see p199) are also listed. The **Österreich Werbung** (Austrian Tourist Board) publishes information on over 500 hotels and pensions.

HOTEL PRICES

Accommodation in Vienna can be expensive. Many hotels and pensions in prime locations are highly priced. However, you can expect to pay approximately a fifth to a quarter less for a room in an establishment just outside the Ringstrasse, and less still if you stay further afield.

Most facilities do have rooms at a variety of prices, depending on their size, aspect and, in pensions, whether they have en suite bathrooms. Single rooms are about three-quarters the cost of double rooms. Some places will put an extra bed in the room on request, which can cost less than the price of a single room. Other hotels offer family or triple-bedded rooms.

Vienna's low season is from November-March (excluding Christmas and New Year) and July-August. Few hotels lower prices in summer, although half have winter rates up to

Penthouse suite No. 663 in the Bristol Hotel (see p199)

25% lower. Most of the large chain hotels reduce the room tariff during quiet periods and offer weekend specials.

Out of season, it is worth asking for a discount for payment in cash. Many places offer discounts for longer stays, and it's possible to find packages such as three nights for the price of two.

The **Österreich Werbung** has international offices and provides details of tour operators that offer all-inclusive Vienna packages.

Opulent lobby of the Imperial Hotel (see p199)

HIDDEN EXTRAS

Apart from most five-star hotels, breakfast is included in the tariff. Rates will always include taxes such as VAT (or MWSt). Beware if changing money at your hotel: the official exchange rate could be as much as 10% better.

Parking fees can also mount up. Street parking within the Ringstrasse is restricted to 90 minutes and there are no private garages. Pensions generally leave you to your own devices to find an underground car park, but some hotels have designated spaces. At some hotels a reasonable amount is charged for parking, but at others it can be very expensive. Outlying districts do not have such stringent street parking restrictions, and garage parking is cheaper.

Try to avoid making phone calls from your room. Most hotels charge a flat rate, even though the official rate varies from day-time to night-time and week-days to weekends. The surcharge may be up to three and a half times the standard rate, so it is worth using a public telephone.

Every other Viennese on the street seems to have a four-legged friend, so many of the hotels allow dogs in the rooms. There may be a charge for this.

HOW TO BOOK

Easter, May, June, September, October, Christmas and New Year are considered peak season during which accommodation may be fully booked as early as two months in advance.

Making direct hotel reservations are easy, since many hotel personnel speak English. If you cancel once the booking is made, you may be charged for the room. Check in advance. If arriving after 6pm, let the hotel know or they may re-let your room to someone else.

The **Wiener Tourismusverband** (Vienna Tourist Board) on the corner of Albertinaplatz,

Statue in the reception area of the Hotel Regina *(see p197)*

Sign of a well-known Viennese hotel

Tegethoffstrasse and Meysedergasse *(see p239)*, can reserve hotel rooms in advance. It is also possible to book accommodations by calling the Tourist Board at 24555 or online by visiting www.wien.info. Otherwise, contact the hotel directly. If the hotel accepts credit cards, a phone call to book will suffice; if not, you may have to send booking confirmation to the hotel in writing. Different hotels have different procedures.

FACILITIES

Hotels are rated one to five stars, pensions on a four-star system; a three-star hotel corresponds to a four-star pension. The rating also attempts to cover the quality and ambience of the hotel or pension. Five-star hotels are upscale and well-run. Many three- and four-star hotels refer to themselves as *Palais*, which equates to a fine town house. At the cheaper end of the scale, small pensions above two stars are often more salubrious than cheap hotels. One- or two-star hotels and pensions tend to cater for travellers on a budget and are generally less pleasant.

Usually, only the top hotels have a full range of public rooms; restaurant, bar, coffee shop and sitting room. In many smaller establishments, the lounge is little more than an extension of the reception. Even if there is no bar, you may find that drinks are served. Almost all hotels and pensions have a breakfast room. While low-priced pensions provide continental breakfast, most hotels offer a hot and cold breakfast buffet.

The Anna Sacher restaurant at the Hotel Sacher *(see p198)*

Because many hotels occupy old buildings, no two bedrooms are the same. Rooms almost always have a phone, though not necessarily a television. Mid-range hotel rooms often have cable TV, mini-bar and a bathroom with a shower or bathtub. Many Viennese buildings back onto quiet courtyards so you can select a peaceful room, or one with a view.

In the 19th century there was a restriction on building heights. To circumvent the regulation, lower floors were (and still are) called *Hochparterre* and *Mezzanin*. Consequently, you may find that the "first floor" is up three stair flights. Additionally, in pensions a communal lift serves the whole building.

The quality of service in the best luxury hotels is as good as anywhere in the world. Wherever you stay, it could be well worth befriending the concierge (by perhaps giving him or her a tip early on in your stay). He or she can be invaluable in directing you to interesting restaurants and bars, and conjuring out of thin air a ticket to the Winter Riding School or a seat at the opera when they have been sold out for months. In general, most of the hotel staff speak English, but the standard of service is variable.

TRAVELLING WITH CHILDREN

Almost all hotels and pensions have cots (some charge) and can arrange a babysitter. Some may charge the same rate for putting a child's bed in the parents' room as they would for an adult's bed. Usually only the larger hotels allow children under various ages to stay free in their parents' room.

DISABLED TRAVELLERS

Information concerning wheelchair access to hotels relies on the individual hotel's assessment of their suitability and it is advisable to check before travelling. The **Wiener Tourismusverband** publishes a detailed leaflet.

HOSTELS

Youth hostels are available in Vienna. The **Wiener Tourismusverband's** youth hostel and camping brochure lists their facilities. Those with better facilities cost around €10–€15 per night including breakfast. Most hostels expect residents to be in by midnight. An International Youth Hostel Federation membership card is required, which can be obtained beforehand or at the hostel. Contact **Österreichischer Jugendherbergsverband** for more information.

SAISONHOTELS

Annually from 1 July to 30 September, two dozen students' hostels become Saisonhotels or seasonal hotels, rated on a scale of one to three stars. At the three-star level expect fairly decent rooms. You may make enquiries at any time of the year at two of the main chains, **Academia Hotels** and **Rosen-Hotel**. Try to reserve well in advance and expect to pay up to €75 for a double room in one of the better places.

CAMPING

Five well-equipped campsites can be found within a radius of 8-15 km (5-9 miles) from the city centre. Most campsites have kitchen facilities; some have a supermarket. For additional camping information, contact the **Wiener Tourismusverband**, **Camping** und **Caravaning Club**

The handsome yellow exterior of the Hotel Josefshof *(see p198)*

Austria, and **Österreichischer Camping Club**. **Wiener Tourismusverband** also produces a camping and youth hostel brochure that provides more details on these sites.

SELF-CATERING

For those who are keen to "go it alone" there are limited opportunities for self-catering in the city. **Pego**, a company that rents homes throughout Austria, has two apartment blocks and a range of flats spread in and around the city; their brochure will give you all the details. You can book by telephone, by fax or in writing. Some apartments have a combined living and sleeping space and most also have a television and telephone. Expect to pay less per night than the price of a pension.

STAYING IN PRIVATE HOMES

It is possible to book a stay in a private home through the **Wiener Tourismusverband**, but the booking has to be made in person. **Mitwohnzentrale**, a private company, offers the same service. Normally you need to stay a few nights and should expect to pay around €36 per person per night.

CHAIN HOTELS

Chain hotels are mostly geared towards business people; rates usually vary according to their level of occupancy, rather than the season. Familiar names include the **Inter-Continental Wien** (see p199), **K+K** (see p195) and the **Vienna Marriott** (see p195) as well as some others listed on pages 194–199.

View of a campsite at No. 40 Huttelbergstrasse

DIRECTORY

INFORMATION

Österreich Werbung
Margaretenstrasse 1,
A-1040. **Map** 4 D2. **Tel**
0810101818. **Fax**
5886620.
www.austria.info

Wiener Tourismusverband
Corner of Albertinaplatz,
Tegethoffstrasse and
Meysedergasse, A-1010.
Map 4 D1 & 6 C4.
Tel 24555. **Fax** 24555-666.
www.wien.info

SAISONHOTELS

Academia Hotels
Pfeilgasse 3a, A-1080.
Map 1 A5. **Tel** 4017655.
Fax 4017620. **www**.
academia-hotels.co.at

Rosen-Hotel
Schelleingasse 36, A-1040.
Map 4 E4. **Tel** 501520.
Fax 50152709.
www.rosenhotels.at

YOUTH HOSTELS

Österreichischer Jugendherbergs-verband
Gonzagagasse 22, A-1010.

Map 2 D4.
Tel 5335353. **Fax** 5350861.
www.oejhv.or.at

CAMPING

Camping und Caravaning Club Austria
Mariahilfer Strasse 180,
A-1150. **Map** 3 A3. **Tel**
89121262. **Fax** 89121274.
www.cca-camping.at

Österreichischer Camping Club
Schubertring 1–3, A-1010.
Map 4 E2 & 6 D5.
Tel 7136151.
Fax 711992754.
www.campingclub.at

SELF-CATERING

Pego
Rathausgasse 11, A-6700
Bludenz. **Tel** 05552
65666. **Fax** 05552
656665. **www**.pego.at

PRIVATE HOMES

Mitwohnzentrale
Westbahnstrasse 19,
A-1070. **Map** 3 A2.
Tel 4026061.
Fax 402606111.

CHAIN HOTELS

Austria Hotels Hotel de France
Schottenring 3, A-1010.
Map 2 D4. **Tel** 313680.
Fax 3195969.
www.hoteldefrance.at

Austria Trend Parkhotel Schönbrunn
Hietzinger Hauptstrasse
10–20, A-1131.
Tel 87804. **Fax** 878043220.
www.austria-trend.at

Clima Cityhotel
Theresianumg 21a,
A-1040. **Map** 4 E4.
Tel 5051696. **Fax** 5043552.
www.climacity-hotel.com

Hilton Vienna
Am Stadtpark, A-1030.
Tel 717000. **Fax** 7130691.
www.hilton.com

Hotel Ibis Wien Mariahilf
Mariahilfer Gürtel 22–24,
A-1060. **Tel** 59998.
Fax 5979090.
www.ibishotel.com

The Imperial Riding School Vienna, A Renaissance Hotel
Ungargasse 60, A-1030.

Map 4 F1. **Tel** 711750.
Fax 711758143.
www.renaissance
hotels.com

Johann Strauss
Favoritenstrasse 12,
A-1040. **Map** 4 D3.
Tel 5057624. **Fax** 5057628.
www.hotel-johann-strauss.at

Novotel Wien West
Am Auhof, A-1140. **Tel**
97925420. **Fax** 9794140.
www.accorhotels.com

SAS Palais Hotel
Parkring 16, A-1010. **Map**
4 E1 & 6 E4. **Tel** 515170.
Fax 5122216.
www.radissonsas.com

Sofitel Hotel Vienna
Am Heumarkt 35–37,
A-1030. **Tel** 716160.
Fax 71616844.
www.accorhotels.com

Wien Hotel Renaissance
Ullmannstrasse 71, A-1150.
Tel 89102. **Fax** 89102300.
www.renaissance
hotels.com

Choosing a Hotel

The hotels listed here have been selected across a wide price range for their good value, facilities and location. All areas and price categories are covered, and there is additional information to help you choose. Under each area, hotels are listed in alphabetical order within each price category. For map references, *see pp262–5.*

PRICE CATEGORIES
Price categories for a double room with bathroom per night, including tax and service

€ Under €75
€€ €75–110
€€€ €110–145
€€€€ €145–200
€€€€€ over €200

STEPHANSDOM QUARTER

Pension Christina €€
Hafnersteig 7, 1010 **Tel** *533 29 61* **Fax** *533 29 61 11* **Rooms** *33* **Map** *2 E5, 6 E2*

Located on a quiet, cobbled side street just within the Stephansdom Quarter, this small unassuming pension is decorated in Art Deco style. Its larger-sized rooms feature proper baths. It is a friendly kind of place where you will be offered a cup of coffee on your arrival. **www.pertschy.com**

Post €€
Fleischmarkt 24, 1010 **Tel** *515 83 0* **Fax** *515 83 80 8* **Rooms** *107* **Map** *2 E5, 6 D2*

Located on the site of a former inn patronized by Mozart, Richard Wagner and Friedrich Nietzsche, this traditional hotel has rooms in contemporary style. There are also business rooms with broadband Internet access, and a restaurant/café. Wheelchair accessible. **www.hotel-post-wien.at**

Am Schubertring €€€
Schubertring 11, 1010 **Tel** *717 02 0* **Fax** *713 99 66* **Rooms** *36* **Map** *2 F5, 6 D5*

This Ringstrasse-style building contains one of the few Jugendstil hotels in the city. The bedrooms have thick carpets and high-quality reproduction furniture. Some bedrooms are furnished in Jugendstil fashion with dark wood, others in lighter Biedermeier style. Quiet rooms at the back are available. Pets are permitted. **www.schubertring.at**

Austria €€€
Fleischmarkt 20, 1010 **Tel** *515 23* **Fax** *515 23 506* **Rooms** *46* **Map** *2 E4, 6 D2*

Up a cul-de-sac and close to the Old University is this roomy hotel with high ceilings. A plus point is that it is extremely quiet. Downstairs are a few small sitting rooms and a breakfast room with a fountain. The bedrooms are spacious and have modern furniture and decent, old-fashioned bathrooms. **www.hotelaustria-wien.at**

Domizil €€€
Schulerstrasse 14, 1010 **Tel** *513 31 99 0* **Fax** *512 34 84* **Rooms** *40* **Map** *2 E5, 6 D3*

Located in central Vienna, near shops, restaurants and a casino, this is a traditional Viennese hotel. Room amenities include a TV, Telephone, mini-bar, and in-room safe. A bar is also on site and bicycles are for rent. The staff are friendly and accommodating. Pets are permitted. Wheelchair accessible. **www.hoteldomizil.at**

Hotel Schweizerhof €€€
Bauernmarkt 22, 1010 **Tel** *533 19 31* **Fax** *533 02 14* **Rooms** *55* **Map** *6 D2*

This family-run hotel, close to St Stephen's Cathedral, aims to spoil its guests with first class service. The friendly staff will organise concert and opera tickets, city tours, restaurant reservations and car rentals, and children under 16 stay free of charge in a room with their parents. **www.schweizerhof.at**

Hotel Tigra €€€
Tiefer Graben 14-20, 1010 **Tel** *533 96 41 0* **Fax** *533 96 45* **Rooms** *79* **Map** *2 D5, 5 C2*

Located close to Stephansdom, this hotel is located in a historic building which once housed Mozart, as a plaque on the building makes clear. The rooms, however, have been completely modernized. Pets are permitted. Children under the age of 12 can stay for free when accompanied by two adults. **www.bestwestern.at**

Kärntnerhof €€€
Grashofgasse 4, 1011 **Tel** *512 19 23* **Fax** *513 22 28 39* **Rooms** *43* **Map** *2 E5, 6 E3*

A few cafés adjoin this well-run hotel in a cul-de-sac. A gate at the end leads to the lovely Heiligenkreuzerhof where you can park a car. The 19th-century building's best feature behind its imposing façade is a fine Art Deco elevator, enclosed within a spiral staircase. Breakfast is served in rustic, beamed surroundings. **www.kartnerhof.com**

Marc Aurel €€€
Marc-Aurel Strasse 8, 1010 **Tel** *533 36 40 0* **Fax** *533 00 78* **Rooms** *31* **Map** *2 E5, 6 D2*

This smaller hotel offers simple but comfortable rooms as well as an on-site restaurant, café and, in the summer, a garden to dine in. All the rooms can be rented monthly at a discount price. rooms with a kitchenette are also available. Pets are permitted. Wheelchair accessible. **www.hotel-marcaurel.com**

Key to Symbols *See back cover flap*

Zur Wiener Staatsoper

Krugerstrasse 11, 1010 **Tel** *513 12 74* **Fax** *513 12 74 15* **Rooms** *22*   **Map** *4 E1, 6 D5*

A tall, thin 19th-century building on a pedestrian street off Kärntner Strasse houses this small hotel. Its façade is great fun, with caryatids over the porch and faces peering out of the plaster-work above. Inside, the breakfast room, bedrooms and bathrooms (all with showers) are squeezed into the space available. **www.zurwiener-staatsoper.at**

Capricorno

Schwedenplatz 3-4, 1010 **Tel** *533 31 04 0* **Fax** *533 76 71 0* **Rooms** *46*   **Map** *2 E5, 6 E2*

Located close to shops as well as to the subway, this hotel offers elegantly appointed rooms, most of which feature a balcony. Room amenities include Internet access. The staff are very helpful and friendly and are available round the clock. Wheelchair accessible. **www.schick-hotels.com**

Hotel am Parkring

Parkring 12, 1015 **Tel** *51 48 00* **Fax** *51 48 04 0* **Rooms** *58*   **Map** *4 E1, 6 E4*

Located on the "Ring" in the upper floors of a building, this hotel offers a magnificent view of the city below. Most rooms include either a balcony or a terrace where you can enjoy a quiet moment to yourself. The hotel's restaurant features fine brandies and an assortment of Austrian wines *(see p212)*. Pets are permitted. **www.bestwestern.at**

Mailberger Hof

Annagasse 7, 1010 **Tel** *512 06 41* **Fax** *512 06 41 10* **Rooms** *40*   **Map** *4 E1, 6 D4*

This is a lovely hotel that is converted from medieval houses. You can dine in the striking vaulted restaurant or, in the summer, in the garden under parasols. A wide, stone staircase leads to the bedrooms; most overlook the courtyard, are tastefully furnished and have plenty of space. **www.mailbergerhof.at**

Schlosshotel Römischer Kaiser

Annagasse 16, 1010 **Tel** *512 77 51 0* **Fax** *512 77 51 13* **Rooms** *24*   **Map** *4 E1, 6 D4*

This terraced house, a classic example of a Viennese miniature Baroque palace, was built for the imperial chancellor in 1684. Stylish public rooms, with chandeliers and rugs on tiles, occupy the ground floor. Upstairs, the bedrooms are cheerful and airy. There are also less expensive attic rooms. Bicycles can be rented. **www.hotel-roemischer-kaiser.at**

Starlight Suiten Hotel Salzgries

Salgries 12, 1010 **Tel** *535 92 22* **Fax** *535 92 22 11* **Rooms** *50*   **Map** *2 E5, 6 D2*

Available here are home-like suites, each with a living room, bedroom, bathroom and work area, and a mini-bar, microwave oven, telephones and TVs – ideal for a longer-term stay. Café and sauna on site. Wheelchair accessible. Children up to the age of six can stay for free when accompanied by their parents. **www.starlighthotels.com**

Wandl

Peterplatz 9, 1010 **Tel** *534 55 0* **Fax** *534 55 77* **Rooms** *138*   **Map** *2 D5, 5 C3*

This charming, old-fashioned hotel is located close to Peterskirche and has been in the same family for generations. Some of the building's finer stuccoed features are in a few of the bedrooms and in the covered courtyard that serves as a breakfast room. Other rooms are more simple but large, and feature parquet floors. **www.hotel-wandl.com**

Am Stephansplatz

Stephansplatz 9, 1010 **Tel** *534 05 0* **Fax** *534 05 71 0* **Rooms** *56*   **Map** *2 E5, 6 D3*

This hotel features rooms in a sleek, modern style with dark, parquet floors and light-coloured furniture. It was re-designed in 2005, using ecologically friendly building materials. Taking this a step further, the hotel uses high-quality Grander water throughout for all purposes. Wheelchair accessible. **www.hotelamstephansplatz.at**

Kaiserin Elisabeth

Weihburggasse 3, 1010 **Tel** *512 26 0* **Fax** *515 26 7* **Rooms** *63*   **Map** *4 E1, 6 D4*

This fetching townhouse is located on a side street close to Stephansdom. It dates from the 14th century and in the 1800s played host to many famous musicians such as Wagner and Liszt. The *fin-de-siècle*-style bedrooms are smart, and Persian rugs lie on parquet floors in the public rooms. Pets are permitted. **www.kaiserinelisabeth.at**

K&K Palais

Rudolfsplatz 11, 1010 **Tel** *533 13 53* **Fax** *533 13 53 70* **Rooms** *66*   **Map** *2 E4, 6 D1*

Canary yellow walls abound in this successful, modern establishment that is set within a fine 19th-century building. An impressive, glass-fronted lobby leads to a smart breakfast room and bar, and up a marble staircase to simple, fresh bedrooms. The hotel is situated on a quiet, grassy square in a business area. **www.kkhotels.com**

König von Ungarn

Schulerstrasse 10, 1010 **Tel** *515 84 0* **Fax** *515 84 8* **Rooms** *33*   **Map** *2 E5, 6 D3*

In this quality hotel, framed signatures of famous visitors from past centuries cover the walls and Mozart is said to have composed *The Marriage of Figaro* here. The covered central courtyard, with its elegant bar/sitting room, is one of Vienna's loveliest. Most bedrooms are large with appealing rustic furniture. **www.kvu.at**

Palais Coburg

Coburgbastei 4, 1010 **Tel** *518 18 0* **Fax** *518 18 100* **Rooms** *35*   **Map** *6 E4*

Located in an architecturally stunning old-world building dating from the 1800s, this is an elegant hotel which was reopened in 2003 after extensive restoration work and now offers 35 suites of varying size. There is also a unique rooftop spa, which includes an indoor pool. Pets are permitted. **www.palaiscoburg.at**

Radisson SAS Palais Hotel

Parkring 16, 1010 **Tel** *515 17 0* **Fax** *512 22 16* **Rooms** *247*

Map *4 E1, 6 E4*

Located across from the Stadtpark and housed in a former Viennese palace, this hotel offers tastefully appointed rooms with amenities that include heated bathroom floors. Also provided are a sauna and a spa that offers massages and other beauty treatments. Pets are permitted. Wheelchair accessible. **www.radissonsas.com**

Vienna Marriott

Parkring 12a, 1010 **Tel** *515 18 0* **Fax** *515 18 67 36* **Rooms** *313*

Map *4 D1, 6 E4*

Numerous shops, cafés, bars and restaurants *(see p212)* fill the open-plan atrium of this modern glass hotel on the Ringstrasse. The hotel lacks a dedicated business centre, but it does have business facilities and a swimming pool. The bedrooms are large; some rooms may be noisier than others. **www.viennamarriott.com**

HOFBURG QUARTER

Pertschy

Habsburgergasse 5, 1010 **Tel** *534 49 0* **Fax** *534 49 49* **Rooms** *55*

Map *2 D5, 5 C3*

This pension combines simple decor with features of a 300-year-old building. You enter a courtyard through ancient gates and ascend a wide, stone staircase. A walkway connects the bedrooms, which have Rococo-style furnishings. The breakfast room is decorated in dark wood in coffee house style. Pets are permitted. **www.pertschy.com**

Graben

Dorotheergasse 3, 1010 **Tel** *512 15 31 0* **Fax** *512 15 31 20* **Rooms** *41*

Map *4 D1, 5 C4*

An inn since the 18th century, the Graben has attracted literary figures such as Franz Kafka and Max Brod. Today, it features comfortable rooms with stylish Italian furniture. There is also a business centre, where you can check your emails, and a pizzeria and Italian restaurant. Pets are permitted. **www.kremslehnerhotels.at**

Pension Nossek

Graben 17, 1010 **Tel** *533 70 41 0* **Fax** *535 36 46* **Rooms** *31*

Map *2 D5, 5 C3*

You will need to book well in advance to obtain a room with a balcony overlooking the Graben in this elegant, but simple, family-run pension that is spread over three floors. Most bedrooms have basic bathrooms, but rugs cover the parquet floors and period furniture and tasteful paintings abound. **www.pension-nossek.at**

Ambassador

Neuer Markt 5, 1010 **Tel** *961 610* **Fax** *513 299 9* **Rooms** *86*

Map *4 D1, 6 D4*

Vienna's best located five-star hotel has a 19th-century façade looking on to Kärntner Strasse, with an *al fresco* café terrace. Marble pillars, tapestries and chandeliers add to the hotel's regal magnificence. Some of the bedrooms have their own sitting rooms, which are screened behind heavy drapes. Wheelchair accessible. **www.ambassador.at**

Astoria

Kärntner Strasse 32-34, 1015 **Tel** *515 77* **Fax** *515 77 58 2* **Rooms** *118*

Map *5 C4*

This is a cosy turn-of-the-century hotel. The panelled Jugendstil foyer leads to a grand dining room on the first floor. There are some splendid bedrooms, many of which feature their own brass letter boxes. It is worth going to this hotel for the extra space and the interesting period furnishings. **www.austria-trend.at/asw**

Radisson SAS Style Hotel

Herrengasse 12, 1010 **Tel** *22 78 0* **Fax** *22 78 07 7* **Rooms** *78*

Map *2 D5, 5 B2*

Conveniently located, this hotel is in contemporary style and offers uniquely designed rooms with amenities that include a flat-panel LCD TV and a CD/DVD player. The hotel also provides free WiFi facilities as well as a sauna, massage parlour and beauty treatments. Pets are permitted. Wheelchair accessible. **www.style.vienna.radissonsas.com**

SCHOTTERING AND ALSERGRUND

Arcotel Boltzmann

Boltzmanngasse 8, 1090 **Tel** *316 12 0* **Fax** *316 12 81 6* **Rooms** *70*

Map *1 C3*

A small, charming hotel with all of the amenities of a four-star establishment, the Boltzmann is situated close to the romantic Strudelhof Steps. It is surrounded by gardens and parks and is a short ten-minute walk from the historic centre. The hotel also offers cosy rooms full of atmosphere and a private little garden. **www.arcotel.at**

Golderner Bär

Türkenstrasse 27, 1090 **Tel** *317 51 11* **Fax** *31 75 11 122* **Rooms** *27*

Map *1 C4*

This is a simple but comfortable small hotel located close to the "Ring". Here you can enjoy a peaceful night's rest in a room designed and decorated in modern style and with sound-proof windows. Amenities include free Internet access. The staff are particularly friendly and helpful. **www.goldbaerhotel.com**

Key to Price Guide *see p194* **Key to Symbols** *see back cover flap*

Mozart ⎙ €€
Nordbergstrasse 4, 1090 **Tel** *317 15 37* **Fax** *317 24 77* **Rooms** *56* **Map** *1 C2*

Housed in a building that served as quarters for Allied troops after World War II, this hotel uniquely features water that is heated using solar energy. The rooms are tastefully decorated and have contemporary furniture. A private house bar is available. Pets are permitted. Wheelchair accessible. **www.hotelmozart-vienna.at**

Hotel Harmonie ⎙ P ⏸ €€€
Harmoniegasse 5-7, 1090 **Tel** *317 66 04* **Fax** *317 66 04 55* **Rooms** *68* **Map** *1 C3*

Situated in a quiet location, this hotel offers friendly service. Rooms are simple but comfortable, and are designed in a modern style. There is a café and bar, and the staff will assist you in obtaining tickets to concerts. Pets are permitted. Children under the age of 12 can stay for free when accompanied by two adults. **www.bestwestern.at**

Regina ⎙ ▤ ⏸ ✦ €€€€
Rooseveltplatz 15, 1096 **Tel** *404 46 0* **Fax** *408 83 92* **Rooms** *164* **Map** *1 C4, 5 A1*

The inside of this hotel has a certain grandeur, with brass chandeliers and classical statues. The building has been a hotel since 1896 and in the restaurant there is a photo of its staff in 1913. Today, the hotel caters mainly to tourist groups. The old-fashioned bedrooms are plain but comfortable. **www.kremslehenerhotels.at**

MUSEUM AND TOWNHALL QUARTER

Academia ⎙ €
Pfeilgasse 3a, 1080 **Tel** *401 76 55* **Fax** *401 76 20* **Rooms** *72* **Map** *1 A5*

During the academic year, this establishment serves as a student residence. However, during the summer break (July 1 to September 30), it opens its doors to the public as a hotel. The rooms are modern and airy, and have a telephone, and some include a balcony. Wheelchair accessible. **www.academia-hotels.co.at**

Arpi P €
Kochgasse 15, 1080 **Tel** *405 00 33* **Fax** *40 50 03 337* **Rooms** *20* **Map** *1 B4*

This is a family-owned, centrally located hotel that was renovated recently and features rooms in contemporary style. The staff are friendly and will assist you in obtaining tickets to theatres and concerts; they can also help you with arranging sightseeing tours of the city. **www.hotelarpi.com**

Hotel Korotan ⎙ P ✦ €
Albertgasse 48, 1080 **Tel** *403 41 93* **Fax** *403 41 93 99* **Rooms** *61* **Map** *1 A5*

This smaller hotel has an extremely modern and airy style, and friendly staff. All rooms have access to the Internet. Also on the premises are a chapel, library and gallery, making the hotel more of an experience than just a place to sleep. Wheelchair accessible. **www.hotel.korotan.com**

Alpha ⎙ P ⏸ €€€
Buchfeldgasse 8, 1080 **Tel** *403 52 91* **Fax** *403 52 91 62* **Rooms** *58* **Map** *1 B5*

Near the centre of the city, close to the Austrian Parliament building, this is a simple and modern hotel with newly renovated rooms in a modern and comfortable style. The breakfast room is light and airy. Internet access is available in the public areas. Wheelchair accessible. **www.hotelalpha.at**

Museum ⎙ €€€
Museumstrasse 3, 1070 **Tel** *523 44 26* **Fax** *523 44 26 30* **Rooms** *15* **Map** *3 C1*

Behind a fine façade with wrought-iron balconies, and set above a cinema, is this classic Viennese pension. It is right on the doorstep of the main museums. The spartan, but massive, bedrooms have high ceilings and wooden floors, and the sitting and breakfast rooms have ornate fireplaces and chandeliers. **www.hotelmuseum.at**

Zipser ⎙ P €€€
Lange Gasse 49, 1080 **Tel** *404 54 0* **Fax** *404 54 13* **Rooms** *53* **Map** *1 B5*

This pension in the Josefstadt area has smart modern carpets and furniture throughout, and the atmosphere is very friendly. Ask for one of the larger, quieter bedrooms at the rear of the hotel; they have excellent bathrooms and big wooden balconies, which are high up and overlook an attractive leafy courtyard. **www.zipser.at**

Altstadt Vienna ⎙ €€€€
Kirchengasse 41, 1070 **Tel** *522 66 66* **Fax** *523 40 01* **Rooms** *42* **Map** *3 B1*

Situated in an interesting old quarter just west of the main museums, this hotel in a 19th-century patrician house is an extremely popular place to stay. Designer lighting, boldly coloured walls, and striking modern furnishings bring life to the ample rooms. The bedrooms at the rear of the hotel are peaceful. Excellent service. **www.altstadt.at**

Cordial Theaterhotel Wien ▦ ⛭ P ⏸ ✦ €€€€
Josefstädter Strasse 22, 1080 **Tel** *405 36 48 0* **Fax** *405 14 06* **Rooms** *54* **Map** *1 A5*

Simple but comfortable rooms are to be found at this hotel, close to the Josefstadt Theater. The hotel also has a bar, sauna and solarium. Breakfast can be served in your room for a small, additional fee and the friendly staff will assist you in planning any excursions in and around Vienna. Wheelchair accessible. **www.cordial.at**

Mercure Josefshof Wien   🔲 🗏 🛗   €€€€
Josefsgasse 4-6, 1080 **Tel** *404 19* **Fax** *404 19 15 0* **Rooms** *121*   **Map** *1 B5*

This hotel is on a quiet back street, close to Vienna's English Theatre. There is a marble and glass entry hallway, and the bedrooms are smart with high-quality reproduction furniture and parquet flooring. Pets are permitted. Children under the age of 12 can stay for free when accompanied by an adult. Wheelchair accessible. **www.josefshof.com**

Rathaus   🔲 P 🛗   €€€€
Lange Gasse 13, 1080 **Tel** *400 11 22* **Fax** *400 11 22 88* **Rooms** *40*   **Map** *1 B5*

Located in a historic townhouse in Josefstadt, but with a modern interior, the Rathaus is dedicated to wine and wine culture. Each luxurious double room is named after an Austrian vintner (whose wines are in the mini-bar) and is stocked with wine cosmetics. The service is excellent; expect to be pampered. **www.hotel-rathaus-wien.at**

OPERA AND NASCHMARKT

Terminus Hotel   🔲   €€
Fillgradergasse 4, 1060 **Tel** *587 73 86 0* **Fax** *587 73 86 76* **Rooms** *41*   **Map** *3 C2*

Located close to the subway, this is a smaller hotel that offers adequate accommodation with the usual range of amenities, such as a TV and telephone. Each room is decorated in a different style. The staff are helpful and pleasant. In the lobby there are vending machines selling a variety of items. Pets are permitted.

Hotel Beethoven   🔲 P 🗏 🛗   €€€€
Millöckergasse 6, 1060 **Tel** *587 44 82 0* **Fax** *587 44 42* **Rooms** *36*   **Map** *3 C2*

In this stylishly decorated and conveniently located hotel, which is situated across the street from the Theater an der Wien, you can enjoy professional and friendly service. Internet access is available in the rooms and the staff will assist you in obtaining tickets to the theatre and concerts. Pets are permitted. **www.hotel-beethoven.at**

Le Meridien Vienna   🔲 🍴 🍽 P 🗏 🔢 🛗   €€€€€
Opernring 13-15, 1010 **Tel** *588 90* **Fax** *588 90 90 90* **Rooms** *294*   **Map** *4 D1, 5 B5*

This elegant hotel has rooms that are tastefully decorated in shades of blue, green and pink. In addition to the standard amenities, bathrobes, slippers and umbrellas are provided. There is also a wellness centre with Jacuzzi, sauna and steam room. Pets are permitted. Expect a first-class stay here. **www.lemeridien.com**

Sacher   🔲 🍴 P 🗏 🔢 🛗   €€€€€
Philharmonikerstrasse 4, 1010 **Tel** *514 56 0* **Fax** *514 56 81 0* **Rooms** *109*   **Map** *4 D1, 5 C5*

Since 1876, the Sacher has been a haunt for the wealthy. Now its café is full of tourists and locals who stop by for a slice of their famous chocolate *Sacher Torte (see p215)*. Both the public rooms and more expensive bedrooms are opulent; even the standard rooms have a regal air. The staff provide outstanding service. **www.sacher.com**

BELVEDERE QUARTER

Suzanne   🔲 🗏   €€
Walfischgasse 4, 1010 **Tel** *513 25 07* **Fax** *513 25 00* **Rooms** *26*   **Map** *4 D1, 6 D5*

This popular pension is just a few steps from the Kärntner Strasse and the Opera House. It is above a couple of local shops. However, the bedrooms, with paintings and comfortable armchairs, have old-fashioned charm and are spread over a number of floors. The more expensive rooms have kitchenettes. **www.pension-suzanne.at**

Clima Cityhotel   🔲 P   €€€
Theresianumgasse 21a, 1040 **Tel** *515 16 96* **Fax** *504 35 52* **Rooms** *37*   **Map** *4 E4*

Quiet despite its central location, this hotel offers a great view of the city from the upper floors. Its sleek and airy bedrooms, with good-sized bathrooms, ensure a comfortable and relaxing stay. The staff are friendly and will assist you in obtaining tickets to events. **www.climacity-hotel.com**

Hotel Erzherzog Rainer   🔲 P 🔢 🛗   €€€
Wiedner Hauptstrasse 27-29, 1040 **Tel** *221 11 1* **Fax** *221 11 35 0* **Rooms** *84*   **Map** *3 C5*

This conveniently located hotel, near the Künstlerhaus, offers traditional Austrian hospitality. The large rooms are decorated tastefully and are quiet as they have sound-proof windows. There is also a comfortable coffee house and bar in which to relax *(see p215)*. Pets are permitted. **www.bestwestern.at**

Hotel Kaiserhof Wien   🔲 🍴 P 🗏 🛗   €€€€
Frankenberggasse 10, 1040 **Tel** *505 17 01* **Fax** *505 88 75 88* **Rooms** *74*   **Map** *4 D2*

In a central location, this hotel offers tastefully decorated and elegant rooms, all with modern conveniences and some with WiFi Internet access. Pleasant staff are also on hand. For exercise buffs, there is a fitness room, sauna, steam room and sanarium, which features special coloured mood lighting. **www.bestwestern.at**

Bristol

Kärntner Ring 1, 1015 **Tel** *515 16 0* **Fax** *515 16 55 0* **Rooms** *140*   **Map** *4 D2, 6 D5*

The Bristol is a very luxurious hotel. The location is also excellent: on the Ringstrasse and opposite the Opera. Marble, gilt, antiques and paintings are everywhere, creating an atmosphere of dignified opulence. The bedrooms include top-floor penthouses and superb business suites. Wheelchair accessible. **www.starwoodhotels.com**

Imperial

Kärntner Ring 16, 1015 **Tel** *501 10 0* **Fax** *501 10 41 0* **Rooms** *138*   **Map** *4 D2, 6 D5*

The grandest of Vienna's top hotels exudes an air of exclusivity and, if you stay here, you may well be sleeping under the same roof as a head of state or two. In the 1950s, two extra floors were added, containing smaller rooms designed in cherry wood. Small pets are permitted. Wheelchair accessible. **www.imperial.viennahotels.it**

FURTHER AFIELD

Lindenhof

Breitenleer Strasse 256, 1220 **Tel** *734 36 37* **Fax** *734 29 80* **Rooms** *24*

Family-owned since 1928, this is a cosy hostelry in a 15th-century building that provides old-world hospitality and simple, but comfortable, rooms. There are also ample dining facilities, including an indoor restaurant and outdoor terrace. Live music and other events take place here occasionally. **www.lindenhof-breitenlee.com**

Roter Hahn

Landstrasser Hauptstrasse 40, 1030 **Tel** *713 25 68 0* **Fax** *713 25 68 19 0* **Rooms** *48*   **Map** *6 F4*

This hotel is in a historic national monument. Each room is uniquely decorated and has a full range of amenities. The staff will provide assistance in obtaining tickets to sights and events in town. There is also a separate luggage room. Pets are permitted. Wheelchair accessible.

Gartenhotel Glanzing

Glanzinggasse 23, 1190 **Tel** *470 42 72 0* **Fax** *470 42 72 14* **Rooms** *14*

Built in the 1930s, this interesting ivy-festooned hotel has a rambling garden and stands in leafy suburbs close to the wine villages. It also features big bedrooms and a grand piano in its main room. Pets are permitted. Children under the age of 15 can stay for free when accompanied by an adult. **www.gartenhotel-glanzing.at**

Hotel Fürstenhof

Neubaugürtel 4, 1060 **Tel** *523 32 67* **Fax** *523 32 67 26* **Rooms** *58*

Very friendly service and clean and comfortable rooms are provided by this family-run hotel that is housed in an early 20th-century building. The recently renovated rooms are decorated in both traditional and contemporary styles, and some have chandeliers. Worth a visit. **www.hotel-fuerstenhof.com**

Hotel Jäger

Hernalser Hauptstrasse 187, 1170 **Tel** *486 66 20 0* **Fax** *486 66 20 8* **Rooms** *17*

Owned and operated by the Jäger family for over 90 years, this cosy hotel offers first-class and friendly service in a traditional Austrian environment. The accommodation includes apartments with a kitchen. Pets are permitted. Children under the age of 12 can stay for free when accompanied by two adults. **www.hoteljaeger.at**

Hotel Stefanie

Taborstrasse 12, 1020 **Tel** *211 50* **Fax** *211 50 16 0* **Rooms** *122*   **Map** *2 F4, 6 E1*

Dating back to 1703, this is the oldest 4-star hotel in Vienna. It is also conveniently located close to Stephansdom. Designed in Classic Viennese or contemporary style, all the bedrooms are comfortable. WiFi Internet access is available in some, as well as in public areas. Pets are permitted. Wheelchair accessible. **www.schick-hotels.com**

Landhaus Fuhrgassl-Huber

Neustift am Walde, Rathstrasse 24, 1190 **Tel** *440 30 33* **Fax** *440 27 14* **Rooms** *38*

This family-run quaint hotel lies in a typical Austrian wine village. There is a *Heuriger (see p201)* next door, and the hotel owner has his own *Heuriger* just up the street. The hotel is prettily decked out in pine, with tiled floors and stencilled furniture. A bus to Vienna is available just outside the hotel. **www.fuhrgassl-huber.at**

Mercure Grand Hotel Biedermeier Wien

Landstrasser Hauptstrasse 28, 1030 **Tel** *716 71 0* **Fax** *716 71 50 3* **Rooms** *203*   **Map** *4 F1*

This hotel occupies the whole complex of a superbly restored Biedermeier passage courtyard that lies off one of Vienna's main shopping streets. The large, spacious bedrooms, almost all looking down on the cobbled passage, are particularly quiet. Bicycles are available to rent. Pets are permitted. Wheelchair accessible. **www.accor.com**

Inter-Continental Wien

Johannesgasse 28, 1037 **Tel** *711 22 0* **Fax** *713 44 89* **Rooms** *453*   **Map** *4 E1, 6 E5*

The Inter-Continental is a modern and cosmopolitan chain hotel, just a two-minute walk from the Ringstrasse. Classical music is played nightly in the bar area of the elegant, chandeliered foyer, and the upper-floor bedrooms have good views across the Stadtpark. Wheelchair accessible. **www.vienna.intercontinental.com**

RESTAURANTS, CAFÉS AND BARS

The Viennese know how to eat well. The staples of Vienna's cuisine are assimilated from the cooking styles of the Habsburg Empire, and so include *Schnitzels*, originating as North Italian escalopes; dumplings that are a speciality of Bohemia; Hungarian goulash; and even Balkan grills and sausages (*Cevapcici*). Balkan cuisine is a result of the post-Second World War immigration that has multiplied the ethnic cuisines now available in the city. The range of gastronomy is vast, from gourmet nouvelle cuisine down to the booths *(Würstelstände)* selling sausages and beer on street corners. You can take your choice of atmosphere from old-fashioned sumptuous splendour to tavern gardens or Baroque wine-cellars. Mealtimes are also flexible and in the city centre you will always find somewhere serving hot meals between 11:30 a.m. and midnight. The listings *(see pp 210–17)* are divided by area and by price, with the emphasis being on local cuisine, but there is a generous choice of alternatives as well.

Papier-mâché waitress outside restaurant

TYPES OF EATING PLACE

The humble *Würstelstände* sell hot dogs and *Leberkäse* (only for the adventurous) which is somewhat alarmingly described as "meat remnants worked into an undefined formless mass". On a slightly higher gastronomic level are the numerous small eateries selling sandwiches, filled rolls, pastries and soft drinks. Mouth-watering open sandwiches are the speciality of **Duran** (several outlets, *see p218*) and the celebrated **Trzesniewski** *(see p218)*, with a coffee or a miniature Pfiff (⅛ of a litre) of beer to accompany them.

Wine cellar sign

If something a little more sustaining is required, the numerous *Stehbeisln* (stand-up counters) at some butchers' and food stores offer fresh dishes and sometimes a welcome bowl of hot soup on a winter's day. Some upmarket restaurants advertise a *Gabelfrühstück* (fork breakfast) serving hot delicacies mid-morning. Another extra repast discovered by the Viennese is the *Jause*, typically cold meats and cheese eaten outside regular mealtimes. All these options are preferable for the budget-conscious traveller to the museum restaurants and cafés which, however good, tend to be more expensive.

Local musician at the Augustinerkeller *(see p218)*

Many self-service restaurants offer a wide selection of cold and hot dishes, including grills made to order, and can be recommended. Among them is **Markt-Restaurant Rosenberger**, which is located in Maysedergasse behind the Opera House. Others can be found in the Ringstrassen shopping mall. Some close early so are better for a quick lunch, while a bustling coffee-house or wine-cellar might be more appealing in the evenings.

WINE CELLARS AND HEURIGEN

Wine cellars represent good value, with cold buffets and a limited range of hot dishes on offer to

Open sandwiches available at Zum Schwarzen Kameel *(see p214)*

accompany local wine from the barrel. The atmosphere is informal, and even more so in the gardens of the *Heurigen* (taverns) in the villages at the periphery of the city at Neustift am Walde, Grinzing, Salmannsdorf, and elsewhere. In theory, *Heurigen* serve only the wine from their own vineyards and of the current vintage. *Heuriger* has two meanings: it refers to the youngest available vintage of the local wine and it also refers to the venues that sell such wines by the glass. According to regulations laid down by Emperor Joseph II, pine twigs placed over or by the door (*ausg'steckt*) remained as long as the vintage lasted, after which they were removed and the tavern closed for the year. You will still see such taverns, but in practice the larger ones are open all year and serve

Garden scene at a *Heuriger* where local wine growers are licensed to sell their own wine

Typical sausage stand (or *Wurst-stand*) in the city centre

an extensive buffet with hot and cold cuts of meat. The wine is mostly white, often a blend of local grapes (the *gemischter Satz*) and is a true *Heuriger* until 11th November of the year after harvest. To sample a genuine local product, look for *Eigenbau* by the entrance.

COFFEE HOUSES AND KONDITOREIEN

Vienna's legendary coffee houses (*see pp58–61*) are culturally specific: politicians favour **Landtmann**, whilst literati swap ideas in **Hawelka** (*see p218*). Coffee is served in different ways depending on the strength and addition of hot milk or water required.

Prices vary according to location and type: a Ringstraßen café is more expensive than a smoke-filled den with a billiard table at the rear, or somewhere like the **Café Ministerium** (*see p218*) patronised by the proverbially parsimonious bureaucrats from the nearby ministries.

While coffee houses serve a small range of simple hot dishes, the *Konditoreien* concentrate on pastries and cakes, though a few also do a good light lunch. The great *Konditoreien* in the centre can be rather a scrum in the tourist season, but the fare is irresistible (diabetics also catered for). Since there is a complicated nomenclature for the *Konditoreien* themselves, it is best to go to the display counter and point to the item you want. A cheaper alternative is the Aida chain found throughout Vienna, with less comfortable seating but lower prices, even for the *Sachertorte*.

THE VIENNESE BEISL

What the trattoria is to Italy the *Beisl* is to Vienna, a simple restaurant offering local specialities in an agreeably informal atmosphere. The name is thought to be of Jewish origin (in the 18th century,

many inn-keepers were Jewish). Unfortunately many *Beisln* have gone up-market and their prices have lifted accordingly. All of them serve typical Viennese specialities like *Tafelspitz* (boiled beef), *Vanillirostbraten* (pot roast with garlic), *Kalbsbeuschel* (calf's lung and heart) and of course *Schnitzel*, together with enticingly named desserts: *Powidltascherln* (pasta envelopes with plum jam) or *Zwetschkenknödel* (plums in potato dumpling). Viennese cooking is strong in the soup department, one of the more popular soups being *Eierschwammerlsuppe* made with chanterelle mushrooms. Huge portions of *Wiener Schnitzel* are served at **Figlmüller** (*see p210*).

The most aspiring *Beisln* should have just as good food as a mid-priced restaurant.

A trendy city bar, the Tunnel (*see p219*), on Florianigasse

The 7th-floor Do & Co restaurant *(see p212)*, with a splendid view of the Stephansdom

MID-PRICED AND ETHNIC RESTAURANTS

The top end of the *Beisln* merge with what Austrians somewhat misleadingly call "*gutbürgerliche Küche*", or "good plain cooking", since at many places so identified, such as **Zum Herkner** in outlying Hernals *(see p217)*, the food is more than good and rather sophisticated. Establishments like **Kern's Beisl** *(see p210)* and **Restaurant Sperl** *(see p215)* offer extremely good value, as do many of the ethnic restaurants throughout the city: **Beim Czaak** *(see p210)* with its roots in Bohemian cuisine, or the Hungarian **Ilona Stüberl** *(see p213)* in the Bräunerstraße. Some restaurants offer great value

One of the city's many *Café-Konditoreien*

because they only accept cash. The authentic Greek restaurants, such as **Kostas** *(see p215)*, also tend to be inexpensive. The same cannot always be said for the up-market Asian and Japanese restaurants and sushi bars that have enjoyed a boom over the last few years. Some are so popular that they are often booked weeks in advance. Among them are **Tenmaya** *(see p212)*, which offers a traditional Japanese setting, including women dressed in kimonos, and **Kim Kocht** *(see p217)*, which features a tempting gourmet food shop on the premises.

Pizza and pasta establishments are ubiquitous, but many of the genuine Italian restaurants tend to be found at the luxury end of the market. This may be at least partly due to the unique environments in which the food is served; in **Da Capo** *(see p210)*, an authentic wood burning oven is used to cook the pizzas and guests can dine in the restaurant's attractive cellar.

Vegetarian restaurants are slowly on the increase, and one of the longest established is **Wrenkh** *(see p212)*. Other restaurants gaining in popularity are those, such as **Cantino Restaurant**, which offer Spanish cuisine that includes authentic paella and tapas *(see p215)*, and Balkan and Turkish establishments. In **Restaurant Dubrovnik** *(see p216)*, guests can dine on Croatian specialties such as *pljeskavica* and other meals derived from south-east European recipes. Meanwhile, the restaurant **Aux Gazelles** *(see p215)* not only offers authentic French/Moroccan cuisine, but presents a whole North African experience, including Turkish steam baths and a café, bar, bazaar shop and nightclub.

LUXURY RESTAURANTS

Gourmet eating in Vienna generally retains a local flavour. Seriously good cuisines may be found at luxury hotels like the **Hotel Sacher** *(see p198)* or the **Imperial** *(see p216)*. The city's most prestigious restaurant for seafood is the **Kervansaray-Hummerbar** *(see p215)*, where fresh lobster, scallops and oysters can be had at a price and the menu changes daily. **Steirereck** *(see p217)*, which is located in the leafy surroundings of the Stadtpark, is still considered one of the best gourmet restaurants in the country. Its menus have a strong Austrian theme. In comparison, **Trattoria Martinelli** *(see p214)* serves traditional Tuscan specialties, which can be enjoyed in the Baroque ambience of the Harrach Palace.

Rote Bar, one of two restaurants at the luxurious Hotel Sacher

READING THE MENU

The three main divisions of the menu are *Kalte* or *Warme Vorspeisen* (cold or hot hors d'oeuvres), *Hauptspeisen* (main courses) and *Mehlspeisen* (desserts). There may be separate entries for soups (*Suppen*), fish (*Fisch*), beef (*Rindfleisch*) and pork (*Schweinefleisch*). Many restaurants have a children's menu and usually a selection of vegetarian dishes. Menus may change with the season to make use of the best and freshest produce, and the waiter will often tell you about the day's specialties (*Tagesangebot*) which are not usually mentioned on the standard menu. These are often worth ordering and can be particularly good value for money. You may also see the phrase *Fertige Speisen* for dishes that are not on the fixed-price menu. A specifically Austrian phrase frequently encountered is *Schmankerin*, which implies regional delicacies. Portions tend to be on the generous side, although there is a trend to lighter eating in the more up-market establishments offering nouvelle cuisine.

The house wines are usually served in glasses which hold exactly a quarter of a litre, though smaller glasses may also be served, and half a litre may come in a carafe. Most restaurants, at least in the city centre, have menus in English but if this is not the case, there is usually a member of staff who can help.

Traditional Austrian musicians in a garden restaurant

Sign for the famous Café-Konditorei Demel

HOW MUCH TO PAY

Vienna's restaurants generally represent good value for money. However over-indulgence in tempting little delicacies (*Leckerbissen*) can make a big dent in the wallet; small items like coffee are also relatively expensive and a cup in one of the congenial old coffee houses or *Konditoreien* costs around €2.5 to €3. Add in an alcoholic drink, such as apricot schnaps, and your costs could easily double. Snack meals and fast-food outlets provide adequate sustenance at around €5, while double that should buy a modest meal in one of the self-service restaurants or less touristy wine cellars. A reasonably priced *Beisl* might cost €20 a head with a glass of wine, but sticking to the fixed-price menu will probably reduce that significantly. There is a large middle swathe of restaurants where you might expect a bill of up to €36, while luxury and gourmet establishments have prices that accelerate well beyond the €40 mark. Prices can be more expensive in the evening or duing peak tourist seasons and holidays.

Most restaurants with a regular international clientele take credit cards, but many of the *Beisln* and standard Viennese restaurants only take cash. It is always best to check in advance as to the payment method accepted.

BOOKING AND SERVICE

Always telephone and confirm any special requests especially wheelchair access and facilities for the disabled, if non-smoking seats are available and whether children are catered for. Facilities may be limited and some of the older establish-ments may have narrow corridors or steps. Booking a day ahead or even on the day is usually sufficient. Even a simple *Beisl* can have a faithful local clientele and you may be disappointed if you wander in and expect to find a free table. Assiduous, service is the hallmark of many Viennese restaurants. Tips are traditionally 10% and are mandatory everywhere except in the few places where you may find that the service is included.

Restaurant in the Altwienerhof Hotel on Herklotzgasse

The Flavours of Vienna: Savoury Dishes

Austrian cuisine is a direct legacy of the country's imperial past, when culinary traditions from many parts of Europe influenced Viennese cooks. As a result, it is far more varied and flavoursome than most people realize. There are Italian and Adriatic influences, Polish- and Hungarian- inspired dishes, and even a rich seam of Balkan flavours running through much of the Austrian kitchen repertoire. *Schnitzel*, for example, may have come to Austria via Milan, which was once under Austrian control, while *Gulasch* is the Austrian version of a Hungarian dish that became popular in Vienna in the 19th century.

Chanterelle mushrooms

Cheese stall at a local Austrian farmers' market

MEAT, POULTRY & DAIRY

Beef is narrowly ahead of pork as the nation's favourite meat. Austrian cattle farmers have a long and proud heritage of producing fine beef, which is used in many dishes, such as paprika-rich *Gulasch*. That most famous of Austrian dishes, *Wiener Schnitzel*, is traditionally made with veal. Pork is used primarily to make hams and sausages. The classic Austrian way with pork is to cure it, smoke it and leave it to mature for months in the clean air of the high Alpine pastures. The result is called *Speck*. Lean *Speck* is similar to Italian *prosciutto*, though with a distinctive smoky tang, while fattier cuts are more like *pancetta* or streaky bacon. *Bratwurst*, made with beef, pork and veal, are Austria's preferred sausages, but other types such as *Frankfurters* are also common. Chicken is almost always served breaded *(Backhendl)*, but *Grillhendl* is a whole chicken roasted over an open fire, or on a spit. Duck *(Ente)* is often served with sweet sauces, but sometimes with sour accompaniments such as pickled red cabbage.

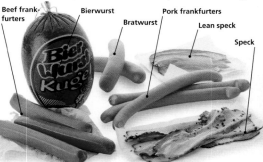

Beef frank-furters | Bierwurst | Bratwurst | Pork frankfurters | Lean speck | Speck

Selection of typical Austrian cured pork, sausages and salami

AUSTRIAN DISHES AND SPECIALITIES

Tafelspitz *is silverside of beef, boiled with root vegetables and served thickly sliced with gherkins and sauerkraut.*

While most classic Austrian dishes (especially those originating in Vienna) are found all over the country, there are some regional differences. *Knödel* are more popular in the east, as are carp, game and pork, while beef and lamb appear more often the further west (and higher up the mountains) you travel. Beef is essential for *Tafelspitz*, often called the national dish. *Speck* is used to make *Speck Knödel*, small, dense dumplings, but the one part of the pig that Austrians do love to eat uncured is the knuckle, called *Stelze*, roasted and served chopped with heaps of sauerkraut. *Fischgröstl* is a mix of fish and seafood, fried together with onion, potato and mince (usually leftovers). It is rarely found on menus, but you may be lucky enough to try it in an Austrian home.

Paprika

Spectacular array of vegetables on display in a Viennese market

Roast goose *(Gänsebraten)* is also popular, as are goose livers. The milk of Austrian dairy cows, grazed on sweet Alpine pastures, gives some excellent artisan cheeses, such as fruity Wälder.

FISH

While not great seafood lovers, Austrians have developed a number of their own fish dishes. Trout *(Forelle)* is the most popular fish, usually served grilled with boiled potatoes. Herring *(Hering)* is pickled and eaten as an appetizer. *Heringsschmaus*, a smoked herring and apple salad, is hugely popular at Easter. Carp *(Karpfen)* is a favourite Christmas dish, but is eaten all year, as is plaice *(Scholle* or *Goldbutt)*, which is often served with a rich vegetable-based sauce.

VEGETABLES

Vegetables in Austria are of the highest quality and so, while imported produce is available all year round, seasonality is still important to Austrians. That is truest of all

Bunches of pale spears of Austrian *Spargel* (asparagus)

for the nation's favourite, asparagus *(Spargel)*. Only local produce is used, and so is found on menus only during the harvesting season, from the end of April to early July. Austrians use asparagus in every way imaginable at this time of year. Wild mushrooms are another seasonal prize, especially chanterelles *(Eierschwammerl)*. Potatoes *(Erdäpfel)* feature widely, often in the form of *Knödel*. These are dumplings made of potatoes or stale white bread and are served with venison or pork dishes. White cabbage is often pickled *(Sauerkraut)* and red cabbage is served with venison and most game dishes.

SAVOURY SNACKS

Liptauer: Goat's or sheep's milk cheese is mixed with paprika, caraway seeds, capers, mustard, chives and onions to create this paste, a staple of Austrian wine bars.

Maroni: Roast chestnuts are a winter treat; the aroma of them, toasting over a brazier on a snowy day, is somehow quintessentially Vienna.

Blunzen: Blood sausage is marinated in vinegar and thinly sliced and served with brown bread. A popular "beer snack".

Schmaltzbrot: Brown bread spread thickly with beef or pork dripping, and eaten with onions and pickles.

Wiener Schnitzel *should classically be veal, breaded and fried. In Austria is is never served with sauce.*

Rindsgulasch *is the beef version of Hungarian goulash, a rich stew flavoured with paprika and caraway.*

Forelle Blau, *literally "blue trout", is made by poaching an unscaled fish in stock, which gives it a blueish hue.*

The Flavours of Vienna: Sweet Foods

Few cities in the world can rival Vienna's devotion to all things sweet. The Viennese enjoy cakes mid-morning or afternoon, and set aside time for between-meal snacks. The finest *torten* (gâteaux), pastries and cakes tend to be found in *Konditoreien (see p201)* and are usually consumed with a cup of coffee. Traditional Viennese desserts can be found in all good restaurants, and are typically rich. From the classic Viennese *Apfelstrudel* to *Gugelhupf* from the Tirol, Austrian desserts all carry a regional influence. In Vienna, pastries take pride of place while, to the west, the Italian influence is strong and cakes, ice creams and meringues are preferred.

Poppy seeds

Relaxing over coffee and cake in an elegant Viennese café

CAKES

The Austrian tradition of cake-baking goes back centuries, with competition fierce between towns and cities to produce the finest. Even in small villages, bakeries would try to outdo each other with their sweet creations. Almost every Austrian city now has its trademark cake, with its

citizens quick to boast that theirs is the best. The most famous Austrian cake is a Viennese creation, the *Sacher-torte*, a rich chocolate cake invented by chef Franz Sacher for Chancellor Metternich in 1832. The signature dish of many an Austrian chef, it should be the first cake the visitor tries – with so much choice on offer, it will be difficult to decide on the second. While the Viennese

rave about *Sachertorte*, over in Linz the locals insist their own *Linzertorte* – an almond based cake usually topped with raspberries – is superior. The people of Linz also say that the *Linzertorte* is older, dating back – legend has it – to the 17th century. Around the Hungarian border, they are proud of their *Dobostorte*, named for the Budapest chef who created it in the 19th century. Its layers of sponge

Linzertorte   Stollen   Sachertorte   Dobostorte   Esterházytorte

Some of the many mouthwatering Austrian cakes available

VIENNESE DESSERTS

From *Topfentascherl* (curd cheese envelopes) to *Kastaniereis* (chestnut purée), Vienna's dessert cuisine uses rich and varied ingredients. Fruits such as plums and apples fill featherlight dumplings, pancakes, fritters and strudels, and although *Mehlspeisen* (puddings) translates literally as "dishes without flour", ground hazelnuts or almonds can be used in its place. Nuts play a key role, especially hazels and pine nuts,

Hazelnuts

the latter often featuring in *Apfelstrudel*. More unusual desserts include sweet "pasta" served with poppyseeds to create *Mohnnudeln*, and *Bohmische Omeletten* (Bohemian omelettes) served with whipped cream and prune sauce. Conversely, *Palatschinken* may also be a savoury snack.

Mohr im Hemd, *a hazelnut and chocolate pudding, is served with chocolate sauce and whipped cream.*

Display of traditional pastries and cakes in a *Konditorei*

and chocolate butter cream are topped with a caramel glaze. From Salzburg, the cake of choice is baked meringue, known as *Salzburger Nockerl*, or Salzburg Soufflé. *Esterházy-torte* also features meringue, layered with a rich hazelnut cream. Stollen is a marzipan-filled fruit bread originally from Germany and now an integral part of an Austrian Christmas. Regional or not, you'll now find all these classic cakes in Vienna and across the country.

PASTRIES

In the perfect global village, a place on the main street would always be reserved for an Austrian pastry and coffee shop. That the French collective name for sweet pastry is *Viennoiserie* under-lines the noble Viennese

tradition of sweet baking. Austrian legend has it that the nation's café habit began when the Turks left all their coffee behind as they aban-doned Vienna after the failed siege of 1529. The *Kipfel*, a light, crescent-shaped pastry (which later became famous

Entrance to one of the world-famous Mozart chocolate shops

as the croissant) also dates from the time of the Turkish siege, its shape being based on the crescent moon in the Ottoman flag. While such symbolism is often lost today, the importance of the café in Austrian society is not. Modern-day Austrians view cafés as extensions of their home, and spend hours reading, chatting and even watching television in them. Treats on offer in cafés will generally include a classic *Apfelstrudel*, *Cremeschnitte* (slices of puff pastry filled with custard and glazed with strawberry fondant), and *Punschkrapferl*, a calorie-packed, pink-fondant-topped pastry laced with rum.

MOZARTKUGEL

Fine chocolates, presented in colourfully decorated boxes carrying the portrait of Mozart, are probably the quintessential Austrian souvenir. Known in Austria as *Mozartkugel*, the chocolates originated in Salzburg, where Mozart lived while composing *Cosi fan Tutti*, the opera in which he worships chocolate. In 1890, master confectioner Paul Fürst made the first Mozart choco-lates by forming small balls of marzipan which he coated in a praline cream and then dipped in warm chocolate. Viennese confectioners soon adopted the technique and even today producers vie with one another as to whose *Mozartkugel* are the best and most authentic.

Apfelstrudel *rolls paper-thin pastry with apple, sultanas, cinnamon and sometimes pine nuts or poppyseeds.*

Palatschinken *are fat, fluffy crêpes that may be filled with fruit or jam, or served with vanilla or chocolate sauce.*

Topfenknödel *are light curd cheese dumplings rolled in breadcrumbs and served with fruit compôte.*

What to Drink in Vienna

Austria is a source of excellent wine and good rich beers.

Vienna itself is a wine-growing region. It is surrounded by vineyards which supply the *Heurige (see p200–1)* in villages on the edge of the city with young local wines. Fine Austrian wines are found in good restaurants *(see* Choosing a Restaurant, *p210).* Home-produced wine is mainly white but there are some excellent local red wines, especially from the Burgenland and Carnuntum districts. Sweet *Eiswein* is made from grapes left on the vines until the first frosts. Fruit brandies and schnapps, many of them first class, are also produced.

Beyond the villages north and west of Vienna lie vineyards producing *Heurige* wines

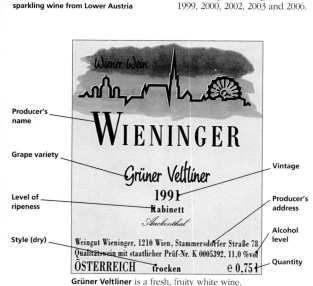

Chardonnay from Styria and sparkling wine from Lower Austria

AUSTRIAN WINES

The most popular wine in Austria is Grüner Veltliner *(see below).* Other wines include superb dry Rieslings, especially from the Wachau, and rich Weissburgunder (Pinot Blanc) from Burgenland. Red wines tend to be soft and lush – robust reds come from the Blaufränkisch grape *(see below).*

Recent good vintages were 1999, 2000, 2002, 2003 and 2006.

Riesling from the Wachau can be light, or full bodied like the Smaragd style.

Producer's name

Grape variety

Level of ripeness

Style (dry)

WIENINGER

Grüner Veltliner

1991

Kabinett

Auckenthal

Weingut Wieninger, 1210 Wien, Stammersdorfer Straße 78
Qualitätswein mit staatlicher Prüf-Nr. K 0005392, 11,0 %vol

ÖSTERREICH *trocken*   ℮ 0,75 l

Vintage

Producer's address

Alcohol level

Quantity

Grüner Veltliner is a fresh, fruity white wine. It is widely grown in Austria and is usually made in a dry style. It also makes excellent *Eiswein.*

St Laurent is a soft red wine; at its best it is rich and stylish.

Blaufränkisch is a quality local red – the best comes from Burgenland.

Krügel or ½ litre tankard

Seidl or standard ⅓ litre measure

Krügel or ½ litre of pale beer

Pfiff or ⅛ litre beer glass

AUSTRIAN BEERS

Vienna has been producing good malty beers for more than 150 years. Viennese lagers are bronze in colour and sweet in flavour. They make an excellent accompaniment to the hearty soups and stews found in *Beisln (see p201)*. The local Ottakring brewery's *Gold Fassl* is typical of the style, although lighter Bavarian-type beers such as *Weizengold* are also commonly available. One of Austria's most popular beers is *Gösser*, produced in Styria and found in the pubs and restaurants of Vienna. Speciality beers include the Styrian *Eggenberger Urbock*, one of the strongest beers in the world. It is made by the Schloss Eggenberg brewery founded in the 17th century.

Kaiser beer, a light beer

Weizengold wheat beer

Gösser Spezial is rich

Bierhof beer mat advertising a pub in the Haarhof.

Null Komma Josef is a local alcohol-free beer.

OTHER AUSTRIAN DRINKS

Austria offers a good range of non-alcoholic fruit juices such as *Himbeersaft* (raspberry syrup) or *Johannisbeersaft* (blackcurrant juice). Fruit is also the basis of many types of schnaps (sometimes called *Brand*). This powerful eau de vie is distilled from berries such as juniper and rowan as well as apricots *(Marillen)* and quince *(Quitten)*. It's worth paying the extra to sample the exquisite fruit schnaps produced by the dedicated specialists. *Almdudler* (herbal lemonade) is also a speciality. For a few weeks in autumn, fermenting grape juice, *Sturm*, is available. Milky in colour and quite sweet, it is more alcoholic than its grape flavour suggests.

Apricot schnaps

The Wiener Rathauskeller is a popular restaurant serving a number of beers

Choosing a Restaurant

The restaurants in this guide have been selected
because of their good value, good food and attractive
interiors. They are listed below by area, and in
alphabetical order within each price category. Some
of the specialities they serve are mentioned. All have a
no-smoking area. For map references, *see pp262-5*.

PRICE CATEGORIES
Price categories for a three-course meal
for one, excluding drinks, but including
all unavoidable extra charges such as
cover, service and tax.
€ Under €20
€€ €20-30
€€€ €30-40
€€€€ €40-50
€€€€€ over €50

STEPHANSDOM QUARTER

Bettelstudent   €
Johannesgasse 12, 1010 **Tel** *513 20 44* **Fax** *513 20 44 2*   **Map** *4 E1, 6 D4*

Established in 1986, this is an interesting, lively and inexpensive restaurant that features Austrian wines and over 30
different types of beer. Also on offer are local specialities and international cuisine, such as lasagne and spare ribs.
The restaurant is well-known for serving meals into the early hours.

Beim Czaak   €€
Postgasse 15 / Corner Fleischmarkt, 1010 **Tel** *513 72 15* **Fax** *512 74 64*   **Map** *2 E5, 6 E3*

Owned by the same family since 1920, this is a delightfully informal place offering Viennese cuisine and some dishes
in the Czech tradition. It has the pleasing atmosphere of the old-style *Beisl*, with few concessions to comfort in the
seating. Friendly service, and pets are permitted too. Closed Sun.

Da Capo   €€
Schulerstrasse 18, 1010 **Tel** *512 44 91* **Fax** *512 44 91-4*   **Map** *2 E5, 6 D3*

An Italian pizzeria and restaurant which feels more up-market than many, Da Capo has a wood-burning oven and
offers attractive seating in its cellar. Besides pizza, specialities include antipasti, pasta, meat dishes and seafood. A
seasonal menu is also available. Reservations are recommended.

Da Conte   €€
Kurrentgasse 12, 1010 **Tel** *533 64 64* **Fax** *532 69 97*   **Map** *5 C2*

This is a traditional Italian restaurant that is well-known for its pasta, lamb and veal dishes, as well as its fresh
fish. For dessert, you might also want to try the *tiramisu* or *crema caramella*. Business lunches are also available.
Reservations are recommended. Closed Sun.

East to West   €€
Seilerstätte 14, 1010 **Tel** *512 91 49* **Fax** *512 91 49*   **Map** *4 E1, 6 D4*

In this popular Asian restaurant, with an attractively understated modern interior, you can enjoy many selections of
tongue-tingling Chinese, Japanese and Thai dishes. The food is light and aromatic, and there is a good selection of
appropriate wines. Reservations are recommended.

Figlmüller   €€
Wollzeile 5, 1010 **Tel** *512 61 77* **Fax** *320 42 57 20*   **Map** *2 E5, 6 D3*

This is a cosy restaurant and wine tavern that specializes in traditional Austrian fare. It is most famous for its huge
Wiener Schnitzels and its a good place to experiment with wines by the glass. Meals for a gluten-free diet are also
available. Pets are permitted. Closed Aug.

Gulaschmuseum   €€
Schulerstrasse 20, 1010 **Tel** *512 10 17* **Fax** *512 10 18*   **Map** *2 E5, 6 D3*

For those who cant get enough of the ever-popular goulash, the Gulaschmuseum is definitely the place to go.
It offers many variations of this classic Viennese dish, made with different meats and vegetables. Reservations
are recommended.

Kerns Beisl   €€
Keeblattgasse 4, 1010 **Tel** *533 91 88*   **Map** *2 D5, 5 C3*

Popular, cosy and busy, this *Beisl* serves up a variety of authentic Austrian and Viennese dishes, including fried
chicken, *Schnitzels*, and beef goulash. There is also an extensive and varied Austrian wine and spirits list. For an
extra special treat, try the gingerbread for dessert. Closed Sat & Sun.

Mandarin   €€
Singerstrasse 11, 1010 **Tel** *512 28 04* **Fax** *513 60 84*   **Map** *4 E1, 6 D3*

This is a popular and busy Asian restaurant that serves up delicious Oriental food in an elegant environment.
It specializes in Szechuan and Cantonese cuisine and always has some interesting specials on the menu.
Reservations are recommended.

Key to Symbols *See back cover flap*

Toko-Ri
V 🍴 €€

Salztorgasse 4, 1010 **Tel** *532 77 77* **Fax** *532 77 77-17* **Map** *2 E4, 6 D2*

A popular Japanese restaurant - one of a chain of four - Toko-Ri features *sashimi, maki, tempura* and more. The interior exudes a sleek modern Japanese minimalism and boasts a sushi counter doubling as an aquarium. It is a good place for devotees of Japanese fish dishes.

Weibels Wirtshaus
🔥 **V** 🍴 €€

Kumpfgasse 2, 1010 **Tel** *512 39 86* **Fax** *512 39 86* **Map** *4 E1, 6 E3*

Austrian cooking at a very high level can be enjoyed in this traditional restaurant with an intimate wood-panelled interior and cosy sitting niches. The menu includes seasonal dishes. When available, try the pumpkinseed soup. Excellent Austrian wines can be ordered by the glass. Reservations are recommended.

Zanoni Luciano
V 🍴 €€

Lugeck 7, 1010 **Tel** *512 79 79* **Fax** *512 79 79-76* **Map** *6 D3*

This popular, casual and inexpensive eatery serves breakfast as well as sandwiches, *crêpes*, ice cream, pastries and cakes. It is a great place to stop if you are in a rush and want a fast meal. Also available are some food items "to go".

Cantinetta Antinori
V 🍴 €€€

Jasomirgottstrasse 3-5, 1010 **Tel** *533 77 22* **Fax** *533 77 22-11* **Map** *2 D5, 6 D3*

Part of an up-market restaurant chain with locations in Italy, Switzerland and Russia, this restaurant offers classic Tuscan dishes, including pasta and fish, and wine from its own vineyards. Both the ambience and service have a discreet Italian stylishness. Reservations are required.

Enoteca Cinque Terre
V 🍴 €€€

Marc-Aurel-Strasse 10, 1010 **Tel** *533 82 65* **Fax** *533 82 65* **Map** *2 E5, 6 D2*

In this small, but popular, Mediterranean restaurant, watching your meal being cooked is part of the experience. The emphasis is on Italian cuisine, and specialities include pasta in cream sauces, and mouth-wateringly prepared fish. Also on offer are excellent Austrian, Italian and Spanish wines. Closed Sat lunch & Sun.

Fadinger
V 🍴 🈳 €€€

Wipplingerstrasse 29, 1010 **Tel** *533 43 41* **Fax** *532 44 51* **Map** *2 D4, 5 C2*

Solid international, vegetarian and regional specialities are served in this elegant restaurant with an airy "Winter Garden" room. The chef is well-known for making creative use of original sauces and seasonings. Closed Sat & Sun. Reservations are recommended.

Griechenbeisl
🔥 **V** 🍴 🎵 🈳 €€€

Fleischmarkt 11, 1010 **Tel** *533 19 77* **Fax** *533 19 77-12* **Map** *2 E5, 6 D2*

Since 1447, Viennas oldest inn has been serving generous portions of traditional Viennese fare to its guests. Now this family-run business has added some international dishes to the menu. Try the pumpkin cream soup, and take a look at the framed autographs on the walls of the Mark Twain room. Closed Dec 24.

Ofenloch
🔥 🍴 🈳 €€€

Kurrentgasse 8, 1010 **Tel** *533 88 44* **Fax** *532 98 22* **Map** *5 C2*

Classic Viennese dishes are served in this historic restaurant with a well-kept *Wirtshaus* interior. The dishes are prepared using only the very best local products, which are largely organically grown. Weather permitting, diners can eat outside on one of Viennas oldest streets. Closed Sun.

Oswald & Kalb
🔥 **V** €€€

Bäckerstrasse 14, 1010 **Tel** *512 13 71* **Fax** *512 13 71 10* **Map** *2 E5, 6 D3*

This small but friendly restaurant behind the Stephansdom has a reputation as a meeting place for artists. While here, you can enjoy some traditional Austrian and regional fare, including *Wiener Schnitzels*. Both house wine and a range of beers are also available.

Plachutta
🔥 **V** 🍴 🈳 €€€

Wollzeile 38, 1010 **Tel** *512 15 77* **Fax** *512 15 77-20* **Map** *2 E5, 6E3*

Typical Viennese cuisine is served in elegant, yet comfortable, green and cream-coloured surroundings. The restaurant specializes in meat dishes and is most well-known for its *Tafelspitz*, which is a boiled beef dish. Formal dress is required; men must wear a jacket and tie. Reservations are recommended.

Salut
🔥 **V** 🍴 🈳 €€€

Wildpretmarkt 3, 1010 **Tel** *533 13 22* **Fax** *533 13 22* **Map** *2 D5, 6 D3*

There are few French restaurants in Vienna. However, Salut, which offers classic French dishes, does something to restore the balance. The decor attempts to transplant a little of Paris to the Danube shore. Fish is a speciality, including *bouillabaisse*. Menu specials are available for lunch. Closed Sun.

Salzamt
🔥 **V** 🍴 🈳 €€€

Ruprechtsplatz 1, 1010 **Tel** *533 53 32* **Map** *2 E5, 6 D2*

Austrian and Viennese cuisine is served in this popular restaurant that opened in the 1980s. Today, its a favourite watering hole of sophisticates who linger into the night at the stylish bar. Excellent meat dishes, pastas, fresh fish and desserts are served here daily. Reservations are recommended.

Wrenkh
♻ V ♿   €€€

Bauernmarkt 10, 1010 **Tel** *533 15 26* **Fax** *535 08 40*   **Map** *2 E5, 6 D3*

One of the best vegetarian restaurants in Vienna, with a comfortable feel and a modern ambience, the Wrenkh not only serves interesting vegetarian meals but also tasty fresh fruit drinks. Daily specials are available, as are menus in English. Closed Sat lunch & Sun. Reservations are recommended.

Zum Basilisken
V ♿ ⊞   €€€

Schönlaterngasse 3-5, 1010 **Tel** *513 31 23* **Fax** *513 31 23*   **Map** *6 E5*

A restaurant, bar and café, Zum Basilisken offers traditional Viennese and regional cuisine in a cosy wood-panelled interior. Specialities include turkey fillets, pork scallops and veal as well as *Tafelspitz*. For something really unique, try the wild boar dish. For dessert, the pancakes with cranberries are recommended.

Zum Schwarzen Kameel
V ♿ ⊞   €€€

Bognergasse 5, 1010 **Tel** *533 81 25* **Fax** *533 81 25-23*   **Map** *2 D5, 5 C3*

This popular, family-owned restaurant, bar and café serves both international and regional cuisine, with classics such as *Tafelspitz* (boiled beef) competing with lighter fare, such as delicious ham sandwiches. There are daily fish specials. The Art Deco dining room is a particularly enjoyable place to sit. Closed Sun.

Do & Co
♻ V ♿   €€€€

Stephansplatz 12, 1010 **Tel** *533 39 69* **Fax** *535 39 59*   **Map** *2 E5, 6 D3*

Part of a catering empire as well as a Viennese institution, Do & Co is on the 7th floor of the Haas-Haus building and has a striking view of the Stephansdom. Excellent international and regional dishes are served, and the specialities include kebabs. Reservations are required.

Drei Husaren
♻ V ♿ ♻   €€€€

Weihburggasse 4, 1010 **Tel** *512 10 92* **Fax** *512 10 92-18*   **Map**

Touted as Vienna's oldest luxury restaurant, Drei Husaren offers fine Viennese cuisine in an environment fit for a Habsburg. Meat, fish and other fare is prepared and served elegantly. For dessert, try the *Drei Husaren Torte*. Men must wear a jacket and tie. Reservations are recommended.

Fabios
♻ V ♿   €€€€

Tuchlauben 6, 1010 **Tel** *532 22 22* **Fax** *532 22 25*   **Map** *2 D5, 5 C3*

This is a very popular international restaurant with a bar and lounge, which offers a variety of food that includes homemade *ravioli*, risotto, venison, rack of lamb and beef fillets. Also on offer is a cookbook featuring some of the restaurant's famous recipes. Closed Sun. Reservations are required.

Himmelsstube
V ♿   €€€€

Parkring 12, 1010 **Tel** *514 80 41 7* **Fax** *514 80 40*   **Map** *4 E1, 6 E4*

On the 12th floor of the Hotel Am Parkring, this restaurant serves traditional Austrian cuisine and Viennese specialities while giving diners an exceptional view of the city. Local wines and brandies are also on offer. Four-course menus are available for a set price. Closed lunch Jul–Aug.

König von Ungarn Restaurant
♻ V ♿   €€€€

Schulerstrasse 10, 1010 **Tel** *515 84 15* **Fax** *515 848*   **Map** *2 E5, 6 D3*

Located in the historic König von Ungarn Hotel *(see p195)*, in a 16th-century building, this restaurant offers international and regional cuisine either *à la carte* or from a set menu. Try the roasted wild duck or stuffed veal fillet. Alternatively, the platter of roasted mixed meats is recommended.

Parkring Restaurant
♻ V ♿   €€€€

Parkring 12a, 1010 **Tel** *515 18-6653* **Fax** *515 18-6736*   **Map** *4 D1, 6 E4*

Located in the Vienna Marriott Hotel *(see p196)*, this formal restaurant offers fine dining as well as splendid views of the Stadtpark. Viennese cuisine and *à la carte* international dishes are served in an elegant yet relaxed environment. A perfect place to end a busy day. Open Wed–Sun for evening meals and Sun for brunch.

Tenmaya
V ♿ ⊞   €€€€

Krugerstrasse 3, 1010 **Tel** *512 73 97* **Fax** *512 46 86*   **Map** *6 D5*

Popular with locals and tourists alike, this Japanese restaurant features numerous Asian delicacies, including sushi and *teppanyaki*. The traditional Japanese setting, which includes women dressed in kimonos, also helps to create an enjoyable dining experience. Reservations are recommended.

Walter Bauer
V ♿   €€€€

Sonnenfelsgasse 17, 1010 **Tel** *512 98 71* **Fax** *512 98 71*   **Map** *6 E3*

Popular with Austrian celebrities and other locals, this restaurant serves international and gourmet cuisine as well as traditional and regional specialities. Dishes include yellow-fin tuna, salmon, lobster and rack of venison. For dessert, try the walnut *Schmarrn*. Closed Mon lunch, Sat & Sun. Reservations are recommended.

Le Siècle
♻ V ♿ ♫   €€€€€

Parkring 16, 1010 **Tel** *515 170* **Fax** *512 22 16*   **Map** *4 E1, 6 E4*

Located in the exceptional Radisson SAS Palais Hotel *(see p195)*, this is an award-winning and elegant international restaurant that also serves a number of regional specialities. For a special evening, order their Candlelight Dinner Menu. Closed Sat, Sun and holidays and for two weeks in summer.

Key to Price Guide *see p210* **Key to Symbols** *see back cover flap*

HOFBURG QUARTER

Ilona Stüberl
🏷️ Ⓥ 🍷 📶   €

Bräunerstrasse 2, 1010 **Tel** *533 90 29* **Fax** *533 90 29-6*   **Map** *2 D5, 5 C3*

In this small and popular family-owned restaurant that specializes in Hungarian cuisine, large helpings of goulash, stuffed cabbage, paprika chicken and other dishes are served up. Outside, there are tables on a pedestrian-only street. Pets are permitted. Closed Mon Oct-Mar.

Reinthaler's Beisl
🏷️ 📋 📶   €

Dorotheergasse 2-4, 1010 **Tel** *513 12 49*   **Map** *2 D5, 5 B3*

This typical, down-to-earth Viennese Biesl restaurant is good value, with lunchtime dishes of the day and a wide range of local specialities. There is outside seating in warmer weather, and reservations are recommended, especially at lunchtime. Closed Sun.

Café Hofburg
🏷️ Ⓥ 🍷 📶   €€

Hofburg-Innerer Burghof 1, 1010 **Tel** *241 00-420* **Fax** *241 00-419*   **Map** *4 D1, 5 B4*

Conveniently located in the Hofburg Palace, this elegant café and restaurant serves traditional Viennese cuisine, including beef goulash, sausages, salads and a variety of pancakes. Try the Emperor's Pancakes filled with apple sauce and plums.

Regina Margherita
🏷️ Ⓥ 🍷 📶   €€

Wallnerstrasse 4, Palais Esterhazy, 1010 **Tel** *533 08 12* **Fax** *533 08 12-20*   **Map** *2 D5, 5 B3*

This is a popular Italian restaurant and pizzeria that is located just off Kohlmarkt. It claims to serve "perfect pizzas" as they are freshly baked in an authentic Napolitan pizza oven. The Italian staff provide friendly service. Reservations are recommended.

Yugetsu
🏷️ Ⓥ 🍷   €€

Führichgasse 10, 1010 **Tel** *512 27 20* **Fax** *512 27 20-21*   **Map** *4 D1, 5 C4*

The number of Japanese patrons inspires confidence in the authenticity and quality of the food served in this Japanese restaurant with an ultra-modern interior. There is a sushi bar on the ground floor and *teppanyaki* on the first floor. Some say this is the best Japanese restaurant in Vienna.

Ephesus
🏷️ Ⓥ 🍷 📶   €€€

Bräunerstrasse 8, 1010 **Tel** *533 90 91* **Fax** *533 90 91*   **Map** *2 D5, 5 C3*

In the arched interior of Ephesus, with its elegant wall friezes in imitation of the Ephesos ruins, Turkish food returns to the traditions of the Ottoman kitchen. As well as Levantine dishes, there are Turko-Greek standbys such as *tsatsiki* and *moussaka*. The wines are Austrian, Turkish, Greek and Italian. Closed Sun.

Novelli Bacaro con Cucina
Ⓥ 🍷 📶   €€€€

Bräunerstrasse 11, 1010 **Tel** *513 42 00* **Fax** *513 42 00-1*   **Map** *5 C3*

This upmarket Mediterranean restaurant, located in a palace, specializes in Italian cuisine and has a lovely interior styled with terracotta from Tuscany. The classic Italian dishes on offer include antipasti, homemade pasta, lamb and beef. There is also an excellent wine list. Pets are permitted. Closed Sun.

Palmenhaus
Ⓥ 🍷 🎵 📶   €€€€

Burggarten, 1010 **Tel** *533 10 33* **Fax** *533 10 33-10*   **Map** *4 D1, 5 B4*

In a great location – inside the Palm House and next to the Butterfly House in the Burggarten – this restaurant features a wide variety of international dishes, with something to suit all appetites, including soups, salads, fish and veal.

Sky Restaurant
🏷️ Ⓥ 🍷 🎵   €€€€

Kärntnerstrasse 19, 1010 **Tel** *513 17 12-40* **Fax** *513 17 12-20*   **Map** *4 D2, 5 C5*

Right at the top of the Steffl building, this impressive restaurant, café and bar offers a splendid view of the surrounding area and serves up Austrian and international cuisine. For a treat, try the lamb and steak dishes or the meals made in a wok. Reservations are recommended. Open for dinner only. Closed Sun.

Mörwald im Ambassador
🏷️ Ⓥ 🍷   €€€€€

Kärntnerstrasse 22, 1010 **Tel** *961 61 161* **Fax** *961 61 160*   **Map** *5 C4*

Located in the Ambassador Hotel *(see p196)*, this restaurant serves traditional and modern Viennese fare and is popular with locals as well as tourists. Specialities incude pork and veal dishes. There is a a range of unique desserts, including dumplings and pancakes with fruit. Reservations are required.

Sapori Restaurant
🏷️ Ⓥ 🍷   €€€€€

Herrengasse 12, 1010 **Tel** *22 780* **Fax** *227 80 79*   **Map** *2 D5, 5 B2*

Located in the Radisson SAS Style Hotel *(see p196)*, the Sapori serves an *à la carte* breakfast as well as fine Italian cuisine in a comfortable and modern environment. A seasonal menu is also available, as are business lunches. Closed lunch and pm Sun & public hols.

SCHOTTENRING AND ALSERGRUND

Flein
V 　　　　　　　　　　　　　　　€

Boltzmanngasse 2, 1090 **Tel** *319 76 89* **Fax** *319 76 89*　　　　　　　**Map** *1 C3*

Conveniently situated in the gardens of the *Lycée Franêais de Vienne* is this pleasant restaurant that is well-known for serving up delicious, but inexpensive, traditional Austrian and French food. Popular with locals. Try the lunch specials and some of the coffees as well. Closed Sat & Sun.

Rembetiko
€€

Porzellangasse 38, 1090 **Tel** *317 41 27* **Fax** *317 41 27*　　　　　　　**Map** *1 C3*

For those who hanker after Greek lamb and grilled fish, this may be the place to restore spirits. The homey interior in Grecian blue and white, along with the friendly service, attracts plenty of regular customers. Another plus is the considerable choice of Greek wines.

Stomach
€€€

Seegasse 26, 1090 **Tel** *310 20 99* **Fax** *310 20 99*　　　　　　　**Map** *1 C3*

The choice of food in this restaurant is eclectic and large (as are the portions). Standard fare is Viennese with some international and seasonal selections. Located in a Biedermeier house, the courtyard is one of the most attractive in Vienna for summer dining. Reservations are recommended. Closed Mon, Tue & lunch Wed-Sat.

Trattoria Martinelli
€€€

Freyung 3, Palais Harrach, 1010 **Tel** *533 67 21* **Fax** *533 67 21-20*　　　　　**Map** *2 D5, 5 B2*

The priority of this elegant restaurant is to offer fine and authentic Tuscan cuisine in a genuinely Italian ambience. Among the specialities are the celebrated *osso buco* and the delicious and unique wild duck *ravioli*. Worth visiting if you desire a taste of Italy. Extensive Italian wines are also on offer.

MUSEUM AND TOWNHALL QUARTER

Lux-Gasthaus-Café-Bar
€€

Schrankgasse 4 / Spittelberggasse 3, 1070 **Tel** *526 94 91* **Fax** *526 09 84*　　　**Map** *3 B1*

With its choice of seating areas (glass atrium, *Gasthaus*, bistro with red leather benches), this restaurant/café/bar is excellent value. The regional and international cuisine includes seasonal dishes, soups, various salads and wonderful fish.

Spatzennest
€€

St. Ulrichsplatz 1, 1070 **Tel** *526 16 59* **Fax** *526 16 59*　　　　　　　**Map** *3 B1*

This quaint *Beisl* is in a pleasant location near St Ulrich's church and close to the lively Spittelberg pedestrian area with its eateries and stalls. It offers appetizing, traditional Viennese and regional specialities, including *Wiener Schnitzels*, smoked pork dumplings and roasted chicken. Daily specials are also served. Closed Fri & Sat.

Zu ebener Erde und erster Stock
€€

Burggasse 13, 1070 **Tel** *523 62 54*　　　　　　　　　　　　　　**Map** *3 B1*

Enjoy first-rate Viennese cooking and seasonal specials in the romantic ambience of this charming Biedermeier house. The ground floor resembles a traditional *Beisl* and offers less expensive fare, while the floor above offers more elegant dining. Reservations are required. Closed Sat lunch & Sun.

Lebenbauer
€€€

Teinfaltstrasse 3, 1010 **Tel** *533 55 56* **Fax** *533 55 56-11*　　　　　　**Map** *1 C5, 5 B2*

This is an award-winning, popular, comfortable and airy vegetarian and natural foods restaurant. Here, you can select from a wide variety of attractively-served and healthy meals. Fish is also available. A pleasant outdoor patio is available for warmer weather dining. Reservations are recommended. Closed Sat & Sun.

Schnattl
€€€

Lange Gasse 40, 1080 **Tel** *405 34 00* **Fax** *405 34 00*　　　　　　　**Map** *1 B5*

A popular restaurant that features Stryian (southern Austrian) fare, the Schnattl also makes an effort to offer organic produce. Try the salad with pumpkinseed oil dressing or some game. The interior is in post-modern style. Styrian wines are available, as are daily lunch specials. Reservations are required.

Selina
€€€

Laudongasse 13, 1080 **Tel** *405 64 04* **Fax** *408 04 59*　　　　　　　**Map** *1 A4*

Close to City Hall, this restaurant has a pleasant and elegant interior. It specializes in Austrian cuisine as well as some international dishes, and is well-known for its Mediterranean and vegetarian meals. Also good are the fish and seafood specials. Reservations are recommended.

Key to Price Guide *see p210* **Key to Symbols** *see back cover flap*

OPERA AND NASCHMARKT

Hungerkünstler
Gumpendorfer Strasse 48, 1060 **Tel** *581 03 70*
Map *3 B3*

This is a simple neighbourhood *Beisl* that offers traditional Viennese and regional cuisine along with some Italian and international specialities. The noodle dish with melted cheese is worth sampling. The interior of the restaurant is pleasant, with antique chandeliers, making for a relaxed dining experience. Closed Sun.

Kostas
Friedrichstrasse 6, 1010 **Tel** *586 37 29*
Map *4 D2*

Close to the Secession building and the Naschmarkt, this little Greek restaurant has been winning laurels for its authentic fare (the lamb dishes are particularly good). It provides better value than many less genuine rivals. Recorded Greek music adds to the ambience. Small portions are available on request. Closed Sun.

Restaurant Shambala
Opernring 13, 1010 **Tel** *588 900* **Fax** *588 90 90 90*
Map *4 D1, 5 B5*

This French restaurant in Le Meridien hotel *(see p198)*, near the Hofburg Palace, offers fine dining in an ultra sleek and modern environment. The nightly specials feature both healthy ingredients and classic French flair. Particularly delicious are the desserts and pastries.

Aux Gazelles
Rahlgasse 5, 1060 **Tel** *585 66 45* **Fax** *585 66 45-39*
Map *3 C2, 5 A5*

In a unique North African-themed complex, you can relax with a candlelit dinner and indulge in some authentic Moroccan and French cuisine before going to one of the other venues nearby. Among them are Turkish steam baths, a café, bar, bazaar shop and nightclub. Reservations are recommended. Closed Sun.

Restaurant Anna Sacher
Philharmonikerstrasse 4, 1010 **Tel** *514 56 0* **Fax** *514 56 810*
Map *5 C5*

In the elegant surroundings of the Sacher Hotel *(see p198)*, this gourmet restaurant offers an international menu that includes veal, chicken and beef dishes. Especially tantalizing is their world-renowned *Sacher torte*. Seven-course meals are available. Men must wear a jacket and tie. Reservations are required. Closed Mon.

BELVEDERE QUARTER

Salm Bräu
Rennweg 8, 1030 **Tel** *799 59 92* **Fax** *799 59 92*
Map *4 F3*

There's a busy and friendly atmosphere in this good-value regional restaurant and beer-cellar in the former stables of the monastic buildings flanking the Salesianerinnenkirche. The *Surstelze* (smoked pork joint) for two is a speciality, as are the beers, which are brewed on the premises.

Cantino Restaurant
Seilerstätte 30, 1010 **Tel** *512 54 46* **Fax** *512 55 50-28*
Map *4 E1, 6 D5*

This is a popular restaurant that specializes in Mediterranean and Spanish cuisine and is well-known for the tantalising variety of tapas it offers. Also worth trying are the paella and fresh sheep cheese with paprika. Closed Sat lunch & Sun pm.

Restaurant Sperl
Karolinengasse 13, 1040 **Tel** *504 73 34* **Fax** *504 73 34-30*
Map *4 E4*

A cosy, traditional wooden interior provides the ideal setting for food from an extensive Viennese and Austrian menu. The spinach dumplings, pork medallions, vegetarian meals, and specialities from the grill are all recommended.

Wiener Wirtschaft
Wiedner Haupstrasse 27-29, 1040 **Tel** *501 11-364* **Fax** *501 11 350*
Map *3 C5*

Located in the Hotel Erzherzog Rainer *(see p198)*, this restaurant serves traditional Austrian cuisine. A speciality is the goulash, of which 14 different types are available. A "Goulash Fest" for larger groups consists of five different goulashes plus side dishes. Coffee and cake are available all day.

Restaurant Hummerbar
Mahlerstrasse 9, 1010 **Tel** *512 88 43* **Fax** *512 88 43-75*
Map *4 E1, 6 D5*

This popular seafood restaurant specializes in fresh oysters, scallops and lobster, and has a daily changing menu. Desserts include fresh fruit served with liquor, ice cream or cream. Advance orders can be given for meals that are prepared on request. Reservations are recommended. Closed Sun.

Korso
⌧ V 🍴 T   €€€€

Mahlerstrasse 2, 1010 **Tel** *515 16 546* **Fax** *515 16 575*   **Map** *4 D1, 5 C5*

Located in the Hotel Bristol *(see p199)*, the Korso features traditional Viennese cooking plus international dishes. The wine list is formidable. The ambience is one of elegance and wealth, and the service is excellent. Men must wear a jacket and tie. Reservations are required. Closed Sat lunch & Sun lunch in Jul.

Restaurant Imperial
⌧ V 🍴 🎵   €€€€

Kärntner Ring 16, 1015 **Tel** *50110 356* **Fax** *501 10 410*   **Map** *4 D2, 6 D5*

Located in the Imperial Hotel *(see p199)*, this is a gourmet restaurant that features both Austrian and international cuisine. Particularly famous is the chocolate-covered Imperial *Torte* (cake). Cigars are also on offer. So, too, are set lunches and brunch; check with the hotel for when they are available.

FURTHER AFIELD

Das Móbel
V 🍴   €

Burggasse 10, 1070 **Tel** *524 94 97* **Fax** *524 94 97-13*   **Map** *3 A1, 5 A3*

The most unique feature of this popular and friendly café and restaurant is that you can buy any of the chairs you sit on, which are all made by Austrian designers. Otherwise, it's worth a visit to try one of the quiches on the international menu.

Schweizerhaus
⌧ V 🍴 🎵 🚇   €

Prater 116, 1020 **Tel** *728 01 52* **Fax** *728 01 52-29*

Regional and Eastern European fare is served up in generous portions in this well-loved restaurant and beer garden inside the Prater Park. Try the beef stew or Slovakian cabbage soup. Beer-lovers may want to sample the Czech Budweiser Budvar beer. Closed Nov-mid-Mar.

Babu
V 🍴 🚇   €€

Stadtbahnbogen 181-184, 1090 **Tel** *479 48 49*

For those who thrive on late-night action, it's good to know that Babu offers a variety of regional and international cuisine almost round the clock in an interesting setting, underneath the elevated tracks of the subway. Babu also has a popular local bar.

Gmoa-Keller
V 🍴 🎵   €€

Am Heumarkt 25, 1030 **Tel** *712 53 10* **Fax** *712 53 10*   **Map** *4 E2*

Featuring both regional Austrian fare and seasonal dishes, this is a popular restaurant. Among the specialities are soups, veal and beef, plus fruit or chocolate pancakes for dessert. It is a friendly place that is much favoured by the musical fraternity from the nearby concert halls. Closed Sun.

Motto Club Restaurant-Bar
⌧ V 🍴   €€

Schönbrunner Strasse 30, 1050 **Tel** *587 06 72* **Fax** *587 06 72-11*   **Map** *3 A4*

A variety of dishes based on regional, Asian and Mediterranean cooking styles is provided in this chic and cosy restaurant and bar. Try the spinach salad or *teriyaki* tofu dish for a unique treat. Also worth trying is the mousse for dessert. DJ music is played nightly.

Restaurant Dubróvnik
⌧ V 🍴 🎵 🚇   €€

Am Heumarkt 5, 1030 **Tel** *713 71 02* **Fax** *713 71 02-14*   **Map** *4 E2, 6 E5*

Croatian specialities, including marinated sardines and *pljeskavica* with *ajvar* (spiced meat patties with a roasted pepper spread), are served in this lively restaurant and bar. If you're looking for authentic south-eastern European food, this is the place to go. Live Dalmatian music features occasionally.

Schloss Concordia
V 🚇   €€

Simmeringer Hauptstrasse 283, 1110 **Tel** *769 88 88* **Fax** *769 88 22*

Typical Austrian cuisine is served in a restaurant in an untypical location – across the street from the Central Cemetery. However bizarre the location, the food is delicious and relatively inexpensive, with an emphasis on extra large *Wiener* and chicken *Schnitzels*. A choice of beers is available.

Silberwirt
V 🍴 🚇   €€

Schlossgasse 21, 1050 **Tel** *544 49 07* **Fax** *548 84 66*   **Map** *3 C4*

Silberwirt is part of a complex of eateries built on the site of Schloss Margareten, which was devastated by the Turks during the 1683 siege of Vienna. Time-hallowed Viennese dishes are cooked with care and flair, and served in a relaxed ambience. A variety of Austrian wines are on offer too. Reservations are recommended.

Stadtwirt
⌧ V 🍴 🚇 T   €€

Untere Viaduktgasse 45, 1030 **Tel** *713 38 28* **Fax** *713 38 28-4*

This is a bustling restaurant, popular with locals, that has cosy corner seats and tables for groups. Also provided is superb Viennese and regional cooking at affordable prices, plus house wines, draught beer and brandies. Reservations are required. Closed Sat lunch & Sun.

Key to Price Guide *see p210* **Key to Symbols** *see back cover flap*

Tempel

☑ 🍴 🔲   €€

Praterstrasse 56, Inner Courtyard, 1150 **Tel** *214 01 79* **Fax** *214 01 79*   **Map** *2 F4, 5 F2*

Tempel restaurant offers a wide choice of dishes, ranging from seafood to beef and veal. The good value set menu, sophisticated desserts and excellent Austrian wines makes this a popular eating place. There is outdoor seating in warmer weather. Closed Sat lunch, Sun, Mon.

Zu den drei Buchteln

♿ ☑ 🍴   €€

Wehrgasse 9, 1050 **Tel** *587 83 65*   **Map** *3C3*

The ambience here lives up to the Bohemian/Moravian culinary aspirations.Try some *svickova* (beef with seasoned cream sauce) and *brimsenbaluska* (sheep cheese dumplings), not to mention the irresistible desserts. Wash it all down with some Czech beer or Moravian wine. Closed Sun, last week Jul, first 2 weeks Aug.

Zum Herkner

♿ 🍴   €€

Dornbacher Strasse 123, 1170 **Tel** *485 43 86* **Fax** *485 43 86*

For many, the long trek out to Zum Herkner is certainly worth it. Good "bourgeois Viennese fare" as well as international cuisine is served at moderate prices in a rustic and unstuffy ambience. The seasonal menu is strong on veal dishes, chanterelle mushrooms and carp. Reservations are required. Closed Sat & Sun.

Eckel

☑ 🍴 🔲   €€€

Sieveringer Strasse 46, 1190 **Tel** *320 32 18* **Fax** *320 66 60*

This charming traditional Viennese restaurant offers a cosy interior in the winter and a garden in the summer. Viennese cooking is at its best here, with international specialities, such as lobster and crayfish, also featuring. There is a superb list of wines, mostly Austrian. Reservations are required. Closed Sun.

Green Cottage

☑   €€€

Kettenbrückengasse 3, 1050 **Tel** *586 65 81* **Fax** *586 65 81*   **Map** *3 C3*

Jugendstil meets the Orient (the interior) and *nouvelle cuisine* goes Chinese (the menu)! The food here ranges from a *Sichuan* version of Mongolian lamb and seasoned grilled fish to deliciously light, rice-based desserts. Some dishes may be salty for the average taste. The staff are friendly and attentive. Closed Sun.

Kronprinz Rudolf

♿ ☑ 🍴 🔲   €€€

Taborstrasse 12, 1020 **Tel** *211 50-423* **Fax** *211 50-160*   **Map** *2 F4, 6 E1*

Located in the Hotel Stefanie (*see p199*), this restaurant offers traditional Viennese and Austrian cuisine in an elegant and refined setting. It is well-known for preparing meals from recipes used during the days of the Austro-Hungarian Empire. When the weather is good, try dining in the courtyard garden.

Mediterraneo Restaurant

♿ ☑ 🍴   €€€

Johannesgasse 28, 1037 **Tel** *711 22 110*   **Map** *4 E1, 6 D4*

Besides preparing a good selection of regional dishes, this restaurant serves up a wide variety of international favourites in a relaxed setting, including Italian, French, Spanish, Greek and Turkish cuisine. Breakfast is also on offer.

SteirerStuben

♿ ☑ 🍴   €€€

Wiedner Hauptstrasse 111, 1050 **Tel** *544 43 49* **Fax** *544 08 88*   **Map** *3 C5*

Fine dining and international cuisine is what is offered at the Steirerstuben. Try their Alpine lamb, char (*Saibling*) in wild garlic sauce, or carp *gelée*. Among the excellent desserts is pineapple with mango sorbet. All meals and desserts are prepared artistically. Reservations are recommended. Closed Sun.

Vikerl's Lokal

📋 ♿ 🍴   €€€

Wüffelgasse 4, 1150 **Tel** *894 34 30* **Fax** *892 41 83*

Viennese cooking is amiably served in this family-run restaurant. When available, try the quail, calf's liver or venison. Don't be deterred by the restaurant's location. The menu changes every two weeks. Reservations are recommended. Closed Sun Jun-Aug.

Kim Kocht

☑ 🍴 📋 🔲   €€€€

Lustkandlgasse 6, 1090 **Tel** *319 02 42* **Fax** *319 02 42*   **Map** *1 B2*

This popular upmarket Asian restaurant is often booked weeks in advance. Specialities include Asian fusion food, artistically prepared. Try some sushi and the sorbet for dessert. A gourmet food shop is also on the premises. Music is played from 6pm in the restaurant's bar. Reservations are required. Closed Sat-Tue.

Vincent

♿ ☑ 🍴   €€€€

Grosse Pfarrgasse 7, 1020 **Tel** *214 15 16* **Fax** *212 14 14*   **Map** *2 E3*

The name bespeaks the owner's passion for modern art, specimens of which adorn the walls. The excellent organic fare is a *nouvelle cuisine* influenced version of Viennese, and decidedly creative. When available, try the mussels or the veal kidneys cooked in port wine. Reservations are required. Closed Sun.

Steirereck

♿ ☑ 🍴 🔲   €€€€€

Meierei im Stadtpark, 1030 **Tel** *713 31 68* **Fax** *713 31 68-2*   **Map** *6 F4*

With its atmospheric location, fabulous service and culinary artistry, this restaurant may be one of the best in Vienna. Menus of stunning flair show both Austrian and international influences. If you appreciate a meal that is staged as a performance, this is the place for you. Reservations are required. Closed Sat & Sun.

Choosing a Café

This section lists a broad cross-section of Viennese cafés, wine cellars, sandwich/self-service bars and *Konditoreien (see pp200-1)*. Both the traditional and the new and fashionable are included; bars are not listed, but some of the places featured do have lively bars. For coffee and cake expect to pay more in the famous cafés, for example Café Konditorei Demel. The main attraction of a Viennese coffee house is that once you have bought something you can relax and stay as long as you like.

STEPHANSDOM QUARTER

Café-Konditorei Gerstner
Kärntnerstrasse 13-15, 1010 **Tel** *512 49 63-77* **Fax** *512 49 63-44*　　　　　　　　　　**Map** *4 D1, 6 D4*

One of the great "Imperial and Royal" *Konditoreien*, which has a marvellous selection of pastries that are not only delicious but are decorated quite artistically. Try the *Nusstorte* or *Topfenstrudel* for a special treat. Also available are confections, such as petits fours and marzipan.

Café Ministerium
Georg-Coch-Platz 4, 1010 **Tel** *512 92 25*　　　　　　　　　　　　　　**Map** *2 F5, 6 F3*

Moderately-priced Austrian home cooking, including vegetarian selections, can be had at this café. Also on offer is a good selection of coffee drinks. Other attractions are chess and billiards, plus live music on Wednesdays and Thursdays. Free WiFi Internet access is available for those who want to surf the net. Closed Sat & Sun.

Duran Sandwiches
Rotenturmstrasse 11, 1010 **Tel** *533 71 15* **Fax** *533 71 15*　　　　　　　　　**Map** *2 E5, 6 D3*

No-frills eat-in and takeaway restaurant, with quite a following, which offers a great selection of open sandwiches for an incredibly low price. Whether meat, fish or vegetarian, they appeal to the eye as well as the taste buds. Those on the go can fax in their order. Closed Sun.

È Tricaffè
Rotenturmstrasse 25, 1010 **Tel** *533 89 90* **Fax** *533 89 85*　　　　　　　　**Map** *2 E5, 6 E2*

All the cafés in this trendy chain (see also Am Hof 2/Corner Bognergasse) serve excellent Italian-style specialities, such as antipasto and *tiramisu*. Most notable is the wine selection, from which you can choose Italian wines by the glass. The espresso is good too.

Vis-à-Vis
Wollzeile 5, 1010 **Tel** *512 93 50* **Fax** *512 93 50*　　　　　　　　　　　**Map** *2 E5, 6 D3*

One of Vienna's most loved, and oldest, wine bars, where more than 300 wines are on offer. Don't be fooled by the size of the place; a visit is essential for any wine connoisseur looking to sample something special. Sparkling wines are especially noteworthy and the glassware is top notch. Closed Sat & Sun.

HOFBURG QUARTER

Café Bräunerhof
Stallburggasse 2, 1010 **Tel** *512 38 93* **Fax** *513 05 49*　　　　　　　　　**Map** *4 D1, 5 C3*

Old-fashioned café that has an *à la carte* menu and also serves breakfast. It's reputed to be the favourite café of Austria's most celebrated author, Thomas Bernhard. Games of chess and billiards round out the offerings here. Live music on weekends.

Café Hawelka
Dorotheergasse 6, 1010 **Tel** *512 82 30*　　　　　　　　　　　　　　　　**Map** *2 D5, 5 C3*

A Viennese institution, with a spartan but cosy interior, this is the preferred café of the city's Bohemians and their dogs. Try the café's most famous speciality, their *Buchteln*, which is a bun made from yeast dough and filled with apricot jam: simply delicious. Closed Tue.

Café-Konditorei Demel
Kohlmarkt 14, 1010 **Tel** *535 17 17-0* **Fax** *535 17 17 26*　　　　　　　　　**Map** *2 D5, 5 C3*

Founded in 1776, this famous "Royal and Imperial" confectioners offers a light lunch of sandwiches and a huge selection of pastries and confections. The elegant Neo-Classical interior adds to the enjoyment of a visit here, and it's a particularly popular spot for tourists.

Key to Symbols *see back cover flap*

Trzesniewski

Dorotheergasse 1, 1010 **Tel** *512 32 91* **Fax** *513 95 65*

Map *2 D5, 5 C3*

Famous stand-up fast-food eatery (eight branches are located throughout Vienna) that specializes in all sorts of open sandwiches. The fillings are made from organic produce and the food is always fresh. Lots of variety at a low cost. Great for a quick meal on the run. Closed Sun.

SCHOTTENRING AND ALSERGRUND

Tunnel

Florianigasse 39, 1080 **Tel** *947 57 20* **Fax** *405 34 65*

Map *1 A5*

This three-storey eatery and art gallery in Josefstadt serves a selection of cold sandwiches and warm food as well as a breakfast buffet. The international and varied cuisine (including pizzas) is generally inexpensive. A variety of drinks rounds out the menu.

MUSEUM AND TOWNHALL QUARTER

Café Landtmann

Dr Karl Lueger-Ring 4, 1010 **Tel** *241 00-111* **Fax** *532 06 25*

Map *1 C5, 5 B2*

A popular coffee-house, the Landtmann was once patronized by Sigmund Freud. Press conferences are frequently held here and it is always crowded in the evenings. An extensive menu includes breakfast. Coffee and tea specialities, homemade desserts, and pastries for diabetics are available.

Sluka

Rathausplatz 8, 1010 **Tel** *405 71 72* **Fax** *406 88 94-4*

Map *1 C5, 5 A3*

Tucked under the arches of the Neo-Gothic Town Hall, this café and confectioner offers a light lunch and buffet of *hors d'oeuvres*. It is also well-known for its caviar sandwiches. While here, don't forget to try at least one cake; those made of fruit are especially good. Extensive selections for diabetics. Closed Sun.

OPERA AND NASCHMARKT

Café Mozart

Albertinaplatz 2, 1010 **Tel** *241 00-211* **Fax** *241 00 219*

Map *4 D1, 5 C4*

Located next to the State Opera House, the building that houses Café Mozart was first established as a café in 1794. Today it is still a popular dining establishment among locals as well as tourists, offering traditional Austrian and gourmet cuisine and pastries in an elegant environment.

FURTHER AFIELD

Heuriger Zimmermann

Armbrustergasse 5, 1190 **Tel** *370 22 11* **Fax** *370 61 30*

Cosy and fashionable *Heuriger* of great character that offers a range of Viennese warm dishes as well as the typical *Heurigen* buffet in a friendly environment. Vegetarians will like the extensive salad buffet. The outdoor dining area is also a good place to relax on a sunny day.

Jazzland

Franz Josefs Kai 29, 1010 **Tel** *533 25 75*

Map *2 D4, 6D1*

The oldest jazz club in Austria and located in a 500-year-old cellar, Jazzland features local and international musicians nightly. Food ranges from traditional Austrian fare to pasta and salads, with Serbian *cevapcici* (ground fried meat shaped like sausages) a speciality. Live music from 9pm; the cover charge varies. Closed Sun.

Mayer am Pfarrplatz

Pfarrplatz 2, Heiligenstadt, 1190 **Tel** *370 12 87* **Fax** *370 47 14*

Popular wine tavern in the village where Beethoven wrote his "testament". Among rustic surroundings you can enjoy a delicious cold buffet or a choice of hot meals that include homemade sausages. Historians will admire the wine press dating from 1617.

SHOPS AND MARKETS

Since Vienna is a compact city, it is a pleasant place to shop. The main shopping area is pedestrianized and full of pretty cafés, and although it is not in the same league as London, Paris and New York when it comes to international stores, you can browse around at a more leisurely pace. Austrian-made glassware, food and traditional crafts all make for good buys. However, the shops tend to cater for comparatively conventional and mature tastes and purses. Vienna has a range of markets selling a variety of produce and wares from exotic fruit to old trinkets. The pedestrian shopping areas of Kärntner Strasse, the Graben, and Kohlmarkt house the more expensive shops and are pleasant to wander around. For more details of shops and markets see the Directory on page 225.

Augarten porcelain Lipizzaner

BEST BUYS

Many of the best buys in Vienna are small and readily transportable: coffee addicts shouldn't forget to buy freshly ground coffee – the city imports some of the best.

If you have a sweet tooth, you couldn't be in a more appropriate city. It is justly famous for its cakes, pastries and *Torten (see p206–7)* and any good *Café-Konditorei* (cake shop and café) will post cakes back home for you. In November and December, try the buttery Advent *Stollen* available from **Julius Meinl am Graben** *(see p223)* or any good baker. Stuffed with fruit and nuts and dusted with icing sugar, it is a tasty Christmas loaf. Alternatively, buy some prettily-packaged *Sachertorte (see p207)*, available year round. The specialist chocolate shops *(see p223)* are worth a visit, both for the unusual packaging and the chocolate itself.

Sweet *Eiswein* (so-called because the grapes are left on the vines until the first frosts) is an unusual and delicious dessert wine. **Zum Schwarzen Kameel** *(see p223)* sells the rarer red version as well.

Other Austrian-made goods include clothes manufactured in the felt-like woollen fabric known as *Loden (see p223)*. If you feel like treating yourself and have space in your car or suitcase, buy custom-made sheets or high-quality down pillows or duvets made in Austria *(see p222)*. Petit point embroidery, which adorns anything from powder compacts to handbags, is a Viennese speciality *(see p222)*.

Glassware – including superb chandeliers – and **Augarten** porcelain *(see p222)* tend to be highly original, although expensive. Many people collect crystal ornaments made by Swarovski. **Ostovics** *(see p222)* is a good cookery and glass shop for such items.

Trachten (Austrian costume) shops *(see p223)* are fun; they have a wide selection of hats, children's dresses, jackets and blouses. **Gilhofer** *(see p223)* stocks old prints and maps. Early editions of works by writers such as Freud, Kraus or Rilke can be found in Vienna's antique bookshops *(see p223)*.

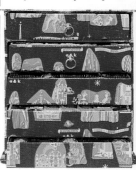

Chest of drawers chocolate box from Altmann & Kühne *(see p223)*

OPENING HOURS

Shops usually open at 8:30 or 9 in the morning and close at 6 or 7 in the evening. Some of the smaller shops close for an hour at lunch time. Traditionally stores were required to close at noon on Saturday, though all now stay open until 5pm. Shops are still closed on Sundays and public holidays, although you can buy items such as groceries, flowers, camera film, books and newspapers at the major railway stations. The supermarkets at the airport and Wien Nord station are open seven days a week.

J & L Lobmeyr's glass shop on Kärntner Strasse *(see p222)*

HOW TO PAY

Vienna is now more credit (and debit) card-orientated, with many shops accepting the major cards. Some also take Eurocheques (with a card), but it is still wise to carry some cash as an alternative.

WHERE TO SHOP

The pedestrian shopping areas of Graben, Kohlmarkt and Kärntner Strasse have many of the most well-known and expensive shops in Vienna.

The more cheaply priced area is along Mariahilfer Strasse, with department stores selling household goods, and well-known chain stores such as H & M.

View down Kohlmarkt, one of Vienna's pedestrian shopping streets

RIGHTS AND SERVICES

If a purchase is defective you are usually entitled to a refund, provided you have proof of purchase. This is not always the case with goods bought in the sales – inspect them carefully before you buy. Many shops in Vienna will pack goods for you – and often gift-wrap them at no extra charge – and send them anywhere in the world.

VAT EXEMPTION

VAT (value added tax) or MWSt (Mehrwertsteuer) is normally charged at 20%. If you reside outside the European Union (EU), you are entitled to claim back the VAT on goods purchased in Austria. This is only the case, however, if the total purchase price (this can include the total cost of several items from one shop) exceeds €73. Take along your passport when shopping and ask the shopkeeper to complete Form U34 at the time of sale. This should also bear the shop's stamp and have the receipt attached. You may have the refund credited to your credit card account, have it posted home, or pick it up at the airport.

Purchased goods must not be used prior to exportation. If you leave Vienna by air, present the form at Customs before checking in, and have it stamped as proof of export. You may also have to show your purchases at Customs, so pack them somewhere accessible. Then post the stamped form to the Austrian shopkeeper or collect the refund at the airport (there is a handling fee). If leaving by car or train, present the form to Customs at the border, where you can also claim a refund. If you are not disembarking the train at the border, there is sometimes a customs official on the train to stamp your form.

When you have goods sent directly to your home outside the EU, VAT is deducted at the time of purchase.

One of the famous *Loden* coats from Resi Hammerer (*see p223*)

Since Austria joined the EU in 1995, EU citizens can no longer claim back VAT.

SALES

The bi-annual sales are held in January and July. The best bargains can usually be found in fashions. Electrical and household goods are also much reduced.

SHOPPING CENTRES

Shopping centres are a fairly recent innovation in Vienna. The most modern are the **Ringstrassen Galerien**, the splendid **Haas Haus** and the spruced-up **Generali Centre**. Built in the same style as the Café Central (*see pp58–61*), **Freyung Passage** is an arcade of elegant shops in the Palais Ferstel (*see pp108 and 110*).

ADDRESSES

Generali Centre
Mariahilfer Strasse 77–79. **Map** 3 A3.

Haas Haus
Stock-im-Eisen-Platz 4.
Map 2 D5 & 5 C3.

Freyung Passage
Palais Ferstel 1, Freyung 2.
Map 2 D5 & 5 B2.

Ringstrassen Galerien
Kärntner Ring 5–7. **Map** 6 D5.

Shops and Boutiques

Even if Vienna does not boast the wide range of shops you find in many other European capitals, it does offer certain goods that are hard to beat elsewhere. Austrian glassware is justly famous and cut-glass gifts are of a high quality. A few shops, such as **Knize** (in the Graben), designed by Adolf Loos, are in themselves worth a visit simply to admire the Jugendstil architecture. It's best to speak English in shops unless you are fluent in German – you will probably receive quicker service!

SPECIALITY SHOPS

Vienna still manufactures leather goods, although nowadays a lot are imported from Italy. **Robert Horn** designs and manufactures leather travel cases and accessories. He maintains that even he has been unable to improve on the design of a briefcase carried by Metternich at the Congress of Vienna, which he has only slightly modernized.

Petit point embroidery is another Viennese speciality. Some of the most attractive can be found at **Petit Point** (where even the shop's door handle is embroidered) and at **Maria Stransky**.

A marvellous place for party tricks, and much beloved by practical jokers, is **Zauberklingl**. **Kober** (see p232) is a "serious" toy shop which sells well-made dolls and toys. Or combine a visit to the novelty and joke shop called **Witte** with a trip to the Naschmarkt. Witte stocks masks, fancy dress outfits, and beautiful old-fashioned paper decorations that are ideal for festivals. **Metzger**, a shop specializing in beeswax, sells its own candles and candlesticks. It also stocks certain gift items, such as honey cakes and boxes of chocolates.

MUSIC

As you would expect in "the City of Music", the range of recordings available is rich and varied. The shops with the widest range of classical CDs are **EMI** and **Gramola**. However, don't expect to find many bargains: CDs and tapes are more expensive in Austria than in other countries in Europe.

Arcadia specializes particularly in opera and operetta. The staff in all these shops are usually very knowledgeable. **Doblinger** is excellent for sheet music; it also has a second-hand department and CD shop.

JEWELLERY

Viennese jewellers have long been famous for their fine workmanship. Fruit and flower brooches carved in semi-precious stones and sometimes studded with diamonds, are a more recent Austrian innovation. **Juwelier Wagner** always has a good selection. Both **Köchert** and **Heldwein** were jewellers to the Imperial Court and still produce beautiful jewellery in their own workshops today. Köchert also sells antique pieces and Heldwein are known for their multi-coloured chains of semi-precious stones. A few years ago, one of the pieces designed by **Schullin** won the prestigious Diamonds International award organized by De Beers for innovative design. Their small window usually attracts a crowd of admirers to view their latest creations. Don't let that put you off – prices start at a reasonable level.

GLASSWARE

The Chandeliers at Vienna's Opera House and the Metropolitan Opera in New York are by **J & L Lobmeyr**, as are the chandeliers in numerous palaces throughout the world – including the Kremlin. This company – now run by a fifth generation of the same family – has produced beautiful glasses and crystal chandeliers since the early 19th century, often commissioning famous artists. One range of glasses still in production today was designed by Josef Hoffmann (see p56) in Jugendstil style. Its famous *Musselinglas*, a type of glass so fine that it almost bends to the touch, is exquisite. There is a small but superb glass museum on the first floor apart from its own glassware, Lobmeyr also sells select items of Hungarian Herend porcelain.

INTERIORS

Vienna's porcelain makers, **Augarten**, are the second oldest in Europe. The company was founded in 1718 and taken over by the House of Habsburg in 1744. Ever since, its products have been marked with their banded shield coat of arms. Each piece of porcelain at **Schloss Augarten** is still hand finished and painted: patterns and shapes are based on original models from the Baroque, Rococo, Biedermeier and Art Deco periods and on designs created by present-day artists. The Schloss Augarten factory is open to visitors. **Ostovics** stocks glass and porcelain as well as kitchen-ware, and is good for gifts.

Founded in 1849, **Back-hausen** is known for its exclusive furnishing fabrics, woven in the original Jugend-stil patterns, and for its silk scarves and matching velvet handbags. In addition it has a good selection of duvets and household linens. Quality bedding and linens are available at **Gans**, which conveniently has a shop at Vienna's Schwechat airport for last-minute purchases. **Gunkel** stocks household linen and bath robes, and for generations the Viennese have patronized **Zur Schwäbischen Jungfrau**, founded in 1720, where fine linens can be made to order as well as purchased ready-made.

FOOD AND WINE

One of Vienna's most renowned and almost revered food and wine shops, **Zum Schwarzen Kameel** (see p212), sells mouth-watering produce.

Julius Meinl am Graben food hall, on the pedes-trianized Graben, also offers a wide selection of delicacies. Enter via its Lukullus Bar in Naglergasse if you decide you would like to stop for a snack and a drink.

There is also a good chain of wine merchants called **Wein & Co**, one of which is situated on the Jasomir-gottstrasse.

Altmann & Kühne is famous for its tiny, hand-made chocolates sold in beautiful boxes shaped like miniature chests of drawers, books, horses and angels.

GIFTS

Successor of the famous Wiener Werkstätten, the outfit called **Österreichische Werkstätten** has a selection of almost exclusively Austrian goods. In stock are a range of enamelled jewellery designed by Michaela Frey, ceramics, mouth-blown glass, candles and, from late autumn onwards, Christmas tree decorations. The arts and crafts markets (see p224) are also good hunting-grounds for picking up knick-knacks. The Tirol-based firm of **Swarovksi** produces high quality crystal. Their necklaces, pins and earrings are popular worldwide, as are their animal figurines and accessories.

BOOKS

Located in the Jewish District is **Shakespeare & Co**, which stocks an extensive selection of books in English, as does **Thalia** (which has several branches) and **Frick International**. For music books in English, visit **Doblinger** (see p222). Rare old books – as well as new ones – can be purchased at **Heck**. Old prints and maps are available at the specialist **Gilhofer**.

Taschenbuchladen bookshop stocks a range of paperbacks.

NEWSPAPERS AND PERIODICALS

Most newspaper kiosks located within the Ringstrasse stock foreign newspapers – and so do the best coffee houses, where they can be read free of charge. There is no English-language Viennese newspaper. **Morawa** sells a variety of newspapers and periodicals in practically any language.

CLOTHES AND ACCESSORIES

Viennese clothes are well-made and tend to be quite formal. **Resi Hammerer** is famous for jackets, coats and capes made from *Loden*. This is a warm, felt-like fabric traditionally in dark green or grey, but now produced in a range of colours.

Tostmann is best known for traditional Austrian costumes or *Trachten: its Dirndl* (dresses) are made from a variety of fabrics including beautiful brocades. Its clothes for children are particularly delightful.

Fürnkranz has several branches throughout Vienna, but its main shop providing elegant day and evening wear is in Kärntner Strasse, with the shop at Neuer Markt stocking more sporty styles. **gty** can always be relied upon for simply-tailored dresses and suits in silk and fine wool.

A trusted and old-established Viennese name is **Knize**. In imperial times this was a famous tailoring establishment, but the shop now stocks ready-to-wear clothes for men and women. It also sells its own scent. **Kettner** – almost hidden down a nearby side street – stocks casual daywear for both men and women at all its branches.

All the shoes at **Bally** are imported from Italy; the quality, as you would expect, is excellent. **D'Ambrosio**, which has several branches located in the first district, stocks trendy, up-market Italian-style shoes for both men and women at moderate prices. **Kurt Denkstein** is another shoe retailer with stock at reasonable prices.

Younger, trendier shoppers should head straight to Judengasse – this street has plenty of reasonably priced boutiques with styles to suit every taste. For menswear in particular, **D G Linnerth** stocks informal and sporty clothes designed for teenagers upwards. The branch of the trendy clothes chain **H & M**, on Graben, is worth a visit if only to view the gilded birdcage of a lift.

An optician called **Erich Hartmann** bought a shop with a large stock of horn and tortoiseshell back in 1980. Today he sells a range of hand-made spectacles, combs and chains, all made from horn. His shop looks like a coffee house and is well-known in the city.

SIZE CHART

For Australian sizes follow British and American convention.

Women's clothes

Austrian	36	38	40	42	44	46	48	50
British	10	12	14	16	18	20	22	24
American	8	10	12	14	16	18	20	22

Shoes

Austrian	36	37	38	39	40	41	42	43
British	3½	4	5	5½	6½	7½	8	9
American	5	5½	6½	7	8	9	9½	10½

Men's shirts

Austrian	44	46	48	50	52	54
British	34	36	38	40	42	44
American	S	M	M	L	XL	XL

Antiques, Auctions and Markets

Many districts in Vienna have their own markets – and a few have several – where you can buy arts and crafts, food, flowers and imported and second-hand goods. The city is also known for its Christmas markets, popular with locals in the evenings. If you are interested in antiques and bric-a-brac, it is worth looking in both the specialist antique shops and the main auction house. Alternatively, enjoy browsing round the bustling ethnic stalls and mix of cultures in the Naschmarkt, Vienna's main food market.

ANTIQUES

Vienna is justly famous for its antique shops. Most are located in the Stephansdom Quarter as well as along Schönbrunner Strasse, where stock ranges from valuable antiques to simply second-hand. The **Dorotheum** *(see Auctions)*, the **Kunst und Antikmarkt** and the Floh-markt *(see Artisan Markets)* should not be missed. Jewellery and antique paintings can be particularly good finds. One of the best shops for antique jewellery is the **Galerie Rauhenstein**. It stocks rare and beautiful pieces up to and including the 1940s.

If you are interested in old jewellery and silver and other antiques, **Herbert Asenbaum** is worth a visit. For larger pieces and shops on a larger scale, try **Subal & Subal** on Spiegelgasse or **Reinhold Hofstätter** on Bräunerstrasse. They are both well established and have a good selection of fine antique furniture.

AUCTIONS

Opened in 1707 as a pawn-brokers for the "new poor", and appropriately called the *Armen Haus* (poor house), Vienna's **Dorotheum** is now the city's most important auction house. In 1788 it moved to the site of a former convent called the Dorotheerkirche, which had an altar-piece of St Dorothea in it – hence the name. This is an interesting place to browse around, and since buying is not restricted to auction times, you can often purchase items over the counter. It has other branches dotted around the city.

FOOD MARKETS

Between the Linke and Rechte Wienzeile, the **Naschmarkt** *(see p138)* is worth visiting even if you don't buy anything. Exotic fruit and vegetables, notably Greek, Turkish and Asian specialities, crowd the stalls and are piled high in the shops. It is a fascinating place to wander around and observe life. Open all year round, it acts as a meeting point for people of different nationalities who come to buy and sell fruit and vegetables, tea, herbs and spices. The section near the Karlsplatz contains the more expensive Viennese-run stalls. These gradually give way to stands run by colourful Turkish stall-holders as you move further towards the flea market.

In addition to the exotic food stalls, you will see Czechs selling hand puppets, Russians selling Babushka dolls and Turks with stalls piled high with eastern clothes. The market is also a good spot for late-night revellers to feast on highly-spiced fish snacks in the early hours of the morning.

Food-lovers should not miss the farmers' market known as the **Bauernmarkt**. A whole range of organic and other country produce is on sale here on Saturday mornings.

ARTISAN MARKETS

Antique markets and arts and crafts markets are fairly new to Vienna, but the Flohmarkt (flea market) at the end of the **Naschmarkt** *(see p138)* and the **Kunst und Antikmarkt** are established hunting grounds for second-hand goods and antiques. The price quoted is probably not the price that you are expected to pay – it's usually assumed that you will bargain.

For the better quality hand-crafted goods, head to the Spittelberg market *(see p117)* near the Volkstheater. Here artists and craftspeople sell their own products rather than mass-produced factory goods. This is a fashionable and attractive part of Vienna and, although the market is small, you are likely to find gifts of good quality. There are also small galleries and cafés where artists exhibit their works.

The **Heiligenkreuzerhof** *(see p75)* art market is in a quiet, secluded courtyard where a small, select group of exhibitors is on hand should you wish to discuss the work. The stalls sell jewellery, ceramics and other hand-made goods. Further entertainment and atmosphere is provided by an Austrian folk singer dressed in traditional clothes playing his accordion.

FESTIVE MARKETS

Christmas markets in Vienna are very special, the most famous of all being the **Christkindlmarkt** *(see p64)* held in front of the Rathaus. Attractions vary from year to year, but there are always sideshows, decorated trees, performances on a temporary stage and lots of stalls, as well as a workshop for making Christmas presents and baking goodies. Items for sale include honey cakes, bees-wax candles, Christmas decorations and various crafts, although the main attraction is the joyous atmosphere. It is especially magical at night when everything is lit up.

The **Alt Wiener Christ-kindlmarkt** *(see p64)* at the Freyung is a smaller affair. Two weeks before Easter there is also an Easter market here with a large selection of blown and hand-painted eggs. Four other Christmas markets take place in the Spittelberg area, in front of Schloss Schönbrunn, at Karlskirche and at the Heiligenkreuzerhof.

DIRECTORY

SPECIALITY SHOPS

Kober
Graben 14–15. **Map** 2 D5 & 5 C3. **Tel** 53360180.

Maria Stransky
Hofburg Passage 2.
Map 5 C4. **Tel** 5336098.

Metzger
Stephansplatz 7. **Map** 2 E5 & 6 D3. **Tel** 5123433.
One of two branches.

Petit Point
Kärntner Strasse 16.
Map 4 D1 & 6 D4.
Tel 5124886.

Robert Horn
Bräunerstrasse 7.
Map 5 C4. **Tel** 5138294.

Witte
Linke Wienzeile 16.
Map 3 A4. **Tel** 58643050.

Zauberklingl
Führichgasse 4. **Map** 5 C4. **Tel** 5126868.

MUSIC

Arcadia
Kärntner Strasse 40.
Map 4 D2 & 5 C5.
Tel 5139568.

Doblinger
Dorotheergasse 10.
Map 5 C3. **Tel** 515030.

EMI
Kärntner Str 30. **Map** 4 D1 & 6 D4. **Tel** 51236750.

Gramola
Graben 16. **Map** 2 D5 & 5 C3. **Tel** 5335034.

JEWELLERY

Heldwein
Graben 13.
Map 5 C3. **Tel** 5125781.

Juwelier Wagner
Kärntnerstrasse 32.
Map 4 D1. **Tel** 5120512.

Köchert
Neuer Markt 15.
Map 5 C4. **Tel** 51258280.

Schullin
Kohlmarkt 7. **Map** 2 D5 & 5 C3. **Tel** 53390070.

GLASSWARE

J & L Lobmeyr
Kärntner Str 26. **Map** 2 D5 & 6 D4. **Tel** 5120508.

INTERIORS

Augarten
Stock-im-Eisen-Platz 3–4.
Map 2 D5 & 5 C3.
Tel 5121494.
One of several branches.

Backhausen
Schwarzenbergstrasse 10.
Map 6 D5. **Tel** 514040.

Gans
Brandstätte 1–3. **Map** 4 D1 & 6 D3. **Tel** 5333560.
One of several branches.

Gunkel
Tuchlauben 11. **Map** 2D5 & 5 C3. **Tel** 53363010.

Ostovics
Stephansplatz 9. **Map** 6 D3. **Tel** 5331411.

Schloss Augarten
Obere Augartenstrasse 1.
Map 2 E2. **Tel** 211240.

Zur Schwäbischen Jungfrau
Graben 26. **Map** 2 D5 & 5 C3. **Tel** 5355356.

FOOD AND WINE

Altmann & Kühne
Graben 30. **Map** 2 D5 & 5 C3. **Tel** 5330927.
One of two branches.

Julius Meinl am Graben
Graben 19. **Map** 2 D5 & 5 C3. **Tel** 5323334.

Wein & Co
Jasomirgottstrasse 3–5.
Map 6 D3. **Tel** 5330916.

Zum Schwarzen Kameel
Bognergasse 5.
Map 5 C3. **Tel** 5338125.

GIFTS

Österreichische Werkstätten
Kärntner Str 6. **Map** 4 D1 & 6 D4. **Tel** 5122418.

Swarovski
Kärntnerstrasse 8. **Map** 6 D4. **Tel** 5129032.

BOOKS

Frick International
Schulerstrasse 1-3 .
Map 6 D3. **Tel** 5126905.

Gilhofer
Rathausstrasse 19 .
Map 1 C5. **Tel** 40961900.

Heck
Kärntner Ring 14. **Map** 4 E2 & 6 D5. **Tel** 5055152.

Shakespeare & Co
Sterngasse 2. **Map** 2 E5 & 6 D2. **Tel** 5355053.

Thalia
Mariahilferstrasse 99.
Map 3 A2. **Tel** 5954550.
One of several branches.

NEWSPAPERS AND PERIODICALS

Morawa
Wollzeile 11. **Map** 2 E5 & 6 D3. **Tel** 515620.

CLOTHES AND ACCESSORIES

Bally
Kärntnerstrasse 9.
Map 6 D5. **Tel** 516490.

D'Ambrosio
Jasomirgottstrasse 6.
Map 6 D3. **Tel** 5330416.

D G Linnerth
Lugeck 1–2. **Map** 6 D3.
Tel 5125888.

Erich Hartmann
Singerstrasse 8, Corner of Lilieng. **Map** 6 D3.
Tel 5121489.

Flamm
Neuer Markt 12.
Map 5 C4. **Tel** 5122889.

Fürnkranz
Kärntner Str 39.
Map 6 D4 & 5 C5.
Tel 4884426. One of several branches.

H & M
Graben 8. **Map** 2 D5 & 5 C3. **Tel** 5125505. One of several branches.

J&R Denkstein
Stephansplatz 4. **Map** 6 D3. **Tel** 5127465.

Kettner
Plankengasse 7. **Map** 5 C4. **Tel** 5132239.

Knize
Graben 13. **Map** 2 D5 & 5 C3. **Tel** 51221190.

Resi Hammerer
Kärntner Str 29–31. **Map** 4 D1 & 5 C5. **Tel** 5126952.

Tostmann
Schottengasse 3a.
Map 5 B2. **Tel** 53353310.

ANTIQUES

Galerie Rauhenstein
Rauhensteingasse 3.
Map 6 D4. **Tel** 5133009.

Herbert Asenbaum
Kärntner Str 28. **Map** 4 D1 & 6 D4. **Tel** 5122847.

Reinhold Hofstätter
Bräunerstrasse 12.
Map 5 C4. **Tel** 5335069.

Subal & Subal
Spiegelgasse 8. **Map** 4 D1 & 5 C4. **Tel** 5131349.

AUCTIONS

Dorotheum
Dorotheergasse 17. **Map** 4 D1 &5 C4. **Tel** 51560.

MARKETS

Alt Wiener Christkindlmarkt
Freyung. **Map** 2 D5 & 5 B2. ◻ 17 Nov–24 Dec: 9:30am–7:30pm daily.

Bauernmarkt
Freyung. **Map** 2 D5 & 5 B2. ◻ Mar–end Oct: 10am–6:30pm Tue & Thu.

Christkindlmarkt
At the Neues Rathaus.
Map 1 C5 & 5 A2. ◻ Mid-Nov–24 Dec: 10am–7pm daily.

Heiligenkreuzerhof
Map 2 E5 & 6 E3. ◻ Apr–Sep: first Sat & Sun of each month; end Nov–Mar: 10am–6pm Sat & Sun.

Kunst und Antikmarkt
Donaukanal-Promenade.
Map 6 F2. ◻ May–end Sep: 2–8pm Sat, 10am–8pm Sun.

Naschmarkt
Map 3 C2. ◻ 6am–6:30pm Mon–Fri, 6am–6pm Sat.

ENTERTAINMENT IN VIENNA

Vienna offers a wide range of entertainment, particularly of the musical variety. There is grand opera at the Opera House – Staatsoper *(see pp140–1)* – or the latest musical at the Theater an der Wien *(see p138)*. Dignified orchestral concerts and elegant Viennese waltzes take place at the great balls during the Carnival season, and waltzes are played in the relaxed atmosphere of the Stadtpark. Even the famous Lipizzaner horses perform to Viennese music and no visit to the city is complete without a trip to the

Pipo at the Ronacher *(see p228)*

Winter Riding School *(see pp98–9)*. Vienna also has excellent theatres, two of which perform in English, and several cinemas which specialize in classic films. Restaurants close early, but you can still be entertained around the clock at one of Vienna's many nightspots. Within the Ringstrasse, the city buzzes with late-night revellers enjoying jazz clubs, such as the Roter Engel, discos, casinos and bars with live music. Or you can end your day sipping coffee and nibbling pastries at a late-night café *(see also pp217–19)*.

The stage of the Theater in der Josefstadt *(see p116)*

PRACTICAL INFORMATION

A monthly guide to Vienna is issued free by the Wiener Tourismusverband (main Vienna Tourist Office – *see p238*). Posters which list the weekly programmes for the opera houses and theatres are pasted on billboard columns and displayed in most hotel lobbies. They also list casts for all the performances. Each day the four main newspapers in the city, *Die Presse, Kronenzeitung, Standard* and *Kurier* *(see p239)* publish programme listings. All four also give details of daily cinema performances and concerts as well as the main sporting events.

BOOKING TICKETS

You can buy tickets direct from the appropriate box office (check opening hours, since these vary), or reserve them on the telephone. The phone numbers and addresses for the booking offices are listed in the Music, Theatre and Cinema directories *(see pp229–30)*. The four state theatres, the Burgtheater *(see p132)*, the Akademietheater *(see p230)*, the Opera House *(see pp140–1)* and the Wiener Volksoper *(see p229)*, all have

Billboard column

one central booking office, the **Bundestheaterkassen** *(see p229)*. However, tickets for performances at any of these four theatres can also be purchased at the box office of the Wiener Volksoper and the Burgtheater.

Tickets usually go on sale a week before the performance. Tickets for the Vienna State Opera are sold from one month in advance. However, bear in mind that tickets for September performances are sold during the month of June.

Phone reservations for credit-card holders can be made from six days in advance. Written applications for tickets for the state theatre must reach the Vienna State Opera ticket office (address as Bundestheaterkassen) no later than three weeks before the date of the performance.

Standing-room tickets are sold at the evening box office one hour before the start of the performance.

Tickets for the state theatres, the Theater an der Wien *(see p138)*, the **Raimund Theater** *(see p229)* and **Konzerthaus** *(see p228)* can be used on public transport for two hours before, and six hours after, all performances. Agencies are reliable – try **Reisebüro Mondial** *(see p229)* – and hotel staff may be able to obtain tickets. Otherwise try the box office for returns.

AT THE THEATRE

If you visit the theatre in person, you will be able to see the seating plan and make your choice accordingly. The monthly programme for the state theatres also contains individual seating plans and it is a good idea to have them in front of you when booking your tickets by telephone. Most hotel porters will also have copies of seating plans for the principal venues.

If you book by telephone remember that *Parkett* (stalls) are in front and are usually the most expensive. In some theatres the front rows of the stalls are known as *Orchestersitze*. The *Parterre* (back stalls) are cheaper and the dress circle (the grand or royal circle) is called *Erster Rang*, followed by the *Zweiter Rang* (balcony). At the Burgtheater and Opera House, there are two extra levels called the *Balkon* and *Galerie*. The higher you go, the cheaper the seats are.

Casino Wien in Esterházy Palace

Boxes are known as *Logen* and the back seats are always cheaper than the front seats.

At the **Wiener Volksoper** *(see p229)* they still have *Säulensitze*, seats where the view is partly obscured by a column. These cheap tickets are bought by music lovers who come to listen rather than to view. There are four tiers of boxes at the Volksoper, known in ascending order as *Parterre, Balkon, Erster Rang* and *Zweiter Rang*.

Buffets at Vienna's principal theatres provide alcoholic and non-alcoholic drinks, and tasty snacks which range from open sandwiches at the **Akademietheater** *(see p230)* and Volksoper to the more elaborate

Busker beneath the Pestsäule

concoctions at the Opera House and Burgtheater. Small open sandwiches with caviar, egg, smoked salmon, cheese and salami on Vienna roll-style bread are also common. Glasses of *Sekt*, a sparkling wine, are always available.

Buffets are usually open for up to one hour before the start of a performance and are often fairly empty. They are an ideal place for relaxing with a snack and a drink, and the coffee is extremely good.

It is not usual to tip ushers at theatres, unless you are being shown to a box, but you may round up the price of a theatre programme.

Coats and hats have to be left in the cloakroom before you go to your seat. There is usually no fixed charge, and tipping is at your discretion.

FACILITIES FOR THE DISABLED

A number of venues offer wheelchair access or help for those with hearing difficulties. Be sure to make your needs very clear when booking tickets.

A booklet, *Wien für Gäste mit Handicaps* (Vienna for handicapped guests), is published by the Wiener Tourismus-verband *(see p238)* and provides information on facilities at entertainment venues, museums, hotels, restaurants, cafés, cinemas, post offices and so on.

TRANSPORT

Buses and trams run until around 11:30pm, while the underground continues until about midnight *(see Getting Around Vienna, pp250–55)*. Night buses are popular, with eight routes operating around the city and into the suburbs. They start at 12:30am from Schwedenplatz, the Opera and Schottentor, and continue every half hour until 4am. Tickets usually cost around one euro and are sold on the bus *(see p255)*.

You can phone for a taxi from your venue, or take one from outside. Taxis usually line up outside theatres after a performance, otherwise you can go to one of the many taxi ranks which are found on most street corners. Taxis which do not stop when hailed are already booked.

CASINOS

Casinos Austria has become the hallmark for superbly run casinos all over the world (you will even find them aboard luxury liners), but **Casino Wien** is a showcase. It is set in the Baroque Esterházy Palace *(see p80)* and you can play French or American roulette, baccarat and poker there. The complex includes a bar, a restaurant and the **Jackpot Casino**, which is a typically Viennese addition.

Casino Wien

Kärntner Strasse 41. Map 4 D1.
Casino ☐ *3pm–4am daily.*
Jackpot Casino ☐ *10am–1am daily.* **Tel** *5124836.*

Dancing at the grand Opera Ball *(see p141)*

Music in Vienna

The Vienna Opera House *(see pp140–41)* is one of the greatest of its kind in the world and, like all four state theatres, is heavily subsidised. The acoustics are excellent – the world-famous conductor Arturo Toscanini advised on the rebuilding of the theatre after it was destroyed at the end of the last war. The house orchestra, the Vienna Philharmonic, performs while the Opera House is open from September until June. Most operas are sung in the original language. The city supports two principal orchestras, the Vienna Philharmonic and the Wiener Symphoniker. There are also a number of chamber music ensembles and visiting artists. Church music is often of concert quality. You can hear more informal music in the Stadtpark, where a small orchestra regularly plays waltzes in summer. Live rock music is popular in discos, and there is an annual jazz festival *(see p63)*.

OPERA AND OPERETTA

Seat prices at the Vienna Opera House range from €10 to €192. Tickets are sold one month in advance of a performance, except standing-room tickets, which are on sale one hour before the performance starts. These are good value, but because of this there is usually a long queue. After buying your ticket you can mark your space by tying a scarf around the rail, leaving you free to wander around. The New Year's Eve performance is always *Die Fledermaus* by Johann Strauss, and famous guests sometimes make surprise appearances during the second act.

The **Wiener Volksoper** is renowned for its superb operetta productions of works by composers ranging from Strauss, Millöcker and Ziehrer to Lehár and Kálmán. There are also performances of musicals and light opera by Mozart, Puccini and Bizet, sung in German. Prices can range from €3 to €58, and the season is exactly the same as the Opera House.

Concealed in a small side street in the Stephansdom Quarter is one of Vienna's great little opera houses the **Wiener Kammeroper**. Many international singers such as Waldemar Kmentt, Eberhard Waechter and Walter Berry started their careers here. You can expect anything to be peformed here from the early works of Rossini to classic operetta, as well as rock versions of familiar operas such as *Tales of Hoffmann* and *Carmen,* and opera parodies.

Since 2006, another venue for opera is the **Theater an der Wien**. Musicals had previously been staged here. These are now put on at the historic **Ronacher**, once Vienna's most glamorous theatre, and the large **Raimund Theater**. In May and June, the Wiener Festwochen *(see p63)* presents theatre and music theatre productions in a variety of venues, most notably Halle G at the MuseumsQuartier.

July sees opera performances by **Oper Klosterneuburg** in the Kaiserhof courtyard of Klosterneuburg, the palatial religious foundation a short way north of Vienna. The festival **Seefestspiele Mörbisch** *(see p63)* takes place every weekend in July and August on a stage projecting on to Lake Neusiedl.

CLASSICAL CONCERTS

The principal venues for classical concerts are the **Musikverein** (including the Brahmsaal and the new halls of Gläserner Saal and Steinerner Saal) and the concert halls of the **Konzerthaus**. Performances are also held in places such as Schubert's birthplace in Nussdorf *(see p185)* and in many historic palaces.

The New Year's Concert *(see p65)* is televised live from the Grosser Musikvereinsaal in the Musikverein every year. You can apply for tickets by writing direct to the **Wiener Philharmoniker**. However, applications must be received on 2 January (not before, not after) for the next year's concert. You can order from abroad by telegram.

Waltz concerts and operetta, which include stars from the Vienna Volksoper, can be heard at the Musikverein, the Neue Burg *(see p95)* and the Konzerthaus on Tuesdays, Thursdays and Saturdays from April until October. Mozart and Strauss concerts are performed on Wednesdays at the Neue Burg. All tickets are the same price, so the best thing to do is to get there early if you want to make sure of getting the best seat. The Konzerthaus and Musikverein concert seasons run from October to June (for events from July to September, see p63).

CHURCH MUSIC

Details of the many church concerts performed in Vienna are published in all the daily newspapers. Look out particularly for details of Sunday mass at the following places: Augustinerkirche *(see p102)*, Minoritenkirche *(see p103)*, the Jesuitenkirche/ Jesuit church *(see p70 and 73)*, Stephansdom *(see p76)* and Michaelerkirche *(see p92)*. In July and August, many other churches hold organ recitals.

The Vienna Boys' Choir *(see p39)* can be heard during mass at the Burgkapelle *(see p103)* every Sunday and religious holiday at 9:15am except from July to mid-September. (Tickets are available from the Burgkapelle; the box office is open the Friday before). You can also hear them at the **Konzerthaus** every Friday at 3:30pm in May, June, September and October. Buy tickets from hotel porters and from **Reisebüro Mondial**. Book well in advance.

INFORMAL MUSIC

The description just outside **Konzert-Café Schmid Hansl** reads, "the home of Viennese song". The original owner of this small café, which serves hot food until it closes, was Hansl Schmid, a very fine singer and musician. Guests would often visit the café just to hear him sing, and sometimes a famous artist might join him in a duet or give a solo performance. The present owner, Hansl Schmid's son, once a member of the Vienna Boys' Choir, has kept up this tradition, and you may well encounter opera stars coming in to perform unexpectedly.

Another Viennese favourite is the **Wiener Kursalon**. Dinner and waltz evenings with the Johann Strauss Salonorchester are held daily throughout the year along with classical ballet performances. Concerts take place in the Stadtpark during the summer months.

ROCK, POP AND JAZZ

What is popular one week in Vienna's lively music scene may very well be out of fashion the next. Many discos have live music on certain nights or for a limited period.

U4 disco has a different style every night (from industrial to flower power) and Thursday is gay night. **Tanzcafé** and **Volksgarten Club Disco** are the oldest in town with live hip-hop and salsa. Also still popular is **Take Five. Roter Engel** in the Bermuda Triangle has live music every night and there is a midnight show at **Nachtwerk**.

Live concerts are held at the **Café Szene**, **Jazzland**, and on Sundays at **Chelsea**. Popular among artistic circles is the **Broadway Piano Bar** which has live music every night. Monday is Jazz night and Saturday is Night Line featuring renowned performers. A must for jazz fans is **Porgy & Bess**, with live music and dancing, and the **Jazzfest** held in the first two weeks of July, with concerts in various venues such as the Opera House (*see pp140–41*), the Volkstheater (*p230*) and the Neues Rathaus (*p130*) as well as many open-air events. All styles, electro and house as well as alternative music can be found at **Café Leopold**, **Schikaneder Bar** and **Flex**.

DIRECTORY

OPERA AND OPERETTA

Bundestheaterkassen
Central Ticket Office.
Operngasse 2, A-1010.
Map 5 C4. *Tel 5131513.*
⏰ 8am–6pm Mon–Fri,
9am–noon Sat, Sun & hols.

Oper Klosterneuburg
Kaiserhof Courtyard,
Klosterneuburg.
Tel 02243444425.

Raimund Theater
Wallgasse 18, A-1060.
Tel 58885. **www.**
musicalvienna.at

Reisebüro Mondial
Faulmanngasse 4.
Map 4 D2. *Tel 58804141.*

Ronacher
Seilerstatte 9, A-1010.
Map 4 E1 & 6 D4.
Tel 58885.
www.musicalvienna.at

Seefestspiele Mörbisch
Mörbisch am,
Neusiedlersee, Burgenland.
Tel 02685 8181
(Jul & Aug). **www.**
seefestspiele-moerbisch.at

Wiener Kammeroper
Fleischmarkt 24, A-1010.
Map 2 E5 & 6 D2.
Tel 51201-0077. **www.**
wienerkammeroper.at

Wiener Volksoper
Währinger Strasse 78,
A-1090. **Map** 1 B2.
Tel 514443670.
www.volksoper.at

CLASSICAL CONCERTS

Konzerthaus
Lothringerstrasse 20,
A-1030. **Map** 4 E2 & 6 E5.
Tel 242002.
www.konzerthaus.at

Musikverein
Bösendorferstrasse 12.
Map 6 D5. *Tel 5058190.*
www.musikverein.at

Orangery at Schönbrunn
Tel 81250040
⏰ Apr–Oct: concerts
8:30pm daily. **www.**
imagevienna.com

Wiener Hofburgorchester
Margaretenstrasse 3.
Map 4 D2. *Tel 5872552.*
www.hofburgorchester.at

Wiener Philharmoniker
Bösendorferstrasse 12,

A-1010. **Map** 4 E2 & 6 D5.
Tel 50565250. **www.**
wienerphilharmoniker.at

INFORMAL MUSIC

Konzert-Café Schmid Hansl
Schulgasse 31. **Map** 1 A2.
Tel 4063658.
⏰ 8pm–4am Tue–Sat.

Wiener Kursalon
Johannesgasse 33.
Map 6 E5. *Tel 5125790.*
www.soundofvienna.at

ROCK, POP AND JAZZ

Broadway Piano Bar
Bauermarkt 21.
Map 5 D3.
Tel 5332849.

Café Leopold
Museumsplatz 1.
Map 5 A5. *Tel 5236732.*

Café Szene
Hauffgasse 26.
Tel 7493341.

Chelsea
Stadtbahnbogen 29–31,
A-1080. **Map** 4 D2.
Tel 4079309.

Flex
Donaukanal
Augartenbrücke.
Map 1 D3. *Tel 5337525.*

Jazzfest
See text for venues. *Tel 588660 for information.*

Jazzland
Franz-Josefs-Kai 29.
Map 2 E5 & 6 E2.
Tel 5332575.

Nachtwerk
Dr-Gonda-Gasse 9.
Tel 6168880.

Porgy & Bess
Riemergasse 11. **Map** 5 E4.
Tel 5128811.

Roter Engel
Rabensteig 5. **Map** 6 D2.
Tel 5354105.

Schikaneder Bar
Margaretenstrasse 22–24.
Map 3 C3. *Tel 5852867.*

Take Five
Annagasse 3a. **Map** 4 D1
& 6 D4. *Tel 5129277.*

Tanzcafé Volksgarten
Burgring/Heldenplatz.
Map 3 C1 & 5 B4.
Tel 5330518.

U4
Schönbrunner Strasse 222.
Map 3 A4. *Tel 8158307.*

Theatre and Cinema

Vienna has a good choice of theatres, with an eclectic mix of styles ranging from classical drama to the avant-garde. Some places, like the early 19th-century Josefstadt Theater *(see p116)*, are well worth visiting for their architecture alone. You can see productions in English at the English Theatre or, if you understand German, you can go and watch one of the many fringe performances. Some cinemas screen films in their original language. The classic film which is usually showing somewhere in the city is *The Third Man*, set in Vienna during the Allied occupation.

THEATRES

Viennese theatre is some of the best in Europe and the **Burgtheater** *(see p132)*, one of the City's four state theatres, is the most important venue. Classic and modern plays are performed here and even if your understanding of German is limited, you will still enjoy a new production (which can often be avant-garde) of a Shakespeare play. For classic and modern plays go to the **Akademietheater**, part of the Burgtheater.

The **Josefstadt Theater** *(see p116)* is worth a visit for the interior alone. As the house lights slowly dim, the crystal chandeliers float gently to the ceiling. It offers excellent productions of

Austrian plays as well as classics from other countries, and the occasional musical. **Kammerspiele** is the Josefstadt's "little house". The old and well-established **Volkstheater** offers modern plays as well as the occasional classic and some operetta performances.

Vienna has a wide range of fringe theatre from one-man shows to *Kabarett* – these are satirical shows not cabarets – but fairly fluent German is needed to appreciate them. German-speakers will also enjoy the highly recommended **Kabarett Simpl**, which has recently reopened.

Theatres that give performances in English include **Vienna's English Theatre** and

the **International Theater**. Plays at the English Theatre are cast and rehearsed in London or New York before opening in Vienna. Some run for a short period only, but they often feature famous international stars.

The International Theater has a Vienna-based ensemble of English-speaking actors. The company presents a wide range of works, with an emphasis on the 20th century. There is also a new production of Charles Dickens' *A Christmas Carol* every year.

CINEMAS

A cinema that screens the latest films in their original language is the **Burg Kino**, while the **Haydn Cinema** and the **Artis International** show new releases in English only. Cinemas that specialize in showing old and new classics as well as the more unusual films are the **Österreichisches Filmmuseum**, **Filmhaus Stöbergasse**, **Filmcasino**, and **Votiv-Kino** (which has a special cinema breakfast on Sundays). The **Apollo Center** is a modern complex and has the largest cinema screen in Austria.

DIRECTORY

THEATRES

Akademietheater
Lisztstrasse 1, A-1030.
Map 4 E2.
Tel 514444740.

Burgtheater
Dr Karl-Lueger-Ring,
A-1014. **Map** 1 C5 &
5 A2. *Tel 514444145.*

International Theater
Porzellangasse 8, A-1090.
Map 1 C3.
Tel 3196272.

Josefstadt Theater
Josefstädt Strasse 26, A-1080. **Map** 1 B5.
Tel 427000.

Kabarett Simpl
Wollzeile 36,
A-1010.
Map 2 E5 & 6 E3.
Tel 5124742.

Kammerspiele
Rotenturmstrasse 20,
A-1010. **Map** 2 E5 & 6 E2
Tel 42700300.

Vienna's English Theatre
Josefsgasse 12, A-1080.
Map 1 B5. *Tel 4021260.*

Volkstheater
Neustiftgasse 1,
A-1070.
Map 3 B1.
Tel 52111400.

CINEMAS

Apollo Center
Gumpendorfer Strasse 63.
Map 3 A4 & 5 B5.
Tel 5879651.

Artis International
Schulgasse 5,
A-1010.
Map 1 A2.
Tel 5356570.

Burg Kino
Opernring 19.
Map 4 D1 & 5 B5.
Tel 5878406.

Filmcasino
Margaretenstrasse 78.
Map 3 C3.
Tel 5879062.

Filmhaus Stöbergasse
Stöbergasse 11–15.
Map 3 B5.
Tel 5466630.

Haydn Cinema
Mariahilfer Strasse 57.
Map 3 B2.
Tel 5872262.

Österreichisches Filmmuseum
Augustinerstrasse 1.
Map 4 D1 & 5 C4.
Tel 5337054.

Votiv-Kino
Währinger Strasse 12.
Map 1 C4
Tel 3173571.

Sport and Dance

Outdoor activities are extremely popular. Football is followed by many locals – especially since the pre-war victories of the famous "Wonder Team". Visitors who enjoy swimming can take advantage of the pools the city has to offer. Horse racing and ice-skating also attract many locals. Flat racing takes place at the Freudenau in the Prater. The well-equipped **Stadthalle** is ideal for spectator sports like boxing and wrestling and houses its own pool, bowling alleys and ice rink. Many of Vienna's dance schools hold special waltz classes during the Carnival season (see p65).

ICE-SKATING

Outdoor ice-skating is very-popular in Vienna. Locals make good use of the open-air rinks at the Eislaufanlage Engelmann and the Wiener Eislaufverein (see p234).

SWIMMING

Vienna can be very warm in summer and has many outdoor pools, including the **Schönbrunner Bad** in the Schönbrunn Palace park (see pp172–73). The **Krapfenwald-bad** has wonderful views over Vienna, and the **Schafbergbad** holds underwater gymnastics every Tuesday and Thursday. The **Thermalbad Oberlaa** has three open-air pools and an indoor pool. The Kinderfreibad Augarten (see p234) is popular with children,

and they can be left at the Kinderfreibad to be watched by the attendants. Beach huts on the Alte Donau coast can be hired daily from **Strand-bad Gänsehäufel** or **Strand-bad Alte Donau**, where you can also hire boats. Strandbad Gänsehäufel has a beach, a heated pool, table tennis and Punch and Judy shows. For relaxing beaches, the world's longest water slide, barbecues and a night bus at weekends, visit **Donauinsel**.

FOOTBALL

The Viennese are enthusiastic football fans, and there are two huge covered football stadiums in the city. The **Ernst Happel Stadion** (which seats 48,000) is in the Prater and the **Hanappi Stadion** (which seats 20,000) is at Hütteldorf.

HORSE RACING

The prater offers a wide range of activities (see pp162–63), including trotting races at the **Krieau**.

DANCING AND DANCE SCHOOLS

During the Carnival season (see p65) many balls, and some fancy dress dances, are held in Vienna. Venues include the Hofburg, the Neues Rathaus (see p130) and the Musikverein (see p229). The grandest event is the Opera Ball (see p141), which takes place on the Thursday before Ash Wednesday. The opening ceremony includes a perfor-mance by the Opera House ballet. An invitation is not needed, you just buy a ticket. The Kaiserball is held at the Neue Burg on New Year's Eve (see pp65 and 95). A special ball calendar is issued by the Wiener Tourismusverband – Vienna Tourist Office (see p238).

The Summer Dance Festival (see p63) runs from July to August. You can learn a range of dances, including rock 'n' roll, at some dance schools in the city. During the Carnival season, some schools hold Viennese waltz classes. The **Elmayer-Vestenbrugg** also teaches etiquette.

DIRECTORY

GENERAL

Stadthalle
Vogelweidplatz 15.
Swimming pool
Tel 98100433.
◻ 8am–9:30pm Mon, Wed, Fri, 6:30am–9:30pm Tue & Thu, 7am–9:30pm Sat, 7am–6pm Sun & public hols.

ICE-SKATING

Eislaufanlage Engelmann
Syringgasse 6–8.
Tel 4051425. ◻ 3rd week Oct–1st week Mar: 9am–6pm Mon,

9am–9:30pm Tue, Thu, Fri, 9am–7pm Wed, Sat, Sun.

SWIMMING

Krapfenwaldbad
Krapfenwaldgasse 65–73.
Tel 3201501.
◻ May–Sep: 9am–8pm Mon–Fri, 8am–8pm Sat & Sun.

Schafbergbad
Josef-Redl-Gasse 2.
Tel 4791593.

Strandbad Alte Donau
Strandbad Alte Donau, Arbeiterstrandbad-strasse 91.
Tel 2636538.

Strandbad Gänsehäufel
Moissigasse 21.
Tel 2699016.

Thermalbad Oberlaa
Kurbadstrasse 14.
Tel 680099600.
◻ 8:45am–10pm Mon–Sat (7:45am–10pm Sun & public hols).

Donauinsel
U1 stop – Donauinsel.

FOOTBALL

Ernst Happel Stadion
Meiereistrasse 7.
Tel 72808540.

Hanappi Stadion
Kaisslergasse 6.
Tel 9145519.

HORSE RACING

Krieau
Prater: trotting
Nordportalstrasse 247.
Tel 7280046 (enquiries).
(see pp64 & 160).

DANCING AND DANCE SCHOOLS

Elmayer-Vestenbrugg
Bräunerstrasse 13.
Map 5 C4.
Tel 5127197 (3–8pm).
◻ 3–8pm Mon–Sat, 5–10pm Sun.

CHILDREN'S VIENNA

Traditionally, the Viennese have a reputation for preferring dogs to children. But negative attitudes towards children are gradually disappearing as the number of families has increased since the 1960s baby boom. Most restaurants serve children's portions, and in some of the more expensive places they can eat Sunday lunch at half price. Eating out at a *Heuriger* is less formal, and you can sit outside in summer. Vienna has many playgrounds and almost all museums offer tours that cater for children. Further out there are large parks, a zoo, swimming pools and ice rinks. Various children's activities are organized throughout the year.

Children pay half price on trams

PRACTICAL ADVICE

Traffic in Vienna can be fast and drivers are not automatically obliged to stop at pelican crossings. Always cross the road at traffic lights, and watch out for speeding cyclists in the bicycle lanes.

Children up to the age of six can travel for free on public transport. Those between the ages of six and 14 must buy a half-price ticket. During the summer holidays (the end of June to the end of August) children under 18 can travel free provided they can show some form of identification when buying a ticket.

It is a good idea to carry some small change, as you will need it to use public lavatories. These are usually clean.

In shops, the assistants may offer children boiled sweets, but do not feel obliged to accept these.

The concierges at many hotels, particularly the larger establishments, can arrange for a baby-sitter. If they cannot, they may be able to suggest a reliable local agency. If you get back from an evening out after about 10 or 11pm, you may have to pay for the baby-sitter's taxi home.

CHILDREN'S SHOPS

Traditional Austrian clothing, which is still worn by some children in Vienna, can be purchased from **Lanz Trachtermoden** on Kärntner Strasse. Traditional dress includes *Lederhosen*, leather shorts, for boys and the *Dirndl*, a traditional dress, for girls. The *Dirndl* is worn with a white lace blouse and an apron. A little bag is sometimes carried as well. Lanz Trachtenmoden also stocks a range of beautiful knitwear in a myriad of colours and designs. Children will particularly like the fine embroidered woollen slippers made in the Tyrol.

Dohnal sells Austrian-made clothes for children up to the age of 16. In addition, the large international chains such as **012 Benetton**, **Jacadi** and **H & M** stock a wide selection of good-quality children's clothes.

Haas & Haas sells delightful craft-like presents, including wooden toys and puppets. They also have a conservatory-style tea house which is an ideal place to treat your

Children on a day out visiting Josefsplatz in the Hofburg

children to lunch, or a delicious cake or *Palatschinken (see pp206–7)*. A more conventional toy shop is **Kober** on the Graben. Kober stocks a superb selection of toys and games, but at high prices.

Dressing up at the Maxim Kinderfest, part of Fasching (see p65)

EATING OUT

Generally speaking, the restaurants in Vienna are not as tolerant of noisy or boisterous children as establishments in many other cities, but there are still a large number of places where children are welcome. It is worth noting that some of the more expensive hotel restaurants offer special Sunday lunch deals for families. The best is probably the **Vienna Marriott** *(see p196)*, where children under 6 eat free and 6 to 12-year-olds eat for half price. The hotel also provides a playroom with a child minder. The **SAS Palais Hotel** offers a similar lunch deal, but does not have a playroom.

Heurige, where you can sit outside in summer, are usually less formal and therefore

Visitors watching the penguins at Vienna's zoo

a better option for families with small children. The best time for families is from 4pm, when most of them open, as they are likely to get busier as the evening goes on. **Heuriger Zimmermann** *(see p219)* has a small zoo where children are permitted to stroke the animals.

There are also a number of well-known fast-food restaurants, including **McDonald's** and **Da Bizi**, which are an option you may decide to go for if your children are fussy about food. Most of them have special children's menus and some offer free gifts for children, especially on their birthdays. The **Wienerwald** Viennese chicken restaurants also have a children's menu. Open until 11:30pm, **Lustig Essen** also caters for children.

Delicious hot chocolate

SIGHTSEEING WITH CHILDREN

Vienna has an amazing variety of attractions that will appeal to children of all ages, including theme parks, funfairs, museums, sports and the zoo.

It usually costs around half the adult entrance fee for children to get into museums. However, be warned that if children touch or get too close to the exhibits, the museum attendants are likely to make a fuss.

Vienna has plenty of parks, but some are designed more for admiring from the pathways than running around in. Watch out for signs warning *Bitte nicht betreten,* which means "Please don't walk on the grass". Details of some of the more child-friendly parks and nature reserves are given on page 234, and there are several playgrounds along the first stretch of the Prater Hauptallee. A picnic in one of these parks is an ideal way to entertain children. Picnic foods and drinks can easily be obtained from a supermarket, and the delicious cakes and pastries that Vienna is famous for can be bought in a *Konditorei* (café and cake shop), of which there are many.

Children's playgrounds in Vienna are generally safe and well equipped. However, it is advisable to avoid the Karlsplatz and Stadtpark play areas because of drug dealing in the vicinity.

Details of some of the more child-friendly parks and nature reserves are given on page 234

DIRECTORY

CHILDREN'S SHOPS

012 Benetton
Goldschmiedgasse 9. **Map** 5 C3.
Tel 5339005.

Dohnal
Kärntner Strasse 12.
Map 4 D1 & 6 D4. *Tel 5127311.*

H & M
Kärntner Strasse 11–15. **Map** 4 D1.

Haas & Haas
Teehandlung, Stephansplatz 4.
Map 2 E3 & 6 D3. *Tel 5129770.*

Jacadi
Trattnerhof 1. **Map** 5 C3.
Tel 5358866.

Kober
Graben 14–15. **Map** 2 D5 & 5 C3.
Tel 5336019.

Lanz Trachtenmoden
Kärntner Strasse 10.
Map 4 D1 & 6 D4. *Tel 5122456.*

EATING OUT

Da Bizi
Rotenturmstrasse 4.
Map 6 D3. *Tel 5133705.*

Lustig Essen
Salvatorgasse 6. **Map** 2 E5 & 6 D2.
Tel 5333037.

McDonald's
Singerstrasse 4.
Map 4 E1 & 6 D3. *Tel 5139279.*

SAS Palais Hotel
Parkring 16. **Map** 4 E1 & 6 E4.
Tel 515170.

Wienerwald
Annagasse 3.
Map 4 D1 & 6 D4. *Tel 5123766.*
Goldschmiedgasse 6.
Map 6 D3. *Tel 050151515.*

Family out cycling, a familiar sight at the Prater

Elephants at Tiergarten Schönbrunn in the palace gardens *(see pp172–73)*

THE ZOO, PARKS AND NATURE RESERVES

Situated in Schönbrunn Palace gardens *(see pp172–73),*this fine zoo *(Tiergarten)* combines historic features with a thoroughly up-to-date layout and the benefit of spacious reserves for the animals. The garden also has a superb maze, which was laid out between 1698 and 1740, and a labyrinth with various games and riddles. With its frescoed ceilings, the central pavilion serves as a charming cafe.

In the Vienna Woods, the Lainzer Tiergarten *(see p171),* is a nature reserve where children can see deer, wild boar and horses. There are playgrounds and a pond. An easy walk takes you to Hermes Villa hunting lodge, with its café and nature-based exhibitions.

FUNFAIR AND CHILDREN'S CITY

An ideal venue for a family outing is the atmospheric **Prater** *(see pp162–63).* Its big wheel is magical at night, and busier than by day. The Prater park also has sandpits, play-grounds, ponds and streams.

Minopolis is a child-size city, with a bank, hospital, supermarket, and fire and police stations where childen aged four to 12 can play at being adults.

Minopolis
Cineplexx Reichsbrücke, Wagramerstrasse 2. **Tel** 2633000. 2–7pm Thu, Fri; 10am–7pm Sat, Sun & hols except Dec 25 & Jan 1.

CHILDREN'S SPORTS

Vienna has some excellent swimming baths, free for children under six, such as the Dianabad *(see p231).* The **Kinderfreibad Augarten**

Ice-skating at Wiener Eislaufverein

is a shallow pool and free for children between the ages of six and 15. However, it is not open to anyone else, except accompanying adults. The

Stadionbad has three children's pools and a water slide and is free to children under 15 on Wednesdays.

In summer, you can swim in the Donauinsel coves *(see p231).* During winter, you can bathe in the hot geysers at Thermalbad Oberlaa *(see p231).*

Between October and March you can go ice-skating at **Wiener Eislaufverein** or at **Eislaufanlage Engelmann**. Then enjoy hot chocolate in a Ringstrasse coffee house like Café Prückel *(see pp58–61)* or Café Schwarzenberg *(see pp60–61)* on Kärntner Ring.

Eislaufanlage Engelmann
Syringgasse 6–8. **Tel** 4051425. 3rd week Oct–1st week Mar: 9am–6pm Mon, 9am–9:30pm Tue, Thu, Fri, 9am–7pm Wed, Sat, Sun.

Wiener Eislaufverein
Lothringerstrasse 28. **Map** 4 E2. **Tel** 71363530. Oct–Mar: 9am–9pm Tue, Thu, Fri, 9am–8pm Sat–Mon, 9am–10pm Wed.

ENTERTAINMENT

Although most theatre is performed in German, the **Märchenbühne der Apfelbaum** marionette theatre sometimes puts on shows in English of favourite fairy tales. Fairy stories with music and song can also be seen at the **Lilarum** puppet theatre. The **Wiener Konzerthaus** and Musikverein hold regular

The big wheel forms a familiar landmark in the Prater park *(see pp162–63)*

concerts for children six times a year on Saturday or Sunday afternoons. In November and December the Opera House *(see pp140–41)* and the Wiener Volksoper *(see p229)* have traditional children's programmes *(Kinderzyklus)*. Productions include Mozart's *The Magic Flute* and Engelbert Humperdink's *Hansel and Gretel*.

Several cinemas in Vienna show films in the original languages – look in the *Standard* newspaper's foreign films section. See also *Entertainment in Vienna* on pp226–31.

SPECIAL ACTIVITIES AND WORKSHOPS

The Rathaus *(see p130)* has children's activities once a month (details from the town hall), and from mid-November there is a Christmas market *(see pp224–5)* which includes a children's train, pony rides and stalls selling toys, chestnuts and winter woollens. A Christmas workshop is held at the Volkshalle in the Rathaus from 9am to 6pm (7pm at weekends). The activities include baking, silk painting and making decorations.

MUSEUMS

Vienna has a range of museums for children to enjoy. The Natural History Museum *(see pp128–9)* boasts an impressive collection of fossils. The **Haus des Meeres** (Vienna Aquarium) contains over 3,000 sea creatures, including piranhas, crocodiles and sharks. Feeding time is 3pm.

Popular exhibits at the Völkerkundemuseum *(see p95)* include exotic musical instruments, African masks and figurines, and Montezuma's treasures. Children aged 13 and under are allowed to enter the **Kunsthaus Wien** free. Designed by Friedensreich

Attacus atlas at the Natural History Museum (see pp128–9)

A Christmas market stall in front of the Rathaus *(see p130)*

Hundertwasser, this colourful private gallery has undulating floors and bright paintings. The **Wiener Strassenbahn museum** (Vienna Tram Museum) houses the largest collection of vintage trams and buses in the world. Details of tours are available from information offices at Karlsplatz and Westbahnhof *(see p238)*.

The Heeresgeschichtliches Museum *(see pp166–7)* contains a range of war memorabilia and the ZOOM Kinder-museum *(see p120)* offers interactive exhibits such as the Zoom Lab. Other options include the **Zirkus und Clownmuseum**, dressing up events at the Sisi Museum in the Hofburg and at Schönbrunn Palace, experimenting with sight and sound at the Haus der Musik *(see p80)* and learning about the mechanics of theatre on a back stage tour at the Austrian Theatre Museum in Lobkowitz Palace *(see p104)*.

Montezuma's headdress in the Völkerkundemuseum *(see p95)*

DIRECTORY

SWIMMING

Kinderfreibad Augarten
Karl-Meissl-Gasse entrance,
Augarten Park.
Map 2 E1. **Tel** 3324258.
☐ 10am–6pm Mon–Fri.

Stadionbad
Prater, Krieau. **Tel** 7202102.
☐ May–Oct: 10am–6pm daily.

ENTERTAINMENT

Lilarum
Göllnergasse 8. **Tel** 7102666.

Märchenbühne der Apfelbaum
Kirchengasse 41.
Map 3 B1. **Tel** 523172920.

Wiener Konzerthaus
Lothringerstrasse 20.
Map 4 E2 & 6 E5. **Tel** 242002.

MUSEUMS

Haus des Meere
Esterházypark. **Map** 3 B2.
Tel 5871417. ☐ 9am–6pm daily.

Kunsthaus Wien
Untere Weissgerberstrasse 13.
Tel 7120491. ☐ 10am–7pm daily.

Wiener Strassenbahn museum
Erdbergstrasse 109. **Tel** 7909 41800. ☐ May–beginning Oct: 9am–4pm Sat, Sun & public hols. (For tours see p237).

Zirkus und Clownmuseum
Karmelitergasse 9. **Map** 2 E4 & 6 E1. **Tel** 2110602127.
☐ 5:30–7pm Wed, 2:30–5pm Sat, 10am–noon Sun.

The exterior of Karl-Lueger-Kirche in winter ▷

SURVIVAL GUIDE

PRACTICAL INFORMATION

The best way to get around the centre of Vienna is on foot because many of the sights are in close proximity to each other. Museums and galleries are often crowded at weekends, so it might be a good idea to plan your visits during the week if possible. Sights are sometimes being refurbished, so it is a good

Sign for tourist information

idea to check in advance that they are open before visiting. Tourist offices have a useful free museums leaflet containing up-to-date information. Most shops in the centre are open Monday to Friday 8am to 6pm, and are open until 5pm on Saturdays. Banks are shut all weekend. Embassy details are listed on page 239.

CUSTOMS INFORMATION

Nationals from most European and many overseas countries do not need a visa to enter Austria, but it is advisable to check your requirements before travelling. Dogs and cats require a rabies vaccination certificate with a German translation. Motorists need a Green Card as proof of third-party insurance. For information on tax-free goods, *see p221.*

TOURIST INFORMATION

You can plan your trip to Vienna by getting in touch with travel agencies and the representatives of **Österreich Werbung** (the Austrian National Tourist Office) in your own country, or you can approach the **Wiener Tourismusverband** (Vienna Tourist Board) directly. The office is located on Albertinaplatz.

For assistance in organizing day trips from Vienna (*see p176–7*), contact the Österreich Werbung. Tourist information is also available from the offices of Austrian

Airlines (*see p247*). There is also an information office at **Westbahnhof** station, from where you can make hotel reservations. The arrivals hall at Schwechat Airport has a tourist information office where you can reserve rooms and pick up a city map that contains diagrams of the public transport network (*also see inside back cover*).

For cheaper accommodation and information about youth hostels or tickets for pop concerts, the multilingual team at **Jugendinformation Wien** provides assistance and leaflets in various languages.

TOURS AND EXCURSIONS

The main guided tour operators are **Vienna Sightseeing** and **Cityrama**. Trams are a good way of seeing the 19th-century buildings in the Ringstrasse because you can choose where to get on and off (*see p252*). Group tours in a 1920s tram are organized by **Oldtimer Tram** and leave from Otto Wagner's Pavilions on Karlsplatz (*see pp146–7*). The **DDSG-Blue Danube** organizes tours on the Danube and Danube Canal to sights such as Otto Wagner's Nussdorf locks. From June to October the **Twin City Liner**, a high-speed catamaran, makes a round trip to Bratislava three times a day. In the summer there are a lot of guided walking tours, in English, French or Italian, with a

A guided walking tour around the Hofburg (*see pp96–101*)

variety of themes. From May to September, cycling enthusiasts can book tours through **Pedal Power** (*see p252*). Tours are run in German or English, but Italian or French can be arranged.

SIGHTSEEING TIPS

Entrance prices vary considerably between museums. Any major exhibitions put on by museums will involve an extra charge. Children pay roughly half price and there are also reductions for senior citizens and students with identity cards. The only day on which the entrance fee is reduced or free is 26 October – the Austrian National Day. Many museums are closed on a Monday, but it is wise to check opening times, and if you are still in doubt, ring the museum itself. For information on booking theatre and musical perfomances *see pp224–9.*

One of the information offices in central Vienna

DISABLED VISITORS

Services for the disabled have improved greatly in recent years. Most of the major museums have special entrances and ramps for wheelchairs, and detailed information is available from the Vienna Tourist office. Trams that are easily accessible for wheelchairs and pushchairs alternate with the classic Viennese tram, especially along the Ringstrasse. The same applies to buses. Most major underground stations provide lifts unless otherwise indicated.

STUDENT INFORMATION

Vienna's main theatres offer cheap standing-room and unsold tickets at the evening box office prior to the performance. For popular shows you may need to queue for several hours. A university identity card as well as an international student card also entitles students to a variety of discounts. Tourist offices will provide information about the cheaper hotels and pensions as well as a list of Vienna's youth hostels (see p195).

RADIO AND NEWSPAPERS

Austria has two main radio stations. Ö1 plays classical music and Ö3 plays popular music. Radio FM4 transmits in English from 1am to 2pm daily on 103.8 MHz. Vienna Cable Radio transmits on FM 100.8.

The main listings magazine is *Falter*, but the two chief newspapers, *Die Presse* and *Standard*, list films daily. You can buy papers in a *Tabak Trafik* (newsagent), a kiosk or, on Sundays, on street-corners. Foreign film cinemas include Artis International, Burg Kino and Haydn (see p228). Many foreign newspapers are available from kiosks.

Shakespeare & Co sell English-language books and **Frick** has a good collection of books in English.

Foreign newspapers are on sale at central kiosks

ELECTRICAL ADAPTORS

The voltage in Austria is 220V AC. Plugs have two small round pins. It is a good idea to buy a multi-adaptor before coming to Vienna.

PUBLIC LAVATORIES

These are generally clean but are not free, so make sure you carry some small change with you. The Jugendstil lavatory on the Graben was designed by Adolf Loos and is worth a visit. All major underground stations have lavatories, which are open late.

DIRECTORY

TOURIST OFFICES

Österreich Werbung
Margaretenstrasse 1.
Tel 58866363.
www.austriatourism.com

Schwechat Airport
Arrivals Hall.
Tel 700722233
www.viennaairport.com

Wien Xtra-Youth Info
Babenbergerstrasse 1
A-1010.
Map 3 C1 & 5 B5.
Tel 1799.
www.wienxtra.at

Wiener Tourismusverband
Corner of Albertinaplatz,
Tegethoffstrasse and
Meysedergasse.
Map 4 D1 & 6 C4.
Tel 24555 or 211140.
www.wien.info

FOREIGN AUSTRIAN TOURIST OFFICES

London
30 St George Street,
London
W1R 0AL.
Tel 071 629 0461.

New York
500 Fifth Avenue,
Suite 2009–2022,
New York
NY 10110.
Tel 212 944 6880.

Sydney
36 Carrington Street,
1st floor,
Sydney
NSW 2000.
Tel 02 299 3621.

Toronto
2 Bloor Street East,
Suite 3330,
Toronto,
Ontario
M4W 1A8.
Tel 416 967 3381.

TOUR OPERATORS

Cityrama
Börsegasse 1.
Map 2 D4 & 5 B1.
Tel 534130.

DDSG-Blue Danube
Handelskai 265.
Tel 58880.

Vienna Sightseeing Tours
Stelzhamergasse 4–11.
Map 4 F1 & 6 F3.
Tel 7124683.

Oldtimer Tram
Schwendergasse 51.
Tel 7909105.

Twin City Liner
Schwedenplatz,
Marienbrücke 103.
Map 6 E2.
Tel 72710137.

EMBASSIES & CONSULATES

Australia
Mattiellistrasse 2–4.
Map 4 E2. *Tel* 506740.

Canada
Laurenzerberg 2.
Map 6 E2. *Tel* 531383000

Ireland
Rotenturmstrasse 16–18.
Map 6 D3. *Tel* 7154246.

New Zealand
Salesianergasse 15.
Map 4 F2. *Tel* 3138505.

United Kingdom
Jaurèsgasse 12.
Map 4 F2. *Tel* 71615151.

United States of America
Boltzmanngasse 16.
Map 1 C3. *Tel* 31339.

INTERNATIONAL BOOKSHOPS

Frick
Graben 27.
Map 5 C3.
Tel 5339914.

Shakespeare & Co
Sterngasse 2.
Map 2 E5 & 6 D2.
Tel 5355053.

Personal Security and Health

Pharmacy sign

Although tourists are unlikely to encounter any violence in Vienna, it is always advisable to take care when out walking. The police and emergency services are easy to contact if need be. Pharmacists are respected and their advice is often sought by locals. A visit to the pharmacy, unless the problem is serious, is the easiest choice. Specialist services available include Befrienders, a telephone helpline for English speakers who may be feeling lonely, an AIDS Helpline and an English-speaking Alcoholics Anonymous group.

SOS sign on U-Bahn platforms

MEDICAL TREATMENT AND INSURANCE

Tick-borne encephalitis is a possible danger wherever there are deciduous trees in Austria and most Austrians and foreign residents are inoculated against it. Inoculation is done in stages, but is not usually recommended for tourists. Only a tiny proportion of ticks carry the disease, which may cause brain damage and in some cases lead to death. The risk is minimal, but to be on the safe side, if you are bitten you should not remove the tick but go to an outpatients department. The Lobau, the Lainzer Tiergarten and Vienna Woods are tick areas, so it is a good idea to wear a hat and long shirt sleeves here.

Red Cross sign

Britain has a reciprocal arrangement with Austria whereby emergency hospital treatment is free upon presentation of a British passport. In theory, visits to doctors, dentists or

EMERGENCY NUMBERS

AIDS Helpline
Tel 599370.

Alcoholics Anonymous
Tel 7995599.
Ask for English language AA.

Befrienders
Tel 7133374.

Dentist
Tel 5122078.
Night and weekend line.

Ambulance
Tel 144.

Doctor on Call
Tel 141.

Fire
Tel 122.

Police
Tel 133.

Vienna Medical Emergency Service
Tel 40144.

Motorway Breakdown
Tel 120.

PERSONAL SECURITY AND PROPERTY

There are a few places to steer clear of in Vienna. The underground is generally safe by day and night. Karlsplatz station, however, which is renowned as a drug centre, is quite unsavoury, particularly at night when it is best avoided. There may be some upsetting sights, although you are unlikely to be bothered. Last trains can be very crowded and the passengers a bit unruly. All under-

ground stations have SOS points for emergencies from which you can call the station supervisor or halt trains. In the Prater, care should be taken at night as it is known for pickpocketing and for fights. Areas around the main railway stations can be unpleasant, though not really dangerous. The red light district is on the Gürtel between the Westbahnhof and the Südbahnhof.

Recent years have seen an increase in pickpocketing throughout the city so take care of your property and do not go out with a lot of cash (travellers' cheques are the safest way of carrying large sums of money). Care should also be taken when withdrawing money at cash point machines. For robbery, assault or missing persons, visit the nearest police station. Contact your consulate if you lose your passport.

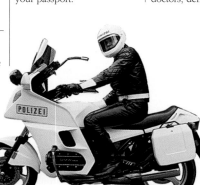

Police motorcycle

Policeman

Fire engine

Police car

Ambulance

DIRECTORY

CRISIS INFORMATION

Lost Property Bureau
Bastiengasse 36.
Tel 40008091.
◯ *8am–3:30pm Mon–Fri.*

**Pharmacy
Information Line**
Tel 1550.

Vienna General Hospital
Währinger Gürtel 18–20.
Map 1 C4 & 5 A1.
Tel 40400.

PHARMACIES

Internationale Apotheke
Kärntner Ring 17.
Map 4 E2 & 6 D5.
Tel 5122825.

**Schweden-Apotheke,
Pharmacie-Internationale**
Schwedenplatz 2.
Map 2 E2 & 6 E2. *Tel* 53329110.

Zum Heiligen Geist
Operngasse 16.
Map 4 D2.
Tel 5877367.

Zur Universität
Universitätsstrasse 10.
Map 1 C4 & 5 A1.
Tel 40252980.

Policewoman   **Fireman**

outpatient departments are also free, but obtaining free treatment can involve a lot of bureaucracy. It is best to take out full health insurance which will also cover flights home for medical reasons. There are several private hospitals in Vienna, but the main hospital (and the largest in Europe) is the Vienna General Hospital in the ninth district. In the case of a medical emergency, call an ambulance *(Rettungsdienst)* or the local **Doctor on Call**.

PHARMACIES

If you are not in an emergency, go to an *Apotheke* (pharmacy) for advice on medicines and treatment. They all display a red "A" sign and operate a night rota system. Any closed pharmacies will display the address of the nearest one open, and the **Pharmacy Information Line** also has details of some which are open. If the problem is serious, call **Vienna Medical Emergency Service**.

Façade of pharmacy

LOST PROPERTY

Go to the nearest police station in the first instance. If they do not restore your property within seven days (and you are still in Vienna), then try the lost property bureau. For property lost on the railways and the Schnellbahn, ask at the Westbahnhof, which is open from 8am to 3pm Monday to Friday. You have to go there in person.

Banking and Local Currency

Bank Austria logo

Since the 1990s, Viennese financial systems have become more accessible. There are now several money-changing machines *(see Directory)*, and you can take any amount of euros or foreign currency in or out of the country. Cash tends to be used rather than credit cards.

BANKING AND EXCHANGE

The best place to change money is at a bank. Although you can use travel agents, bureaux de change *(Wechselstuben)* and hotels, banks offer a better rate. Exchanging a large amount of money at one time can save on commission because there is often a minimum charge or a handling fee of around €3.60. You can also exchange foreign bank notes for euros at one of the automatic money-changing machines (Change-o-mats).

Most banks stay open from 8am to 12:30pm and from 1:30 to 3pm (5:30pm on Thursdays). A few of them (for example, the main Bank Austria-Creditanstalt bank on Schottengasse) do not close for lunch. Some banks, generally those at the main railway stations and at airports *(see Directory)*, stay open longer than usual.

CREDIT AND DEBIT CARDS

You can pay for items with major credit cards, such as VISA, MasterCard, American Express and Diners Club, in most hotels, shops and major restaurants. Most shops accept debit cards. However, credit cards are not used as frequently as, for instance, in the UK or France, so it is a good idea to carry some cash on you at all times. This can be obtained using a credit or debit card at most cash point machines. Just look for the logo of your card on the front of a machine to check that you can use it. Cash machines give instructions in German, English and French, and some may also have instructions in Italian, Swedish and Spanish.

If you are planning to use a credit card to pay for something, make sure it is accepted first, especially if you carry MasterCard or Euro-Card. Also be aware that some establishments set a minimum expenditure that can be paid for by credit card.

Be sure to report lost or stolen cards to your own or the nearest Austrian bank.

TRAVELLER'S CHEQUES

Traveller's cheques are the safest way to carry large sums of money, with the advantage that you can change as much or as little as you need at any one time. Choose a well-known name such as American Express, Visa, Travelex or cheques issued through a bank. Traveller's cheques can be changed for cash in most Austrian banks and are useful for paying for your room at many of the larger hotels. There is, however, a minimum commission charge, which may make changing small sums of money uneconomical. It is worth checking the exchange rates before you travel to decide whether sterling, dollar or euro cheques are the most appropriate for your trip.

DIRECTORY

AFTER-HOURS EXCHANGE COUNTERS

Opera-Karlsplatz Passage
Map 4 D1 & 5 C5.
⬜ *8am–7pm daily.*

Schwechat Airport
⬜ *6am–9pm daily.*

Südbahnhof
Map 4 F4.
⬜ *7am–9pm daily.*

Westbahnhof
⬜ *7am–10pm daily.*

AUTOMATIC MONEY-CHANGING MACHINES

Die Erste Bank, Graben 21.
Map 2 D5 & 5 C3.

Bank Austria,
Kärntner Ring 1.
Map 4 D2 & 6 C1.

Bank Austria,
Mariahilfer Strasse 54.
Map 3 B2.

Bank Austria, Stephansplatz 2.
Map 1 D5 & 6 D3.

FOREIGN CREDIT CARD MACHINES

Bank Austria,
Schottengasse 6.
Map 1 C4 & 5 B2.

Bank Austria,
Schubertring 14.
Map 4 E2 & 6 D5.

AMERICAN EXPRESS

Kärntner Strasse 21–3.
Map 4 D1 & 6 D4.
Tel 515670.

Autobank automatic money-dispensing machine

Currency conversion machine which accepts foreign banknotes

THE EURO

The Euro (€) is the common currency of the European Union. It went into general circulation on 1 January 2002, initially for 12 participating countries. Austria was one of those 12 countries taking the Euro in 2002, with the Austrian schilling phased out in the same year.

EU members using the Euro as sole official currency are known as the Eurozone. Several EU members have opted out of joining this common currency.

Euro notes are identical throughout the Eurozone countries, each one including designs of fictional architectural structures. The coins, however, have one side identical (the value side), and one side with an image unique to each country.

Bank Notes

Euro bank notes have seven denominations. The €5 note (grey in colour) is the smallest, followed by the €10 note (pink), €20 note (blue), €50 note (orange), €100 note (green), €200 note (yellow) and €500 note (purple). All notes show the stars of the European Union.

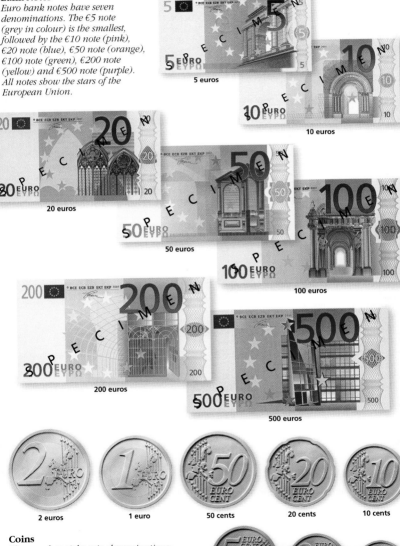

5 euros

10 euros

20 euros

50 euros

100 euros

200 euros

500 euros

2 euros

1 euro

50 cents

20 cents

10 cents

Coins

The euro has eight coin denominations: €1 and €2; 50 cents, 20 cents, 10 cents, 5 cents, 2 cents and 1 cent. The €2 and €1 coins are both silver and gold in colour. The 50-, 20- and 10-cent coins are gold. The 5-, 2- and 1-cent coins are bronze.

5 cents

2 cents

1 cent

Communications

Austria's telecommunications network and postal service are now run by two separate companies. The many post offices are easily identified by the yellow post office sign. Phoning abroad at peak times can be problematic as there are not enough telephone lines, although the number is being increased. Many phone numbers have been changed as a result, so if you cannot get through ring directory enquiries *(see below)*. To phone outside Austria, try using a telephone booth at a post office. You do not need change as you pay at the counter.

Emergency phone sign

Coin-operated phone

Sign for cardphone

USING THE TELEPHONE

Telephones are mainly push-button, and most of them have instructions in four languages: German, English, French and Italian. Austria has one of the most expensive telephone systems in Europe, so make sure you have plenty of change or take a phone-card with you. The coin-operated telephones take 10 cent, 20 cent, 50 cent, €1 and €2 coins.

Phonecards can be purchased from any post office or from newsagents. For international calls, it is best to avoid hotels as they tend to add a hefty surcharge on top of the cost of the call.

Cheap rate calling times from Vienna are between 6pm and 8am Monday to Friday and all day on Saturday, Sunday and public holidays. To make a reverse charge call, for which a fee is payable, go to the nearest post office.

Telephone boxes

There are telephone booths at every post office. Yellow-striped public telephone boxes take coins or phonecards and are found throughout the city. Directories are usually available in telephone boxes, but can be too tatty to use. If you need to find a number, post offices always have legible directories available or contact directory enquiries.

USING A CARD PHONE

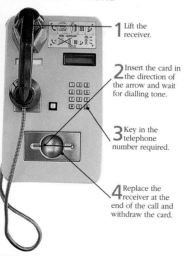

1 Lift the receiver.

2 Insert the card in the direction of the arrow and wait for dialling tone.

3 Key in the telephone number required.

4 Replace the receiver at the end of the call and withdraw the card.

USING A COIN-OPERATED PHONE

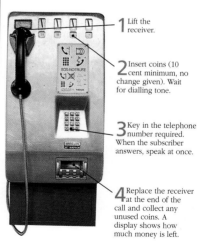

1 Lift the receiver.

2 Insert coins (10 cent minimum, no change given). Wait for dialling tone.

3 Key in the telephone number required. When the subscriber answers, speak at once.

4 Replace the receiver at the end of the call and collect any unused coins. A display shows how much money is left.

REACHING THE RIGHT NUMBER

- For directory enquiries in Austria, the EU and neighbouring countries, dial 118877.
- For international information, dial 0900 118877.
- All directory enquiries cost €1.35 per minute.
- For international or national telegrams, dial 0800 100190.
- For wake-up service, dial 0900 100100.
- To ring the **USA**, dial 001 followed by the number.

- To ring the **UK**, dial 0044 followed by the number (omit the 0 from the area code).
- To ring **Australia**, dial 0061 followed by the number.
- To ring **New Zealand**, dial 0064 followed by the number.
- To ring the **Irish Republic**, dial 00353 followed by the number.
- The front pages of the A–Z telephone directory list codes for each country. The cost of calls is available at post offices.

Mail and Postal Services

Decorative stamp

The post office provides postage stamps *(Briefmarken)*, telegrams and registered letters, as well as arranging the delivery of packages. There is also an express delivery *(Eilbriefe)* service, but this is a lot more expensive and may only be a day quicker. In addition, the post office sells phonecards and collectors' stamps. You can collect correspondence marked *Post Restante* or *Postlagernd* (to be called for) but you will need proof of identity, such as a passport. You can cash travellers' cheques and giro cheques up to a maximum of €180 per cheque. Main post offices will also change foreign currency into euros and vice versa. Many post offices also have fax machines.

Post office sign

SENDING A LETTER

The Austrian postal system is reliable, verging on the pedantic, and posting a letter can take some time. Each

Display showing pick up times

Yellow letter box

individual letter is carefully weighed and every size and shape coded separately. Very few letters are sent at the set European rate of 65 cents.

Most post offices in Vienna are open between 8am and noon and 2pm and 6pm from Monday to Friday (but there

are no financial dealings after 5pm). Precise opening times are displayed at every post office. The main post office in each of the city's 23 urban districts *(Bezirke)* is open from 8am to 10am on Saturdays (but not for financial dealings). The **Central Post Office** in the first district is open 24 hours, and those at **Westbahnhof** and **Südbahnhof** open daily from 6am to 11pm and 7am to 10pm respectively, but not all services are available after normal opening hours. The airport post office is open from 7am to 8pm daily.

You can buy postage stamps at newsagents or post offices, which also have stamp-vending machines. Letters for Europe weighing up to 20 g cost 65 cents, as do postcards. Registered letters cost €2.10. You should add the standard

vehicle country code (for example, "D" for Germany) before the post code.

E-MAIL AND THE INTERNET

Vienna has a variety of internet cafés, where you can collect your email in relative comfort, often with a cup of coffee or a snack. Charges are most reasonable during off-peak times.

USEFUL ADDRESSES

Central Post Office
Fleischmarkt 19. **Map** 2 E5 & 6 D2.
Tel 515090.

Südbahnhof
Wiedner Gürtel 10. **Map** 4 F4.
Tel 501810.

Westbahnhof
Gasgasse 2.
Tel 8923260.

Tel 8921020 (for general information).
www.post.at

Surfland Internet Café
Krugerstrasse 10.
⭘ *10am–11pm daily.*

Vienna's Districts

Vienna is divided into 23 urban districts or Bezirke, *as shown on this map. The district number is incorporated into the Vienna postcode. For example, the 23rd district is written as A-1230. The inset area shows the part of Vienna covered by our Street Finder maps 1–4 (see pp262–5).*

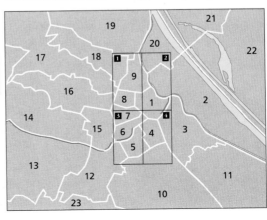

GETTING TO VIENNA

As a popular tourist destination and a major link between Eastern and Western Europe, Vienna is well served by air and rail. There are direct flights from every major European city as well as from North America, Canada, Japan and Australia. However, visitors from New Zealand need to change planes at London or Frankfurt and visitors from Ireland must transit at London or Munich. Vienna

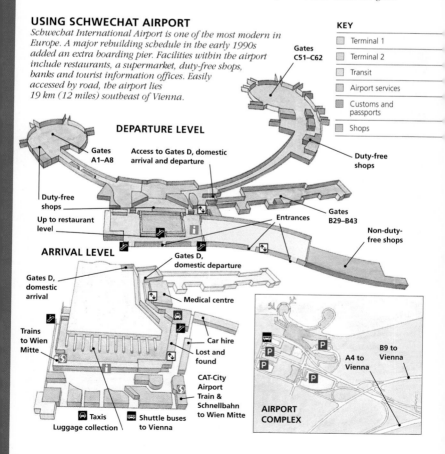

Austrian Airlines aeroplane

also has coach and rail links with the rest of Europe, but this usually involves overnight travel. If you are not eligible for student or special rates, travelling by train is not significantly cheaper. Vienna has good motorway routes to the rest of Europe, but if you are arriving from Germany, do not forget that the Austrian motorway speed limit is only 130 km (80 miles) per hour.

ARRIVING BY AIR

There are several flights a day between London Heathrow airport and Vienna's airport at Schwechat. British Airways is the main British airline with regular flights to

Vienna, and the main Austrian carrier is Austrian Airlines. Aer Lingus operates daily flights from Gatwick to Vienna from April to October.

If you fly from the United States, there are direct flights with Delta from New York,

Orlando and Atlanta. Austrian Airlines flies direct to New York and Chicago. There are also direct flights from Sydney and Toronto.

It is not necessary to pay full price for a scheduled ticket. There are good

USING SCHWECHAT AIRPORT

Schwechat International Airport is one of the most modern in Europe. A major rebuilding schedule in the early 1990s added an extra boarding pier. Facilities within the airport include restaurants, a supermarket, duty-free shops, banks and tourist information offices. Easily accessed by road, the airport lies 19 km (12 miles) southeast of Vienna.

KEY

- Terminal 1
- Terminal 2
- Transit
- Airport services
- Customs and passports
- Shops

Gates C51–C62

DEPARTURE LEVEL

Gates A1–A8

Access to Gates D, domestic arrival and departure

Duty-free shops

Duty-free shops

Up to restaurant level

Gates B29–B43

Entrances

Non-duty-free shops

ARRIVAL LEVEL

Gates D, domestic departure

Gates D, domestic arrival

Medical centre

Trains to Wien Mitte

Car hire

Lost and found

CAT-City Airport Train & Schnellbahn to Wien Mitte

Taxis

Luggage collection

Shuttle buses to Vienna

B9 to Vienna

A4 to Vienna

AIRPORT COMPLEX

The modern exterior of Schwechat International Airport

deals if you shop around the discount agencies; you can get APEX tickets if you book two weeks in advance; and charter flights are available at very competitive prices. Weekend package offers, including the price of two nights at a good Viennese hotel, can also prove to be excellent value, sometimes costing less than the economy-class ticket price.

Schwechat International Airport transit area

SCHWECHAT AIRPORT

Vienna has one airport, Schwechat International. It is 19 km (12 miles) from the city centre and is about a 20-minute ride with the City Airport train, which is located at Wien Mitte station. This modern airport is very easy and quick to use. The airport supermarket is often used by Viennese caught out by the restricted shopping times in the city and is open 7 days a week from 7:30am until 7pm, including holidays.

GETTING INTO TOWN

The simplest way to get to the city centre is by taxi or by the CAT-City Airport Train. When you come out of customs you will see signs for taxis and the CAT. There are always plenty of taxis available and they take about 20 minutes to reach the centre of Vienna. The CAT train runs between the airport and Wien Mitte and costs €10 each way if you pay on the train and €8 if you buy online. It departs from the basement level of the airport. Further information on the CAT can be obtained by calling 25250 or visiting www.cityairporttrain.com.

There are buses running from approximately 6am to midnight every 30 minutes to Schwedenplatz, Südbahnhof and Westbahnhof stations. (If you want the exact time-table, phone Vienna Airport Lines. Alternatively, you can get this information from the Vienna Airport website.)

The fare for the buses is around €6, including baggage, which you pay the driver when you get on. The Schnellbahn train, which also departs from the basement level of the airport, is the cheapest option. However, it only goes every half hour. This train takes approximately 30 minutes to connect with Wien Mitte and stops at Praterstern-Wien Nord.

DIRECTORY

AIRLINES

Air France
Kärntner Strasse 49.
Map 4 D1 & 6 D5. **Tel** 50222 2400. Airport **Tel** 700732065.

All Nippon Airways
Argentinierstrasse 214.
Map 4 E3. **Tel** 79567360 Airport **Tel** 700733733.

Austrian Airlines
Kärntner Ring 18.
Map 4 E2 & 6 D5. **Tel** 517661000. Airport **Tel** 700762520.

British Airways
Kärntner Ring 10.
Map 4 E2 & 6 D5. **Tel** 79567567. Airport **Tel** 700732646.

Delta
Odeongasse 2a/1. **Tel** 79567023.
Map 2 E4 & 6 E2.

Iberia
Opernring 1. **Map** 4 D1 & 5 C5.
Tel 79567722. Airport **Tel** 70073552.

Lufthansa
Mariahilferstrasse 123. **Map** 3 A3. **Tel** 0810 10258080. Airport **Tel** 700735711.

Flight Information
Tel 7007 or 700722233.

Vienna Airport Lines
0810 222333 or 7007 32300
www.viennaairport.com
www.postbus.at

Shopping mall at Schwechat International Airport

ARRIVING BY RAIL

Like London and Paris, Vienna has several mainline railway stations, three of which serve international connections.

Most Eurocity services charge a supplement if you buy your ticket less than 72 hours before departure. Many of the train services to Vienna are over-night and, for a small fee, it is possible to reserve a seat or a bed up to two months before travelling. Often there are no buffet facilities on overnight trains, but snacks are some-times sold by the steward.

Generally, the Westbahnhof handles trains from the west and includes some Budapest services. Southern and eastern

Travel agency (Reisebüro) at Westbahnhof

areas are served by the Süd-bahnhof, and trains from the north arrive at Franz-Josefs-Bahnhof (see Major Rail and Coach Stations *opposite).*

Westbahnhof has inter-changes with the U3 and U6 underground lines, the Schnell-

Exterior view of the Franz-Josefs-Bahnhof, which services trains from Prague and northern Austria

Rail route into Vienna with abbey at Melk (see p179) in the background

Sign at Westbahnhof showing how to get to the exit, Regionalbahn, Schnellbahn, ticket machines and Regionalbus station

bahn and several tram and bus routes. The Südbahnhof is linked to the Schnellbahn and several tram and bus lines, while Franz-Josefs-Bahnhof is served by the Schnellbahn and the cross-city D tram, which goes directly to the Ringstrasse. All the stations have taxi ranks.

The travel agency (*Reisebüro)* at Westbahnhof is open from 8am to 7pm on weekdays and from 8am to 1pm on Saturdays and can provide in-formation as well as helping with booking hotel rooms.

The travel agency at the Südbahnhof, which is open from 8am to 7pm on weekdays and from 8am to 1pm on Saturdays (with shorter hours from November to April), offers a similar service. In Vienna there is a telephone number for obtaining railway infor-mation in English.

Railway information
Tel 051717.

Austrian Federal Railways
Tel 93000 051717.
www.oebb.at

ARRIVING BY COACH

Vienna's main coach station, the Vienna International Bus terminal (VIB), is close to Erdberg U3 underground station. Services run to most Eastern European cities (such as Bratislava, Budapest and Prague) and also to Berlin,

Eurolines coach

London and Paris (see www. eurolines.com for schedules). Südbahnhof station handles routes within Austria (*see p255).*

ARRIVING BY ROAD

All drivers in Austria must carry their driver's licence, car registration document and insurance papers. Visitors need to carry an overseas extension of their annual insurance, such as a Green Card. An inter-national driver's licence is required for people whose language is written in a script other than Roman. Wearing seatbelts is compulsory, and children up to the age of 12 or under 1.5 m (5 ft) may not sit on front seats unless with special child seats or seat belts. To travel on motorways in Austria you must have a

Sign on the Gürtel indicating the direction of the city centre

vignette sticker, available at petrol stations and tobacconists, attached to the inside of your windscreen. *Vignettes* are available for 10 days (€7.60), two months (€22) or one year (€72.60). All rented cars will have a *vignette* provided. Visitors arriving by road from the south arrive on the A2 and A23 southern motorways (Südautobahn), from the north on the A22 Danube motorway (Donau-uferautobahn), from the west on the A1 western motorway (Westautobahn) and from the east (including Schwechat International Airport) on the A4 eastern motorway (Ostautobahn). The city centre is marked Zentrum. The motorways converge on the outer ring road (Gürtel), sections of which are quite seedy. A *Parkscheine* is needed to park on inner-city streets and is available from tobacconists.

ARRIVING BY BOAT

From April to October you can arrive by boat along the Danube from Bratislava, the Wachau and Budapest. The

Sign showing direction to the ferry terminal

boat docks at the Donaudampfschiffsgesellschaft (DDSG-Blue Danube) shipping line's landing station at the Reichsbrücke bridge *(see p238)*. It is close to the Vorgartenstrasse U-Bahn station on the U1 line. There is a DDSG-Blue Danube information counter at the dock which can provide city maps.

DDSG-Blue Danube ferry arriving in Vienna from eastern Europe

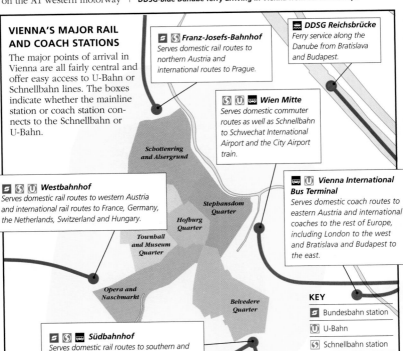

VIENNA'S MAJOR RAIL AND COACH STATIONS

The major points of arrival in Vienna are all fairly central and offer easy access to U-Bahn or Schnellbahn lines. The boxes indicate whether the mainline station or coach station connects to the Schnellbahn or U-Bahn.

Franz-Josefs-Bahnhof
Serves domestic rail routes to northern Austria and international routes to Prague.

DDSG Reichsbrücke
Ferry service along the Danube from Bratislava and Budapest.

Wien Mitte
Serves domestic commuter routes as well as Schnellbahn to Schwechat International Airport and the City Airport train.

Westbahnhof
Serves domestic rail routes to western Austria and international rail routes to France, Germany, the Netherlands, Switzerland and Hungary.

Vienna International Bus Terminal
Serves domestic coach routes to eastern Austria and international coaches to the rest of Europe, including London to the west and Bratislava and Budapest to the east.

Südbahnhof
Serves domestic rail routes to southern and eastern Austria and international routes to Italy, Slovenia, Croatia and Slovakia, with some routes to Budapest and Prague. Domestic coach routes to southern and southwestern Austria leave from here.

Schottenring and Alsergrund

Stephansdom Quarter

Hofburg Quarter

Townhall and Museum Quarter

Opera and Naschmarkt

Belvedere Quarter

KEY

- Bundesbahn station
- U-Bahn
- Schnellbahn station
- Coach and bus station
- River boats

GETTING AROUND VIENNA

Walking is generally the easiest and most enjoyable way to get around the compact centre of Vienna. There is so much to see, and when you feel tired or hungry there is always a café or *Konditorei* just a few steps away. The good news for pedestrians is that the normally asser-tive Viennese drivers are dissuaded from driving through the city centre by a com-plicated and frustrat-ing one-way system, pedestrian zones and

Viennese Fiaker

strict parking limits. If you would rather not walk around the main sights, a net-work of minibuses crisscrosses the city centre. The public transport system is clean, efficient and easy to use. Run by the City of Vienna Transport Authority, it con-sists of a tram, bus and under-ground network. All the services operate from 5am to 12:30am, but it is best to check individual timetables, which are very reliable, before travelling.

WALKING IN VIENNA

Walking is an excellent way to see the city, but there are a few points to remember. Traffic rarely stops at pedestrian crossings so you should proceed with care. British and Australian visitors should remember that motor-ists drive on the right. On the Ringstrasse, trams run against the traffic, so it is necessary to look both ways. Try to use subways or crossings where there are signals. If you ignore the red figure meaning "Do not cross" you could be fined on the spot by a police-man, even if there is no sign of traffic at the time. In addition, keep an eye out for cyclists; they share the pavement with pedestrians and, if they are travelling at some speed, may not have time to stop if you stray onto their section of the pavement.

Do not cross

Cross

There are at least 50 guided walking tours in and around Vienna on offer throughout the summer months. They explore themes such as Biedermeier, Baroque or Vienna 1900 and are available in German, English, French and Italian. For a variety of information on walking tours,

contact the Wiener Touris-musverband *(see p238)*.

THE CITY BY FIAKER

Traditional horse-drawn open carriages or *Fiakers*, many driven by a crusty, bowler-hatted and bewhiskered coachman, are a novel and relaxing way to get around. Take into account that part of the route is on the busy Ringstrasse. You can hire a *Fiaker* at Stephans-platz, Heldenplatz and Albertinaplatz, but to avoid an unpleasant surprise agree the terms (price and length of trip) before you set off. Even a short trip can be costly.

VIENNA BY BICYCLE

Vienna is great for cyclists, as long as you avoid the main roads and tramlines by sticking to the cycle paths. A 7-km (4-mile) cycle path round the Ringstrasse takes you past many sights and there are bike paths to the Hundert-wasser Haus *(see p164)* and to the Prater *(see pp162–63)*. A booklet called *Rad Wege* shows all Vienna's cycle routes and is available from bookshops. Bikes can be hired at some train stations and discounts are given with a train ticket, or from various Citybike stations (see www.citybikewien.at). City cycle tours run during summer *(see p238)*. Pedal Power's 3-hour city tours leave from the Prater Ferris wheel at 10am daily.

Traffic signal for cyclists

Cycle lane

Cycling along bicycle lanes in the Prater

Beginning of no-parking zone

End of no-parking zone

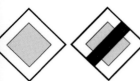

Priority to traffic on the right cancelled

Priority to traffic on the right restored

DRIVING IN VIENNA

Drivers are aggressive in Vienna, so you will need to be alert as cars race and cut in front of you. Priority is always to the right unless a "yellow diamond" indicates otherwise. You must give way to trams, buses, police cars, fire engines and ambulances. It is useful to belong to an internationally affiliated automobile association or you will be charged by the ÖAMTC (the Austrian motoring association) for breakdowns or repairs. Traffic news is on most radio stations except Ö1, and FM4 broadcasts traffic news in English. The speed limit in Vienna is 50 km (30 miles) per hour. Police carry out checks with infra-red guns and can fine you on the spot. The limit for alcohol is 0.5 mg per ml of blood (about $\frac{1}{3}$ litre of beer or 1–2 glasses of wine). There are spot checks and you could be fined a considerable sum and have your licence confiscated if you exceed the limit.

Only lead-free petrol and diesel are widely available. A few garages take credit cards, but tend to prefer cash or payment by debit card.

PARKING PLACES

Apart from Sundays, when shops are closed, finding a parking spot in Vienna is frustrating and time-consuming. *Anfang* and *Ende* signs can be seen everywhere. You

are not allowed to park between them. Do look carefully as the *Ende* sign may be around a corner or facing the wrong way. If your car is clamped or towed away, telephone or go to the police, who will tell you which of the city's two pounds to go to. The City of Vienna operates a park and pay scheme in districts 1 to 9 and 20 from 9am to 10pm Mondays to Fridays *(see p245)*. You can buy parking disks from newsagents *(Tabak Trafiken)*, some banks and petrol stations. Usually, a maximum of two hours is allowed in any space. In other districts, a blue line by the kerb indicates a pay and display scheme. Car parks in Vienna tend to be expensive.

CAR HIRE

To hire a car, you will need your passport and a driver's licence that has been issued for at least one year. International licences are required for languages in a script other than Roman.

Major car hire firms have outlets at the airport and in the city centre. Car hire is more expensive at the airport, but it is the only place where you will be able to hire a car late at night or at weekends.

Car park sign

TAXIS

You can recognize a taxi by the TAXI sign on the roof. They are usually saloon cars, often Mercedes. If a taxi is for hire, the sign on its roof will be illuminated. In the centre of Vienna it is easier to get a taxi at one of the city's ranks, rather than by hailing one in the street. Alternatively you can call one of three numbers (31300, 40100 or 60160) to order a taxi, which will usually come in a few minutes. The operator tells you when to expect it and you should be waiting, as it may drive off if you are not there. A short trip costs from €7 to €10. There are additional costs for more than one passenger, luggage, and late-night and weekend journeys. A trip to the airport costs up to €34. It is usual to tip about 10 per cent of the fare, rounding up the sum to the nearest euro.

Taxi meter

Basic fare

Supplement fare

Vienna's taxis are usually saloon cars, often Mercedes

TICKETS AND TRAVEL CARDS

Finding your way around Vienna's transport system is fairly simple, but buying the right ticket at the right price can be a bit more confusing. It is easiest to buy your tickets in advance, either from a newsagent *(Tabak Trafik)*, from a ticket machine or over the counter at an underground or Schnellbahn booking office. A standard ticket covers all areas of Vienna (zone 100). With this you can change trains and lines as often as you like, and even change from the underground to a tram or a bus, but you are not allowed to break your journey.

A weekly season ticket is valid for all areas of Vienna (zone 100) and from Monday to Sunday. This is a good buy if you plan to use public transport for more than four days. One advantage of this ticket

24-hour ticket

72-hour ticket

Weekly season ticket

Streifenkarte, or strip ticket, valid for four journeys

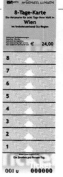
8-Tage-Karte valid for eight days' travel or for up to eight people on the same day

is that it need not be used just by the person who bought it. More useful for parties of visitors are the green *8-Tage-Karte*. Each card consists of eight strips which, when stamped, are valid for a day on Vienna's public transport. Up to eight people may stamp the same ticket. It is important that you

start with strip one – stamping strip eight first will invalidate the other seven. Also available are 24-hour tickets and a strip ticket for four rides.

The Vienna Card is a 72-hour ticket valid on all transport. You only need to punch it once, and it comes with additional discounts and benefits.

1 Use the touch screen to change the language and to select your ticket type.

2 Follow the instructions and insert coins, notes or a credit card to pay for your ticket.

Vienna Transport Authority ticket machine

Insert your ticket in the direction of the arrow. Wait for the pinging noise to confirm that your ticket has been validated.

Ticket-stamping machine

DIRECTORY

CAR HIRE

Avis City
Südbahnhof.
Map 4 F4. Tel 5876241.
Airport Tel 7007 32700.
www.avis.at

Budget City
Vienna Hilton.
Map 4 F1 & 6 F4.
Tel 7146565.
Airport Tel 7007 32711.
www.budget.at

Europcar
Schubertring 9.
Map 6E5. Tel 7146717.

Airport Tel 7007 32699.
www.europcar.at

Hertz City
Kärntner Ring 17.
Map 4 D1 & 5 C5.
Tel 512 8677.
Airport Tel 7007 32661.

BIKE TOURS/ RENTAL

City Bike
www.citybikewien.at

Pedal Power
Ausstellungstrasse 3.
Tel 7297234.
www.pedalpower.at

CAR PARKS

Wollzeile 7.
Map 2 E5 & 6 D3.

Am Hof.
Map 2 D5 & 5 C2.

Morzinplatz.
Map 2 E4 & 6 D2.

Dr-Karl-Lueger-Ring.
Map 1 C5 & 5 A2.

Börsegasse.
Map 2 D4 & 5 C1.

Other car parks are shown on the Street Finder map (see pp262–7).

24-HOUR PETROL STATION

Börsegasse 11.
Map 2 D4 & 5 C1.

BP Morzinplatz 1.
Map 2 E4 & 6 D2.

TAXIS

Taxi-Booking
Tel 31300.
Tel 40100.
Tel 60160.

Limousine Service
Flughafen-Taxi
Tel 5127000.

Travelling by Underground

U-Bahn station symbol

Construction of Vienna's underground, or U-Bahn, system, one of the most modern in Europe, began in 1969 and continues to the present day. Though Vienna is a compact city and many of the major sights can be reached on foot or by tram and bus, the U-Bahn is a clean, fast and reliable way of crossing the city. It is also useful for travelling further afield. The U-Bahn currently comprises five lines, and line U2 now runs to Prater Stadien and line U1 has been extended to Leopoldam.

manually and you will need to pull hard as they are stiff and heavy. The U-Bahn is generally safe (*see p240*), but in case of emergencies there are help points on most platforms. You are not allowed to smoke on U-Bahn platforms or on the trains (smoking is also forbidden on trams and buses).

THE UNDERGROUND SYSTEM

Displays above the train doors show stations and connections, and a recorded voice announces stops and also connections to trams and buses. Be aware, though, that this announcement may be a station behind. Prams can be stored by the doors; a picture of a pram indicates where. Bicycles are also allowed, but only on a few carriages and at set times. Doors are opened

Emergency help point on a Vienna U-Bahn platform

MAKING A JOURNEY BY UNDERGROUND

1 To determine which line to take, travellers should look for their destination on a U-Bahn map. The five lines are distinguished by colour and number. Simply trace the line to your destination, making a note of where you need to change lines. Connections to other forms of transport are also shown.

2 Tickets can be bought from a newsagent, ticket vending machines or ticket offices. To get to the trains, insert your ticket into the ticket-stamping machine in the direction of the arrow. Wait for the ping indicating that it is validated, and pass through the barrier. Follow the signs (with the number and colour of the line) to your platform.

3 On the platform, check the direction and destination of the train on an electronic destination indicator.

4 Stops along the line are shown on a plan. A red arrow in the corner shows the direction in which the train enters the station.

5 At your destination follow the *Ausgang* signs to reach street level.

Pull handle to open door

The door opens out to the side

Sign showing stops on line 3 of the U-Bahn, including connecting stops

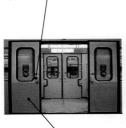

6 At stations with more than one exit, use the map of the city to check which street or square you will come out at.

Travelling by Tram

Viennese tram

The city's red and white trams are a familiar sight, and the Viennese know winter has arrived when tram drivers put up their leather screens against the icy wind that blows through the doors. Sadly many lines are being pulled up to make way for cars, and development of the U-Bahn means that some lines are no longer needed. A visit to Vienna would not be complete without a tram ride, as it offers not only an excellent view of the city, but a nostalgic journey into Vienna's past.

Trams in a busy Vienna street

USING A TRAM

Using Vienna's trams is a delightful way to get around the city. There are still some old-style trams in use with wooden seats and old-fashioned interiors. A recorded voice announces the stops (as on the underground and buses), and each tram has its route clearly displayed with all the stops marked. The doors are opened by pressing the button beside them. Single-journey tickets

Westbahnhof

STRASSENBAHN HALTESTELLE

9 Tram stop

can be bought from machines at the front of the tram, but regular passengers tend to use passes or

strip tickets *(see p252)*, which work out cheaper and are more convenient.

Tram exit button   **Tram entrance button**

SIGHTSEEING BY TRAM

A good way to see the parade of handsome 19th-century public buildings on the Ringstrasse is on the tram network. A trip on tram lines 1, 2 and D will take you past

buildings ranging in style from Greek Neo-Classical to Jugendstil *(see p54–7)*. The Tram Museum gives organized tours of Vienna in a 1920s tram (including a visit to Vienna's Tram Museum itself). The meeting point is at Otto Wagner's Karlsplatz Pavilions *(see p146)*, and prospectuses are available from information offices. Private groups may also hire a vintage tram (built between 1913 and 1958) to take them to the Prater or a *Heuriger* or simply to tour the city.

Tram Museum
Tel 790944903.

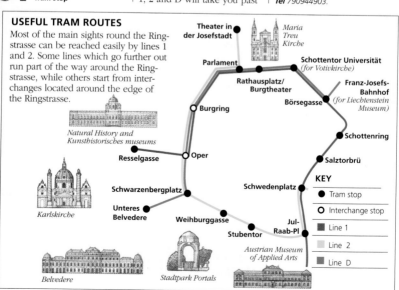

USEFUL TRAM ROUTES

Most of the main sights round the Ring-strasse can be reached easily by lines 1 and 2. Some lines which go further out run part of the way around the Ring-strasse, while others start from inter-changes located around the edge of the Ringstrasse.

Natural History and Kunsthistorisches museums

Karlskirche

Belvedere

Theater in der Josefstadt

Maria Treu Kirche

Parlament

Rathausplatz/ Burgtheater

Burgring

Resselgasse

Oper

Schwarzenbergplatz

Unteres Belvedere

Weihburggasse

Stadtpark Portals

Stubentor

Schottentor Universität *(for Votivkirche)*

Franz-Josefs-Bahnhof *(for Liechtenstein Museum)*

Börsegasse

Schottenring

Salztorbrü

Schwedenplatz

Jul-Raab-Pl

Austrian Museum of Applied Arts

KEY

●	Tram stop
O	Interchange stop
■	Line 1
■	Line 2
■	Line D

Travelling by Bus

Route number
Destination

Little hopper buses serve the centre of Vienna and larger buses go from the inner suburbs, Ringstrasse and Prater to the outer suburbs. Some buses run along old tram routes, and they are the same municipal red and white colour as the trams. Bus stops are also in the same red and white colours as tram stops.

Bus stop

Viennese hopper bus

BUS TICKETS

Tickets for buses, like tram tickets, can be purchased from the driver when you get on, but it is more advisable to buy a pass or a strip ticket from Schnellbahn or U-Bahn stations, or from a newsagent, beforehand *(see p252)*. Ticket machines on trams and buses are identical. Tickets other than those bought on the bus or tram need to be stamped in the blue ticket-stamping machine in order to validate them. If you have already made part of your journey by tram or U-Bahn, there is no need to stamp your ticket again. Limited services run on holidays and Christmas Day. On New Year's Eve, buses and other forms of public transport run all night.

2 Insert money in the slot

1 Choose your ticket

3 Collect your ticket and change here

Tram machine

can board one of the orange-coloured federal buses *(Postbusse)* that run to a variety of destinations in eastern Austria. The main coach companies that organize excursions and tours in and around Vienna are Cityrama and Vienna Sightseeing *(see p238)*, and their buses and coaches, full of tourists, are a common sight on the roads of central Vienna, especially during the summer months.

COACHES

Vienna's main coach station is Busbahnhof Wien, situated near Südbahnhof/ Südtirolerplatz *(see p248)*, where you

NIGHT BUSES

Night buses operate every night of the week starting at half past midnight and then at 30-minute intervals until 4am in the morning. There is some variation between the service operating on weekday nights (Sunday night through to Thursday night) and that operating at the weekend and on public holidays. All night buses in Vienna start from Schwedenplatz, the Opera and Schottentor, and travel to most suburbs of the city. All types of bus tickets are valid for travel on the city's night buses.

If you are staying some distance from a night bus route, it is possible to arrange for a taxi to pick you up from your destination stop. Taxis can be booked through the Transport Office in Schwedenplatz.

Travelling by Train

Schnellbahn logo

Bundesbahn logo

The Austrian Federal Railways or Bundesbahn, with its familiar red and white logo, has about 5,800 km (3,600 miles) of railways, and offers frequent direct connections to all European countries *(see p248)*. Within Austria, it offers good connections to tourist destinations such as Salzburg and Innsbruck. Further afield destinations *(see pp158–79)* can be reached by Schnellbahn or Bundesbahn lines.

The Schnellbahn (known as the S-Bahn for short), with its distinctive blue and white logo, is really a commuter service. It has stops in the centre of Vienna interconnecting with mainline railway stations

(see p249), but is of most use as a means of getting to sights that are further afield. The local Bundesbahn is also a commuter service, when it is sometimes called the Regionalbahn on maps and timetables

in order to distinguish it from national routes. Timetable information is available from station information offices and is displayed on station departures and arrivals boards.

Schnellbahn train

STREET FINDER

The map references for all the sights, hotels, restaurants, bars, shops and entertainment venues described in this book refer to the maps in this section. A complete index of street names and all the places of interest marked on the maps can be found on the following pages. The key map *(right)* shows the area of Vienna covered by the *Street Finder*. This map includes sightseeing areas as well as districts for hotels, restaurants and entertainment venues.

All the street names in the index and on the *Street Finder* are in German – *Strasse* translating as street and *Gasse* meaning lane. *Platz* or *Hof* indicate squares or courtyards. Throughout this guide, the numbers of the houses follow the street names, in the same way that you will find them in Vienna.

View of Vienna's roof tops from Am Hof *(see p87)*

KEY TO STREET FINDER

▮	Major sight
▮	Places of interest
▢	Other building
Ⓤ	U-Bahn station
🚆	Bundesbahn station
🚋	Badner Bahn stop
Ⓢ	Schnellbahn station
🚌	Bus and coach station
Ⓟ	Parking
ℹ	Tourist information office
✚	Hospital with casualty unit
🔲	Police station
✝	Church
✡	Synagogue
⊠	Post office
═	Railway line
	Pedestrian street

**SCALE OF MAPS
1–4 & 5–6 RESPECTIVELY**

0 metres	250	
0 yards	250	**1:14,000**

0 metres	125	
0 yards	125	**1:9,000**

Section of the Austria fountain (1846) by Schwanthaler (left) and side view of the Schottenkirche *(see p110)*

0 kilometres	1
0 miles	0.5

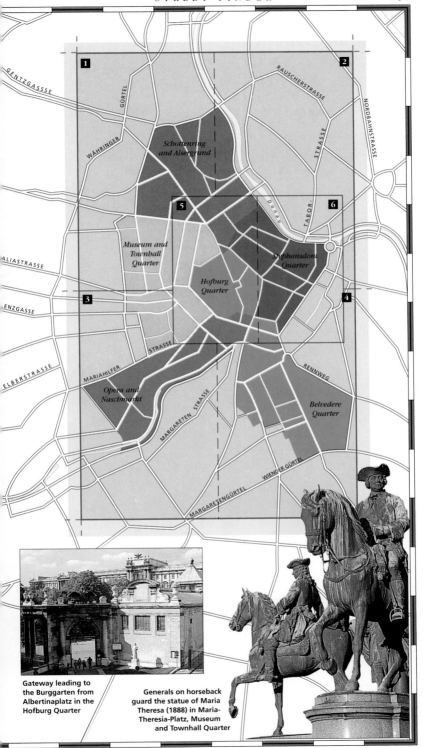

Gateway leading to the Burggarten from Albertinaplatz in the Hofburg Quarter

Generals on horseback guard the statue of Maria Theresa (1888) in Maria-Theresia-Platz, Museum and Townhall Quarter

Street Finder Index

Vienna's street and place names are generally spelt as one word; -platz, -strasse or -kirche are put at the end of the name, as in Essiggasse for example. Occasionally they are treated as separate words, for instance Alser Strasse. Abbreviations used in this index are Dr as in Doctor-Ignaz-Seipel-Platz, and St as in Sankt Josef Kirche. Some entries have two map references. The first refers to the smaller scale map that covers the whole of central Vienna, the second refers to the large-scale inset map that covers the Stephansdom and Hofburg Quarters.

USEFUL WORDS

Gasse	street
Strasse	road
Platz	square
Hof	court
Kirche	church
Kapelle	chapel
Dom	cathedral
Denkmal	monument
Markt	market
(often the sight of an old market)	
Brücke	bridge

A

Abraham-a-Sancta-
Clara-Gasse **5 B3**
Academy of Fine Arts
4 D2 & 5 B5
Academy of
Sciences **2 E5 & 6 E3**
Adambergergasse **2 E3**
Ahornergasse **3 A2**
Akademie der Bildenden
Künste **4 D2 & 5 B5**
Akademie der Wissen-
schaften **2 E5 & 6 E3**
Akademiestrasse
4 E2 & 6 D5
Akademietheater, see
Konzerthaus
Albertgasse **1 A5**
Albertplatz **1 A4**
Albertina **5 C4**
Albertinaplatz **4 D1 & 5 C4**
Alexander-Nehr-
Gasse **1 C1**
Allgemeines
Krankenhaus **1 A3**
Alois Drasche Park **4 D5**
Alpen-Garten **4 F4**
Alser Strasse **1 A4**
Alser Strasse station **1 A4**
Alserbachstrasse **1 C2**
Alsergrund District **1 B2**
Alte Backstube **1 B5**
Altes Rathaus **2 D4 & 6 D2**
Althanstrasse **1C1**
Altlerchenfelder
Kirche **3 A1**
American Bar **4 D1 & 6 D3**
Amerlingstrasse **3 B2**
Am Gestade **2 D4 & 5 C2**
Am Heumarkt **4 E2 & 6 E5**
Am Hof **2 D5 & 5 C2**
Am Modenapark **4 F2**
Am Stadtpark **4 F1 & 6 F4**
Am Tabor **2 F2**
An-der-Hülben **6 E4**
Anastasius-Grün-
Gasse **1 A1**
Andreasgasse **3 A2**
Annagasse **4 D1 & 6 D4**
Annakirche **4 D1 & 6 D4**
Anton-Frank-Gasse **1 A1**
Antonigasse **1 A5**
Anzengrubergasse **4 D5**
Apollogasse **3 A2**
Arbeiterkammer **4 E3**
Arbeitergasse **3 A5**
Argentinierstrasse **4 E4**
Arndtstrasse **3 A5**
Arsenalstrasse **4 F5**
Aspernbrücke **2 F5 & 6 F2**
Aspernbrücken-
gasse **2 F4 & 6 F2**
Auerspergstrasse **1 B5**
Augarten Palace **2 E3**
Augarten Palais **2 E3**
Augarten Park **2 E2**
Augartenbrücke **2 D3**
Augasse **1 C1**
Augustinerkirche
4 D1 & 5 C4
Augustinerstrasse

4 D1 & 5 C4
Austrian Museum of
Applied Arts
2 F5 & 6 F3
Austrian Tourist
Board **4 D2**
Autobus Bahnhof
4 F1 & 6 F3
Ayrenhoffgasse **1 B1**

B

Babenbergerstrasse
3 C1 & 5 B5
Babenbergerstrasse
station **3 C1 & 5 A5**
Bacherplatz **3 B4**
Bäckerstrasse **2 E5 & 6 D3**
Badgasse **1 C2**
Ballgasse **6 D4**
Ballhausplatz **5 B3**
Bandgasse **3 A2**
Bankgasse **1 C5 & 5 B3**
Barbaragasse **6 E3**
Barnabitengasse **3 B2**
Bartensteingasse **1 B5**
Bäuerlegasse **2 E1**
Bauernfeldplatz **1 C3**
Bauernmarkt **2 D5 & 6 D3**
Bayerngasse **4 F2 & 6 F5**
Beatrixgasse **4 F2 & 6 F5**
Beethoven-Denkmal **6 E5**
Beethovengasse **1 C3**
Bellariastrasse **5 A4**
Belvedere Garten **4 F3**
Belvederegasse **4 E4**
Benno-Floriani-Platz **1 A5**
Bennogasse **1 A4**
Berggasse **1 C4**
Bernardgasse **3 A1**
Bestattungsmuseum **4 E4**
Biberstrasse **2 F5 & 6 F2**
Bindergasse **1 B2**
Blechturmgasse **4 D4**
Bleichergasse **1 B2**
Blumauergasse **2 F3**
Blumenmarkt **3 C4**
Blutgasse **6 D3**
Bognergasse **5 C3**
Bohemian Court
Chancery **2 D5 & 5 C2**
Böhmische
Hofkanzlei **2 D5 & 5 C2**
Boltzmanngasse **1 C3**
Borschkegasse **1 A3**
Börse **2 D4 & 5 C1**
Börsegasse **2 D4 & 5 B1**
Börseplatz **2 D4 & 5 C1**
Bösendorferstrasse
4 D2 & 5 C5
Botanical Gardens **4 F3**
Botanischer Garten **4 F3**
Botanisches Institut **4 F3**
Brahmsplatz **4 D3**
Brandmayergasse **3 B5**
Brandstätte **2 D5 & 6 D3**
Bräuhausgasse **3 A4**
Bräunerstrasse **5 C4**
Breite Gasse **3 C1**
Breitenfelder Gasse **1 A4**
Brigittagasse **2 D1**

Brigittenau District **2 D1**
Brigittenauer Lände **1 C1**
Brückengasse **3 A4**
Brünnlbadgasse **1 A4**
Buchfeldgasse **1 B5**
Bundes-Lehr-und
Versuchsanstalt **6 D5**
Bundeskanzleramt
1 C5 & 5 B3
Bundesministerium
für Finanzen **6 D4**
Bundesmobilien-
sammlung **3 A2**
Bürgerspitalgasse **3 A3**
Burggarten **4 D1 & 5 B4**
Burggasse **3 A1 & 5 A3**
Burgkapelle **4 D1 & 5 B4**
Burgring **3 C1 & 5 A4**
Burgtheater **1 C5 & 5 A2**

C

Café Landtmann
1 C5 & 5 B2
Canisius Kirche **1 B1**
Canisiusgasse **1 B2**
Canongasse **1 A2**
Canovagasse **6 D5**
Castellezgasse **2 F3**
Castelligasse **3 B4**
Cathedral Museum
2 E5 & 6 D3
Chemisches Institut **1 B3**
Christinengasse
4 E2 & 6 E5
Churhausgasse **6 D3**
City Air Terminal
4 F1 & 6 F4
Clock Museum
2 D5 & 5 C2
Clusiusgasse **2 D2**
Cobdengasse **6 E4**
Coburggasse **6 E4**
Colloredogasse **1 A1**
Concordiaplatz
2 D4 & 5 C1
Corneliusgasse **3 B3**
Czerningasse **2 F4**

D

Damböckgasse **3 B3**
Dammstrasse **2 E1**
Danhausergasse **4 D3**
Darwingasse **2 F3**
Daungasse **1 A4**
Demel-Konditorei
2 D5 & 5 C3
Denisgasse **2 D1**
Deutschordenskirche
2 E5
Diehlgasse **3 A5**
Dietrichsteingasse **1 C3**
Diplomatische Akademie,
Politische Kommission
4 E3
Doblhoffgasse **1 B5**
Döblergasse **3 B1**
Döblinger Hauptstrasse
1 B1
Domgasse **6 D3**

Dominikanerbastei
2 F5 & 6 E3
Dominikanergasse **3 A4**
Dominikanerkirche
2 E5 & 6 E3
Dom- und Diözesan-
museum **2 E5 & 6 D3**
Donaukanal **2 D2 & 6 D1**
Donaukanal-Promenade
6 E2
Donnergasse **6 D4**
Dorotheergasse
4 D1 & 5 C4
Dr-Ignaz-Seipel-Platz **6 D3**
Dr-Karl-Lueger-Platz **6 E4**
Dr-Karl-Lueger-Ring
1 C5 & 5 A2
Dr-Karl-Renner-Ring
1 C5 & 5 A3
Drahtgasse **5 C2**
Dreifaltigkeitskirche **1 B4**
Dreimäderlhaus
1 C5 & 5 B2
Dresdner Strasse **2 F1**
Dumbastrasse **6 D5**
Dürergasse **3 B3**

E

Ebendorferstrasse
1 C5 & 5 A2
Edelhofgasse **1 A2**
Einsiedlergasse **3 A5**
Einsiedelplatz **3 B5**
Elektrotechnisches
Institut **4 D3**
Elisabethen-Spital **4 F1**
Elisabethkirche **4 E4**
Elisabethstrasse
4 D1 & 5 B5
Embelgasse **3 A4**
Ephesos Museum **5 B4**
Erzherzog Karl
Denkmal **5 B4**
Eschenbachgasse
3 C2 & 5 B5
Essiggasse **6 D3**
Esslinggasse **2 D4 & 5 C1**
Esterházypark **3 B2**
Esterházygasse **3 B3**
Ethnological Museum
5 B4

F

Fahnengasse **5 B3**
Falkestrasse **6 E3**
Färbergasse **5 C2**
Fasangasse **4 F4**
Fassziehergasse **3 B1**
Faulmanngasse **4 D2**
Favoritenstrasse **4 D3**
Fechtergasse **1 C2**
Felderstrasse **1 C5**
Feldgasse **1 A4**
Fendigasse **3 B5**
Ferdinandstrasse
2 F5 & 6 F2
Ferstelgasse **5 A1**
Fichtegasse **4 E1 & 6 D5**
Figarohaus **2 E5 & 6 D3**

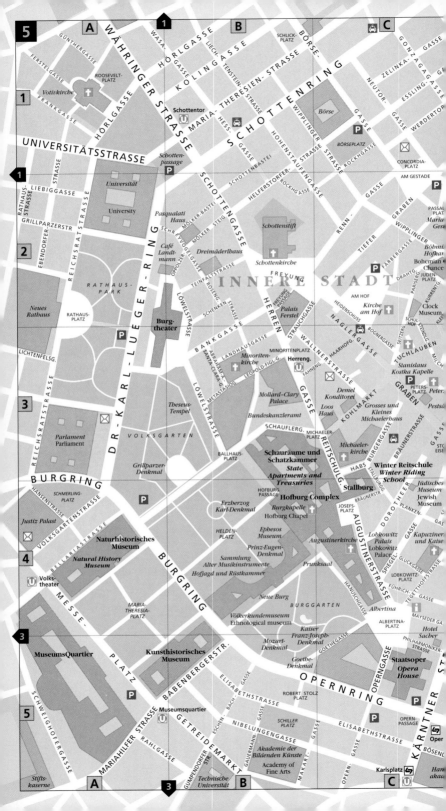

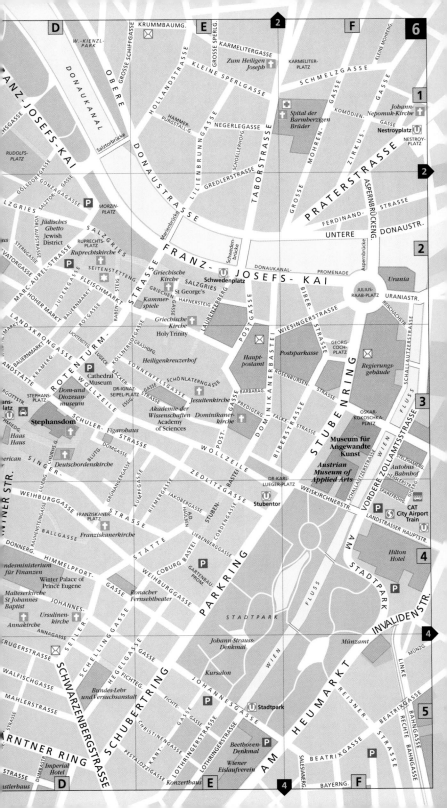

General Index

Acknowledgments

Dorling Kindersley wishes to thank the following people who contributed to the preparation of this book.

Main Contributor
Stephen Brook was born in London and educated at Cambridge. After working as an editor in Boston and London, he became a full-time writer in 1982. Among his books are *New York Days, New York Nights; The Double Eagle; Prague, L.A. Lore* and books on wine. He also writes articles on wine and travel for many newspapers and periodicals.

Additional Contributors
Gretel Beer, Rosemary Bircz, Caroline Bugler, Dierdre Coffey, Fred Mawer, Nicholas Parsons.

Proof Reader
Diana Vowles.

Design and Editorial
Managing Editor Carolyn Ryden
Managing Art Editor Steve Knowlden
Senior Editor Georgina Matthews
Senior Art Editor Vanessa Courtier
Editorial Director David Lamb
Art Director Anne-Marie Bulat
Consultant Robert Avery
Language Consultant Barbara Eichberger

DTP
Vinod Harish, Vincent Kurian, Azeem Siddiqui.

Design and Editorial Assistance
Ros Angus, Claire Baranowski, Jane Edmonds, Gadi Farfour, Fay Franklin, Rhiannon Furbear, Sally Gordon, Emily Green, Alistair Gunn, Elaine Harries, Melanie Hartzell, Paul Hines, Laura Jones, Priya Kukadia, Joanne Lenney, Carly Madden, Hayley Maher, Ella Milroy, Kate Molan, Melanie Nicholson-Hartzell, Catherine Palmi, Helen Partington, Sangita Patel, Alice Peebles, Marianne Petrou, Robert Purnell, Nicki Rawson, Sadie Smith, Sands Publishing Solutions, Simon Ryder, Andrew Szudek, Samia Tadros, Lynda Warrington, Susannah Wolley Dod.

Additional Illustrations
Kevin Jones, Gilly Newman, John Woodcock, Martin Woodward.

Cartography
Uma Bhattacharya, Mohammad Hassan, Jasneet Kaur, Peter Winfield, James Mills-Hicks (Dorling Kindersley Cartography)
Colourmap Scanning Limited, Contour Publishing, Cosmographics, European Map Graphics, Street Finder maps: ERA Maptec Ltd (Dublin).
Map Co-ordinators Simon Farbrother, David Pugh
Cartographic Research Jan Clark, Caroline Bowie, Claudine Zante.

Additional Photography
DK Studio/Steve Gorton, Ian O'Leary, Poppy, Steve Shott, Clive Streeter.

Fact checker
Melanie Nicholson-Hartzell

Special Assistance
Marion Telsnig and Ingrid Pollheimer-Stadtlober at the Austrian Tourist Board, London; Frau Preller at the Heeresgeschichtliches Museum; Frau Wegsch-eider at the Kunsthistorisches Museum; Frau Stillfried and Mag Czap at the Hofburg; Herr Fehlinger at the Museen der Stadt Wien; Mag Schmid at the Natural History Museum; Mag Dvorak at the Österreichischer Bundestheaterverband; Dr Michael Krapf and Mag Grabner at the Österreichische Galerie; Robert Tidmarsh and Mag Weber-Kainz at Schloss Schön-brunn; Frau Zonschits at the Tourismusverband.

Photography Permissions
Dorling Kindersley would like to thank the following for their kind permission to photograph at their establishments:

Alte Backstube, Bestattungsmuseum, Schloss Belvedere, Bundesbaudirektion, Deutschordenskirche and Treasury, Dom und Diözesanmuseum, Sigmund Freud Gesellschaft, Josephinum Institut für Geschichte der Medzin der Universität Wien, Kapuzinerkirche, Pfarramt St. Karl, Stift Klosterneuburg, Wiener Kriminalmuseum, Niederösterreichisches Landesmuseum, Österreichischer Bundestheaterverband, Österreichische Postsparkasse (P. S. K.), Dombausekretariat Sankt Stephan, Spanische Reitschule and Museum für Volkskunde. Dorling Kindersley would also like to thank all the shops, restaurants, cafés, hotels, churches and public services who aided us with photography. These are too numerous to thank individually.

Picture Credits
t = top; tl = top left; tc = top centre; tr = top right; cla = centre left above; ca = centre above; cra = centre right above; cl = centre left; c = centre; cr = centre right; clb = centre left below; cb = centre below; crb = centre right below; bl = bottom left; b = bottom; bc = bottom centre; br = bottom right; d = detail.

Works of art have been reproduced with the permission of the following copyright holders: *Brunnenhaus* Ernst Fuchs © DACS, London 2006; *The Tiger Lion* 1926 Oskar Kokoschka © DACS, London 2006 155t; © the henry moore foundation: 144b.

The Publishers are grateful to the following individuals, companies and picture libraries for permission to reproduce their photographs:

4corners Images: Damm Stefan 11br; A1 PIX: Rainer Binder 11cl; Alamy Images: imagebroker/ Christian Handl 205tl; INSADCO: Photography/ Martin Bobrovsky 205c; Art Kowalsky 10cla; John Lens 176cr; Barry Mason 207c; mediacolor's 176 cla, 206cl; David Noble 207tl; Robert Harding Picture Library Ltd/ Richard Nebesky 204cla; Ken Welsh 10bc; WoodyStock/ Helmet Ebner 180; Graphic Sammlung Albertina, Wien: 26–7; Ancient Art and Architecture Collection: 24b(d), 25t, 29ca; Akg-Images: 8–9, 16(d), 17t, 19tc(d), 19br(d), 21b, 22–3, 24t, 24–5, 25cb, 25bl, 26ca, 26br(d), 27t, 28t, 28c, 28br(d), 29t, 28–9, 29cl, 29bl, 30t(d), 30cl, 32cl, 32br, 33b, 34br, 36tl, 38br, 55b(d), 67 inset, 87b(d), 98cla, 110b(d), 149ca, 152cb, 172b, 237 inset; Erich Lessing 11tl, 38cb, 39cr, 98cla; Austrian Airlines: 246t; Austrian Archives: 35tl.

Belvedere,Vienna: 156crb; Thomas Preiss 157cla; Bildarchiv Preussischer Kulturbesitz, Berlin: 23bl, 35cbl, 92t; Casa Editrice Bonechi, Firenze: 167ca;

CHRISTIAN BRANDSTÄTTER VERLAG, Wien: 20ca, 31c(d), 33tl, 34bl, 83t, 99c; BRIDGEMAN ART LIBRARY, London: 133b(d); Albertina, Wien 46br; Bonhams, London 24ca; British Library, London 4t(d), 19bl(d); Kunsthistorisches Museum, Wien 19tr(d), 46cr; Museum der Stadt Wien 33tr, 38car(d), 38bcl, 39cl; Österreichische Galerie 35tr; HOTEL BRISTOL: 190cr; ©1999 BUNDESGÄRTEN, WIEN: 172tl; BUNDESMINISTERIUM FÜR FINANZEN: 27cb(d); BURGHAUPTMANNSCHAFT IN WIEN: 101ca, 101cb, 101b.

COURTESY OF CAFÉ MUSEUM: 58br; ARCHÄOLOGISCHER PARK CARNUNTUM: 21tr; CASINOS AUSTRIA: 227c; CEPHAS PICTURE LIBRARY: Mick Rock 161b, 208tl; Wine Magazine 240br; CONTRAST PHOTO: Milenko Badzic 65t; Franz Hausner 166b; Michael Himml/ Transglobe 152tr; Hinterleitner 227b; Peter Kurz 63b, 141tl, 233b; Boris Mizaikoffl/Transglobe 63t; Tappeiner/Transglobe 234c; H Valencak 178b. DDSG-DONAUREISEN GMBH: 249c; K.U. K Hofzuckerbäcker CH. Demel's Söhne GmbH: 203c; DK IMAGES:(c) Judith Miller/ Sloan's 10tc; ET ARCHIVE, London: 38br; Museum für Gestaltung, Zurich 34cl; Museum der Stadt Wien 26bl, 31tl, 38cl; EUROLINES (UK) Ltd: 248cb; EUROPEAN COMMISSION: 243; MARY EVANS PICTURE LIBRARY, London: 18tl, 18bl, 18br, 19tl, 22c, 25br, 27br, 30cr, 30bl, 30br, 32t, 35b, 38t, 39t, 76tr, 175b, 189 inset.

F. A. HERBIG VERLAGSBUCHHANDLUNG GMBH, München: 98bl, 98br, 99bl, 99br. ROBERT HARDING PICTURE LIBRARY: Larsen Collinge International 42cb, 232t; Adam Woolfitt 62t, 137t, 150t, 178t, 256tl; HEERESGES-CHICHTLICHES MUSEUM, Wien: 47b, 166t, 166b, 167t, 167cb, 167b; HEINZ HEIDER, VOR: 252cl; HISTORISCHES MUSEUM DER STADT WIEN: 17b, 20t, 21ca, 21cbr, 26t, 28cb, 32cr, 32bl, 33ca, 33cb, 43t, 47tl, 49c, 141tc, 141tr, 145ca, 169t; HOTEL SACHER: 202cr; HULTON-DEUTSCH COLLECTION: 28bl, 36tr(d), 38bcr(d), 168ca; HUTCHISON LIBRARY: John G Egan 200t. THE IMAGE BANK, London: GSO Images 11b; Fotoworld 41bl; HOTEL IMPERIAL: 190b. JOSEFSTADT THEATRE: 226c. WILHELM KLEIN: 23t, 26cb; KUNSTHAUS WIEN: Peter Strobel 48t; KUNSTHISTORISCHES MUSEUM, Wien: 24cb, 41cbr, 46cl, 48b, 56c, 95t, 95b, 99t, 100 all, 122–3 all, 124–5 all, 126–7 all, 175tl.

J & L LOBMEYR, Wien: 49t; LEOPOLD MUSEUM-PRIVATSTIF-TUNG: Selbstbildnis, 1910, by Egon Schiele 46bla, Hockender Weiblicher Akt, 1910, by Egon Schiele 120tr, Self Portrait with Chinese Lantern, 1912, by Egon Schiele 118t, Die Schnitter, 1922 by Egger-Lienz 120t; LONELY PLANET IMAGES: Richard Nebesky 233tl; MAGNUM PHOTOS: Erich Lessing 18tr, 20c, 20bl, 20br, 21tl, 21cbl, 22cb, 23cal, 26c, 29br, 30–1, 31b; MANSELL COLLECTION, London: 9 inset; MUSEUM JUDENPLATZ: Votava/PID 86tl; MUSEUMSQUARTIER,

ERRICHTUNGS-UND BETRIEBSGESMBH: Lisi Gradnitzer 118br; Rupert Steiner MQ E+B GesmbH 41br, 119t, Martin Gendt MQ E+B GesmbH 119bl; MUMOK, MUSEUM OF MODERN ART LUDWIG FOUNDATION VIENNA: Homme accroupi, 1907, by André Derain, © ADAGP, Paris & DACS, London 2006, 119br; The Red Horseman, 1974 by Roy Lichtenstein, © Estate of Roy Lichtenstein/DACS, London 2006, 120b. NARODNI MUSEUM, Praha: 18bc; NATURHISTORISCHES MUSEUM, Wien: 46t, 128–9 except 129br, 235cb.

ÖSTERREICHISCHE BUNDESBAHNEN: 248t, 255b; ÖSTERRE-ICHISCHE GALERIE, Wien: 47cb, 154c, 155 all, 156bl, 157 all; ÖSTERREICHISCHES MUSEUM FÜR ANGEWANDTE KUNST, Wien: 28ca, 47tl, 56t, 57c, 82–3 all except 83t; ÖSTERREICHISCHE NATIONALBANK: 243cal, 243cac; ÖSTER-REICHISCHE NATIONALBIBLIOTHEK, Wien: 20cb, 22t, 23cb, 36c; ÖSTERREICH WERBUNG: 5bl, 27ca, 31tc, 31tr, 34ca, 44b, 98cbl, 101t, 140b, 163cb, 163b, 172t, 179b, 203t, 232cr. POPPERFOTO: 37tc; RAIFFEISENBANK WIEN: Gerald Zugman 34cr; RETROGRAPH ARCHIVE, London: Martin Ranicar-Breese 193br; REX FEATURES, London: Action Press 36bl, Adolfo Franzo 37tl, Sipa Press 121b, Sokol/Sipa Press 121b; GEORG RIHA: 77t; RONACHER VARIETY THEATRE/CMM: Velo Weger 226t.

HOTEL SACHER: 194t; SCHLOSS SCHÖNBRUNN KULTUR-UND BETRIEBSGES MBH, Wien: Professor Gerhard Trumler 172c, 173 all except 173b, 174 all, 175tr; SCHLOSS SCHÖNBRUNN KULTUR- UND BETRIEBSGES MBH 1999: Wolfgang Voglhuber 139b; SCIENCE PHOTO LIBRARY, London: Geospace 10t; SYGMA: Habans/ Orban 37tr, Viennareport 37ca; TRAVEL LIBRARY: Philip Entiknapp 66–7, 221t, 250t. UNICREDIT BANK AUSTRIA AG: 242tl; WERNER FORMAN ARCHIVE: Museum der Stadt Wien 60c; St Stephens Cathedral Museum 23car; WIENER LINIEN GMBH &CO KG: 252 cl; WIEN MUSEUM: 86br, Longcase Clock c.1762-69 David A.S. Cajetano 86c; WIENER SÄNGERKNABEN: 5cbr, 39b, 64b; WIENER STADT- UND LANDESBIBLIOTHEK, Wien: 36tc, 36bl; WIGAST AG: 193tl, 193cr. VIENNASLIDE: Harald A Jahn 232b; Karl Luymair 230cl; MUSEUM FÜR VÖLKERKUNDE, Wien: 49b, 235b; VOTAVA, Wien: 163t; ZEFA: 153c; Anatol 98–9; Damm 248b; G Gro-Bauer 179t; Havlickek 177c; Sibelberbauer 62b; Streichan 37cb; Studio Mike 206t; V Wentzel 41cbc. ZOOM KINDERMUSEUM: Alexandra Eizinger 118cla.

JACKET: Front - DK IMAGES: Peter Wilson cbl; SUPERSTOCK; agefotostock main image. Back - DK IMAGES: Peter Wilson tl, cla, clb, bl. Spine - DK IMAGES: Peter Wilson b; SUPERSTOCK: agefotostock t.

All other images © Dorling Kindersley. For further information see: www.dkimages.com

---

SPECIAL EDITIONS OF DK TRAVEL GUIDES

DK Travel Guides can be purchased in bulk quantities at discounted prices for use in promotions or as premiums. We are also able to offer special editions and personalized jackets, corporate imprints, and excerpts from all of our books, tailored specifically to meet your own needs.

To find out more, please contact:
(in the United States) **SpecialSales@dk.com**
(in the UK) **travelspecialsales@uk.dk.com**
(in Canada) DK Special Sales at **general@tourmaline.ca**
(in Australia) **business.development@pearson.com.au**

Phrase Book

In Emergency

Help!	Hilfe!	hilf-er
Stop!	Halt!	hult
Call a doctor	Holen Sie einen Arzt	hole'n zee ine'n artst
Call an ambulance	Holen Sie einen Krankenwagen	hole'n zee ine'n krank'n-varg'n
Call the police	Holen Sie die Polizei	hole'n zee dee pol-its-eye
Call the fire brigade	Holen Sie die Feuerwehr	hole'n zee dee foy-er-vair
Where is the nearest telephone?	Wo finde ich ein Telefon in der Nähe?	voh fin-der ish ine tel-e-fone in dair nay-er?
Where is the nearest hospital?	Wo ist das nächstgelegene Krankenhaus?	voh ist duss next-g'lay-g'ner krunk'n-hows?

Communication Essentials

Yes	Ja	yah
No	Nein	nine
Please	Bitte	bitt-er
Thank you	Danke vielmals	dunk-er feel-malse
Excuse me	Gestatten	g'shtatt'n
Hello	Grüss Gott	groos got
Goodbye	Auf Wiedersehen	owf veed-er-zay-ern
Goodnight	Gute Nacht	goot-er nukht
morning	Vormittag	for-mit-targ
afternoon	Nachmittag	nakh-mit-targ
evening	Abend	ahb'nt
yesterday	Gestern	gest'n
today	Heute	hoyt-er
tomorrow	Morgen	morg'n
here	hier	hear
there	dort	dort
What?	Was?	vuss?
When?	Wann?	vunn?
Why?	Warum?	var-room?
Where?	Wo/Wohin?	voh/vo-hin?

Useful Phrases

How are you?	Wie geht es Ihnen?	vee gayt ess een'n?
Very well, thank you	Sehr gut, danke	zair goot, dunk-er
Pleased to meet you	Es freut mich sehr, Sie kennenzulernen	ess froyt mish zair, zee ken'n-tsoo-lairn'n
See you soon	Bis bald/bis gleich	bis bult/bis gleyesh
That's fine	Sehr gut	zair goot
Where is...?	Wo befindet sich...?	voe b'find't zish...?
Where are...?	Wo befinden sich...?	voe b'find'n zish...?
How far is it to...?	Wie weit ist...?	vee vite ist...?
Which way to...?	Wie komme ich zu...?	vee komma ish tsoo...?
Do you speak English?	Sprechen Sie englisch?	shpresh'n zee eng-glish?
I don't understand	Ich verstehe nicht	ish fair-shtay-er nisht
Could you please speak slowly?	Bitte sprechen Sie etwas langsamer?	bitt-er shpresh'n zee et-vuss lung-zam-er?
I'm sorry	Es tut mir leid/ Verzeihung	es toot meer lyte/ fair-tseye-oong

Useful Words

big	gross	grohss
small	klein	kline
hot	heiss	hyce
cold	kalt	kult
good	gut	goot
bad	schlecht	shlesht
enough	genug	g'nook
well	gut	goot
open	auf/offen	owf/off'n
closed	zu/geschlossen	tsoo/g'shloss'n
left	links	links
right	rechts	reshts
straight on	geradeaus	g'rah-der-owss
near	in der Nähe	in dair nay-er
far	weit	vyte
up	auf, oben	owf, obe'n
down	ab, unten	up, oont'n
early	früh	froo
late	spät	shpate

entrance	Eingang/Einfahrt	ine-gung/ine-fart
exit	Ausgang/Ausfahrt	ows-gung/ows-fart
toilet	WC/Toilette	vay-say/toy-lett-er
free/unoccupied	frei	fry
free/no charge	frei/gratis	fry/grah-tis

Making a Telephone Call

I'd like to place a long-distance call	Ich möchte ein Ferngespräch machen	ish mer-shter ine fairn-g'shpresh mukh'n
I'd like to call collect	Ich möchte ein Rückgespräch (Collectgespräch) machen	ish mer-shter ine rook-g'shpresh (coll-ect-g'shpresh) mukh'n
local call	Ortsgespräch	orts-g'shpresh
I'll try again later	Ich versuche es noch einmal etwas später	ish fair-zookh-er ess nokh ine-mull ett-vuss shpay-ter
Can I leave a message?	Kann ich etwas ausrichten?	kunn ish ett-vuss ows-rikht'n?
Hold on	Haben Sie etwas Geduld	harb'n zee ett-vuss g'doolt
Could you speak up a little please?	Bitte sprechen Sie etwas lauter?	bitt-er shpresh'n zee ett-vuss lowt-er?

Staying in a Hotel

Do you have a vacant room?	Haben Sie ein Zimmer frei?	harb'n zee ine tsimm-er fry?
double room with double bed	ein Doppelzimmer mit Doppelbett	ine dopp'l-tsimm-er mitt dopp'l-bet
twin room	ein Doppelzimmer	ine dopp'l-tsimm-er
single room	ein Einzelzimmer	ine ine-ts'l-tsimm-er
room with a bath/shower	Zimmer mit Bad/Dusche	tsimm-er mitt bart doosh-er
porter	Gepäckträger/ Concierge	g'peck-tray-ger/ kon-see-airsh
key	Schlüssel	shlooss'l
I have a reservation	Ich habe ein Zimmer reserviert	ish harb-er ine tsimm-er rezz-er-veert

Sightseeing

bus	der Bus	dair booss
tram	die Strassenbahn	dee stra-sen-barn
train	der Zug	dair tsoog
art gallery	Galerie	gall-er-ee
bus station	Busbahnhof	booss-barn-hofe
bus (tram) stop	die Haltestelle	dee hal-te-shtel-er
castle	Schloss, Burg	shloss, boorg
palace	Schloss, Palais	shloss, pall-ay
post office	das Postamt	dee pohs-taamt
cathedral	Dom	dome
church	Kirche	keersh-er
garden	Garten, Park	gart'n, park
library	Bibliothek	bib-leo-tek
museum	Museum	moo-zay-oom
information (office)	Information (-sbüro)	in-for-mat-see-on (-zboo-roe)
closed for public holiday	Feiertags geschlossen	fire-targz g'shloss'n

Shopping

How much does this cost?	Wieviel kostet das?	vee-feel kost't duss?
I would like...	Ich hätte gern...	ish hett-er gairn...
Do you have...?	Haben Sie...?	harb'n zee...?
I'm just looking	Ich schaue nur an	ish shau-er noor un
Do you take credit cards?	Kann ich mit einer Kreditkarte bezahlen?	kunn ish mitt ine-er kred-it-kar-ter b'tsahl'n?
What time do you open?	Wann machen Sie auf?	vunn mukh'n zee owf?
What time do you close?	Wann schliessen Sie?	vunn shlees'n zee?
This one	dieses	deez'z
expensive	teuer	toy-er
cheap	billig	bill-igg
size	Grösse	grers-er
white	weiss	vyce
black	schwarz	shvarts
red	rot	roht
yellow	gelb	gelp
green	grün	groon
blue	blau	blau

Types of Shop

antique shop	**Antiquitäten-geschäft**	un-tick-vi-**tayt**'n-g'**sheft**
bakery	**Bäckerei**	beck-er-**eye**
bank	**Bank**	bunk
book shop	**Buchladen/ Buchhandlung**	bookh-lard'n/ bookh-hant-loong
butcher	**Fleischerei**	fly-sher-**eye**
cake shop	**Konditorei**	kon-ditt-or-**eye**
chemist		
(for prescriptions)	**Apotheke**	App-o-**tay**-ker
(for cosmetics)	**Drogerie**	droog-er-**ree**
department store	**Warenhaus, Warengeschäft**	vahr'n-hows, vahr'n-g'**sheft**
delicatessen	**Feinkost (geschäft)**	fine-kost (g'sheft)
fishmonger	**Fischgeschäft**	fish-g'**sheft**
gift shop	**Geschenke(laden)**	g'**shenk-er(lahd**'n)
greengrocer	**Obst und Gemüse**	ohbst oont g'**moo**-zer
grocery	**Lebensmittel-geschäft**	**layb**'nz-mitt'l-g'**sheft**
hairdresser	**Friseur/Frisör**	freezz-**er**/freezz-**er**
market	**Markt**	markt
newsagent/ tobacconist	**Tabak Trafik**	tab-**ack** tra-feek
travel agent	**Reisebüro**	rye-zer-boo-roe
café	**Cafe, Kaffeehaus**	kaff-**ay**, kaff-**ay**-hows

Eating Out

Have you got a table for… people?	**Haben Sie einen Tisch für… Personen?**	harb'n zee ine'n tish foor… pair-**sohn**'n?
I want to reserve a table	**Ich möchte einen Tisch bestellen**	ish **mer**-shter ine'n tish b'**shtell**'n
The bill please	**Zahlen, bitte**	**tsarl**'n **bitt**-er
I am a vegetarian	**Ich bin Vegetarier**	ish bin vegg-er-**tah**-ree-er
Waitress/waiter	**Fräulein/Herr Ober**	froy-line/hair-**oh**-bare
menu	**die Speisekarte**	dee **shpize**-er-kart-er
fixed price menu	**das Menü**	duss men-**oo**
cover charge	**Couvert/Gedeck**	koo-vair/g'**deck**
wine list	**Weinkarte**	**vine**-kart-er
glass	**Glas**	glars
bottle	**Flasche**	**flush**-er
knife	**Messer**	**mess**-er
fork	**Gabel**	**garb**'l
spoon	**Löffel**	**lerff**'l
breakfast	**Frühstück**	**froo**-shtook
lunch	**Mittagessen**	**mit**-targ-ess'n
dinner	**Abendessen/ Dinner**	**arb**'nt-ess'n/ dee-**nay**
main course	**Hauptspeise**	**howpt**-shpize-er
starter, first course	**Vorspeise**	**for**-shpize-er
dish of the day	**Tageskarte**	**targ**-erz-kart-er
wine garden(s)	**Heuriger (Heurige)**	hoy-rigg-er (-e)
rare	**englisch**	**eng**-glish
medium	**medium**	**may**-dee-oom
well done	**durch**	**doorsh**

Menu Decoder

See also pp 202–11

Apfel	**upf**'l	apple
Almdudler	ahlm-**dood**-ler	herbal lemonade
Banane	bar-**nar**-ner	banana
Ei	**eye**	egg
Eis	**ice**	ice cream
Fisch	**fish**	fish
Fisolen	fee-**soul**'n	green beans (haricot)
Fleisch	**flysh**	meat
Garnelen	**gar**-nayl'n	prawns
gebacken	g'**buck**'n	baked/fried
gebraten	g'**brart**'n	roast
gekocht	g'**kokht**	boiled
Gemüse	g' **mooz**-er	vegetables
vom Grill	fom **grill**	grilled
Gulasch	**goo**-lush	stew
Hendl/Hahn/Huhn	**hend**'l/harn/hoon	chicken
Kaffee	kaf-**fay**	coffee
Kartoffel/Erdäpfel	kar-**toff**'l/**air**-dupf'l	potatoes
Käse	**kayz**-er	cheese
Knoblauch	k'**nob**-lowkh	garlic
Knödel	k'**nerd**'l	dumpling
Kotelett	kot-**lett**	chop
Lamm	**lumm**	lamb
Marillen	mah-**ril**'n	apricot
Meeresfrüchte	**mair**-erz-froosh-ter	seafood

Mehlspeise	**mayl**-shpize-er	dessert
Milch	**milhk**	milk
Mineralwasser	minn-er-**arl**-vuss-er	mineral water
Obst	**ohbst**	fresh fruit
Öl	**erl**	oil
Oliven	o-**leev**'n	olives
Orange	o-**ronsh**-er	orange
frischgepresster Orangensaft	**frish**-g'press-ter o-**ronsh**'n-zuft	fresh orange juice
Paradeissalat	pa-ra-**dice**-sa-lahd	tomato salad
Pfeffer	**pfeff**-er	pepper
pochiert	**posh**-eert	poached
Pommes frites	pomm-**fritt**	chips
Reis	**rice**	rice
Rind	**rint**	beef
Rostbraten	rohst-**brart**'n	steak
Rotwein	**roht**-vine	red wine
Salz	**zults**	salt
Sauce/Saft	**zohss**-er/zuft	sauce
Schalentiere	**sharl**'n-tee-rer	shellfish
Schinken/Speck	**shink**'n/shpeck	ham
Schlag	**shlahgg**	cream
Schnecken	**shnek**'n	snails
Schokolade	shock-o-**lard**-er	chocolate
Schwein	**shvine**	pork
Semmel	**zem**'l	roll
Senf	**zenf**	mustard
Serviettenknödel	ser-vee-**ert**'n-k'nerd'l	sliced dumpling
Sulz	**zoolts**	brawn
Suppe	**zoop**-er	soup
Tee	**tay**	tea
Topfenkuchen	**topf**'n-kookh'n	cheesecake
Torte	**tort**-er	cake
Wasser	**vuss**-er	water
Weinessig	**vine**-ess-igg	vinegar
Weisswein	**vyce**-vine	white wine
Wurst	**voorst**	sausage (fresh)
Zucker	**tsook**-er	sugar
Zwetschge	**tsvertsh**-ger	plum
Zwiebel	**tsveeb**'l	onions

Numbers

0	**null**	**nool**
1	**eins**	**eye**'ns
2	**zwei**	**tsvy**
3	**drei**	**dry**
4	**vier**	**feer**
5	**fünf**	**foonf**
6	**sechs**	**zex**
7	**sieben**	**zeeb**'n
8	**acht**	**uhkht**
9	**neun**	**noyn**
10	**zehn**	**tsayn**
11	**elf**	**elf**
12	**zwölf**	**tsverlf**
13	**dreizehn**	**dry**-tsayn
14	**vierzehn**	**feer**-tsayn
15	**fünfzehn**	**foonf**-tsayn
16	**sechszehn**	**zex**-tsayn
17	**siebzehn**	**zeep**-tsayn
18	**achtzehn**	**uhkht**-tsayn
19	**neunzehn**	**noyn**-tsayn
20	**zwanzig**	**tsvunn**-tsig
21	**einundzwanzig**	ine-oont-tsvunn-tsig
22	**zweiundzwanzig**	**tsvy**-oont-tsvunn-tsig
30	**dreissig**	**dry**-sig
40	**vierzig**	**feer**-tsig
50	**fünfzig**	**foonf**-tsig
60	**sechzig**	**zesh**-tsig
70	**siebzig**	**zeep**-tsig
80	**achtzig**	**uhkht**-tsig
90	**neunzig**	**noyn**-tsig
100	**einhundert**	ine **hoond**'t
1000	**eintausend**	ine **towz**'nt

Time

one minute	**eine Minute**	ine-er min-**oot**-er
one hour	**eine Stunde**	ine-er **shtoond**-er
half an hour	**eine halbe Stunde**	ine-er **hull**-ber shtoond-er
Monday	**Montag**	**mone**-targ
Tuesday	**Dienstag**	**deen**-starg
Wednesday	**Mittwoch**	**mitt**-vokh
Thursday	**Donnerstag**	**donn**-er-starg
Friday	**Freitag**	**fry**-targ
Saturday	**Samstag**	**zum**-starg
Sunday	**Sonntag**	**zon**-targ

Vienna Transport Network

There are five U-Bahn lines running across the city, each identified by a number. The Schnellbahn is essentially a commuter service. Bundesbahn trains to the rest of Austria and Europe run from Vienna's mainline stations. The Badner Bahn operates between its terminal opposite the Opera, and Baden. For more details, see *Getting Around Vienna* on pages 250–55.

KEY

●—	U1
●—	U2
●—	U3
●—	U4
●—	U6
●—	Schnellbahn line
●—	Badner Bahn line
○	Interchange
🚆	Bundesbahn station
🚆	CAT (City Aiport Train)
Ⓢ	Schnellbahn terminus
🚌	Bus Terminal
▪	Major sight

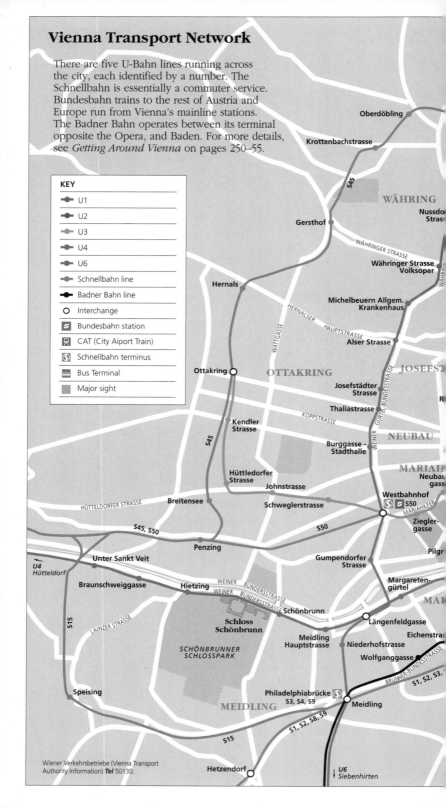

Oberdöbling

Krottenbachstrasse

S45

WÄHRING

Nussdo Stras

Gersthof

WÄHRINGER STRASSE

Währinger Strasse Volksoper

Hernals

Michelbeuern Allgem. Krankenhaus

HERNALSER HAUPTSTRASSE

WATTGASSE

Alser Strasse

Ottakring

OTTAKRING

JOSEFST

Josefstädter Strasse

Thaliastrasse

KOPPSTRASSE

GÜRTEL-BUNDESSTRASSE

WEINER GÜRTEL

Kendler Strasse

Burggasse - Stadthalle

NEUBAU

S45

Hüttledorfer Strasse

Johnstrasse

Breitensee

Schweglerstrasse

S50

MARIAH
Neubau gass

Westbahnhof
Ⓢ 🚆 S50

MARIAHILFER

HÜTTELDORFER STRASSE

Ziegler-gasse

S45, S50

Penzing

Gumpendorfer Strasse

Pilgr

U4
Hütteldorf

Unter Sankt Veit

Margareten-gürtel

Braunschweiggasse

Hietzing

WEINER BUNDESSTRASSE

WEINER BUNDESSTRASSE

Schönbrunn

MAI

Längenfeldgasse

Eichenstra

S15

LAINZER STRASSE

Schloss Schönbrunn

Meidling Hauptstrasse

Niederhofstrasse

Wolfganggasse

BRUNNER-BUNDESSTRASSE

S1, S2, S3,

SCHÖNBRUNNER SCHLOSSPARK

Speising

MEIDLING

Philadelphiabrücke Ⓢ
S3, S4, S9

Meidling

S1, S2, S8, S9

S15

U6
Siebenhirten

Hetzendorf

Wiener Verkehrsbetriebe (Vienna Transport Authority Information) *Tel* 50130.